John y, Lim

March 27, 1999

D0844433

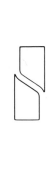

"Black Jack"

John A. Logan and Southern Illinois in the Civil War Era

James Pickett Jones

With a Foreword by John Y. Simon

Southern Illinois University Press
Carbondale and Edwardsville

Copyright 1967 by Florida State University
Reprinted by arrangement with the University Press of Florida
Foreword by John Y. Simon copyright © 1995 by the
Board of Trustees, Southern Illinois University

All rights reserved

Printed in the United States of America

Production supervised by Natalia Nadraga

98 97 96 95 4 3 2 1

Publication of this volume was made possible in part by grants from the
Office of the President, John A. Logan College, and the John A. Logan
College Foundation.

Library of Congress Cataloging-in-Publication Data

Jones, James Pickett.
    Black Jack : John A. Logan and Southern Illinois in the Civil War
era / James Pickett Jones ; with a foreword by John Y. Simon.
        p. cm. — (Shawnee Classics)
    Originally published: Tallahassee : Florida State University,
1967.
    Includes bibliographical references and index.
    1. Logan, John Alexander, 1826–1886. 2. Generals—United States—
Biography. 3. United States. Army—Biography. 4. Illinois—
History—Civil War, 1861–1865. I. Title.
E664.L83J63 1995
973.7′415′092—dc20
[B]
ISBN 0-8093-2001-0   94-42300
ISBN 0-8093-2002-9 (pbk.)   CIP

The paper used in this publication meets the minimum requirements
of American National Standard for Information Sciences—
Permanence of Paper for Printed Library Materials, ANSI Z39.48-1984. ⊚

Frontispiece: John A. "Black Jack" Logan as a brigadier general
in the U.S. Army. Courtesy of the Illinois State Historical Library

To my daughter
Nancy Berlin Jones

CONTENTS

ILLUSTRATIONS

opposite page

MAPS

FOREWORD

Thomas Jefferson believed that the Illinois country was too large and too unshapely to form a single state. In his 1784 plan for the Northwest Territory, he drew rectangles on a map which would have divided present-day Illinois among three projected states: Assenisipia in the north, Illinoia in the center, and Polypotamia in the south. The Ohio River ran diagonally through Polypotamia, uniting southern Illinois with western Kentucky. The outbreak of the Civil War some three-quarters of a century later apparently vindicated Jefferson's plan in terms of political, social, and cultural identity. The southernmost counties of Illinois, called Egypt for reasons that remain obscure, formed part of a borderland between North and South.

The completion of the Illinois Central Railroad in 1856, the longest in the world, had been expected to bring prosperity to southern Illinois, drawing the agricultural wealth of the state to Cairo for transshipment down the Mississippi River to New Orleans, thence out to the markets of the world. Traffic, however, immediately flowed northward to Chicago, connected both by rail and lake steamers to the East Coast. In 1860, Chicago contained a population of 112,172; Cairo, the largest town in Egypt, had 2,188.

While Illinois doubled in population in the decade before the Civil War, Egypt remained relatively stable. Only 5 percent of the population of Egypt was foreign-born, compared to 19 percent for the state. Most people lived on small farms, smaller than those elsewhere in the state, with an assessed valuation per acre lower than the state average. Egypt was a region of subsistence farmers, southern in origin, Protestant in religion, and Democratic in politics.

In 1860, John A. Logan had won reelection to Congress with over 80 percent of the votes. Republican opponent David T. Linegar of Cairo had run slightly ahead of the Republican nominee for president, Abraham Lincoln. Born in Brownsville and educated in southern Illinois except for a brief sojourn at

xi

law school in Louisville, Logan was a Mexican War volunteer and flamboyant lawyer whose talents carried him naturally to the state legislature in the mid-1850s. There he vigorously opposed statewide prohibition on behalf of constituents for whom "the use of intoxicating drinks seems more natural than the use of water," and pushed through a stringent law against black migration to Illinois that strengthened his local popularity.

First elected to Congress in 1858, he gave full support to Stephen A. Douglas. In a debate over enforcement of the Fugitive Slave Act, he denounced Republicans who aided runaway slaves. "You call it the dirty work of the Democratic party to catch fugitive slaves for the southern people. We are willing to perform that dirty work. I do not consider it disgraceful to perform any work, dirty or not dirty, which is in accordance with the laws of the land and the Constitution of the country." Thus he won the nickname "Dirty Work Logan" that followed him in his political career. During the 1860 presidential campaign, when the *Franklin Democrat*, a newspaper in Benton where Logan then lived, attempted to switch allegiance from Douglas to Lincoln, Logan, with the aid of a menacing crowd of supporters, forced the owners to sell out, using implied threats of violence. Afterward, his nickname seemed even more appropriate.

During the secession crisis of 1860–61, Logan denounced both "abolitionist Black Republicans" and Southern extremists, reminding Southerners that the "election of Mr. Lincoln, deplorable as it may be, affords no justification or excuse for overthrowing the republic." In a lengthy speech on February 5, he urged compromise, a position affirmed by his votes through the remainder of the session. Events eliminated compromise, however, when war began at Fort Sumter on April 12. For more than two months, Logan remained uncharacteristically silent about the war. During those months, Egypt was in turmoil. On April 25, Douglas addressed the Illinois legislature urging support of the war. "There can be no neutrals in this war, only patriots or traitors." Douglas won over many Democrats but not Logan. "I opposed war upon the south & invasion last winter as being certain disunion forever, I am still of the same opinion," Logan wrote privately on May 9.

"Judge D[ouglas]. took the same ground then that I did, now he tells me that he is for capturing Richmond and prosecuting a war of subjugation if necessary to compel obedience I can not nor will not agree to it ... " Many were called "rebel & traitor" for not supporting "Lincoln & his policy" and "the attempt now is being made to transfer the democracy to the tail end of an infamous abolition disunion party, I for one shall not, be transferred ... " This recently discovered letter answers persistent questions about Logan's opinions after war began. In the spring of 1861, Logan concealed such views from his constituents while calculating his political future.

During Logan's silence, many other Egyptians said all too much. Following his return from Congress in 1861, Logan moved from Benton, in Franklin County, which had been transferred to a new congressional district, to Marion in Williamson County. At a public meeting in Marion on April 15, a large crowd ratified resolutions drawn up by a committee that included Logan's father-in-law, John M. Cunningham. The resolutions blamed the war upon "the elevation to power of a strictly sectional party" likely to drive "the border Slave States from the Federal Union" into the Confederacy. In that event, Illinois must divide, and the crowd pledged "to use all means in our power to effect the same, and attach ourselves to the Southern Confederacy." Unionists repealed the resolutions the next day, but these were not the same people who had passed them. From Jonesboro and Vienna, as well as Marion, came reports of public rejoicing when Fort Sumter fell.

A meeting in Carbondale denounced the "diabolical, unjust and unholy" war against the South. If the North did not acknowledge the "independence of the Confederate States" then "we of Southern Illinois will consider it our duty and our inalienable right to withdraw from the North and attach ourselves to the Southern Confederacy." This meeting carried added menace as speakers urged cutting the Illinois Central Railroad. They targeted the Big Muddy bridge, four miles north of Carbondale, a point soon guarded by a company of volunteers that Governor Richard Yates sent from Chicago. The main body of Chicago troops continued to Cairo, where the local newspaper protested "the occupation of our city or

xiii

any part of Southern Illinois by troops from either section." Even before fighting began, the *Cairo Gazette* had launched a campaign to create a new and neutral state in southern Illinois.

In response to the Carbondale meeting, Daniel H. Brush, the town's founder, called another. Unlike Marion, Carbondale was a new town, created by the railroad, where Brush had banned all liquor sales and led efforts to build churches and found a college. Brush planned to carry an American flag to a meeting of "all lovers of their country." Urged to cancel the meeting to avoid violence, Brush said that he would attend if nobody else did and "would carry the flag or die in the effort." Cries of "down with the flag" came from across the square, but the meeting concluded with cheers for the Union. Two days later, Brush made a patriotic speech from the roof of his store, ran up an American flag, and soon enlisted as a forty-eight-year-old private in a volunteer company that immediately elected him captain.

Back in Marion, however, Thorndike Brooks and Harvey Hayes recruited for the other side. Assembling a band of about thirty-five, they marched to Paducah in search of a Confederate army to join. Hibert Cunningham, Logan's brother-in-law, marched with them, signaling Logan's support. Brooks's company joined the 15th Tennessee, which fought against Logan's 31st Illinois at Belmont, and Brooks eventually rose to the rank of lieutenant colonel. After the war Thorndike Brooks's father Chauncey, a Baltimore merchant, banker, and philanthropist, former president of the Baltimore and Ohio Railroad (which he established along with Johns Hopkins), father of five Unionist sons and uncle of eleven Union soldiers, wrote to President Andrew Johnson to ask a pardon for his Confederate son, led astray by living in Williamson County, where, he explained, "the population were about all rebels."

Hibert Cunningham also behaved like a young man led astray. By October 1863, he had deserted the Confederate army to join Logan at Vicksburg. Accepting his erring brother-in-law in familial style, Logan let him serve as a captain on his staff during the Atlanta campaign.

In mid-April 1861, the allegiance of Egypt hung in the balance. Political attitudes of previous decades inclined Egyptians toward the South, yet Confederate firing on the American flag at Fort Sumter roused a patriotism that impelled many to volunteer for the Union. The first fully organized southern Illinois regiment, the 18th Illinois, was mustered in on May 21 by Captain Ulysses S. Grant at Anna. He noted "the prevailing opinion abroad that the people of this section of the State are ignorant, disloyal, intemperate, and generally heathenish," but Grant was "agreeably disappointed in the people of Egypt." Under Colonel Michael K. Lawler, the regiment later fulfilled a few of the stereotypes, but when Lawler won promotion to brigadier general and the stern and upright Daniel H. Brush took over, these superb fighters acquired discipline.

By the end of May, Cairo had become an armed camp, troops guarded the Big Muddy bridge, and increasing numbers of young Egyptians had enlisted in the Union army. Opponents of war still trumpeted their opinions but made few converts. War had begun in earnest and the time for doubting had ended. Yet Logan still maintained his ominous silence.

Logan chose a dramatic moment to speak out. After mustering in Illinois volunteers, Grant had traveled to St. Louis, Cincinnati, and Indiana in search of a commission. Finally Governor Yates called on him to command a regiment that Grant had mustered into state service in Mattoon, a regiment that had elected a blowhard colonel incapable of maintaining even a semblance of order. Grant imposed discipline. The troops could still choose whether to extend their enlistments from the original ninety days to the three years the federal government now required. On the day of decision, Democratic Congressman John A. McClernand, accompanied by Congressman Logan, arrived in Springfield to address the volunteers. McClernand's support for the Union was beyond question; what Logan might say was a mystery. Grant hesitated before allowing both to speak. As Grant recalled, Logan spoke with "force and eloquence." Logan conveyed "a loyalty and devotion to the Union which inspired my men to such a point that they would have volunteered to remain in the army as long as an enemy of the country continued to bear arms against it. They entered the United States service almost to a man."

Even after his dramatic speech to the volunteers, Logan continued to blame abolitionists and secessionists for the war, with heavier emphasis on the "impertinent spirit of the anti-slavery party of the North" that had frustrated all efforts for compromise. Logan then left for an emergency session of Congress, vowing to enlist once the session ended. In a letter to his wife from Washington, Logan wrote that "there is no use for northern men to sacrifice themselves by standing out against the storm." He voted for men and money to sustain the war but against a bill that would have allowed the army to protect fugitive slaves.

On August 19, Logan returned to Marion, climbed on a wagon in the town square, and delivered the speech southern Illinois had long waited to hear. "The time has come when a man must be for or against his country," he said. "I, for one, shall stand or fall with the Union and shall this day enroll for the war. I want as many of you as will to come with me." County clerk John H. White had arranged for several men to step forward to enlist. Others muttered in disgust and moved away. Marion remained a bastion of antiwar sentiment throughout the conflict, but elsewhere in Egypt, Logan's conversion carried the day. Logan eventually recruited enough men to fill the 31st Illinois, with eight of ten companies raised in his congressional district. By newspaper account, all but twelve of 1100 men were Democrats.

Logan's long-delayed decision made sound political sense. Public opinion in southern Illinois had swung to support of the war, leaving only diehards dreaming of compromise or secession. Thorndike Brooks's tiny band stood alone, while hundreds had enlisted in the Union army. To secure Democratic support, both Yates and Lincoln had assured Logan of a colonelcy; promotion to brigadier general awaited his first success in the field. Persistent opposition to the war meant political suicide. Federal authorities had already arrested and imprisoned some opponents of the war, a fate that awaited Logan's law partner and successor in Congress, William Joshua Allen.

Logan's long delay had exacerbated turmoil in Egypt. Williamson County Confederates had marched away expecting Logan to take command. His immense popularity in his district, where he seemed to know everybody's name, encouraged his followers to intuit his intentions, and his violent denunciations of Republicans led to belief that he would never fight their war.

After he enlisted, Logan visited his mother in Murphysboro, who "upbraided" him for abandoning his principles. Only one of his brothers supported the Union, and his sister Dorothy was married to Dr. Israel Blanchard, an impassioned opponent of the war. During the war, General Logan intervened with Lincoln to rescue Blanchard from imprisonment. When Logan embarked on a new political career after the war as a Republican, Democrats charged him with Confederate sympathies in the spring of 1861. Logan's sister, Mrs. Blanchard, stepped forward to support the accusation. With Logan's own family and that of his wife arrayed in support of the South, no wonder that his decision proved so difficult.

Nestled between slaveholding Missouri and slaveholding Kentucky, with ties of kinship, friendship, and commerce extending across the Mississippi and Ohio rivers, southern Illinois participated in the turmoil that gripped the neighboring states. Before the war ended, however, more than twice as many Missourians had enlisted in the U.S. Army as had fought for the Confederacy, and the proportion in Kentucky was three to one. Jefferson Davis's reckless decision to fire upon the flag at Fort Sumter, to demolish a virtually defenseless federal outpost that posed no threat to Confederate nationalism, offended the borderland. Union victory in the war owed much to the success of Lincoln's border state policy of waging war to preserve the Union, not to destroy slavery. Under such circumstances, traditional pro-Southern attitudes in Egypt received no encouragement. By August 1861, Logan and almost everybody in southern Illinois except a few extremists had no real alternative but to support the war for the Union.

During the war, Logan rose to major general and converted to the Republican party. When Josh Allen ran for reelection to Congress in 1864, Logan campaigned against his former close friend and partner. Not everybody fully trusted Logan; in 1866 he was defeated in the contest for state commander of the Grand Army of the Republic. That same year, when he ran for congressman-at-large, Democrats revived and embellished every report of Logan's initial sympathy for secession to counter Logan's identification of Democrats with traitors. Democrats denounced "that low vulgar, dirty, and hypocritical Logan. Maggots would sicken on him." In a debate between Logan and his opponent T. Lyle Dickey in Carbondale on September 28, Dickey emphasized Logan's acquiescent attitude toward rebellion early in the war. Both parties besought veterans of the Thorndike Brooks company to write statements either implicating Logan in involvement with Confederate recruiting or exonerating him. Mrs. Logan printed a statement with eight signatures denying such charges against her husband; six of the eight then claimed that their names had been printed without their consent. Reeling from charges of disloyalty, Logan asserted that "the instant the first gun was fired, I left the Democratic Party and went with loyal men to suppress the rebellion."

Logan lied but won the election. As his political career flourished, carrying him to the Senate and to the Republican nomination for vice president in 1884, the story of the turmoil in Egypt at the outbreak of the war receded from memory. Republicans instead emphasized disloyal activity later in the conflict, portraying Democrats as rebel sympathizers or copperheads, and spawning legends of widespread Confederate intrigue in southern Illinois that persist even today. Instead, opponents of the war, strongest near Marion and Jonesboro, opposed the federal government without deliberately aiding the Confederacy. Civil disorder in Williamson and Union counties, no less than the proud record of southern Illinois volunteers in western campaigns, formed part of Logan's legacy in Egypt.

When James Pickett Jones published *"Black Jack"* in 1967, reviewers praised the first scholarly biography of this flamboyant commander and charismatic politician. Most, however, deplored the book's abrupt conclusion on the eve of Logan's major foray into national affairs, a fault Jones remedied in 1982 with publication of *John A. Logan, Stalwart Republican from Illinois*, the second volume of a complete biography. By that time, remaining copies of *"Black Jack"* had succumbed to the gnawing of rats in their Florida warehouse. Long a scarce book, this dramatic account of Logan's rise to political and military eminence deserves a new generation of readers.

John Y. Simon

Southern Illinois University
at Carbondale

PREFACE

The southern Illinois triangle, called "Egypt," was a land of divided loyalties in the Civil War era. Almost surrounded by slave states, with economic and social ties in the slave states, Egypt became a Northern center of pro-Southern sentiment. The Civil War is well known as a "Brother's War" in Kentucky, Virginia, and Missouri, but in the war's first year it was almost equally so in southern Illinois.

John A. Logan, Egypt's most powerful political leader, personified the thoughts, doubts, and frustrations of the divided section. A Democrat before the war, "Black Jack" Logan spoke for Egypt in both the state and national arena. When the conflict came, Logan, like Egypt, was reluctant to fight Mr. Lincoln's war. Gradually, however, both political leader and section roused to support the Union. At the war's end Logan became a Republican and took many once rabidly partisan Democrats into the Republican Party with him. An entire section, once solidly Democratic, began voting Republican. Logan also stands as a prototype of the mid-19th Century American who experienced a change of attitude toward the Negro. His agonizing shift from Negrophobe to Negrophile was typical of many of his fellow citizens in the border states.

While Logan's role in these changes was important, Egypt did not change its political habits merely because of him. Secession, war, Copperheadism, and the new issues created by the war led to the change. But Logan personified the revolution and he led it to his political profit. This study attempts to place Logan in his Egyptian surroundings and examine the section's effect on the man as well as the man's effect on the section.

In addition, this study investigates the role of the political soldier in the Civil War. The tensions produced by professional-amateur command friction profoundly affected the Union war effort. Logan's career affords an excellent view of the problem. From 1861 to 1865 "Black Jack" wrote an amazing martial record. For a man with little training, he showed great aptitude for command. Even those critical of his political career speak glowingly of Logan the soldier. The Union army was shot through with political soldiers. Most of them were poor, many incompetent. Of those who rose to high command, Logan stands out as the ablest. Most West Pointers named Logan the best of the volunteers. Some, Grant included, admitted his record outshone that of many professionals. Few Union commanders won such admiration from their men, and few showed greater personal courage. Still, Logan was an amateur, and despite his success, was looked upon as an amateur by many of his fellow soldiers. Logan's conflicts with George H. Thomas and William T. Sherman produce a classic picture of West Point vs. the political soldier.

Works on Logan are almost non-existent. Most treatments of the soldier-politician are partisan campaign biographies published in the 1880's. In one, Byron Andrews wrote of Logan's "shining mail of untarnished integrity." George F. Dawson, a family friend, dedicated his biography to Logan the "Ever victorious Warrior, and Illustrious Statesman." Published in 1887, the last biography written, Dawson's study is the best known and most often cited life of Logan. It is a totally unbalanced and misleading work. The Logans read the manuscript with the general advising his wife to "pass judgment upon it. . . . If you think it ought to be changed you can make the suggestion to D." Dawson ignored Logan's pre-war career, never stating that Logan was a Democrat. The most deceptive work about Logan was written by his wife. Mary outlived the general and spent her life polishing Logan's "mail of untarnished integrity." No balanced biography of Logan exists.

This work is not a full-scale biography of John A. Logan. It is an attempt to present a man of divided loyalties leading an equally divided section in days of national crisis. In 1982, the University of Florida Press published my second work on the Illinoisan, *John A. Logan, Stalwart Republican from Illinois*. This volume moved "Black Jack" from his arrival in the House in 1867 through his death in 1886. Together, the two volumes are the only scholarly biography of the Illinois soldier-politician.

No writer can hope to acknowledge all those who assisted in the preparation of a manuscript. He can simply recognize those who have been most helpful. I would like to acknowledge my particular indebtedness to Professor William E. Baringer of the University of Florida. This study began under his guidance and he has been a constant source of help in a multitude of ways. I would also like to thank Professors Donald D. Horward, Joseph D. Cushman and Joe M. Richardson, my colleagues at Florida State University, for their encouragement and assistance.

There are several institutions I must recognize for their invaluable contributions to this study. The staff of the Manuscripts Division of the Library of Congress was helpful in making available the extensive Logan collections. The staff of the Illinois State Historical Library was also of great aid in supplying materials, including some of the illustrations reproduced by permission in this volume. Grateful acknowledgment is extended to the Illinois State Historical Society and to *Mid-America* for permission to reprint parts of my articles which appear in Chapters III and XIV, respectively—"John A. Logan, Freshman in Congress, 1859–1861," *Journal of the Illinois State Historical Society*, LVI, No. 1 (Spring 1963), pp. 36–60; "John A. Logan and the Election of 1864 in Illinois," *Mid-America*, XLII, No. 4 (October 1960), pp. 219–30. Lastly I am indebted to the staff of Florida State University's interlibrary loan division. The author is responsible for any mistakes that appear.

J.P.J.

Tallahassee, Florida

CHAPTER I

THE YOUNG EGYPTIAN

Illinois is shaped like a giant flint arrowhead. Its point thrusts deep into the South between the Mississippi and Ohio Rivers. At its tip the two rivers merge in a great confluence. Here North and South meet, and in the triangle of land at the arrowhead's point, called "Egypt," the customs and ideas of North and South were interwoven. John A. Logan was a product of this sectional intermingling.

Egypt runs from Alton and Vandalia on the north to Cairo, standing with "one foot in the Mississippi and the other in the Ohio" one hundred and thirty miles to the South.[1] The section has a long and colorful history. Its first inhabitants were Indians of the Illinois Confederation. The first whites were the French who established forts and missions along the rivers in the seventeenth and eighteenth centuries. They in turn were succeeded by the English after the French and Indian War. Settlement was sparse until the American Revolution when American soldiers came first to expel the English and later as settlers, lured westward by land bounties and the gentle beauty of the terrain. From the Northern states a human tide flowed down the Ohio, to be joined by Southerners moving northward from Virginia, Kentucky, and Tennessee, or later, across the river from Missouri.[2] The first four decades of independence were years of steady growth in southern Illinois. The future of the section seemed limitless; its destiny as the great exchange point between North and South was evident to all.

In 1824 Dr. John Logan crossed the Mississippi into this

---

[1] Baker Brownell, *The Other Illinois* (New York, 1958), 3.

[2] In 1860 the Illinois Census revealed that the 11 states that seceded in 1861 had contributed 94,475 natives to the Illinois population. The three border slave states of Kentucky, Maryland and Missouri had contributed 83,063. Many, perhaps a majority of these immigrants settled in Egypt. *Eighth Census of the United States* (Washington, 1861), 104-105.

burgeoning land. A native of Ireland, he was brought to the
United States in the first decade of the nineteenth century by
his father. The family first settled at Ellicott Mills, Maryland,
but young Logan soon joined the westward rush into the Mississippi Valley, settling in Perry County, Missouri.[3] He studied
medicine with his father and, although he engaged in various
agricultural, business and political ventures in the West, he
never abandoned medical practice.

The doctor left Missouri in 1824 and established his residence on the Big Muddy River at Brownsville, a tiny hamlet
serving as county seat of Jackson County, Illinois. At Brownsville, Logan met Miss Elizabeth Jenkins, daughter of one of
the county's most influential families. She was born in North
Carolina and moved with her family to South Carolina and
Tennessee. Then, following the path of so many slave state
residents, her family crossed the Ohio into Egypt. Elizabeth's
brother, Alexander, later Illinois lieutenant-governor, was one
of Egypt's most prominent lawyers. Her father, a Jackson
County farmer, later held a colonel's commission in the Black
Hawk War.

After a brief courtship, Dr. Logan and Miss Jenkins were
married. Soon after the marriage, the doctor took his bride to
a new home a few miles up the Big Muddy from Brownsville.
Here they settled on a 160-acre farm near the site of the present town of Murphysboro.[4] It was here that their first child,
John Alexander Logan, was born on February 9, 1826.

Jack Logan's childhood was not typical of frontier Illinois.
He grew up in the comfortable two-story house in which he
was born. This relative comfort was made possible by his
father's medical abilities, which gave Dr. Logan a large practice in Jackson County. This income was supplemented by that
of the Logan farm, one of the area's finest.[5] The doctor also
took an active part in local politics as an ardent Jacksonian

---

[3]*Appleton's Cyclopedia, 1886*, 504; George W. Smith, *A History of
Southern Illinois* (Chicago, 1912), III, 1148.
[4]George Smith, *Southern Illinois*, III, 1149.
[5]Daniel H. Brush, *Growing Up With Southern Illinois*, Milo M. Quaife,
ed., (Chicago, 1944), 62. Brush wrote: "The Logan homestead became a
very pleasant place to visit especially in apple and peach time. . . . The
old gentleman [Dr. Logan] was a great lover of horse-flesh and usually
had some good stock."

Democrat. Young Jack found his home a center for all the excitement of politics.

When Jack was two, a boy named Thomas was born, to be followed by nine other children. Jack roamed the quiet forests and streams of the county. He saw spring made beautiful by the blooms of his father's fruit trees and sometimes disrupted by the rising of the Big Muddy. In the fall he tramped the crimson forests with his brothers and accompanied his father in hunting the abundant geese and quail of the area.

Jack's life centered on the farm, but there was time for an occasional excursion into Brownsville. This town of about 300 souls, with its tan yard, salt works, and courthouse, was the metropolis of Jack Logan's youth.[6] Here he saw the yearly militia muster, with its heavy drinking and inevitable fights. Here were held political meetings, at one of which he heard his father speak in his first race for the state assembly. At the conclusion of the campaign in 1834, the eight year old grieved to hear his father had lost to James Harreld in the contest to succeed Alexander Jenkins who was running for lieutenant-governor. Uncle Alexander's victory partially compensated for his father's failure, and the boy thrilled to hear that his uncle would go to Vandalia to help run the state.

Brownsville also provided Jack's first schooling away from the farm. His parents had taught him as much as they could, and at seven he was sent to town, where classes were held in the courthouse.[7] Despite his father's desire that Jack be educated, work on the farm took its share of the boy's time. This was especially true after Dr. Logan's successful second race for the assembly sent him to Vandalia in 1836. Jack began early to assume responsibility, for frequent absences were common in a frontier doctor's family. From Vandalia Dr. Logan wrote Jack charging him with many duties at home.[8]

[6]George Smith, *Southern Illinois*, I, 483; Edmund Newsome, *Historical Sketches of Jackson County, Illinois* (Carbondale, Illinois, 1882), 22.

[7]George Smith, *Southern Illinois*, I, 483.

[8]Dr. John Logan to John and Tom Logan, December 8, 1836, Dr. John Logan Mss., Illinois State Historical Library, Springfield. In 1839 Dr. Logan was a member of the general assembly when a new county was created out of Sangamon County. The new county was: "Logan County . . . named by Abraham Lincoln in honor of his friend, Dr. John Logan. . . . In the Tenth General Assembly despite the fact that Dr. Logan was a Democrat . . . he and Abraham Lincoln became close friends. When

Despite these duties, Jack Logan had time to sail his home-made flatboat on the nearby Big Muddy. He learned to play the fiddle and became one of the best riders of the neighborhood. Dan Brush recalled: "John in his early life became an expert rider and was ever ready to ride a race. I have witnessed races at the Logan tracks many times when John, as a boy, was a rider of one of the horses, and never saw him excelled." And there was the business of the farm. He plowed, felled trees, and when ordered by his father to run squirrels out of the corn, he posted a notice on a tree: " 'I give notice to all squirrels to keep out of the cornfield. If they don't keep out they will be shot.' " When the notice had no effect, Jack returned with a gun to enforce the edict. Dr. Logan won reelection in 1838 and 1840 and during the assembly sessions became one of Egypt's most vocal Democratic spokesmen.[9]

An educated man himself, Dr. Logan continued to provide the best education the region offered for his children. For some time the best seemed to be in Brownsville. This was supplemented by reading and frequent political discussions at home. At a young age the boy espoused his father's political ideas, becoming a staunch Jacksonian Democrat.

The time arrived when a more advanced school was required. In 1842, at sixteen, Jack and his fourteen-year-old brother Tom were sent to Shiloh Academy at Shiloh Hill in nearby Randolph County. The boys remained there for three years studying spelling, grammar, arithmetic, and receiving their first instruction in Latin. Jack also seems to have demonstrated his oratorical ability, speaking on such subjects as drunkenness, which he called a "loathsome leprosy."[10]

Jack's diligence as a student is a matter of debate. Most

Logan County was carved out of Sangamon no name having been suggested by the settlers . . . Mr. Lincoln suggested the name of his friend Logan. As convincing proof of the origin of the name the following item appeared in the *Sangamo Journal* of Springfield . . . in its issue of Feb. 16, 1839, the next day after the passage of the bill creating Logan County: 'Logan County is named in honor of Dr. John Logan, the present representative from Jackson County.' " Lawrence B. Stringer, *History of Logan County, Illinois* (Chicago, 1886), I, 149-150.

[9]Brush, *Growing Up*, 62; George F. Dawson, *The Life and Services of General John A. Logan as Soldier and Statesman* (Chicago, 1887), 5.

[10]Dawson, *Logan*, 6-7; Byron Andrews, *A Biography of General John A. Logan* (New York, 1884), 367; Ms. of a speech by John A. Logan, undated, Dr. John Logan Mss.

of his biographers state that he excelled at his studies and was among the best students in the school. One commentator on Logan's early life, however, felt that "it is doubtful if he was a hard student."[11] In later life Logan frequently referred to his roguish youth. In a speech at Southern Illinois College in 1869 he said: "I well remember in my boyhood days when the same number of men and boys at my college . . . would have been a terror to all hen coops, melon patches, apple and peach orchards . . . without a picket fence, shot gun, and bull dogs."[12] In 1845 Dr. Logan brought the boys home to be educated with the rest of his expanding family. To provide instruction, a private tutor, a frontier rarity, was hired to teach the Logan children.

The years the boys were at Shiloh Academy were eventful ones for Jackson County. They returned on vacation in 1843 to view the burned ruins of the Brownsville courthouse and see the twenty-acre tract their father donated to the county for its new courthouse. The transfer of the county seat aroused considerable opposition. Dan Brush, the most vocal Jackson County Whig, fought the move and called Dr. Logan a "bigoted incompetent."[13] On election day, voters listened to speakers from both sides and voted to accept Dr. Logan's offer. The new courthouse quickly became the center of a new county seat named Murphysboro.

Misfortune struck in 1844. One of the greatest inundations in this land of annual floods hissed and swirled up the Big Muddy partially covering the Logan farm. Further disappointment was caused by Dr. Logan's defeat in his attempt to regain the seat he had given up in 1842. The incumbent defeated him in a close race.

But 1845 and 1846 were crisis years and Jack thrilled to the exciting events. The Mexican problem smoldered through early 1846 and burst into flame in May. Mississippi Valley Democrats supported President Polk's war policy, and young men

[11]Dawson, Logan, 3; Andrews, Logan, 367; James Buel, The Standard Bearers: the Authorized Pictoral Lives of Blaine and Logan (Philadelphia, 1884), 310. The dissent is from Joseph Wallace, "A Biography of John A. Logan," unpublished manuscript biography in the Illinois State Historical Library, Springfield, 4.
[12]Ms. of a speech by John A. Logan, undated, Dr. John Logan Mss.
[13]Newsome, Jackson County, 17; Brush, Growing Up, 132.

were urged to enlist to vindicate "the honor and rights of your country and to repel from your soil a foreign foe."[14] There were also thrilling events of a family nature. The election of 1846 swept Dr. Logan, a zealous war Democrat, back into the Illinois assembly.

Jack, who now preferred to be called John, wanted to join the rush to Mexico. His parents persuaded him to remain at home until the doctor's campaign was over. After his father's victory, young Logan had to postpone his enlistment until Dr. Logan returned from Springfield. Finally, in the spring of 1847, Logan heard that a Jackson County company was being formed. The slight but wiry young man, who was so slender that he appeared consumptive to some, enlisted.[15] He and James Provost, a Jonesboro merchant, were the candidates for lieutenant. Logan coveted the rank and challenged his rival to a foot race, card game or fist fight for the lieutenancy. The struggle was settled when Provost was elected first lieutenant and Logan, second lieutenant.[16]

In May the company was ordered to rendezvous at Alton with other companies of its new regiment. At Alton, Logan became a soldier. His enlistment dated from May 9, when the Jackson County men, Company H, were mustered into service. On June 8 the entire regiment was mustered as the First Regiment of Illinois Volunteers, commanded by Colonel Edward W. B. Newby.[17]

The men settled down to army life with its drills, routine, and occasional illnesses caused by oppressive June heat and change of food and water. As a second lieutenant, Logan had his first command experience at Alton and aided in preparing the 68 men of the company for the trials ahead. Here he met young officers of other companies, many from Egypt. Among them was jovial Captain John Cunningham, former sheriff of Williamson County. Cunningham found in Logan a kindred

[14]Alton *Telegraph and Democratic Review*, May 30, 1846.
[15]Buel, *Standard Bearers*, 310.
[16]May Strong Hawkins, "The Early Political Career of John A. Logan," unpublished masters thesis, University of Chicago, 1934, 7. This story was told Miss Hawkins in 1934 by A. S. Tibbetts, editor of the Jonesboro *Gazette*.
[17]Isaac H. Elliott, *Record of the Services of Illinois Soldiers in the Black Hawk War, 1831-32, and in the Mexican War, 1846-48* (Springfield, 1902), 224. Hereafter cited as *Illinois Adjutant-General's Report.*

Southern Illinois

From S. A. Mitchell's county map of Illinois, 1860
Courtesy of the Illinois State Historical Library

spirit, genial and adventurous. A cordial relationship developed between Logan and the older man, a friendship that grew during their war service.[18]

On June 14, the anxiously awaited marching orders came, and the regiment boarded steamers for Fort Leavenworth. At Leavenworth the novelty of the Missouri River voyage ended and the old routine of camp life caught them again. Logan's friend "Doff" Ozburn indicated some of the difficulty:

> the Captain takes but little responsibility upon himself which makes the other boys from different counties so hopeless in trying to do anything or make any kind of a show, but I hope the day is not far distant when John will be Captain of the company for he justly deserves the station. If John Logan was out of the company I would pray to be at home but he is the same John here that he is at home, he has nothing but if I kneed [sic] it I get a share and that without a murmer [sic].[19]

The prospect of a movement brightened spirits, and the order to march on July 7 was greeted with a cheer. The regiment had been ordered to Santa Fe to occupy that northernmost Mexican outpost and to stand ready to march south if needed as reinforcements. Their route lay across the desolate expanse of the southern Great Plains. For a time the line of march ran through beautiful prairie, but after the Kansas River was left behind on July 10, the country became a desolate, burned wasteland. To most the novelty of the land wore off quickly. The prairie "for the first few days had a most grand appearance, but the only one scene for 27 days gave me a disgust to a Prairie Country."[20]

By August, Logan sweltered in the heat as the column crossed the Cimarron and approached the edge of the Staked Plains. Water was scarce, there were food shortages, and constant fears of Indian attack. But heat was the greatest enemy. The sun rose early, baked the men all day, and set late, followed by chilling nights.

---

[18]*Illinois Adjutant-General's Report*, 208; Mary S. C. Logan, *Reminiscences of a Soldier's Wife* (New York, 1913), 27.

[19]Lindorf Ozburn to Diza Ozburn, July 4, 1847, Ozburn Mss., Illinois State Historical Library, Springfield.

[20]Lindorf Ozburn to Diza Ozburn, July 10, 1847, Ozburn Mss.

As the column neared Santa Fe its situation improved. In early September the extreme heat lessened and the plains gave way to the streams and valleys of northern New Mexico. At last on September 7, the regiment sighted Las Vegas, near Santa Fe, the first town the men had seen in more than a month.

Santa Fe was merely a resumption of the drudgery of Alton and Leavenworth. For men who had struggled through the hardships of the march, a return to camp routine with no prospect of action seemed dull indeed. Sergeant Ozburn voiced the general feeling. "I am in hopes we will not walk so far as we did, come home and say we have done nothing. . . ."[21]

In October, reinforcements were needed to the south, and Colonel Newby took half his force and began the march to El Paso. After their comrades' departure, those remaining settled down to garrison duty with the bleak prospect of boredom and disease until a treaty was signed. Logan, named adjutant of the post at Santa Fe, had increased duties to ease the routine. The position came as recognition of the young lieutenant's popularity and ability. Logan also busied himself by studying Spanish, a language which seems to have lingered with him the rest of his life.[22]

In late October Logan was given a chance to return to Illinois as recruiting officer to enlist replacements for men lost to disease. Logan refused, much to Ozburn's dismay, since the sergeant hoped to accompany his friend back to Egypt. Ozburn did not know the reason for Logan's refusal but stated, "I suppose he wished to win laurels on the field of battle."[23] Logan's letters of this period indicate that the sergeant was correct. On November 5 Logan wrote his father that the war was disappointingly remote. He told his father of the sickness sweeping the troops at Santa Fe, but assured Dr. Logan that he was healthy.[24]

This condition was short lived, and John Logan's Mexican

---

[21]Lindorf Ozburn to Diza Ozburn, October 20, 1847, Ozburn Mss.

[22]Ms. of muster roll for Company H, October, 1847, Ozburn Mss.; Dawson, *Logan*, 3.

[23]Lindorf Ozburn to Diza Ozburn, October 20, 1847, Ozburn Mss.

[24]John A. Logan (Hereafter cited as JAL) to Dr. Logan, Nov. 5, 1847, John A. Logan Mss., Library of Congress.

War battle was fought against disease. During the winter a measles epidemic struck the garrison. Logan contracted the illness, which killed nine of his comrades in Company H.[25] Because of distance Logan's family knew little of his condition. It was not until spring that Dr. Logan received a clear picture of the young lieutenant's illness and recovery. When the doctor discovered how grave his son's illness had been, he wrote Ozburn, "You will pleas [sic] accept my hearty and devout thanks for your kind care and attention on my son John in his illness."[26]

Spring brought his recovery and increased hopes for an end to the war. In February, 1848, Nicholas Trist completed negotiations with the Mexicans and the Illinois soldiers rejoiced at the thought of going home. With the expected ratification of the Treaty of Guadalupe Hidalgo, the Santa Fe occupation force mustered in the city for the last time. In July the order to march moved down the line and the gaping villagers watched the *Americanos* terminate their nine months occupation.

The men again faced a summer march. Dr. Logan, speaking as a veteran of the Black Hawk War, sent his son advice on the return trip. The doctor cautioned him to stay with the others all the way to Alton and warned: "there will be great danger as the Indians are allways [sic] more hostile on the close of a war between us and any other nation than they are at any other time."[27]

The return march was less eventful than the one to New Mexico. Heat, thirst, and Indian danger were still present, but thoughts of homecoming made the discomforts less burdensome.

John Logan had mixed feelings on his return. His happiness at seeing friends and family was tempered by his failure to win glory in battle. In September, the men reached Leavenworth where they boarded transports, and in early October they arrived at Alton. Here they were greeted as soldiers who

[25]*Illinois State Register* (Springfield), Jan. 21, 1848; *Illinois Adjutant-General's Report*, 222.
[26]Dr. Logan to Lindorf Ozburn, March 26, 1848, Ozburn Mss.
[27]Dr. Logan to JAL, April 16, 1848, Logan Mss., Library of Congress.

had given "evidences of heroism and patience."[28] From October 15 to October 18 they were mustered out. There was another happy reception at Murphyboro where the young veteran was welcomed by his family.

Logan returned from New Mexico 22 years old and undecided as to his future. His father wanted him to study medicine, but Logan was more interested in politics.[29] With the support of his father and his uncle, both influential in Jackson County politics, Logan had a good chance for minor office. In 1849, after a brief period of reading law in his uncle's office, Logan entered his first political contest and was easily elected county clerk. This office, however, was temporary, for Logan felt that a successful career in politics demanded further knowledge of the law. His service as clerk was a method of obtaining money to finance a law degree.[30] By 1850 he had accumulated enough money to make it possible for him to resign and enter law school.

Among frontier law schools, Louisville University's was one of the best, and Logan crossed the Ohio in 1850 to begin his studies. Instruction at Louisville was adequate for a frontier barrister. There were recitation examinations and lectures and a moot court twice a week. Board and lodging were reasonable, but Logan was forced to call on his father from time to time for financial aid. In thanking the doctor, Logan predicted that the favor would "receive a ten fold benefit" when he graduated. Logan studied hard and became an able student, especially at courtroom oratory. In February, 1851, he received his diploma and started home, telling his father, "You can tell all who are anxious for my attendance at our court that I am certain to be there if life lasts and money holds out."[31]

Logan returned in time for the spring elections and offered himself as candidate for prosecuting attorney of the Third Judicial District. Prominent in the press were statements by friendly journalists proclaiming Logan's graduation and as-

[28]*Illinois State Register*, October 20, 1848.
[29]Mary Logan, *Reminiscences*, 98.
[30]Thomas W. Knox, *The Lives of James G. Blaine and John A. Logan* (Hartford, Conn., 1884), 269.
[31]JAL to Dr. Logan, Jan. 6, 1851, Logan Mss., Library of Congress.

suring their readers that the young man would be an "orna-
ment" to his profession.[32] His race was successful and in the
summer, at 25, he began his legal career. In order to function
more effectively as prosecutor, Logan moved to Benton in
Franklin County.

Logan's term as prosecuting attorney was brief. After
serving little more than a year he resigned to run as representative in the Eighteenth General Assembly from Jackson
and Franklin Counties, a position his father had held four
times.

This campaign was Logan's first real test in his chosen profession. His political ambitions were boundless. He told his
father, "Politics is a trade and if my few fast friends in Jackson will stand by me, the day is not far distant when I can
help myself and them to pay ten fold."[33]

On the stump in 1852, Logan, known personally to many
voters in the two counties, gave evidence of the qualities necessary for success in Egyptian politics. He was a vigorous man,
about medium height, weighing about 140 pounds.[34] Logan's
appearance led to countless romantic stories. He had bright
eyes, swarthy complexion and straight black hair, features
that led many to claim for him Indian ancestry. This assertion
was unfounded, but it persisted throughout his career.[35]

Logan was popular among the younger voters because of
his fun-loving nature. He joined in the horse-play of militia
day and playfully wrestled town children. Daniel Gill remembered that as a twelve year old he was playing marbles with
Logan's younger brother William when Logan strolled by and
kicked the marbles out of the ring. "Immediately the players
jumped up and knocked the hat from the head of John A.
Logan. A regular sham-battle ensued between John A. and the
players."[36] Some strait-laced members of the community opposed this behavior, but Egypt was a boisterous section and
Logan's reputation as a rollicking spirit aided in public life.

---

[32]Cairo *Sun*, May 29, 1851.
[33]JAL to Dr. Logan, Aug. 31, 1852, Logan Mss., Library of Congress.
[34]H. E. Kimmel, "Sixty-sixth Wedding Anniversary of Daniel Gill and
Lucinda Pyle Gill, DuQuoin, Illinois," *Journal of the Illinois State Historical Society*, XVII, No. 3 (Sept., 1924), 442.
[35]Andrews, *Logan*, 369; Mary Logan, *Reminiscences*, 98.
[36]Kimmel, "Sixty-sixth Wedding Anniversary," 441.

Without abilities in other directions Logan's career might have been short lived. He was an able speaker. Beginning at Shiloh Academy, Logan developed an oratorical style. His voice was sonorous and audible even to the last ranks of a large crowd, so powerful, in fact, that he was able to shout down hecklers, a quality necessary in the rough-and-tumble of Egyptian politics.

He was also blessed with a ready made organization built by his Uncle Alexander Jenkins and Dr. Logan. However, his father's health was poor and Logan had to do much of the organizing. He formed political meetings in his own behalf and for W. A. Denning, candidate for the Democratic nomination to Congress in 1852. Denning, a veteran campaigner, supported Logan, and Logan and his father backed Denning. Denning wrote the doctor:

> If Allen [Willis Allen, Denning's opponent] is nominated his friends have already threatened political death to me and my friends and among others your own son. . . . I hope, and pray Doct. that you will try and get the leading Democrats together . . . and send up some man who can be relied on in any and every emergency.[37]

Logan who was still on the circuit as prosecuting attorney, also urged his father to send a delegate to the district convention who "will do as we want him to. . . . I can't be a delegate, my position will not allow it."[38]

Denning failed to get the nomination, but this did not materially effect Logan's campaign. Logan ran as a Jacksonian Democrat, adopting positions popular in southern Illinois. He was bitterly anti-Negro and promised to fight for a bill excluding free Negroes from Illinois. He also spoke in favor of rigid enforcement of the Fugitive Slave Act. But like his idol, Jackson, Logan and the Egyptian Democrats who supported him were supporters of the Union and not devoted to extreme Southern states rights doctrines. Furthermore, he took the usual Egyptian position on the railroad issue. He opposed "State policy" in favor of a railroad policy that would benefit

---

[37]JAL to Dr. Logan, Aug. 31, 1852; W. A. Denning to Dr. Logan, Sept. 1, 1852, Logan Mss., Library of Congress.
[38]JAL to Dr. Logan, Aug. 31, 1852, Logan Mss., Library of Congress.

St. Louis, the city toward which most of the southern Illinois triangle looked.

Logan indicated his support of the Compromise of 1850, if the Fugitive Slave Act was enforced, and spoke for Stephen A. Douglas, an old friend of Dr. Logan and the hero of Illinois Democrats. Logan promised to vote for the "Little Giant" for the Senate if he was elected to the assembly. Logan's platform was popular; he was well-liked; and his organization was effective. On election day the Democratic voters of Jackson and Franklin Counties gave him a large majority.[39] At 26 John A. Logan's political career moved beyond the boundaries of Egypt.

---

[39]George Smith, *Southern Illinois*, III, 1149.

CHAPTER II

SPRINGFIELD AND MARY

Springfield in the winter of 1853 looked dreary to those arriving in the town that had been the Illinois capital since 1837. Despite its appearance, Springfield was charged with an air of expectancy. Every other year brought a session of the Illinois General Assembly, and legislators had begun arriving from all over the state.

The 18th General Assembly convened January 3 when the legislators were sworn in by Justice Lyman Trumbull. The major opening day business was election of a speaker. The Whigs had been shattered in 1852, and this assembly was heavily Democratic. There were 59 Democrats, 16 Whigs and 1 Free Soiler in the House.[1] This made organization simple. John Reynolds, St. Clair County Democrat and former governor, was elected by acclamation, many feeling that the office was due him because of his long service to the party.[2]

Two days later the assembly met in joint session to elect a senator. Stephen A. Douglas had been in the Senate since 1847 and expected no difficulty in his fight for re-election.[3] The Democrats caucused, and nominated the "Little Giant" by acclamation.

Logan was an enthusiastic Douglas supporter as his father had been before him. He voted for Douglas as the senator won 75-19 over Joseph Gillespie. When committee assignments were made Logan drew two important seats, judiciary committee and committee on banks and corporations. Logan's record in the House was closely watched in Egypt, and Logan's law partner, W. K. Parish, wrote: "I am glad to see that you

---

[1]Newton Bateman and Paul Selby, *Historical Encyclopedia of Illinois and a History of Sangamon County* (Chicago, 1912), II, 189.
[2]W. A. Denning to JAL, Jan. 16, 1853, Logan Mss.
[3]George Fort Milton, *The Eve of Conflict; Stephen A. Douglas and the Needless War* (New York, 1934), 95.

are on the judiciary committee. That will give you additional standing and particularly as a lawyer."[4]

The House got down to work January 6. Logan introduced the bill that became the center of the most acrimonious debate of the session. As a fellow Democrat stated: "He had scarcely warmed his seat when he opened upon some of the exciting topics of the day."[5] Logan's proposal was to instruct the judiciary committee to report a bill to prevent the immigration of free Negroes into Illinois "under the article of the Constitution requiring the legislature to pass such a law."[6] The anti-slave forces from northern Illinois immediately called for a vote to table the bill and lost 54 to 14. The bill went to committee, where Logan would have a hand in its construction.

The stir caused by Logan's exclusion bill quickly subsided and both sides prepared for the final battle. Meanwhile the business of the body continued with private bills filling the agenda. On January 11, Logan proposed an act for the relief of John M. Cunningham which passed unanimously three days later. This measure provided for a one hundred dollar payment to Logan's old friend as reimbursement for his services as marshal of the district court of Massac County.[7]

There was more important business before the House, however, and Logan was active in most of it. There were proposals in favor of adopting a statewide prohibition act modeled on the famous "Maine Law," the pioneer "dry" statute of that state. Logan, and most of the members from Egypt where "the use of intoxicating drinks seems more natural than the use of water," opposed the proposal, and in the debates he introduced several· petitions from citizens urging the legislature to vote against the bill.[8] Because of his great interest in this measure, Logan was named to a special committee to investigate the law as it had been applied in Maine.[9]

All attempts to push through a law of this kind failed when

---

[4]W. K. Parish to JAL, Jan. 16, 1853, Logan Mss.
[5]Usher F. Linder, *Reminiscences of the Early Bench and Bar of Illinois* (Chicago, 1879), 343.
[6]*Journal of the Illinois House of Representatives, Eighteenth General Assembly, 1853*, 3. Hereafter cited as *House Journal, 1853*.
[7]*Illinois Private Laws, 1853*, 494; *House Journal, 1853*, 177.
[8]*House Journal, 1853*, 278, 323; Cairo *Times and Delta*, Feb. 3, 1858.
[9]*House Journal, 1853*, 21.

opposition forces, led by the Egyptian members, tabled every "dry" motion. The last victory for the anti-prohibition men came on January 29 when Logan and 33 others voted successfully to table a proposed statewide "dry" law.

Much House business concerned railroad incorporation. Logan voted in the affirmative 15 times on laws chartering new roads. Most of these bills passed unanimously, but the bill to charter a Terre Haute and Vandalia Railroad Company brought a bitter debate, with Logan and the representatives from Lower Egypt in opposition.

This fight was a renewal of the struggle between "State policy" and the railroad plan advocated in Lower Egypt. The "State policy" forces wanted a cross-state road in southern Illinois, but they opposed building a road that would benefit any out-of-state terminus; consequently they favored constructing a road with Alton as western terminus. The Terre Haute and Vandalia was to be a link in that system.

The opposition to "State policy" centered in the section of the state that looked to St. Louis as an economic center. These representatives had been fighting a losing battle against the "State" forces through the 1840's, and though their strength seemed to have increased by 1853, they were unable to charter a road with St. Louis as terminus or to vote down the Terre Haute and Vandalia bill. Logan voted with the losing bloc.[10]

During the session Logan was pleased to discover that his activities were not being overlooked and that they seemed to be popular in his home district. W. A. Denning, a close friend, and his law-partner Parish kept him in touch with reactions in Jackson and Franklin Counties, and Parish told him, "I have no fears but what we will be able to exert an influence in the political arena in Egypt sufficient for all practical purposes."[11] The Benton newspaper took notice of Logan's record, calling him "our worthy and talented young representative . . . who has demonstrated to the North by his talent and eloquence . . . that we, in the South have interests to foster, guide

[10]Arthur C. Cole, *The Era of the Civil War* (Springfield, 1919), 33, 43; *House Journal, 1853*, 307.
[11]W. K. Parish to JAL, Jan. 16, 1853, Logan Mss.

and protect, and that we have men who are willing and able to do it."[12]

The law of greatest interest to southern Illinois in 1853 was the Negro exclusion bill which emerged as the session's last major business. Egyptians greeted Logan's action with a solid show of support. They viewed the spectre of wholesale Negro immigration into Egypt as a great calamity to be avoided at all costs. Parish wrote Logan, "The move . . . in relation to the immigration of free negroes into the state is one that will reflect credit and distinction in Egypt especially."[13]

In taking the lead in transferring this feeling, almost unanimous in Egypt, into legislative action, Logan became for the first time recognized throughout the state as Egypt's spokesman. His statements in debate came to be regarded as those of the entire section. The Negro bill first skyrocketed Logan into state-wide prominence, won him immense popularity in his home section, but brought condemnation from many quarters.

Anti-Negro feeling had grown in Illinois in the 1840's. The Constitution of 1848 denied Negroes the vote and the right to serve in the militia. Furthermore, there was a provision instructing the legislature to pass laws prohibiting the entrance of Negroes into the state. This provision was separately submitted to Illinois voters for ratification and passed 50,261 to 21,297.[14] Until 1853 the provision was ignored. But in 1853 Logan took advantage of the invitation contained in the 1848 law and moved to end Negro immigration.

There were few Negroes in the state; the 1850 census listed only 5,436, but of this number 3,124 lived in counties included in the Egyptian triangle.[15] These unfortunates existed in pitiful conditions with no legal status whatsoever. In the 1850's northern Illinois abolitionists began to demand increased rights for these Negroes. Egyptians reacted to this pressure by demanding a counterattack that would make a Negro de-

---

[12]Benton *Standard*, quoted in the Quincy *Herald*, March 24, 1853.

[13]N. Dwight Harris, *The History of Negro Servitude in Illinois; and of Slavery Agitation in that State, 1719-1864* (Chicago, 1904), 234; W. K. Parish to JAL, Jan. 16, 1853, Logan Mss.

[14]Cole, *Era of the Civil War*, 225.

[15]Cole, *Era of the Civil War*, 225; *Seventh Census of the United States, 1850*, 702.

luge on their section impossible. Logan's bill was a response to this clamor from his constituents.

By late January, all interest in Springfield centered on the Negro bill. On January 29, Logan reported the bill out of committee. The stage was set and the debate was scheduled for the middle of the following week. On February 2 the speaker announced the bill as the next order of business and heated debate began.

Opposition to Logan's bill came from the representatives from the counties along the northern border, combined with a scattering of support from legislators from north central Illinois. On the first day of debate, the northern men introduced an amendment that would have repealed all of Illinois' "Black Codes." This proposal was beaten 58 to 7.[16] During debate on the amendment, Logan attacked its backers as "abolitionists," and charged that repeal would lead to intermarriage and social and political equality.[17]

Following this exchange, Logan's bill reached the floor for adoption. This law made the introduction of a Negro into the state a crime punishable by a $100 fine. Furthermore it made any Negro entering the state liable within ten days to arrest and fine, and if unable to pay the fine, he was forced to work out the fine and trial costs.[18]

The measure was attacked vigorously by its opponents and Logan was forced to speak out in its defense. Summoning all the arguments Egyptians had been advancing for a decade, Logan began by attacking his adversaries as supporters of racial equality. He stated that history illustrated that Negroes are "not suited to be placed upon a level with white men."[19] Reaching the heart of his argument, he stated that Egypt, surrounded by slave states, would be the only area of the state harmed by mass Negro migration. He proclaimed his constituents' fear that Negroes would migrate into Egypt, become paupers, and ruin the morals of the section. In conclusion Logan lashed out at the pro-Negro legislators:

[16]*House Journal, 1853*, 363.
[17]Ms. of speech delivered in the Illinois legislature in 1853, Logan Mss.
[18]Harris, *Negro in Illinois*, 236.
[19]Ms. of speech delivered in the Illinois legislature in 1853, Logan Mss.

Nor can I understand how it is that men can become so fanatical in their notions as to forget that they are white. Forget the sympathy over the white man and have his bosom heaving with it for those persons of color. It has almost become an offense to be a white man. Unfortunate were these gentlemen in their birth that they could not have been ushered into existence with black skin and a wooly head.[20]

Logan's final roar was a threat. "Unless this bill shall pass you will hear it again next session and again until something shall be done to protect those people from the inundation from the colored population."[21]

Soon after Logan's ringing defense died away, roll call began. It was evident that the bill's opponents had gained strength. Logan's speech had alarmed some members of his own party from northern Illinois who felt that the bill was too harsh. This group was not large enough to create a coalition capable of defeating the measure, and when the vote was tallied the bill passed 45 to 23. Voting "aye" was a solid bloc of representatives from the counties south of Springfield.[22] When the House adjourned, Logan received congratulations on his first major legislative victory. Six days later the Senate passed the bill by a four-vote majority.

Though the victory was popular in Egypt, others in the state said that the law was brutal, too stringent, and passed by the Democrats merely to satisfy southern Illinois and to placate their fellow Democrats from the slave states. Several mass meetings were held in the North to protest the act's passage.[23] The attack came from many quarters; some Democrats joined Whigs and Free Soilers in opposition. John M. Palmer, writing years later, summed up their feeling: "All the provisions of the act are an example of the barbarity which can only be excused by the prejudices of that part, the Southern, of the State of Illinois."[24]

[20]Ibid.
[21]Ibid.
[22]House Journal, 1853, 442-443.
[23]Logan's law did receive staunch support from the Illinois State Register (Springfield), but some Democratic organs in northern Illinois were hesitant in giving the measure their unqualified backing.
[24]John M. Palmer, Personal Recollections (Cincinnati, 1901), 59.

One student of the Negro in Illinois maintains that the bill was probably favored by a majority of the state's population, and that though many opposed the rigid provisions for enforcement, most Illinoisans favored the exclusion of free Negroes in principle. The same writer challenges those who believe that the law was never enforced, citing at least three cases of arrest under the "Logan Negro Law."[25] Gustave Koerner, a leading German politician, also gives evidence of the law's enforcement. Koerner, an opponent of the bill, tells of freeing a Negro about to be arrested under the measure.[26] The law remained in effect until 1863, when it was repealed.

On February 14, the 18th Assembly ended, and Logan returned to Egypt over muddy February roads. The session had given Logan a chance to move up the political ladder. His name was known throughout Illinois, and he had made a record that gave him increased stature in Egypt. The 27 year old returned as a conquering hero who had advanced his section's legislative banner, met the enemy and emerged victorious. His fellow Egyptians were already speaking of the great things the future held for him.

On his return, Logan and Parish settled down to their expanding practice in Benton. Shortly thereafter Logan was summoned to Murphysboro by the news that his father was dying. Within the week, despite the best attention available, Dr. Logan died from an abscessed liver. The young legislator's triumphant return was shattered. The deep affection between father and son is obvious from their correspondence. The doctor had been proud of his son's success; his influence on Logan's youth and early political career was considerable.

Back in Benton, Logan found that increased popularity materially aided him. Logan and Parish defended murderers, took divorce cases and spent most of their time in actions involving small claims.[27] Logan's most famous case was his defense of a prominent citizen of Union County on trial for murder. Hostility toward his client led Logan to ask for a change of venue, and the trial was moved to Golconda. Logan's plea was self-

---

[25]Harris, *Negro in Illinois*, 237.
[26]Gustave P. Koerner, *Memoirs of Gustave P. Koerner* (Cedar Rapids, 1909), II, 31.
[27]Ms. of legal notebooks, 1851-1858, Logan Mss.

defense as the death had taken place during an altercation. The courthouse stood in a field of grazing sheep. As Logan arose to deliver his summation to the jury, a dog chased a lamb into the courtroom. Sensing his opportunity, Logan seized the lamb and, holding it in his arms, likened the defendant to the sacrificial lamb of the Old Testament. The plea was effective and the jury found the defendant not guilty.[28]

But Logan was not long to appear as an attorney for the defense. In 1853 the election for prosecuting attorney of the Third Judicial District was to be held. A victory in this election would give him an excellent chance of improving himself politically, as well as gaining prestige in the legal profession. The Third District included the lower 16 counties of the state and included most of the counties of the Ninth Congressional District. A term as prosecutor would give Logan a chance to spread his influence over the entire area and stand him in good stead for any future attempt at higher elective office. He announced for the office and was easily elected.

In the spring of 1854 Logan began his new duties. As prosecutor, Logan visited the counties of his district for the regular court sessions. Travel over rough roads on horseback was tiring and occasional rheumatism, contracted during the march to Santa Fe was painful.[29]

Court was pure delight to Logan. There was ample opportunity for hearty conviviality, story telling and political discussion. Though his duties occupied a great deal of time, the young attorney was active in Egyptian politics. His leadership in the legislature and his willingness to speak out in defense of the section had made him a growing force in Egypt. The editor of the Cairo *City Times* reported on June 7, 1854 his attendance at court, where he met, "Our old friend John A. Logan, who . . . is performing with universal acceptability the duties of State's attorney."[30]

1854 was an election year and Logan maintained close interest in the Democratic nomination for the House from Lower

[28]Dawson, *Logan*, 9.
[29]Mary Logan, *Reminiscences*, 8. Logan retained his partnership with Parish in name until 1855, when Parish became circuit court judge and the partnership was dissolved.
[30]Cairo *City Times*, June 7, 1854.

Egypt. It went to Scott Marshall, who was chosen to succeed Willis Allen, leaving the House after two terms. Logan had met Marshall on the circuit, and they had become friends. During his campaign, Marshall prominently displayed a list of "intimate acquaintances" who endorsed his candidacy. Logan's name headed the list.[31]

The same year brought the renewal of the debate over slavery in the territories. Most of the Illinois Democrats, Logan included, backed Douglas and popular sovereignty, and endorsed the Kansas-Nebraska Act. When the "Little Giant" returned to Springfield, Logan journeyed to the capital to see the senator, and as Douglas spoke to the large welcoming crowd, Logan stood among the state's party leaders behind him. He enthusiastically applauded Douglas' statement, "I tell you the time has not yet come when a handful of traitors in our camp can turn the great State of Illinois . . . into a Negro worshiping, Negro equality community."[32]

After the meeting Logan returned to Egypt and to his thriving practice. 1854 and 1855 were eventful years for the young lawyer-politician. In the spring of 1855 Logan began a legal association with W. J. "Josh" Allen. Logan's new partner was the son of ex-Congressman Willis Allen and the partnership brought to an end Logan's estrangement from this influential Egyptian political family. Relations had been improving slowly since the 1852 elections, and Logan and "Josh" Allen remained close friends down to the Civil War, though their partnership was terminated in 1859.[33]

Most of Logan's business in early 1855 concerned a murder trial at Jonesboro, but he had time to devote to politics. He lost no occasion to applaud popular sovereignty and to acclaim Douglas a future president. Logan also spoke several times against the Know-Nothings, charging them with intolerance and with attempting to deny constitutional rights to many Americans. One of these speeches, at Metropolis, led the Cairo

---

[31]*Ibid.*, Nov. 1, 1854. Among other names on the list was Marion County Democrat Silas Bryan, father of William Jennings Bryan.

[32]Carl Sandburg, *Abraham Lincoln: The Prairie Years* (New York, 1928), II, 11.

[33]Newsome, *History of Jackson County*, 66; Cairo *City Times*, April 4, 1855.

City Times to exclaim, "John is one of the right sort; a pure patriot and unflinching Democrat."[34]

Perhaps the most important political event of the year in Egypt was Douglas' autumn visit. The "Little Giant" was pleased with Democratic organization in southern Illinois and promised to speak there in September and October.[35] He made several stops and Logan joined the senator in striking out at opposition to "Nebraska" policy. The 29-year-old prosecutor had become Douglas' friend and supporter, and the older man was happy to be associated with the son of his old friend of the 10th General Assembly.[36]

Despite Logan's political interests, law was still his primary concern, and as prosecutor he toured the circuit. These court sessions were pleasant. With the exception of Murphysboro, none gave him greater pleasure than his stops in Shawnee-town, county seat of Gallatin County, a lively village over-looking the Ohio. It had been one of Egypt's earliest ports, and many of the section's pioneers, who drifted down the Ohio, de-barked there. In 1855 it was the site of a thriving land office serving much of southern Illinois.

Registrar of the Shawneetown land office was Logan's old friend, John M. Cunningham, and Logan was always welcome at the captain's home. Logan reminded the captain that during the war he had promised to give him his daughter Mary in marriage. The promise had been in jest since she was only eight at the time, but Logan asked about her and was told she was in school at Morganfield, Kentucky.[37] During the next year Logan returned frequently and in June, 1855, Mary came home and her father invited Logan to meet her. The girl was 17, vivacious and friendly, with a large circle of young friends.

Logan seems to have fallen in love with Mary almost from their first meeting, but Mary, fresh from school, showed signs of uncertainty. Her return from school brought a round of parties with friends, but Logan persisted, and traveled long

[34]Cairo *City Times*, May 2, 1855.
[35]Stephen A. Douglas to Charles Lanphier, July 7, 1855, Lanphier Mss., Illinois State Historical Library, Springfield.
[36]Cairo *City Times*, Sept. 26, 1855; Frank E. Stevens, *The Life of Stephen A. Douglas* (Springfield, 1924), 673.
[37]Mary Logan, *Reminiscences*, 27, 29.

distances to spend weekends with her. In the early summer Logan was able to spend some time in Shawneetown as prosecutor in a murder case and Mary's hesitancy began to fade with his constant attention.

By August Logan was ready to propose and on the sixth he wrote, "Be assured of my sincerity and after mature reflection, say that you will be mine."[38] Mary's answer was not complete acceptance. She still had reservations and later wrote: "To this day I marvel that a young man of Logan's rare ability, ambition, and mature years . . . should hazard his career by marrying a girl of seventeen."[39] Logan's reply to her letter was a panic stricken missive asking if there was a rival for her affections. His fears were quickly allayed, however, and one day later, in Benton, he received her acceptance. November 27 was the wedding date.[40]

From August to November, Logan rode to Shawneetown whenever possible and the two corresponded steadily. They exchanged miniatures, and in October, when Mary spent a week in Kentucky at her old school, Logan journed to Murphysboro, assuring Mary, "I shall have a nice time telling my good old Mother all about My Mary and having her advice to me."[41]

The wedding was simple. Logan's family lived too far to attend and the couple was married by Logan's old partner, Judge Parish, in the presence of a few friends.

The couple lived in Benton after the wedding and Mary found her first months there a constant strain, since she had to act as hostess to large groups of her husband's legal and political friends. "Remembering that Logan's wife must be equal to everything," she later wrote, "I put aside my timidity."[42]

Mary accompanied Logan on the circuit. She endured jolting buggy rides and was entranced with the excitement of court days. Mary became more than a mere traveling companion as she began to read law reports to her husband and write blanks for the indictments used by the prosecutor.

---

[38]JAL to Mary Cunningham, Aug. 6, 1855, Logan Mss.
[39]Mary Logan, *Reminiscences*, 38-39.
[40]JAL to Mary Cunningham, Aug. 15, 16, 1855, Logan Mss.
[41]JAL to Mary Cunningham, Aug. 20, Oct. 5, 1855, Logan Mss.
[42]Mary Logan, *Reminiscences*, 41.

Soon Mary's trips had to cease. In early 1856 Logan learned that he was going to become a father. The cottage in Benton became a lonely place for the young wife and she told Logan she would never get used to his absences.[43] His letters were filled with legal news and regrets at separation. At every possible occasion Logan came to Benton, but 1856 was an important political year and visits became fewer. He kept in close touch with local, state, and national affairs. From Washington a Douglas supporter suggested Logan begin organizing support for the "Little Giant" for president, "so as to show abroad that he stands fair in his own state."[44] Other politicians wrote asking his advice and support; his influence was being courted by office-seekers throughout southern Illinois.[45]

In the summer, Logan joined Illinois Democrats at Springfield to nominate their candidates for state office. They deplored Buchanan's victory over Douglas, but they endorsed "Buck and Breck" against the "Black Republican" Fremont. Logan was named an elector on the Democratic ticket from the Ninth Congressional District, and he was one of the orators chosen to address the mass meeting held after the convention. William A. Richardson was nominated for governor against William Bissell, a former Democrat who had broken with the party on the Kansas issue. The "Nebraska" test of loyalty to Douglas' leadership was applied everywhere by the Democrats, and in Egypt, with the exception of the German counties along the Mississippi, the "Little Giant" received solid support. The loss of the Germans was partially compensated for by the accession to the Democrats of old Whigs whose party had disintegrated.

In Egypt, the Democratic Convention in the Ninth District re-nominated Scott Marshall for the House, a nomination tantamount to election. Logan again stumped southern Illinois for Marshall and the party ticket. In the fall he decided to resign as state's attorney and run for the legislature from his old district. His powerful voice was heard throughout the section as he denounced "Black Republicans" and Know-Nothings

[43]*Ibid.*, 50.
[44]John Hacker to JAL, Feb. 22, 1856, Logan Mss.
[45]Green B. Raum to JAL, Aug. 7, 1856; William H. Snyder to JAL, March 13, 1856, Logan Mss.

with equal fervor.[46] When Douglas spoke in Carbondale in October, Logan joined Marshall in echoing the statements of the senior senator. At Belleville the Democrats invaded the German counties in force and Logan joined John A. McClernand, James Robinson, both congressmen, Don Morrison, and Bob Ingersoll in speaking for the party's candidates. Gustave Koerner remembered Logan as "one of the most vituperative speakers [who] abused Colonel Bissell so as to disgust even his party friends."[47]

Logan's own contest was never in doubt, and on election day he rolled up a greater majority than four years earlier. However, the fate of Buchanan and Richardson in Illinois was uncertain. Despite huge Democratic majorities in Egypt, the Republicans carried the state house and Buchanan barely won the state's electoral votes.[48] While Logan felt that the state was "disgraced" for having voted for Bissell, Republicans gloried in their gains and stated that only the solid vote of backward Egypt the "land of darkness," had kept Illinois out of the Republican column.[49]

The election victory was followed by the excitement of the birth of his first child, John Cunningham Logan. December was the happiest period of the young couple's life. Baby and mother prospered, and the new father looked forward to the opening of the legislature. In January the Logans decided that mother and child should stay in Benton rather than undertake the trip to Springfield.

The 20th General Assembly met in Springfield on January 5, 1857. This time Logan was no longer the obscure son of a former legislator, but a figure of considerable influence. Despite Bissell's victory, the Democrats had captured both houses

---

[46]Cairo *Times and Delta*, July 16, 1856.

[47]Koerner, *Memoirs*, II, 29.

[48]Cairo *Times and Delta*, Nov. 26, 1856; David W. Lusk, *Politics and Politicians of Illinois, 1856-1884* (Springfield, 1884), 35. In Logan's district composed of Franklin and Jackson Counties, Buchanan and Richardson ran far ahead of the Republicans. Buchanan carried Franklin 1051 to 5 and Jackson 1144 to 2. Richardson carried Franklin 1076 to 34 and Jackson 1096 to 46. The vote in Illinois for president was: Buchanan 105,528; Fremont 96,278; Fillmore 37,531.

[49]*Illinois State Journal* (Springfield), Nov. 19, 1856; JAL to Mary Logan, Nov. 9, 1856, Logan Mss.

of the Assembly, and the governor was faced by a hostile legislature. On the Democratic side of the House, outstanding leaders were Logan, John Dougherty, Ebon C. Ingersoll, Bob's brother, and W. R. Morrison. Leaders of the Republicans were C. B. Denio and Isaac Arnold. There was also a small group of six Know-Nothings, led by Shelby M. Cullom.[50]

First business was election of a speaker, and Democrat Samuel Holmes' victory over Isaac Arnold presaged Democratic domination. The House completed its routine business, and Logan and S. W. Moulton, both Democrats, and Cullom were named to conduct outgoing Democratic Governor Joel Matteson to the chair for his message.

The following day committee assignments were made. Logan was appointed to Judiciary, Finance, Penitentiary, Banks and Corporations, and was named chairman of the Committee on Elections. On January 13, the serenity of the chamber was broken and party feelings were inflamed almost to the point of violence. Logan's speech caused the explosion, for which many had been waiting.

Governor Bissell was a victim of a "rheumatic affliction of the lower extremities which prevents me from much walking, without assistance." The partial paralysis was a result of Mexican War injuries, and Bissell decided in 1855, to give up politics. In 1856 he changed his mind when he discovered "an extraordinary and persistent effort being made to wheel Illinois into the ranks of the slavery supporting . . . states."[51]

Bissell had been a Democrat, but renounced Douglas' leadership following the Kansas-Nebraska Act. His switch to the Republicans cost him little support and in 1856 he was elected governor. This was treason, and Democrats were looking for a chance to attack the traitor. Their opportunity came when they discovered that Bissell had once been challenged to a duel by Jefferson Davis of Mississippi in a feud involving their actions in the Mexican War. Since the 1848 Constitution pre-

---

[50]*Journal of the Illinois House of Representatives, Twentieth General Assembly, 1857*, 3-5. Hereafter cited as *House Journal, 1857.*

[51]W. H. Bissell to E. Peck, Jan. 21, 1856, Joseph Gillespie Mss., Illinois State Historical Library, Springfield.

vented a man from taking office as chief executive under these circumstances, the stage was set.[52]

Strangely enough, the Democrats did not press the accusation in the campaign, but Logan and the other Democrats had been preparing their case since the election, and seeking "an orator to execute the unfeeling task." Logan was chosen.[53] This plan of attack was not unknown to the general public since newspapers had been editorializing on Bissell's disqualification for some time.[54]

When the Assembly convened, the state waited for the Democratic challenge. Due to Bissell's infirmity, the governor's message was read for him. It was a moderate speech, but left no doubt that Bissell was opposed to extension of slavery in the territories.[55] Following the reading Logan rose and began his tirade. He condemned Bissell's position on slavery as a surrender to the abolitionist principles of the Republicans, and assaulted the governor as a perjurer, branding him as unfit to hold his high office. Reaching an emotional crescendo, Logan concluded:

> This sir, is my home. Beneath the green and hallowed sod of this beautiful prairie state lie the bones of my aged and venerable father. Shall I stand quietly by, as one of the people's representatives, and see her public morals corrupted, her constitution violated, her honor tarnished, and give no sound of alarm?[56]

His final words were lost in a roar of applause from the Democrats and a storm of boos from the Republicans. Arnold and Denio rose to Bissell's defense, and Koerner condemned the speech as the "coarsest billingsgate." A Republican paper called Logan's effort a "long and frothy speech . . . in which

---

[52]Shelby M. Cullom, *Fifty Years of Public Service: Personal Recollections* (Chicago, 1911), 180; Bateman and Selby, *Sangamon County*, I, 48; Cole, *Era of the Civil War*, 151-152.

[53]Alexander Davidson and Bernard Stuve, *A Complete History of Illinois from 1673 to 1884* (Springfield, 1884), 661; JAL to William R. Morrison, Jan. 13, 1857; William R. Morrison to JAL, Jan. 13, 1857; JAL to Philip B. Fouke, Jan. 6, 1857, Logan Mss.; Robert D. Holt, "The Political Career of William A. Richardson," *Journal of the Illinois State Historical Society*, XXVI, No. 3 (Oct., 1933), 242.

[54]Cairo *Times and Delta*, Nov. 19, 1856.

[55]Cullom, *Fifty Years*, 25.

[56]Ms. of a speech delivered January 13, 1857, in the Illinois State Legislature, Logan Mss.

he has disgusted his own party." Even the Know-Nothings
backed Bissell and Cullom called the speech "cruel and a viru-
lent attack" and recalled, "I became very much prejudiced
against" Logan.[57]

Democrats jumped to Logan's defense. The speech was published, in pamphlet form, with an appendix of letters from
Davis to Bissell, for distribution throughout Illinois. Support
came from many quarters, and Judge I. N. Haynie told Logan
that his speech had been well received in Egypt.[58] Some Democrats, however, were upset by the lack of consideration shown
the sickly governor.

Bissell was a sensitive man, and the attack "deeply wounded
him." He became his own best defender. Instead of answering
charge with charge, he resorted to calm, reasoned argument.
Bissell simply maintained, as he had during the election, that
the constitution did not apply in his case. His defense was that
the technical challenge had not been given or accepted and
that no duel had been fought. Furthermore he claimed that
since the entire affair had taken place outside the state and
not within Illinois' jurisdiction, he was in no way a perjurer
and could take his oath of office.[59]

The turmoil gradually subsided, but the animosities the
speech created remained beneath the surface. The "Bissell
speech" was Logan's major action of the session, and while it
strengthened him at home, its very nature tended to verify
Republican claims that Logan was little better than a bigoted,
cruel rowdy from backward Egypt who merely served as a
henchman for Douglas.[60]

For·the rest of the session, Logan's activity was steady and
unsensational. He led the fight against repeal of a section of
his 1853 Negro exclusion bill, and the motion to repeal was
tabled 46 to 28.[61] Another move popular in Egypt was his active participation in the fight to fend off reapportionment. One
proposal, which would have cut the representatives in Lower

---

[57]Koerner, *Memoirs*, II, 39; Quincy *Weekly Whig*, Feb. 7, 1857; Cullom, *Fifty Years*, 25, 180.
[58]Davidson and Stuve, *History of Illinois*, 661; I. N. Haynie to JAL,
Jan. 17, 1857, Logan Mss.
[59]Koerner, *Memoirs*, II, 39; Cullom, *Fifty Years*, 180.
[60]Cameron Rogers, *Colonel Bob Ingersoll* (New York, 1927), 89.
[61]*House Journal, 1857*, 91.

Egypt from five to four, was tabled 38 to 32.[62] Among the most constructive acts of the session were acts establishing free schools and the law building a new penitentiary. These were passed with little fanfare, and when the solons dispersed February 19, the Logan speech remained the most talked about event of the session.

Mary anxiously awaited the end of business in Springfield. When the session ended, Logan came home to spend what they hoped would be a long sojourn. However, Logan had to make a living, and he soon set off on the circuit, with his partner Josh Allen. He found no dearth of business, and the young barrister who had bearded the Republicans in the capital had as much work as he could handle. He was gradually becoming one of the most sought after lawyers in the southern half of the state. In the summer of 1857, Logan was retained by the prosecution in the case for which he is best remembered.

Shawneetown was a town of violent Democratic factionalism. The local paper, the *Illinoisan*, actively participated in these feuds and served as a mouthpiece for Colonel James C. Sloo, a quarrelsome Democrat who differed with most Egyptians on slavery. Sloo had been at odds with the majority of his party for years, once calling Scott Marshall a "foul mouthed puppy."[63] Leader of the colonel's opponents was John E. Hall, clerk of the county and circuit courts. Hall was a close friend of Captain Cunningham and Bob Ingersoll, his deputy. These three constantly came under attack from the *Illinoisan* and Sloo.[64]

The Hall faction frequently used nearby newspapers to defend itself. In October, 1856, the Marion *Intelligencer* ran an article signed "Vindex," which delivered a scurrilous attack on Colonel Sloo.[65] When Ingersoll asked his superior if he was "Vindex," he received an enigmatic reply. Hall's manner convinced Ingersoll that he had delivered the blast.[66]

---

[62]*Ibid.*, 895.

[63]Shawneetown *Illinoisan*, Sept. 8, 1854.

[64]Ms. of Ingersoll Brothers legal day book, 1856-1857, Robert G. and Ebon C. Ingersoll Mss., Illinois State Historical Library, Springfield; Rogers, *Ingersoll*, 86; Herman Kittredge, *Robert G. Ingersoll; a Biographical Appreciation* (New York, 1911), 36; Shawneetown *Illinoisan* as quoted in the Cairo City *Times*, Oct. 31, 1855.

[65]Marion *Intelligencer*, Oct. 10, 1856.

[66]Rogers, *Ingersoll*, 87; Kittredge, *Ingersoll*, 39.

In November, Colonel Sloo's son Robert returned from West Point and began gunning for "Vindex." One day, as Ingersoll was taking dictation from Hall, Bob Sloo appeared in the doorway. Before either man could move, Sloo fired, and Hall lay dead in Ingersoll's arms. The young assassin made no attempt to escape and was quickly apprehended, but the trial did not begin until the spring of 1857.

In southern Illinois, the excitement of the Dred Scott decision paled into insignificance beside the Sloo trial. As the time approached, Shawneetown was deluged by visitors. The prosecution hired Logan and Allen, and the defense was led by John Dougherty, a leading Democrat and old friend of Colonel Sloo.[67] Logan took the case hesitantly since Mary was slightly ill when he left Benton.

Empaneling a jury took some time, so heated were local passions, and it was late May before the trial began. The defense produced an immediate sensation when it indicated that Sloo's defense would be temporary insanity, a plea Logan considered "a most infamous lie . . . but will not avail him in my judgement."[68] The trial dragged on through the summer until tempers were frayed and passions almost at the breaking point. To make matters more uncomfortable for Logan, Mary's illness lingered and the baby was sick. By August he wrote:

> You can not imagine the distress and uneasiness of mind I am in since reading your letter. Has the Lord determined to destroy our happiness on this earth? I am almost tempted to start home tonight, but . . . I suppose I will have to remain in suspense till I hear again. We are nearly through this week and God knows I will not leave you again.[69]

He also advised her that he was confident that Sloo could not be acquitted and that a hung jury was his only chance of escape.

In early August, Logan wrote that Sloo's defense "have got four abolition doctors here from the North who are going to swear that he is crazy as a bedbug and God knows what effect it will have on the case."[70] The effect was disastrous, and Sloo

---

[67]Cairo *Times and Delta*, June 3, 1857.
[68]JAL to Mary Logan, May 28, 1857, Logan Mss.
[69]Ibid., Aug. 3, 4, 1857, Logan Mss.

was eventually acquitted of the grounds of insanity. This was a pioneer case in the state since it was one of the first acquittals based on insanity. Logan had served the prosecution ably and was disappointed in the verdict, but he was at last free to return to Benton.

He returned to find Mary recovered but his son's condition had worsened. It was soon evident that the baby might never recover, and the autumn was filled with despair when the baby died in late September.[71]

The period following this tragic event were months of crisis for the family. Mary, lonely at home, had borne the brunt of the tragedy and was desolated. She pleaded with her husband not to leave her again, and when he returned to the circuit and the political wars in 1858, her letters ring with supplications. "Politics if you will allow can destroy our happiness together. It will robb [sic] you of all domestic feelings and make you miserable except when in the society of men engaged in the discussion of political subjects."[72]

Logan countered with arguments he used over and over. He told Mary that law and politics were his only trade. He regretted the separations, but they were necessary for him to make a living. Gradually she became reconciled and wrote: "It will sound rather strange to you to see me so much interested about your being a candidate . . . but I am satisfied you will not be contented to lead a quiet domestic life for a few years at least." One reason for this interest was that the candidacy Mary alluded to was the U. S. Congress. She hoped that a victory would keep them together more effectively than had Logan's earlier posts.

In the spring of 1858, rumors spread through Egypt that Marshall would step aside and that Logan would be his successor. Logan's apprenticeship in state politics was coming to a close. As he had moved from local politics to the state level in 1853, so he was prepared to move to the national scene in 1858. While the nation watched Illinois, all Egypt kept an eye on Logan, waiting for confirmation of the rumor.

---

[70]Ibid., July 28, 1857, Logan Mss.
[71]Mary Logan, *Reminiscences*, 58.
[72]Mary Logan to JAL, March 8, 1858, Logan Mss.

CHAPTER III

DIRTY WORK IN WASHINGTON

Egypt had always been a Democratic stronghold. Whigs received little support from small farmers who loudly proclaimed their loyalty to Jacksonian Democracy. In 1856 Republicans showed little power in Egypt. For years, Democrats running for state office had counted on Egyptian landslides to push them to victory. Douglas was no exception, and in 1846 and 1852 the section marched solidly behind him. Then came the renewal of the question of slavery in the territories, which brought a change to the Democrats of Egypt, Illinois, and the nation.

In 1857 Buchanan demanded that the Lecompton Constitution be accepted as the formula for solving the Kansas question. When support of this mockery of popular sovereignty became a test of party loyalty, the Democratic party became divided. In December, Douglas, who would not accept the proslave constitution, arrived in Washington to talk to the president. The two men could not agree, and Buchanan warned the senator of the price of party insurgency.[1]

The Douglas-Buchanan split had immediate repercussions in Egypt. Most southern Illinois Democrats fell in behind Douglas, but there were administration supporters who wrote: "It has been boasted that Mr. Douglas holds Illinois in his breeches pocket, and can lead it away with him in support of whatever vagaries his self-willed head may lead him into. This is a most tremendous mistake."[2]

Logan never hesitated in his support of the "Little Giant," agreeing with the Douglas press which proclaimed, "The people are with him for he is right."[3] As the Douglasites organized for the battle, there was speculation about the Douglas

[1]Philip G. Auchampaugh, "The Buchanan-Douglas Feud," *Journal of the Illinois State Historical Society*, XXV, No. 1 (April, 1932), 12; Milton, *Eve of Conflict*, 273.
[2]Cairo *Times and Delta*, Feb. 24, 1858.
[3]Salem *Advocate*, Jan. 1, 1858.

candidate for the House in the Ninth District. In April, Scott
Marshall declined to run for re-election, announcing that he
had a friend willing to take up the cry against Lecompton.[4] To
most Egyptians the "friend" was obviously Logan, and in a
perceptive view of Egyptian politics the administration press
asked:

> How have our Congressional candidates been nominated
> and elected? Beginning with Willis Allen they have been
> elected by the fiat of a few. Samuel S[cott] Marshall was a
> man of influence and belonged to this clique; John A. Logan
> is a man of influence and belongs to this clique; W. J. Allen
> is a man of influence and belongs to this clique; all were
> aspirants for congressional honors; therefore it was ar-
> ranged between them that Mr. Marshall should first go to
> Congress, Mr. Logan next, each one turning his own influ-
> ence and that of his friends in favor of the one whose turn
> it might be to go to Congress.[5]

There seems to have been such an agreement between Egypt's
Democratic leaders, and Marshall, having stepped aside, looked
forward to Logan's "glorious victory over the Black Republicans and the Chicago Postmaster traitors combined."[6]

Most Illinois Democratic leaders remained loyal to Douglas
and denounced the "Danites" or "Buccaneers" as the administration men were called. Logan took the stump early and, after
a speech in Cairo on April 13, even the hostile local press
called his effort "calm and argumentative and frequently interrupted by cheering."[7] Many leading Democrats wrote Logan
in the spring assuring him of an easy triumph.

The Republicans saw in the Democratic schism a chance for
victory in the Senate race as well as a possibility of gaining
several House seats. The "Danites" were making such extravagant claims in Egypt that some Republican leaders envisioned
possible gains in the Democratic stronghold. These optimists
were warned by D. L. Phillips, a Democrat turned Republican,
that these claims were false and that Egypt was pro-Douglas.

---

[4]William Hacker to JAL, April 11, 1858, Logan Mss.
[5]Cairo *Times and Delta*, April 21, 1858.
[6]S. S. Marshall to JAL, May 2, 1858, Logan Mss. The "Postmaster
traitors" are the "Danites."
[7]Cairo *Times and Delta*, April 14, 1858.

John A. Logan as a member of Congress

Courtesy of the Illinois State Historical Library

He added in a letter to Senator Lyman Trumbull, "The Democracy here are led by the Allens, Marshall, Logan . . . and others, and these are all for Douglas. John Logan is bitter against Buchanan."[8] Republicans began to realize that division in their opponents' ranks might do them little good.

With Logan's nomination a foregone conclusion, he became a target for attacks by both "Danites" and Republicans. The *State Journal* called him "an arrant trickster of the blackguard order." The Republican organ at Chicago agreed and added: "He is a Douglasite . . . and evinces determination to follow that gentlemen unto the end."[9]

Organized campaigning began April 21 when Democrats assembled at Springfield. Douglas' candidacy was endorsed and candidates nominated for state office. After Douglas' nomination, the convention split, the "Danites" calling a meeting for June 9 to name their state ticket. In June the Republicans gathered to name their party's slate, endorsing Abraham Lincoln as Douglas' opponent and jibing at the divided Democrats.

Shortly after the Democratic convention at Springfield, Logan and his fellow Egyptians held their district convention at Thebes. Logan was nominated for the House by acclamation, and despite the absence of opposition, he began stumping the district.

This speaking tour was interrupted in June when Logan and his wife journeyed to Chicago to meet Douglas. On the ninth, amid wild enthusiasm, the "Little Giant" entered the city. There he made his first speech of the canvass and conferred with supporters from all over the state. Logan optimistically reported on conditions in the Ninth District and applauded Douglas' speech in which the senator attacked both Buchanan and the Republicans.[10]

The Douglas caravan moved on to Springfield for the senator's second address. The Logans rode the triumphal train to the capital and again listened to the "Little Giant" excoriate their opponents.

---

[8]D. L. Phillips to Lyman Trumbull, March 2, 1858, Lyman Trumbull Mss., Library of Congress.
[9]*Illinois State Journal*, April 22, 1858; Chicago *Press and Tribune*, quoted in Cairo *Times and Delta*, April 28, 1858.
[10]Mary Logan, *Reminiscences*, 58.

After the Springfield meeting, Logan and Mary returned to Benton to begin the congressional campaign. For the first time since their marriage, Mary was able to accompany him on extended tours and she took an increased interest in her husband's political affairs.

Opponents were slow in appearing against Logan. As early as April, rumors started that John Dougherty, well-known Jonesboro Democrat, would be the "Danite" candidate, but this was denied and in June Dougherty was nominated for state treasurer by the "Danites."[11] The Republican candidate in the Ninth was Ben L. Wiley, who did little campaigning. Deploring this inactivity of the opposition, Scott Marshall wrote Logan praying for a more active fight, promising "to travel over the district and help skin them." He added, "we won't have much fun in Egypt unless you can get up something of this kind."[12]

The first real opponent in the field was Logan's former partner, W. K. Parish, the "Danite" man, whom the Cairo *Times and Delta* predicted would win the seat by a "whooping majority."[13] However, it was obvious to most observers that the "Buccaneers" strength in Egypt was largely imaginary.

Logan soon discovered unexpected campaign help. Lincoln challenged Douglas to a series of joint debates, and the list included two Egyptian towns, Jonesboro and Alton. Logan would have a chance to appear beside the senator and benefit from the luster Douglas would add to his cause. Douglas also stood to gain by appearing with Logan. The senator knew that his lieutenant wielded great power in southern Illinois and that Logan's support would probably mean that no "Danite" legislators would be returned from Lower Egypt.

The first two debates took place at Ottawa and Freeport, and in September the senatorial aspirants turned toward Egypt. Douglas arrived first, meeting Logan at Chester, where Logan spoke for the senator. The group moved on to Cairo, where Logan and Marshall preceded Douglas in addressing a crowd of Democrats.[14]

---

[11]Cairo *Times and Delta*, April 28, 1858.
[12]S. S. Marshall to JAL, May 2, 1858, Logan Mss.
[13]Cairo *Times and Delta*, Aug. 11, 1858.
[14]Cairo *Times and Delta*, Sept. 29, 1858; Linder, *Reminiscences*, 345.

Next day Douglas and his companions moved to Jonesboro to meet Lincoln, who had arrived the previous evening. The Jonesboro meeting was one of the quietest of the debates. Until about noon there was little evidence of any unusual activity. About midday the Douglas carriages, accompanied by a cannon, which boomed at every opportunity, rolled into town. That afternoon, about 2,000 people listened to the two giants renew their arguments.[15] Mary Logan later remembered Douglas' ability to win support by the "magnetism of his personality." She also recalled Lincoln:

> I always like to think of Mr. Lincoln as he was in the days when I saw him with the eyes of an opponent. His awkwardness has not been exaggerated, but it gave no effect of self-consciousness. There was something about his ungainliness and about his homely face, even in a state of tall and ungainly men, which would have made any one who simply passed him in the street or saw him sitting on a platform remember him.[16]

The Jonesboro debate renewed the exchange begun at Freeport. Douglas was constantly cheered by the partisan crowd as he defended popular sovereignty. Lincoln's penetration into Egypt was the signal for the gathering of all Egypt's Republicans. This group, combined with the "Danites," who applauded Lincoln out of hatred for Douglas, was able to muster considerable vocal support for the gangling Republican.[17]

The debate served as a rallying point for Egyptian Democrats and Republicans. After the two debators concluded, local battles began in earnest. Logan took advantage of Douglas' presence, and following the match with Lincoln, the "Little Giant" accompanied Logan to Benton. There Douglas addressed a wildly partisan crowd. With Logan presiding, he and the senator blasted the "Danites" and called on the voters of Franklin to follow the Douglas banner. The party next moved to the state fair at Centralia, which provided a good

---

[15]George Smith, *Southern Illinois*, I, 264, estimates the crowd at 2,000. The Chicago *Press and Tribune* estimated the number at 1,400, but the paper was doing its best to convince voters that Douglas could not even draw a crowd in Democratic Egypt.

[16]Mary Logan, *Reminiscences*, 61.

[17]Paul M. Angle (ed.), *Created Equal? The Complete Lincoln-Douglas Debates of 1858* (Chicago, 1958), 200, 223.

opportunity for a large crowd. Again Logan and Douglas shared the platform, the former delivering a speech which even the Chicago *Press and Tribune* admitted was effective.[18]

With the departure of Lincoln and Douglas, politics settled back to normal. But the Alton *Courier* thought that following Lincoln's appearance, "Egypt is waking up and shaking off the political cloud in which it has so long been enshrouded."[19] The Republican press showed great faith in Lincoln's vote getting powers by predicting that Logan's majority might be cut to 5,000, but not even his bitterest opponents forecast a Logan defeat.[20]

In late September, Republicans entered an active candidate against Logan. Wiley, whose business prevented him from campaigning, withdrew, and D. L. Phillips took the stump. The canvass in the Ninth was typical of northwestern politics. Rallies were accompanied by the usual fights and drinking. Most of the district's towns raised poles flying flags lettered with the names of their favorites, and rowdies tried to saw down poles of the opposition.[21] Usually there were only two poles, but there were three in the Ninth District, and the trio of candidates hurled charge and counter-charge. The "Danites" claimed the Know-Nothings were for Logan, but voters remembering his scourging of the nativists in 1856 were inclined to discount the story.[22] The campaign was to a great extent a battle of personalities, much of the time external personalities. The names of Buchanan, Douglas, and Lincoln appear almost as often as those of the congressional candidates. However, the issue of slavery in the territories and the Negro problem in general did occupy the three men. Logan pointed out that the Republicans were in league with the abolitionists and if elected would bring the feared deluge from across the Ohio. Logan found himself between his two opponents, and from opposite poles Republicans and administration men joined in attacking him.

[18]Chicago *Press and Tribune*, Sept. 19, 1858.
[19]Alton *Courier*, Oct. 2, 1858.
[20]Chicago *Press and Tribune*, Oct. 2, 1858.
[21]Charles B. Johnson, *Illinois in the Fifties* (Champaign, Illinois, 1918), 147.
[22]Cairo *Times and Delta*, Sept. 29, 1858.

Though Logan spent most of his time in his own district, in October he entered the neighboring Eighth District, and at Salem joined Silas Bryan and I. N. Haynie in speaking for P. B. Fouke, Douglasite candidate for Congress. Later, after he spoke at Mound City, that town's paper gave clear insight into Logan's political personality:

Logan is a popular speaker and seems to have espoused, certainly so far as this district is concerned, the popular cause. In addition to this, he is personally popular—is in possession of the desirable faculty of making himself a lion in the social circle, as he is acknowledged to be in the political arena. In him abolitionism finds a foe who will be satisfied only with 'war to the knife, and knife to the hilt.' His hate for that creed is bitter and no man knows how to evince a bitter spirit more completely than John A. Logan.[23]

The last great meeting of the contest was the final Lincoln-Douglas debate at Alton, October 15. Again the Democrats gathered, but this time Fouke, the Douglas candidate from the Alton district, was the chief beneficiary of the Little Giant's presence.

Following this debate, Logan concluded his own campaign. Throughout the canvass he had speculated on Douglas' chances. He realized the race would be close. A Republican governor carried the state in 1856 and Lincoln had the added advantage of a divided Democracy. In the summer, the senator's friends attempted to declare a truce, but Buchanan refused and John Slidell, Louisiana senator, and a close Buchanan lieutenant, furnished money to help undermine Douglas.[24] The "Buccaneers" were particularly active in the close legislative districts, and it was feared that if too many of them fell, Douglas might be beaten.[25]

There was great activity, by all sides, in the crucial central region. There the election would be decided. Republicans were conceded a majority in the North and Douglas was awarded

[23]Mound City *Emporium*, Oct. 14, 1858.
[24]Richard R. Stenberg, "An Unnoted Factor in the Buchanan-Douglas Feud," *Journal of the Illinois State Historical Society*, XXV, No. 4 (Jan., 1933), 281; Milton, *Eve of Conflict*, 346.
[25]James W. Sheahan, *The Life of Stephen A. Douglas* (New York, 1860), 397.

Egypt, and a strong swing in either direction in the region around Springfield could be decisive.

Careful observers like Logan were inclined to take other factors into account. Reapportionment had been slow in Illinois, and the populous north was still dominated in the legislature by the Democratic south. In addition, only half the Senate was to be elected, and though it was rumored that the "Danites" were trying to influence the holdovers to abandon Douglas, the senator's forces were confident of their support.[26]

November 2, election day, was cold and rainy. The Republicans later claimed the rain robbed them of victory, but apportionment more than bad weather handed reelection to Douglas. Though Republicans won the state offices, and Lincoln outdrew Douglas in total vote, the legislature was Democratic.

In Egypt almost all the Douglas men were victorious. Douglas candidates were returned from the two legislative districts of Lower Egypt, and with the exception of German St. Clair County, southern Illinois was solidly Douglasite.[27] Logan's vote was overwhelming. He rolled up 15,878 votes to 2,976 for Phillips, and less than 200 for Parish. The "Danites" were crushed, the Republican gain was insignificant, and Logan was swept into office by a 12,000 vote majority.[28] Logan was beaten in only one county of the sixteen in the Ninth District. In Edwards County, northernmost in the district, he lost by 120 votes; Bissell had carried the county by a similar margin two years earlier. In most counties his margin was immense. Johnson County voted for Logan 1158 to 6.

Victory did not mean an immediate trip to Washington. The 36th Congress did not convene until December, 1859. Logan had an entire year before him, and he returned to the circuit to make a living. In January he went to Springfield to practice. He remained through February, writing Mary to apologize for his absence, but advising her, "there may not be so good an opportunity for us to get some money as now."[29] In

[26]Cole, *Era of the Civil War*, 179; Milton, *Eve of Conflict*, 351.
[27]Chicago *Press and Tribune*, Nov. 5, 1858.
[28]Lusk, *Politics and Politicians*, 45; Chicago *Press and Tribune*, Nov. 18, 1858. Despite Republican claims of increased power in Lower Egypt, Phillips garnered only 600 more votes in the Ninth District than Bissell had in 1856. Alton *Courier*, Nov. 4, 1858.
[29]JAL to Mary Logan, Jan. 30, 1859, Logan Mss.

February Logan was honored by the Democratic state committee. In appreciation of his speech against Bissell, it presented him a gold headed cane inscribed "To John A. Logan from his friends for the advocacy of our rights on the 13th of January, 1857."[30] This was good news for Mary, but she had news of her own for Logan. That winter she joyfully announced they were going to have another child.

The year was quiet in Illinois politics. Both parties were working for 1860. The Democrats were certain that Douglas' victory over Lincoln would win him the presidential nomination, and the Republicans, though depressed at their loss, had been kept alive by the vigor of Lincoln's campaign.[31] It was a quiet year for Logan, and his time was consumed by his practice. It brought him a fair living, but like many frontier attorneys he marked many of his accounts unpaid.[32]

Logan spent a great deal of time in Benton and was with Mary when their daughter, named Dorothy after a paternal aunt, was born. All was happy until summer gave way to autumn and a new crisis arose. The baby was too small to stand the trip to Washington and what Mary had hoped would be time together turned into a long separation. Her disappointment was intense, and the parting a painful one, but Logan promised to send for her as soon as possible. In November he left Benton for Washington and national politics.

The trip, Logan's first into the East, was an interesting experience, especially a brief stop at Harpers Ferry. It had been little more than a month since John Brown raided the town, and bullet holes were still plainly visible. Logan, who bitterly denounced Brown, shuddered as he wrote to his wife, "There is more danger of a rupture in this government now than [there] has ever been before."[33]

Logan arrived in Washington November 26, an unknown freshman congressman from the Northwest.[34] He was cheered

---

[30]JAL to Mary Logan, Feb. 7, 1859, Logan Mss.

[31]William E. Baringer, "Campaign Technique in Illinois, 1860," *Transactions of the Illinois State Historical Society*, No. 39 (1932), 203.

[32]Ms. legal account book, 1859, Logan Mss.

[33]JAL to Mary Logan, Nov. 27, 1859, Logan Mss.

[34]Logan was so obscure that he was listed in the index of the *Congressional Globe* as, "Logan, John A., a Congressman from Indiana." *Congressional Globe*, 36th Congress, 1st Session, pt. 1, lvi.

to hear several Southern congressmen say that Douglas was the only man to handle the national emergency.[35] On December 4 Logan's career in the House began informally in Democratic caucus, where he met many of his party's leaders and voted for Thomas Bocock of Virginia for speaker. The five Illinois Democrats were anti-Lecompton men, and though they initially agreed to back Bocock, they were an unknown quantity in the 36th Congress. Leading the Douglas men in the House was John McClernand, whom Logan knew casually from contacts at political gatherings in Illinois. The other Illinois Democrats in the House were James Robinson, Isaac Morris, and Phil Fouke.

Next day, before packed galleries, the 36th Congress began its chaotic course. An explosion came quickly. After one inconclusive vote for speaker, John B. Clark of Missouri introduced a resolution that any man who favored the views toward slavery expressed in Hinton Helper's work *The Impending Crisis* was unfit to be speaker. Since the leading Republican candidate, John Sherman, had endorsed the book, the resolution was obviously directed at him. The reaction to Clark's proposal made the already difficult speakership election almost impossible. Logan favored the Clark resolution and voted against an attempt to table it.

The speakership fight was made uncertain by the close division of the House. There were 109 Republicans, 101 Democrats, and 27 Whigs and Know-Nothings, the latter holding the balance of power. The second ballot shook the contest down to a two-way fight between Sherman and Bocock, with the two minor parties scattering to prevent a choice. It was obvious to Logan that House organization would be a long and tedious process, and he devoted all his spare time to getting his own affairs organized.

On December 7, taking advantage of a lull in the speakership fight, William Kellogg of Illinois rose to attack the rumored deal between Horace Greeley, editor of the New York *Tribune,* and Senator Douglas. The reported bargain would have sold out Illinois Republicans in the senatorial election of 1858. The story was old, frequently denied by Douglas, and

---

[35]JAL to Mary Logan, Dec. 1, 1859, Logan Mss.

it brought Illinois Democrats to their feet. Logan tried to get the floor to answer Kellogg, but failed, and it was McClernand who finally defended the "Little Giant."[36]

Two days later, Logan got the floor for the first time. His maiden speech was not a notable example of parliamentary oratory, but it did not go unnoticed. The chair recognized the young Democrat with the swarthy skin, jet black hair, and large drooping mustache, and his booming voice made his auditors take notice. Logan began by charging Kellogg with making unfounded charges against Douglas. Choking off Kellogg's interruption, he went on charging that the only reason for dredging up the old story was to ruin Douglas as a presidential candidate. Logan reminded the House that Kellogg's cry was, "Republicanism! Abolitionism! Sewardism!" Stopping Kellogg's attempted interruption again, his voice soared as he cried:

> I tell the gentleman now, since he has refused this morning to bring forward his proof, that from this time forth, I shall never notice it. I scorn to notice it any further, and the reason for it is this. I made a charge once, in the legislature of the State of Illinois, and I stood up and did prove it, when called upon for proof, and did not shrink from responsibility, and like a spaniel cower . . .[37]

Kellogg leaped up shouting, "Does the gentleman call me a spaniel coward?" Amid the confusion and shouts the pair rushed at each other, but friends held the two apart while the chair gaveled for order.[38] Through the din, Logan demanded to be allowed to continue, assuring the chair, "I am in no danger of receiving injury." This brought a demand that provocation cease, and Logan promised to continue in "as mild a temper as I am capable of." When hisses and noise continued, he defiantly shouted, "If I am to be hissed; if I am to be clapped down or if I am to be intimidated in this Hall, allow

[36]Cong. Globe, 36th Cong., 1st Sess., pt. 1, 40.
[37]Ibid., 82-83. The allusion to his own charges are those made in the Bissell speech.
[38]New York Times, Dec. 10, 1859; Allan Nevins, The Emergence of Lincoln (New York, 1950), II, 118; Cong. Globe, 36th Cong., 1st Sess., 83. One study claims Logan drew a pistol during the altercation, but no other contemporary or secondary accounts mention the pistol. See, Emerson D. Fite, The Presidential Campaign of 1860 (New York, 1911), 43.

me to say that I have as many rights, whether they be respected or not as any man on this floor."[39] John Farnsworth, Illinois Republican, then asked that the House not be turned into a "bear garden," and suggested that Logan's remarks were out of order. When a semblance of order was restored, Logan, still on his feet, turned his attack on southern Democrats who had received Kellogg's accusation with "smiles and applause." He accused them of being ungrateful to Douglas, whose efforts had always been in their behalf. When he was asked his position on slavery in the territories, his defense of popular sovereignty received loud applause from Democratic benches.

Turning to Republican violations of federal law, Logan called for rigid enforcement of the Fugitive Slave Act. Continuing on the same subject, he won a nickname:

> Every fugitive slave that has been arrested in Illinois, or in any of the Western states, and I call Illinois a Western state, for I am ashamed longer to call it a Northern state, has been made by Democrats. In Illinois the Democrats have all that work to do. You call it the dirty work of the Democratic party to catch slaves for the Southern people. We are willing to perform that dirty work. I do not consider it disgraceful to perform, dirty or not dirty, which is in accordance with the laws of the land, and the Constitution of the country.[40]

From this day, the Republican press of Illinois called him "Dirty Work" Logan.[41]

Logan continued by condemning expressions of sympathy for John Brown which were sweeping the North. He then made a plea for Democratic unity and the election of a Democratic speaker so as to "snatch power from the anti-Constitution, anti-Union, anti-everything" Republicans. When asked if

---

[39]*Cong. Globe*, 36th Cong., 1st Sess., pt. 1, 83.

[40]*Ibid.*, 85. It is interesting to compare this speech and later speeches by Logan in this session with his post-war writings which constantly attack the brutality of the law, calling it "unnecessarily cruel and harsh." John A Logan, *The Great Conspiracy, Its Origin and History* (New York, 1886), 40.

[41]*Illinois State Journal*, Jan. 11, 1860. The Chicago *Press and Tribune* referred to him as "John A. Logan (d.w.)."

he would support a Democratic nominee in 1860 whose slavery views did not agree with those of Douglas, he answered:

> I am now about twenty-eight years of age. I was born a Democrat; and, all my life, I have learned to believe that the Democratic party, in national convention, never do wrong. (Applause and laughter from the Democratic benches and galleries). I have never known the Democratic party, in national convention to endorse a platform that was not consistent with my views. . . . I came here as a Democrat, and I expect to support a Democrat. I may have differed with gentlemen on this side of the House in reference to issues that are passed; but God knows that I have differed with the other side from my childhood, and with that side I will never affiliate so long as I have breath in my body.[42]

Logan's maiden speech, full of violence, wild charges, and obvious "doughfacism," rang with demagogic appeals for preservation of union at all costs. Logan exhibited an ability to turn embarrassing questions to his own advantage, and showed an intense loyalty to Douglas. The senator acknowledged this support and reiterated that Kellogg's charge was an "unmitigated falsehood."[43]

Illinois took notice of the interchange between its two sons. Democrats greeted Logan's speech with joy, and Republicans denounced it. One paper, commenting on Logan's giving his age as 28, when he was actually 33, called the statement "a kind of spread-eagle flourish to attract attention to his youth."[44] Another Republican organ noted a tone to Logan's speech that had been generally overlooked by Illinois Democrats in their enthusiasm. In commenting on Logan's pro-Southern statements and his advocacy of rigid enforcement of the Fugitive Slave Act, a Quincy daily wrote that Logan's speech "does not sit well on the stomachs of some of the Democracy."[45] Indeed some Democrats had begun to ask them-

---

[42]*Cong. Globe*, 36th Cong., 1st Sess., pt. 1, 86. The slip in age (Logan was thirty-three) could have been unintentional, but it was probably done purposely to draw attention to his youth, which he was fond of emphasizing.

[43]Stephen A. Douglas to John McClernand, Dec. 8, 1859, McClernand Mss., Illinois State Historical Library, Springfield.

[44]*Illinois State Journal*, Jan. 11, 1860.

[45]Quincy *Daily Whig and Republican*, Dec. 11, 1859.

selves if this young congressman was not too pro-Southern. Charles Lanphier, Democratic editor of the *Illinois State Register*, wrote McClernand shortly after Logan's speech, deploring the fact that Logan had declared his intention of suporting any platform or nominee of the Charleston convention. Lanphier called the position "peculiar." He added that he had little fear that the convention would nominate anyone other than Douglas, but "let us not anticipate the adoption of such heresies by pledging our support to any such, should they, by possibility be adopted . . . the expressions mentioned are ill received at home. . . . The real meaning of course we appreciate, but it makes awkward record for us."[46]

Logan was pleased with his first effort and told his wife the speech had given him a reputation of which she could be proud. He added that he and McClernand had become "warm friends," and that he had called on Douglas. Glowing with pride, he wrote, "I think I have more standing today in Congress than any new member in it. . . . I think that I am regarded as the best debater in the House, of my age, on all sides."[47]

On the following day Kellogg and Logan rose to apologize for offending the dignity of the House. Logan hoped the exchange had done nothing to inflame relations between members.

The House deadlock continued. Six ballots were taken, with Sherman usually from four to six votes short of majority. The Democrats, Logan included, clung to Bocock. Yet, after a Democratic caucus on December 17 decided to stick with Bocock, Logan wrote Mary that the Republicans would probably organize the House sooner or later. He also told her of a practical problem which plagued all freshmen in the House, the difficulty of getting the floor. Congress was a far cry from the Illinois legislature, but Logan, undaunted, closed by telling his wife that "it is not a hard matter for a man of ordinary mind to become a considerable man in Washington City."[48]

[46]Charles H. Lanphier to John McClernand, Dec. 29, 1859, McClernand Mss.

[47]JAL to Mary Logan, Dec. 10, 13, 1859, Logan Mss.

[48]JAL to Mary Logan, Dec. 17, 1859, Logan Mss.

The next week, a break came in the Sherman-Bocock duel. Bocock withdrew December 19, and his votes scattered, the Illinoisans going to John Reagan of Texas. On the next day, Logan and the Illinois Democrats voted for McClernand, who garnered 21 votes to run third behind Sherman, who was still four votes short. Logan stuck to McClernand for three ballots, then joined the Democratic rush to John S. Millson of Virginia. For a time there was a feeling that the Know-Nothings would back Millson, but with their refusal the contest went on.[49]

Mary Logan's December letters overflowed with pride at her husband's success. But she did exhibit some fright at the difficulty with Kellogg. She assured him that his actions met with solid support from his constituents and "everyone admired your bravery."[50] When she asked him to come home for Christmas, he replied that if he left Washington before a speaker had been elected, neglect of duty would make a "sweet morsel" for his enemies. In one of her letters, Mary mentioned the possibility of disunion, and Logan replied, "I hope and pray that such may never be the case, I don't as yet apprehend danger of such a thing at any time soon, but if these troubles continue the destruction at some day is inevitable."[51]

The troubles did continue. Heated exchanges occurred daily, and some legislators carried firearms in the House. On December 23 and 24, Illinois members monopolized the floor in an intra-state battle. Farnsworth began the exchange by condemning the return of runaway slaves in Egypt. Logan replied that the Egyptians were obeying federal law, and that he saw nothing wrong with advertising for fugitives.[52] Logan pointed out that Farnsworth had endorsed Brown's raid, and stated that he refused to enforce the Fugitive Slave Act. When the Republican acknowledged the truth of the charge, Logan ac-

---

[49]*Cong. Globe*, 36th Cong., 1st Sess., pt. 1, 197, 209.
[50]Mary Logan to JAL, Dec. 21, 1859, Logan Mss.
[51]JAL to Mary Logan, Dec. 31, 1859, Logan Mss.
[52]Advertisement for fugitives was common in Lower Egypt. In 1851, beneath a runaway horse notice, the Jonesboro *Gazette* advertised for a fugitive slave. Jonesboro *Gazette*, April 25, 1851. Five years later a Cairo paper noted: "The owner is requested to come, prove property, pay charges, and take him away." "Him" was a slave named John who was described to facilitate recognition. Cairo *Times and Delta*, Dec. 3, 1856.

cused him of being a disunionist. Argument concluded the next day with Logan defending Kansas-Nebraska and Douglas. During the discussion, Farnsworth stated that while the Democrats worshiped Douglas, the Republicans were men of principle. This brought Fouke to his feet snarling, "We worship Stephen A. Douglas and you worship Fred Douglass." The Republican answered, "I am inclined to think Fred is the likelier man of the two."[53]

While the Illinois members snapped at each other, sporadic votes were taken, all inconclusive. Logan cast his ballot for McClernand, then for Clement Vallandigham of Ohio. The policy to be followed by the Illinois Democrats was clearly delineated by McClernand in January. Illinois Democrats should "keep themselves within the party organization and conciliate Democrats of all shades of opinion so far as is practicable," wrote McClernand. This policy, he felt, was abetting the Douglas campaign. McClernand wrote Charles Lanphier, "Douglas is gaining ground. The example of his friends in the House from Illinois has done much to knock off the edge and much of the opposition to him in the South."[54]

The new year brought little change. An attempt to limit speeches to 20 minutes to facilitate completion of organization failed as Logan joined the opposition. Rumors swept the capital that Southern Democrats were plotting to hamstring legislation by keeping the House unorganized until 1861 if possible. When deadlock continued into January, fear of secession and civil war gripped the nation.

During the second week of the new year, a proposal was made to decide the issue on plurality. Logan, still having trouble obtaining the floor, rose to speak against the motion, but was not recognized.[55] By January 27, 38 ballots had been taken, and the end of the fight seemed near. Democrats were supporting William N. H. Smith of North Carolina, and his

[53]*Cong. Globe*, 36th Cong., 1st Sess., pt. 1, 237-240. There is some evidence that Logan, as a young man, had taken part in captures of fugitive slaves. Daniel Brush, *Growing Up With Southern Illinois*, 125, says that the Logan boys used their father's race horses in catching runaways.

[54]John McClernand to Charles H. Lanphier, Jan. 3, 14, 1860, Lanphier Mss.

[55]*Cong. Globe*, 36th Cong., 1st Sess., pt. 1, 532.

vote was climbing near majority. When he pledged support of popular sovereignty, Logan and the Illinois Democrats changed to Smith. But there was still a drawback. He was rumored to have been a Know-Nothing, and some spurned him for that reason. Logan announced, on changing his ballot, that Smith himself had assured him that he was a Whig, and had never belonged to the American Party. This brought a few more ballots, and the announced total gave the Southerner a one-vote advantage. Then John Sherman rose to cast his first vote of the session. Democrats hissed as he voted for Thomas Corwin of Ohio, and after a wild vote reshuffling, the clerk announced the total: Smith 112, Sherman, 106, scattering 10. Still no majority.[56]

On the following day, a Saturday, the Republicans caucused and Sherman withdrew. Since it was rumored that three eastern anti-Lecompton Democrats would vote for William Pennington of New Jersey, and since Pennington had not endorsed the Helper book, his election seemed possible. Sunday night Logan wrote his wife, "My opinion is that the Republicans will elect a speaker . . . Pennington of New Jersey."[57]

At noon Monday, the galleries were overflowing with spectators who heard Sherman's withdrawal and Pennington's nomination. Stop-Pennington forces united on McClernand, and Logan voted for his fellow Illinoisan to the last. However, some Southerners would not support McClernand, and unity was impossible. On the 44th ballot, taken on the first day of February, an eastern anti-Lecompton man voted for Pennington, and amid Republican cheers the bitter contest ended. Logan had voted on all 44 ballots and supported the general choice of his party, but he agreed with one of his constituents who wrote, "The defeat of Sherman has afforded us some satisfaction, but we would have been better pleased if in addition we could have had a Democratic speaker." The same correspondent lauded the actions of the Illinois House Democrats, "your own course being particularly commendable."[58] Logan's actions were attuned to public opinion at home, and he lost no

[56]*Cong. Globe*, 36th Cong., 1st Sess., pt. 1, 611-612; New York *Times*, Jan. 28, 1860.
[57]JAL to Mary Logan, Jan. 29, 1860, Logan Mss.
[58]S. Staats Taylor to JAL, Feb. 8, 1860, Logan Mss.

opportunity in taking advantage of the fact. He had copies of his December 9 speech printed for distribution in Egypt for the 1860 election.[59]

Republicans in Illinois had paid close attention to the speakership fight, and they chided Democrats for voting for a supposed Know-Nothing, Smith. In a letter to the *State Journal*, Illinois Democratic House members vowed that they would vote for a Know-Nothing before they would support a "Union destroying Black Republican."[60]

When committee assignments were made, Logan received an unimportant appointment to the Committee on Revisal and Unfinished Business. Through February the freshman congressman took little part in House deliberations. He voted against the abolition of the frank for congressmen, and on February 29 visited the Senate to listen to Douglas speak on Illinois politics. Logan heard the senator explain Republicanism: "The creed is pretty black in the northern end of Illinois; about the center it is a pretty good mulatto; and it is almost white when you get down to Egypt."[61]

Through most of February Logan listened to continued exchanges between Republicans and Southerners, and efforts to halt the vituperation. S. S. Cox later remembered Logan as a moderate who, with McClernand, Vallandigham, and himself, served as a "breakwater against the contending tides."[62]

March brought Logan to his feet again in defense of Douglas against accusations by Kellogg of the supposed Greeley deal in 1858. This defense prompted the *State Journal* to comment, "Your Grecian orator, dirty-work Logan, and Monsieur Fouke . . . seem to feel as though Mr. Douglas was in their especial care."[63] Logan voted in favor of the Homestead Bill as that historic measure passed the House 115 to 65.[64]

On March 26, after a prolonged fight to win the floor, Logan introduced a bill reorganizing the district courts of southern

---

[59]JAL to Mary Logan, Dec. 17, 1859, Logan Mss.

[60]*Illinois State Journal*, Feb. 15, 1860.

[61]*Cong. Globe*, 36th Cong. 1st Sess., pt. 1, 920.

[62]S. S. Cox, *Three Decades of Federal Legislation, 1855-1885* (Providence, 1885), 76.

[63]*Illinois State Journal*, March 28, 1860.

[64]*Cong. Globe*, 36th Cong., 1st Sess., pt. 2, 1115.

Illinois. His frustration at being overlooked by the chair burst forth in debate over the Utah Territory and polygamy. There were several proposals for bills which would outlaw polygamy, but some Southerners refused to support such measures, feeling that if polygamy could be declared a crime in a territory, the precedent might later be used against slavery.[65] After Logan voted with the majority against tabling the whole bill, he got the floor and introduced a compromise amendment. He proposed to divide the territory in half, a solution which Logan felt would make the Mormons a minority in each half. For the next week Logan struggled vainly for recognition to discuss his amendment. Failing to get the floor on April 4 he charged while his colleagues called for order, "the floor has been farmed out to different persons; and members have not been recognized when they rose and addressed the speaker. Gentlemen who desired to speak have been excluded and prevented."[66] On the following day, Logan's amendment was defeated 159 to 36.

When spring came, the attention of the Democrats in Congress was divided between legislative affairs and their national convention, scheduled to begin in Charleston April 23. They requested an adjournment during the convention but the motion failed. After voting for a deficiency appropriation bill April 18, Logan and fellow Illinois Democrats left for Charleston. The battle of 1860 had begun.

---

[65]New York *Times*, March 29, 1860.
[66]*Cong. Globe*, 36th Cong., 1st Sess., pt. 2, 1544.

CHAPTER IV

1860, VICTORY AND DEFEAT

Douglas forces in Illinois had long been preparing for Charleston. Delegates had been selected January 4. Six days later the "Buccaneers" held their convention and nominated a separate slate. Both intended to go to the convention and press their claims as legitimate delegates.

In February, Logan had written Scott Marshall that Douglas' chances for the nomination looked good. Marshall replied that he was gratified, since Douglas' victory "is the only hope for us in the Northwest, and is therefore a struggle for life."[1] Before he left the capital, Logan's optimism faded, and he confided to Mary, "I am not entirely sanguine of success as there is the most infamous combination against our man and if they find he is about to be nominated they will try to break up the convention."[2]

Logan was not a delegate, nor was any Democratic representative from Illinois. In the Illinois delegation were many of Logan's friends: Marshall, William Richardson, Usher F. Linder, and "Josh" Allen. But the Illinois congressmen attended. Led by McClernand and Logan, they worked feverishly to nominate the "Little Giant." Logan felt that it was his "duty to get Illinois a President."[3]

Sunday evening before the meeting, Douglas men congregated at Hibernian Hall, their headquarters. They talked confidently of victory and passed out campaign biographies of their hero written by James Sheahan.[4] The "infamous combination" opposing Douglas was also present in force. Slidell of Louisiana, leader of the administration forces, was attempting to wean the large New York delegation away from Douglas.

---

[1]S. S. Marshall to JAL, Feb. 18, 1860, Logan Mss.
[2]JAL to Mary Logan, April 16, 1860, Logan Mss.
[3]JAL to Mary Logan, April 6, 1860, Logan Mss.
[4]Murat Halstead, *Caucuses of 1860* (Columbus, Ohio, 1860), 5; Milton, *Eve of Conflict*, 431. The biography was James W. Sheahan's work, *The Life of Stephen A. Douglas.*

Fire-eating W. L. Yancey of Alabama was ready to denounce Douglas as little better than the abolitionists.[5]

Douglas forces planned to fight for seating their disputed delegations from Illinois and New York and then to try to write a platform so inoffensive to the South that Douglas would be able to get the two-thirds necessary. They pointed out that Northwestern Democrats had been strong in defending the Fugitive Slave Act. Logan's role in this conciliation was important. As pro-Southern Egypt's representative, he had been in the front line of defense of what he considered the South's constitutional rights. He worked frantically at Charleston to make Douglas palatable to the "South Americans," and to convince them that his election would not be a threat to the South.[6]

On convention eve, Murat Halstead, a perceptive reporter, spied three Illinois leaders, Richardson, McClernand, and Logan sitting "pensive and silent." Logan sat with "his hat tilted far back on his head, his hands in his pockets and his mouth full of tobacco."[7] The reporter evidently observed the silence of confidence; no Illinois leader would discuss a second choice in the event of Douglas' failure.

On April 23, ornate Institute Hall was packed as the convention was called to order with F. B. Flournoy of Arkansas, temporary chairman. When Caleb Cushing became permanent chairman, the battle began. In preliminary skirmishing, Douglas forces had things their own way. After Richardson, Douglas' floor leader, called the delegate contest in Illinois "frivolous and contemptible," the credentials committee voted without dissent to seat the Douglas men.[8] Just as important was the acceptance of the credentials committee's majority report, seating the 35 pro-Douglas delegates from New York. This group, led by Dean Richmond, was seated in place of Fernando Wood's administration supporters.[9] As final evidence of Douglasite power, on April 24 a rule was adopted, 198 to 101,

---

[5]Auchampaugh, "Buchanan-Douglas Feud," 33.
[6]Milton, *Eve of Conflict*, 431; Halstead, *Caucuses*, 6-7, 9; JAL to Mary Logan, May 7, 1860, Logan Mss.
[7]Halstead, *Caucuses*, 9.
[8]*Proceedings of the Conventions at Charleston and Baltimore of the National Democratic Convention* (Washington, 1860), 6.
[9]*Ibid.*, 30.

providing that members of uninstructed delegations might vote individually. This meant the Douglas votes in the uninstructed Massachusetts and Pennsylvania bodies were free of the unit rule and free to support Douglas.[10] Even in delegations clinging to the unit vote, minority Douglas men exerted considerable influence, and it was among them that Logan worked.

Though these procedural victories heartened the Douglasites, the next item of business, platform, loomed as an imposing hurdle. On a raw cold Friday, April 27, majority and minority reports of the platform committee filtered rapidly through the delegates and party workers. The majority report, supported by the slave states, defended slavery in the territories and denied the right of Congress or a territorial legislature to molest it. The minority report reaffirmed the Cincinnati platform of 1856 and popular sovereignty. The crisis was at hand. For two days the platform was debated. Southerners demanded inclusion of a slave-code, and Richardson spoke for the Northwest when he challenged the South to compromise.[11]

The week-end was rife with speculation and attempts to settle the platform wrangle. Though Logan and the Illinoisans continued their efforts to close the rapidly opening abyss, they increasingly felt that if the platform fight drove some of the delegates out of the convention, Douglas might stand a better chance of victory. They reasoned that if they could get a ruling in favor of election by two-thirds of those present and voting, Douglas might easily win.

On Monday morning, May 1, tension in convention hall was almost unbearable. As the vote on the platform proceeded, it was evident the result would be close. When the minority platform passed 165 to 138, Douglas men moved that the planks be voted on separately. When voting began, the convention floor became bedlam. Douglas forces retreated in the face of a Southern walk-out, but the Southerners carried out their threat and seven delegations bolted led by Alabama.

Logan was completely frustrated at this suicidal action. He and other Douglas men ceased conciliation and denounced the Southern men as violently as he customarily did abolitionists.[12]

[10]New York *Times*, April 25, 1860.
[11]*Democratic Convention Proceedings*, 135.
[12]Halstead, *Caucuses*, 87.

Fear of disunion gripped all Northerners at Charleston. Logan was present when Clement Vallandigham forecast that an unhealed party split would inevitably lead to civil war.[13]

The remainder of Logan's time at Charleston was spent in a vain attempt to nominate Douglas. When Cushing refused to rule in favor of election by two-thirds of those voting, Douglas' nomination became an impossibility. His first ballot vote of 145½ rose to 152½, but after 57 ballots brought little change, the convention adjourned to meet in Baltimore, June 18. The New York *Times* commented that the Democratic schism "seems to sever the last link of nationality in the political affairs of the nation."[14] The day he returned to Washington, Logan, tired and disappointed, told Mary, "I have worked at Charleston until I am nearly crazy. . . . Our fight there was terrible. Such a combination has never been met by any man on earth as was met at Charleston."[15]

When Logan returned to the House he was in time for several measures coming to a vote. A bill abrogating New Mexico's slave codes passed 97 to 90 as Logan voted "no." On the same day the House tariff measure passed by a large majority with Logan again in opposition.[16] A week later he rose to make a personal explanation. The *Globe* listed a $25.26 charge for stationery against the Committee on Revisal and Unfinished Business, and Logan, the chairman, informed the House that the committee had never met, and probably never would. To protect the committee against a charge of fraud, he explained that the stationery had been used by another committee which had been using his committee's rooms. As Logan sat down, Illinois Republican Elihu Washburne, losing no chance to criticize Logan, chided his colleague for taking up the House's time with so insignificant a matter.[17]

In late May, Democrats had Congress to themselves. They kept a wary eye on Chicago, where the Republicans assembled to nominate their presidential candidate. After the Republicans had made their choice, Logan wrote Mary, "There is a

[13] James L. Vallandigham, *The Life of Clement L. Vallandigham* (Baltimore, 1872), 138.
[14] New York *Times*, May 4, 1860.
[15] JAL to Mary Logan, May 7, 1860, Logan Mss.
[16] *Cong. Globe*, 36th Cong., 1st Sess., pt. 3, 2046.
[17] *Ibid.*, 2180.

great desire on the part of everyone to get home soon since the Republicans have nominated Abe Lincoln, they are anxious to commence the fight at home."[18]

In May, Logan journeyed to New York City to speak in Douglas' behalf. Since the Charleston convention, rumors had claimed that a portion of the New York delegation would abandon Douglas at Baltimore in favor of a candidate more acceptable to the South. Logan's trip to New York was designed to prevent a change of position by the New Yorkers. While in the city he spoke at Cooper Institute in favor of Douglas for president. The trip was highly successful and Logan wrote McClernand, "the New York delegation have given us every assurance that they will stand firm at Baltimore."[19]

The important business of the session was by no means over, and when Logan returned to Washington the House was considering the Senate's amendments to its Homestead Bill. The House voted to substitute its original bill by an overwhelming vote. Logan was paired, but announced that if he had voted he would vote "aye."[20] In the debate over the Pacific Railroad, Logan opposed Southern claims for a Southern route and voted, with the majority, to send the bill back to committee.

When Republican James McKean of New York spoke of the "Southern masters of the Democratic party," on June 6, Logan stated that he had no master and suggested McKean's entire statement be stricken from the record. Nine days later, during debate over reducing appropriations for lighting Washington streets, a humorous exchange occurred between Logan and Samuel Peyton of Kentucky. When Peyton proposed the reduction, Logan asked, "I want to know why a gentleman who travels so much at night as the gentleman from Kentucky, desires to travel in the dark." Peyton replied, "Those with whom I keep company are honest, and it is not necessary to have them guarded; but perhaps in the gentleman's country— for I believe he comes from Egypt—he may want protection at night."[21]

---

[18]JAL to Mary Logan, May 19, 1860, Logan Mss.
[19]*Illinois State Journal*, May 30, 1860; JAL to John McClernand, June 2, 1860, McClernand Mss.
[20]*Cong. Globe*, 36th Cong., 1st Sess., pt. 3, 2222.
[21]*Ibid.*, pt. 4, 3049.

The six weeks between the Charleston schism and the Baltimore convention were filled with wild party speculation. Logan had not abandoned hope that the party rupture could be healed, and confidently reported, "Alex Stephens and the patriotic men of the South have gone to work and will strike down secession and disunion beyond all question."[22] This was more optimism than the situation warranted, but on the eve of the Baltimore meeting hopes were high that Democrats would reunite. The reconvening Democrats were welcomed by the Baltimore press, which spoke of the occasion as one of the most "momentous" in American history. The *Sun* pleaded for a Democratic compromise; disunion was certain if the party split continued.[23] The Front Street Theatre was the scene of the convention, and extra windows had been constructed to make the building more bearable in the stifling June heat.

The delegations came from most Southern states, one composed of Charleston seceders, and one pro-Douglas group. The radical Southerners were strangely silent as they awaited the credentials committee report. During this period of calm, rumors flew. Some claimed knowledge of a Douglas withdrawal; some stated that Horatio Seymour of New York or Alex Stephens would get the nomination.[24] When the credentials report was made, the majority favored seating Douglas men from the South. All eyes were on Dean Richmond, chairman of the New York delegation, for the large Empire State group could throw great weight in either direction. When the New Yorkers voted for the majority report the second bolt began. Next day a second convention was meeting in St. Andrew's Hall in Baltimore.

Voting for the presidential nomination brought the convention to a quick close. Douglas received 173½ on the first ballot and was victorious. But another vote was taken at the request of Flournoy of Arkansas, to make the vote look, "a great deal stronger."[25] Douglas' total climbed to 181½ and the meeting came to a close. As the last item of business, Logan, speaking for the Democratic National Committee, reminded each state

[22]JAL to Mary Logan, May 16, 1860, Logan Mss.
[23]Baltimore *Sun*, June 18, 1860.
[24]New York *Times*, June 20, 1860; Halstead, *Caucuses*, 194.
[25]*Democratic Convention Proceedings*, 231.

to name a proper person for the national committee.[26] Though party unity seemed shattered beyond repair when the seceders nominated John C. Breckinridge and Joseph Lane, the Douglasites left the city with a show of confidence.

When Logan returned to Washington, little business remained. Logan brought his affairs to a close and answered roll call on adjournment day. He joined his fellow congressmen from Illinois in calling on Douglas and pledging support in the campaign ahead.

Logan's first session in Congress had not been particularly outstanding. He had engaged in several clashes that kept his name in the papers, but as a constructive member of the body his contributions were few. With the exceptions of his trips to Charleston, New York, and Baltimore, his attendance record was good, and he seems to have been conscientious in securing various congressional reports for distribution in his constituency. Despite this lackluster record, typical of many freshmen in the House, he gained in stature with his constituents. Every letter from Egypt told of the hearty support at home. His defense of the Fugitive Slave Act and his attack on Kellogg would serve him well in his campaign for re-election.

Douglas' campaign in Illinois in 1860 began at a disadvantage. His nomination came almost a month after Lincoln's, and the Douglas state candidates, James C. Allen for Governor, and Lewis Ross for Lieutenant-Governor, were not selected until mid-June.[27] In Egypt, however, Logan's campaign for re-election had been initiated by his friends before he returned. In preliminary organization, Mrs. Logan had been a hard worker, and when Logan returned he found much of the ground work complete. He was also relieved to discover Mary and the baby, whom they called "Dollie," in good health.

In July, after he was formally nominated for a second term, Logan took the campaign trail. The canvass began at Shawneetown, where a combined political meeting and barbecue brought together Democrats to hear Logan and Ross attack Breckinridge and Lincoln as disunionists and hold up Douglas as the only hope of the nation.[28] On July 25 Logan traveled to Spring-

[26]Halstead, *Caucuses*, 238.
[27]Cole, *Era of the Civil War*, 196.
[28]Lusk, *Politics and Politicians*, 106.

field where the statewide Douglas ratification meeting was held. In the afternoon a throng of Democrats gathered to hear James Allen, Logan, and McClernand speak for the "Little Giant." Festivities ended with a torchlight procession and fireworks, and the campaign was officially under way.

Shortly after Logan's return from the state capital, Republicans entered David T. Linegar in the race for Logan's seat. The Republicans felt that Linegar would help get out the vote in Egypt. Even if he failed to defeat Logan, the larger Republican vote would aid the national ticket in its battle for the Illinois electoral vote.[29] The state's Republican press sounded an optimistic note on the party's chances in southern Illinois. Correspondents from the section assured readers that the Republicans were organizing and would produce a surprise in November.[30]

One reason for Republican smiles was the bitter feud between Douglas and Breckinridge men reported from Egypt. Union County was a hotbed of anti-Douglas feeling, and the pro-Breckinridge editor of the Jonesboro *Gazette* challenged Logan to a joint debate. The challenge was not accepted.[31] Later in the campaign, when Logan campaigned in that county, he was greeted by wholesale heckling.[32] Supporters of the Baltimore seceders seemed to have considerable support in southern Illinois, and while the fourth party in the election, the Constitutional Union Party, had few adherents in Egypt, its strength in the central counties, still an unknown quantity, was feared by the Democrats. A slight shift in those pivotal counties might decide the election.

Logan left his own district to campaign for Douglas in Marion County where he made a speech dealing "the secessionists such blows as made them bite the dust."[33] One paper reported

[29]Clark E. Carr, *My Day and Generation* (Chicago, 1908), 376-377.
[30]*Illinois State Journal*, July 4, 1860.
[31]Chicago *Press and Tribune*, July 18, 1860. In a later issue, the *Press and Tribune* indicated that it felt that Logan was little better than a Breckinridge man when it called him "one of the . . . meanest doughfaces in the last session of Congress." Named along with Logan were Cox and Vallandigham of Ohio, and Charles H. Larrabee of Wisconsin. Chicago *Press and Tribune*, Aug. 8, 1860.
[32]JAL to Mary Logan, Sept. 15, 1860, Logan Mss.
[33]Salem *Advocate*, Aug. 9, 1860. Logan shared the platform at Salem with Silas Bryan whose son William Jennings had been born in March, 1860.

that Logan offered to campaign throughout the state, but he was told his services were most needed in Egypt.[34] Estimates of the growing power of the Republicans in darkest Egypt were printed constantly in the state and read throughout the nation. They were so convincing that a New York paper reported, "Egypt is almost wiped out as a Democratic stronghold."[35] The *Illinois State Journal* estimated the growth of the Republican Party in Egypt and, in a county by county survey, the paper predicted a gain of some 3,250 votes over Bissell's 1858 total.[36]

Not all the opposition reports were glowing. One Republican journal despaired of Republicanism in Egypt: "Democracy can only flourish in such places as Egypt where the majority are exceedingly illiterate."[37] Even the confident *Press and Tribune* finally admitted that the best the Republicans could hope for would be a reduced majority, blaming Logan's power on ignorance and bad whiskey.[38]

With the campaign well under way, Egypt was invaded by outside politicians. The Republican nominee for governor, Richard Yates, spoke in Jonesboro and Cairo, and S. A. Hurlbut, Joseph Gillespie, and Gustave Koerner, three Lincoln men, were active in the region.[39] A particularly active Lincoln supporter was W. W. Danenhower, who spoke in almost every county of southern Illinois. Since Danenhower was a former Know-Nothing, Democrats feared the 1856 Fillmore vote might go to the Republicans.[40] These speakers were greeted by small groups of Republican marching clubs called "Wide-Awakes," and a Lincoln-Hamlin pole was raised in Jackson County, home of the "notorious John A. Logan."[41]

The Democrats were not without outside support. Candidates for state office joined Logan, and Douglas planned to

---

[34]Chicago *Press and Tribune*, Sept. 1, 1860.
[35]New York *Herald*, Aug. 13, 1860.
[36]*Illinois State Journal*, Sept. 17, 1860.
[37]Oregon *Argus*, Sept. 8, 1860.
[38]Chicago *Press and Tribune*, Oct. 16, 22, 1860.
[39]*Ibid.*, Sept. 1, 1860.
[40]Alton *Courier*, Oct. 28, 1860; Chicago *Press and Tribune*, Aug. 23, 1860.
[41]Johnson, *Illinois in the Fifties*, 174; Chicago *Press and Tribune*, Aug. 1, 1860.

come to Egypt.[42] Before he arrived, October elections in several northern states were won by Republicans. Seeing only one chance remaining to defeat Lincoln, Douglas cancelled his scheduled appearances and turned south to speak in the slave states.[43]

The Douglas campaign never picked up great momentum. Attempts to heal the party breach failed, and while unified Republicans gained, Douglas' chances grew dim. His first campaign speech at Norfolk had caused grumbling from some of his closest supporters. In answer to a question about secession in the event of a Lincoln victory, Douglas emphatically endorsed the union and promised to aid in maintaining the laws of the land against all resistance. This statement was greeted with horror by the South, and William Richardson wrote his wife after hearing Douglas' speech, "Logan was storming around, 'ugly and full of fight.' "[44] While there is little doubt that Logan and many of his fellow Egyptians recoiled at Douglas' speech, there is no evidence to indicate that Logan's efforts in Douglas' behalf were affected.

On the contrary, he seems to have thrown himself wholeheartedly into the fight, going so far as to use unscrupulous methods. The newspaper in Benton, Logan's home, the *Franklin Democrat*, was a small Democratic sheet which, for most of the campaign, endorsed Douglas on its masthead. In September, the editors, A. and G. Sellers, decided that Douglas had no chance, and began shopping for a new candidate. They refused to consider the Southerner, Breckinridge; Bell seemed to have less chance than Douglas. This left Lincoln, and in an effort to help defeat the Southern Democratic ticket, the Sellers brothers decided to come out in favor of Lincoln. When word of this switch reached Logan, then on a speaking tour, he cancelled several talks and returned to Benton determined there would be no Republican organ at home. On the evening the *Democrat* went to press with its first endorsement of Lincoln and Hamlin, Logan went to the newspaper office. He began by trying to persuade the publishers they were making a mistake.

[42]Salem *Advocate*, Aug. 9, 1860.
[43]Milton, *Eve of Conflict*, 497.
[44]*Ibid.*, 492, 493.

When they refused to return to the Douglas fold, Logan shouted, "I'll be d--d if it shall come out for Lincoln." He attempted to buy out the brothers. They set the price at $700, Logan offering $550. At first they declined, but by midnight the haggling had drawn a considerable crowd of Logan's supporters. Sensing the crowd's hostility, the Sellers agreed to Logan's terms.[45]

Two weeks after their expulsion, the Sellers brothers arrived in Springfield, and the *State Journal* gladly published their attack on Logan. Complaining that an attempt at redress through Egyptian courts would be futile due to the Democratic judges and juries, the former publishers challenged:

> Mr. Logan may have succeeded in crushing us for the time being, and throwing us out of employment, but these acts of his will have a voice that will speak in louder tones than we can utter. Go on, Mr. Logan, put down free speech, close up the avenues of free thought, gag the press if you can, trample under foot the sacred guarantees of the Constitution, but you can never stop the march of truth.[46]

Logan and his supporters did not deny the story, and most of the state's Republican press joined in the attack.

If the banished publishers of the *Democrat* meant by the "march of truth" a Lincoln victory, they had their revenge. But their martyrdom had little effect in Egypt, where huge majorities were returned for the Democratic candidates. There was a large turnout on election day, and Logan defeated Linegar 20,863 to 5,207.[47]

The four-cornered race for president also ended in a Democratic landslide in Lower Egypt. Douglas had 17,684 votes to 3,950 for Lincoln, 1,275 for Bell, and 1,056 for Breckinridge.[48] Like Linegar, Lincoln was able to carry only Edwards County in Logan's district. Bell's vote was evenly divided throughout the district, but most of Breckinridge's total came from Union County. Logan carried Union 1,292 to 142, but Douglas narrowly won the county over the combined vote of his three

---

[45]Chicago *Press and Tribune*, Sept. 7, 1860.
[46]*Illinois State Journal*, Sept. 20, 1860.
[47]Chicago *Tribune*, Dec. 5, 1860.
[48]*Illinois State Journal*, Nov. 28, 1860; George Smith, *Southern Illinois*, I, 314, 315.

opponents. All Egyptian legislative districts went Democratic with the exception of the two St. Clair County seats. There the German voters sent two Republicans to the assembly to support the new Republican governor, Richard Yates.

One student of Illinois history has remarked on the astounding rise in Republican strength in Egypt in the election of 1860. However, the 1860 vote in Lower Egypt when compared with 1856 and 1858 Republican totals reveals no significant change. Logan received 84% of the total vote cast in 1858 and 79% in 1860. The Republican gubernatorial candidate, Bissell, in 1856 polled 12% of the vote and Lincoln got 17% in 1860. In both cases there was only a 5% change, hardly a major increase for the Republicans.[49] When the crisis struck the nation shortly after Lincoln's election, the claims that Egypt had been wiped out as a Democratic stronghold proved extravagant. Voters who had cast their ballots for Logan, Douglas, and Breckinridge were soon to prove their Democracy, and it was to be a Democracy with ties south of the Ohio.

As Logan prepared for the return to Washington and the second session of the 36th Congress, he realized that his role in the period at hand would not be an easy one. Many agreed with Charles Lanphier that Logan's position on the problems that plagued the country had been "peculiar." During the 1850's Douglas had been forced to "radicalize" the Democratic Party in the Northwest to maintain himself in power in Illinois. This was also necessary to further his presidential ambitions.[50] As Douglas slowly abandoned his attempts to court Southern Democrats, Logan found it difficult to follow his lead. However, he felt Douglas offered the best hope for the prevention of disunion; furthermore, he had seen the price of party insurgency in Illinois. Yet Logan was an Egyptian, and while the rest of the state's Democrats had followed the new course set by Douglas, Egypt clung to its Southern proclivities. The time was at hand when Egypt, with its split personality

---

[49]Cole, *Era of the Civil War*, 200; Chicago *Tribune*, Dec. 5, 1860; Alton *Courier*, Nov. 4, 1858; Lusk, *Politics and Politicians*, 45; *Illinois State Journal*, Nov. 28, 1860.

[50]Henry C. Hubbart, " 'Pro-Southern' Influences in the Free-West, 1840-1865," *Mississippi Valley Historical Review*, XX, No. 2 (June, 1933), 56-57.

—economic and social ties with the South, and reluctance to see the union destroyed—would be forced to make a choice. With Logan as Egypt's spokesman, it was inevitable that the section's problems would fall heavily upon him in the days of crisis.

CHAPTER V

A PLAGUE ON BOTH YOUR HOUSES

In November, when Logan left for Washington and the opening of Congress, secession hung heavily over the land. Many Democrats agreed with the *Illinois State Register* which had proclaimed, "the election of Mr. Lincoln will be a national calamity."[1]

For the first time since his marriage, Logan planned to have his family join him for a legislative session. Before he left Illinois in November he arranged for his wife and daughter to follow him. Excitedly, Mary awaited the departure date, and in late November she went by rail to Washington.

When the second session of the 36th Congress began on December 3, "stillness pervaded the capital."[2] Good order in the House, contrasting vividly with the chaotic first session, led observers to hope that secession might be averted. December 4 Buchanan's message was received in joint session. It satisfied few and disappointed almost everyone. There is no record of Logan's 1860 opinion of the message, but two decades later he called Buchanan "a weak and feeble old man . . . doubtless a Union man at heart," but lacking in perception, forcefulness, and "nerve."[3]

The young congressman doubtless had mixed feelings in 1860. Like Buchanan, he held secession unconstitutional and opposed coercion. But while Buchanan remained largely inactive, Logan felt swift compromise steps were necessary to save the Union.[4]

Following the presidential message, the House voted to create a committee to investigate the state of the Union. Logan voted for the Committee of Thirty-three, and two days later Republican William Kellogg was named Illinois' representative.

---

[1]*Illinois State Register*, Nov. 7, 1860.
[2]New York *Times*, Dec. 4, 1860.
[3]John A. Logan, *The Great Conspiracy*, 104.
[4]*Cong. Globe*, 36th Cong., 2nd Sess., appendix, 178-181.

The Illinois House delegation presented an unusual bipartisan front in voting for the Homestead Bill which, despite Southern opposition, passed 132 to 76.[5] In the following two weeks the activities of the Committee of Thirty-three and speeches on the crisis occupied the House. Logan took little part in these debates. He sat listening, and like everyone else, closely watched the South Carolina secession convention.

On December 17 Logan voted for a resolution recommending repeal of any statute obstructing the Constitution. Since the resolution included personal liberty laws, Logan gladly voted "aye." Later that day when a similar resolution was proposed, Logan asked that there be no Democratic opposition. He wanted the bill amended to state that "all men" rather than "all law-abiding citizens" should obey the Constitution, remarking that if the wording were not changed some of the members of Congress would not be included as "law-abiding citizens." The reworded resolution passed 136 to 0.[6]

December 20 began calmly enough. All Washington kept a nervous eye on South Carolina, and compromise proposals occupied the House. As it convened, Logan introduced a bill to hold circuit and district courts for the southern district of Illinois at Cairo. When Elihu Washburne objected to the proposal, John Bingham of Ohio assured Washburne that the bill was necessary for swift administration of justice. With Washburne still unconvinced, Logan defended the bill on grounds that much of the business transacted at Springfield concerned the Cairo area. Washburne then proposed postponment of consideration and Logan agreed.[7]

Following this exchange, the House returned to the state of the Union. As speakers droned on, an unusual ripple of noise spread through the chamber. Then came the announcement. South Carolina had passed an ordinance of secession.

The Illinois House delegation stood united against South Carolina's action. In an informal caucus, Logan joined his fellow congressmen in a resolution stating, "the Union must and

[5] Ibid., pt. 1, 16.
[6] Ibid., 109.
[7] Ibid., 160.

should be preserved." Beneath this unanimity, Illinois members were bitterly divided as to the best means of preserving the Union.[8]

The rest of the month brought little change to the House. Compromise efforts continued, but to many the Christmas season brought bleak prospects and fear of war. Illinois Democrats seemed united against secession, but they also condemned the use of force against seceding states. McClernand wrote, "The Northwest cannot afford to submit to disunion except as an unavoidable necessity." Douglas voiced the sentiments of his followers when he added, "I will not consider the question of force and war until all efforts at peaceful adjustment have been made and have failed."[9] Logan was in complete accord with this.

On New Year's Day the Logans attended the White House reception and Mary was impressed with the president's dignity and the graciousness of his niece who extended them a "cordial greeting." The month had been a fascinating one for Mary. She had attended many social events and had helped Mrs. Douglas, to whom she was devoted, receive guests. However, she remembered later that the issues of the day were never forgotten, and every social gathering became a heated discussion.[10]

Logan was troubled over the crisis the new year would bring. He steadfastly opposed secession, but remained equally opposed to force. He agreed with the *State Register*: "Mr. Lincoln, while calling on the Democracy to sustain him must do something himself towards preserving the Union. He must recognize that the Union is endurable as it was originally framed, 'part slave and part free.' "[11]

This opinion harmonized with the Egyptian press which announced its opposition to force and added, "let her [South Carolina] in God's name go peacefully. . . . The sympathies of our people are mainly with the south."[12] In these and other

---

[8]*Illinois State Register*, Dec. 20, 1860.
[9]John A. McClernand to Charles Lanphier, Dec. 21, 1860; Stephen A. Douglas to Lanphier, Dec. 25, 1860, Lanphier Mss.
[10]Mary Logan, *Reminiscences*, 71, 74.
[11]*Illinois State Register*, Dec. 31, 1860.
[12]Cairo *City Gazette*, Dec. 6, 1860.

comments from southern Illinois, Logan saw seeds of trouble that might shatter Egypt. A compromise necessary to preserve the Union was just as necessary for the welfare of Egypt, caught as it was in a maelstrom of sectional animosities.

Logan lost no time in making known his feelings on the nation's problems. On January 1 he wrote Judge I. N. Haynie a lengthy commentary on the times. Logan began by warning Haynie, "My feeble hand is incompetent to portray that fearful future whose rapid approach is now shaking this vast republic to its very center." He dated the beginning of the trouble from the election of Lincoln, "a strictly sectional candidate."

The young congressman told the judge that his only hope was for a moderate majority in each section to prevent extremists from tearing the Union apart. But Logan saw little evidence that moderates were winning the struggle. "Those who dream that this Confederacy can separate peacefully will wake up to the conviction of their sad error I fear too late," he continued.

Logan's hope was that the "old fire of patriotism from the great heart of the people . . . would command the peace." He was particularly adamant that the North should cease its interference with Southern institutions. He attacked both "abolitionist Black Republicans" and Southern "fire-eaters" as creators of civil conflict. Of Lincoln he wrote:

> History informs us that Nero, a royal but insane and blood thirsty man fiddled while Rome was burning, and it does seem to me that the President elect and his friends flushed and drunken with victory are plunging deeper into their fanatical orgies, the nearer our beloved country is undone.

Then he turned to the South. "The election of Mr. Lincoln, deplorable as it may be, affords no justification or excuse for overthrowing the republic." But he felt calm Southerners would realize Lincoln was "harmless," faced by a hostile Congress which would make him a "political puppet."

Logan closed the letter with a plea for Union. Speaking for his section, he concluded, "we of the Northwest having as much, if not more, at stake than any other section can not stand silently by while the joint action of extremists are [sic] dragging us to ruin."[13]

The Logan-Haynie letter was Logan's only clear statement on national problems in the first month of 1861. Through January he took little part in House debates. The first excitement of the new year in the House was a resolution approving Major Robert Anderson's move from Ft. Moultrie to Ft. Sumter. The resolution also pledged support of all constitutional measures taken by Buchanan to preserve the Union. When he voted, Logan cried, "as the resolution receives my unqualified approbation, I vote aye." The resolution carried 124 to 56.[14]

Logan's next business concerned the Cairo court bill. After some discussion on January 9, the bill came up for passage two days later. With Washburne no longer offering opposition, it passed without a roll call.

On January 14 the report of the compromise committee emerged and a long acrimonious debate began. Since no representative of the Douglas Democrats had been named to the group, they viewed the committee's actions with hostility. Nevertheless, once the report was presented, the Douglasites were generally in favor of the proposals. The report called for repeal of personal liberty laws; a guarantee that slavery would be protected in slave states; and immediate entry of New Mexico presumably as a slave state. Following the report, each member demanded the floor to comment. While these speeches droned on, Mississippi, Florida, and Alabama seceded.

During the fortnight after arguments began, Logan again experienced the frustration of the freshman member unable to get the floor. The story of the indignant congressman who announced, "I have been a member of this House three successive terms, and I have caught measels, and influenza, but I never have been able to catch the speaker's eye," seemed appropriate in Logan's case.[15] Night sessions were held to provide time for oratory, and still the Illinois freshman failed to win

---

[13]JAL to I. N. Haynie, Jan. 1, 1861, Logan Mss. This letter was written to Haynie for circulation in Logan's constituency. Its contents reported in the *Illinois State Journal*, Feb. 14, 1861, elicited the comment by that paper that it was evidence of "party pique and partisan hatred."

[14]*Cong. Globe*, 36th Cong., 2nd Sess., pt. 1, 281.

[15]Mary Logan, *Thirty Years in Washington* (Hartford, Connecticut, 1901), 122.

recognition. On the evening of January 28, Logan had a sharp exchange with Henry L. Dawes of Massachusetts, and on the last day of the month, still unrecognized, he lashed out with the fury of his frustration.

When Charles Francis Adams and E. Joy Morris of Pennsylvania made a deal by which Adams, who had the floor, agreed to yield to Morris if he returned the favor next evening, Logan rose to object. He angrily proclaimed:

> I have remained here . . . several evenings for the purpose of obtaining the floor, and I want the speaker now to tell me how many names are registered as entitled to the floor to speak, so that I may know on what evening I shall come here to obtain the floor, by acting decently and respectfully to the speaker.

He continued, "I desire to say that this practice of farming out the floor in advance is infamous, and ought not to be tolerated in any body."[16]

While Logan was having difficulties in Washington, disturbing news arrived from Illinois. The state legislature was considering reapportionment of congressional districts. The Republicans, now in control, wanted to change districts to the detriment of sparsely settled Egypt. Rumors reached Logan that Franklin County, his residence, would be removed from his district to gerrymander him out of Congress.[17]

In January the Democratic state convention at Springfield adopted resolutions of loyalty to the Union while opposing force as a weapon against secession. These sentiments Logan approved; but they were condemned by the Republican press as "semi-secessionist." Strangely enough, the Washington correspondent of the Chicago *Tribune* simultaneously characterized Logan as a "unionist." On February 1 this writer lauded Logan, Morris, and Fouke as men who

> have stood bravely up against those who have been their party friends and associates, but are now seeking to ruin the country. The courage and patriotism of these men, who have broken all political and friendly ties for the sake of

---

[16]*Cong. Globe*, 36th Cong., 2nd Sess., pt. 1, 656.

[17]T. M. Eddy, *The Patriotism of Illinois* (Chicago, 1865), I, 483; Cole, *Era of the Civil War*, 259.

the Union and justice is almost universally commended here.[18]

This would seem to indicate that Republicans were not convinced that Logan was openly secessionist, as they would later charge.

Logan's struggle for recognition continued into February. After a bitter argument with John Sherman, Logan finally got the floor on the evening of February 5. Before crowded galleries he delivered his speech on the state of the nation.[19] This was in many ways a reiteration of the letter to Haynie, but taken as a whole it afforded the most complete view of Logan's position in the crisis.

He again traced the crisis to Lincoln's election, which he called a "golden opportunity" for the South. But the Republicans did not deserve the entire blame. He condemned abolitionists who have "warred upon southern institutions," and "reckless and seditious" Southerners who "have been no less industrious in creating a corresponding hatred of Northern people." He called both sides more partisan than patriotic and demanded rapid compromise efforts. These efforts were necessary, he maintained to avoid the unconstitutional use of force in putting down secession, even though secession itself was "unlawful." On the use of force, Logan declared that resort to arms would forever create permanent hatred between sections. He compared the bitterness felt by the American colonies toward their former masters, the English, after the Revolutionary War, to the situation force would create in 1861. "They are our kinsman," said he of Southerners, "and should be dealt with kindly."

Developing this analogy, he compared Republicans to King George III as oppressors and, by inference, the American patriots of 1776 to the South of 1861 as the oppressed. Since Logan had attacked the extremists in the South, charges later made by Republicans that Logan was defending the "fire-eaters" were not true. This portion of Logan's speech was unfortunate since its distortion in the hands of his enemies

---

[18]Chicago *Tribune*, Jan. 14, 28, Feb. 1, 1861.

[19]*Illinois State Register*, Feb. 11, 1861; *Cong. Globe*, 36th Cong., 2nd Sess., appendix, 178-181. The entire speech is contained in these four pages.

furnished ammunition for harmful attacks.

He then called on members of the House to put aside politics and "satisfy and appease" the apprehensions of the South. This could be done by guaranteeing the South its "peculiar institutions." Such guarantees, he went on, would place weapons in the hands of Southern conservatives which they could use to return their states to the Union.

Descending to specifics, Logan wanted assurances that the interstate slave trade would not be abolished and that prohibition of slavery in the territories would not be enforced.

> It has been said on this floor, by Republicans, that the God of nature has so arranged the soil and climate of those territories that slavery cannot go there. . . . Why, if by the soil and climate, is slavery excluded from the territories, in God's name why insist on this impracticable legislation by Congress?

Logan doubted that Southerners would ever enter the new territory since it would be economically unprofitable to them; but "it is a denial of a right under the Constitution . . . that annoys and chafes them."

He next dealt with several compromise proposals before the country. Mentioning the Crittenden Compromise, the report of the House Committee, and several other proposals, Logan indicated that he would be willing to support any of them.

Logan concluded his long oration with a fervent appeal in the name of Southern and border state conservatives. He likened them to "noble Spartans standing in the breach," and promised "immortality." He forecast lasting infamy for extremists. With another plea to calm men everywhere, Logan closed amid applause from the galleries.

This address defined Logan's position for dark days ahead. From February 5 until June 18, Logan failed to clarify his position in light of rapidly changing conditions. There is little doubt that the speech pleased his constituents. In the main it echoed sentiments of a section deeply concerned with possible civil war. Scott Marshall praised the speech as "highly commendable."[20]

---

[20]S. S. Marshall to JAL, Feb. 26, 1861, Logan Mss.

The address clearly placed Logan in the compromise camp. He recoiled at the prospects of civil conflict and demanded promises to the South necessary to end the danger. Because of the speech, he was condemned as a secessionist and praised as a unionist.

Logan's strong compromise stand increasingly moved him away from fellow Illinois Democrats. He had been very close to Douglas and McClernand in early days of crisis, but now imperceptibly a gap was appearing. McClernand, voicing the thoughts of many Northwestern Democrats, wrote:

> If we become entangled with disunion we will be lost as a party. . . . Any compromise which would enable them [seceding Southerners] to come back into the party as its leaders, will doom the Democratic party to a repetition of its late convulsions and overthrow.[21]

After Logan's speech, McClernand wrote Lanphier that he had talked to Logan and found him a "compromiser."[22] As his friends hardened their attitude toward the South, Logan remained open to any compromise proposal.

Logan said little more during the rest of the session. He rose to defend S. S. Cox's right to speak and voted for Sherman's resolutions guaranteeing that the Federal government would not interfere with slavery where it existed. He opposed a militia bill called by Bocock a "declaration of war." This proposal, for calling out state militia to defend the Union, was held by many to be evidence of the North's determination to use force, and brought solid Illinois Democratic opposition. Unable to table the measure, its opponents finally succeeded in postponing debate until adjournment. Logan voted for postponment as the motion carried 100 to 74.[23]

The final business of the month was the showdown on compromise committee recommendations. Items were voted on singly. The first resolution, calling for effective enforcement of the fugitive slave law, which Logan considered long overdue, passed 137 to 53 with Logan voting for it. He also voted

---

[21]McClernand to Lanphier, Feb. 4, 1861, Lanphier Mss.

[22]McClernand to Lanphier, Feb. 8, 1861, Lanphier Mss.

[23]*Cong. Globe*, 36th Cong., 2nd Sess., pt. 2, 1232; New York *Times*, Feb. 27, 1861.

for a resolution promising no interference with domestic institutions of states.

On Monday, March 1, voting turned against the compromisers. The move to admit New Mexico failed 71 to 115. Logan voted for passage, and its defeat disappointed him. The last item provided for easier extradition procedures. Again Logan and the Illinois Democrats voted "aye," but the bill was decisively defeated.[24] Little of a constructive nature seemed to have been done by the House. Nevertheless, when the body adjourned on March 4, Logan could take heart from the border states, which remained in the Union.

On March 4 these problems became the concern of the new president. When Lincoln arrived in Washington in late February, Logan and Republican Congressman Owen Lovejoy, a strange combination, visited him at Willard's Hotel. Since Lincoln was a friend of Logan's father, Logan had reason to visit the president-elect as a social caller. However, Logan's report of the meeting, written later, when he had become a Republican, invites speculation. Logan stated that he and Lovejoy urged Lincoln to "protect the property of the country, and put down the Rebellion no matter at what cost in men and money."[25] In light of prior statements, and subsequent actions, this is difficult to believe. Logan had called Lincoln's election "deplorable," and likened the president-elect to Nero. The comment that Logan demanded suppression of the rebellion regardless of cost is distortion. Political considerations, not accurate reporting, guided Logan's pen in writing *The Great Conspiracy*. Though there is no evidence to substantiate it, Logan's visit was probably to urge compromise on Lincoln.[26] The entire Illinois congressional delegation called on Lincoln February 23.[27]

With the session at an end, Logan hurried to Illinois, a

---

[24]*Cong. Globe*, 36th Cong., 2nd Sess., pt. 2, 1327.

[25]John A. Logan, *The Great Conspiracy*, 142.

[26]*Ibid.*, 110. Here he states: "There were Republicans in the 36th Congress who courageously expressed their belief that concessions could not be made and that compromises were mere waste paper." He had earlier called these Republicans "drunken with power," and demanded all possible compromise efforts be made. *Cong. Globe*, 36th Cong., 2nd Sess., appendix, 178-181.

[27]*Illinois State Register*, Feb. 26, 1861.

homecoming filled with uncertainty. He had spoken what he thought were the beliefs of his constituents. But had he? Already Egypt gave evidence of serious division. The Salem *Advocate* boldly spoke of the possible secession of southern Illinois, and announced that an army marching from northern Illinois to attack the South could not reach the Ohio.[28] Others gave assurance that Egypt stood solidly for the Union.[29]

Signs of discontent were growing among his constituents. A letter from Carbondale in the *Illinois State Journal* accused Logan of crying "Union" while supporting the South.[30] Other evidences of trouble in Egypt were the increasing number of letters reaching Republican congressmen protesting Logan's position on national issues. One Egyptian asked Washburne for an end to compromise. Another complained that Union men in Egypt "must look away from our own district for 'friends at court.'" A third added that Egypt had no representative who could instill confidence in Union men.[31] Despite such opposition, Logan returned reasonably certain that a majority of his constituents supported him.

But who were his constituents? This was Logan's greatest cause for uneasiness as he left Washington. Charles Lanphier of the *State Register* had written McClernand of a plot to gerrymander Logan out of his district.[32] In February the Illinois press was full of details of proposed new districts. First reports had Franklin County safely tied to the old counties of the Ninth. Then came proposals placing the county in the Eighth Illinois, to the north. This plan would place Logan and James Robinson in the same district. The *State Register* called the plan "unequalled in the history of gerrymandering."[33] When the Logans arrived in Benton in mid-March, the young congressman realized he was facing the greatest crisis of his

---

[28]Salem *Advocate*, Jan. 31, 1861.

[29]Shawneetown *Illinoisan* in the *Illinois State Journal*, Feb. 14, 1861.

[30]*Illinois State Journal*, Feb. 9, 1861.

[31]C. D. Hay to Elihu Washburne, Feb. 4, 1861; R. R. Brush to Washburne, Feb. 24, 1861; Milo Jones to Washburne, Feb. 22, 1861, Elihu Washburne Mss., Library of Congress.

[32]Charles Lanphier to John A. McClernand, Feb. 20, 1861, McClernand Mss.

[33]Chicago *Tribune*, Feb. 9, 13, 1861; *Illinois State Register*, Feb. 9, 1861.

career. But of one thing he was sure. If necessary he would move to stay with his old constituency.

From his return in March, until June, information on Logan's activities is extremely sketchy. In these months when Egypt was full of plots and counter-plots, he was silent. His actions are, for the most part, unreported. This silence led to wild speculation by friends and enemies.

Logan's first act was to move his residence to Marion in neighboring Williamson County. When the bill passed, Franklin, Hamilton, and Wayne Counties were detached, and Logan's district, to be the Thirteenth after 1862, contained the remaining fifteen counties of the old Ninth.[34] The people of Benton regretted his decision to leave, and the "best wishes of the whole community" went with the Logans.[35]

Once he settled Mary and their daughter in Marion, Logan returned to his law practice. He had a living to make and the prestige of congressional service brought him many clients. He became associated with Wiliam H. Green, pro-Southern member of the Illinois assembly. [36] Logan's absences were less oppressive to Mary since moving to Marion. She had been reunited with her family which had recently moved there.

On circuit in March and early April, Logan made several speeches. His remarks were similar to the February 5 address. He called on Lincoln for compromise and continued to abhor coercion. Comparing Lincoln to George III continued to give Republicans ammunition against him.[37]

In early April the eyes of Egypt focused on Charleston harbor. The hostile Chicago *Tribune* advised that if any section of the free states could be lured into secession, Egypt was the place.[38] Logan persisted in his compromise attitudes and attacked abolitionists and secessionists alike. His views were not given wide publication and he seemed to have lapsed into silence.[39]

---

[34]Bateman and Selby, *Historical Encyclopedia*, I, 20.
[35]Benton *Democrat* in *Illinois State Register*, April 9, 1861.
[36]*Illinois State Register*, June 21, 1861.
[37]*Illinois State Register*, June 21, 1861; Edward C. Smith, *The Borderland in the Civil War* (New York, 1927), 138.
[38]Chicago *Tribune*, April 2, 1861.
[39]*Illinois State Register*, June 21, 1861.

On April 12 the explosion came. When South Carolina batteries began to slam shells into Ft. Sumter, many Northerners heretofore opposed to coercion were galvanized into support of the president. Not so in Egypt. Egypt, an area divided socially, culturally, and emotionally, stood with one foot in each camp. While there were no slaves in the triangle, it was in every other way as much a border area as Missouri and Kentucky. Logan himself later admitted that in the border states, tied to the South as they were by bonds of blood, politics, and economics, there was no unanimity of opinion in the April days of 1861.[40] Thus, Logan's lack of immediate resolution was natural. The young Democrat's actions are a mystery. Whether due to failure of his words to be preserved, or possible censorship of his papers, information about Logan is scanty from April to mid-June, 1861.[41] After the war, his 1861 record became involved in politics. Separation of fact from political buncombe is an arduous task. The burden of proof that Logan contemplated or participated in treason rests with those who made the charge. A diligent search of contemporary and secondary material does not uncover irrefutable evidence of Logan's guilt.

It seems reasonable to assume that Logan, after Sumter, remained a man of divided feelings. On June 21 when he broke silence, and in July, in his letters to his wife, Logan's lack of enthusiasm for war is still evident.[42] After Sumter he remained in favor of compromise and opposed to coercion. He perhaps agreed with the Cairo *Gazette* which felt that Egypt should "stand unitedly as mediators between the North and the South."[43] The fact that he did not rush to the colors on April 12 as most of his biographers claim, told against him when used by political opponents.[44]

---

[40]John A. Logan, *The Great Conspiracy*, 208.

[41]Jasper Cross, "Divided Loyalties in Southern Illinois During the Civil War," unpublished doctoral dissertation, University of Illinois, 36; Jasper Cross, "The Civil War Comes to Egypt," *Journal of the Illinois State Historical Society*, XLIV, No. 2 (Summer, 1951), 163. Cross and the author agree as to the possibility of censorship, but no definite proof against Mrs. Logan has been uncovered.

[42]*Illinois State Register*, June 21, 1861; Mary Logan to JAL, July 22, 25, 1861; JAL to Mary Logan, July 4, 4, 6, 10, 16, 1861, Logan Mss.

[43]Cairo *Gazette* in Chicago *Tribune*, April 20, 1861.

[44]See Dawson, Andrews, Knox, and Mrs. Logan.

Egypt, by contrast, made plenty of noise. It was a seething cauldron of intrigue. A public meeting in Pope County endorsed secession.[45] Closer to home, on April 15 at Marion, a meeting was held to protest Lincoln's call for troops. It summoned a public gathering for the 15th to offer up pro-secessionist resolutions. A large crowd was called to order at the court house by James D. Manier. He appointed a committee, which included Logan's father-in-law Captain Cunningham, to draft resolutions.[46] They were already prepared; they were produced and loudly accepted by the crowd.

The Marion resolutions traced the beginning of the nation's troubles to Lincoln's election. They condemned the president's coercion, feeling that this policy would drive the border states out of the union. "In that event, the interest of the citizens of southern Illinois imperatively demands a division of the State. We heartily pledge ourselves to use all means in our power to effect the same and attach ourselves to the Southern Confederacy." In conclusion the meeting called for acknowledgment of the independence of the Confederacy and refused to bear arms against it.[47]

The Marion resolutions were inevitably linked to Logan. There were rumors he had endorsed them and that he was working throughout Egypt to aid the Confederacy.[48] However, a seemingly reliable contemporary states, "John A. Logan was not in the county when these meetings were held, and had not been for several days."[49] Furthermore, in the Chicago *Tribune* story of the Marion affair, names of the leaders are mentioned, and Logan's name does not appear.[50] After the war, a prominent Egyptian Democrat, D. R. Pulley, who participated in the meeting, stated that Logan had no connection with it. Even Manier, who presided, denied that Logan was present.[51]

[45]Wood Gray, *The Hidden Civil War: The Story of the Copperheads* (New York, 1942), 45.

[46]Milo Erwin, *The History of Williamson County, Illinois* (Marion, Illinois, 1876), 253.

[47]Marion *Intelligencer* in Chicago *Tribune*, April 25, 1861.

[48]Gray, *Hidden Civil War*, 58; Koerner, *Memoirs*, II, 124; Cole, *Era of the Civil War*, 260.

[49]Erwin, *Williamson County*, 256.

[50]Chicago *Tribune*, April 25, 1861.

[51]D. R. Pulley to JAL, Oct. 22, 1866, Logan Mss.; Erwin, *Williamson County*, 256.

On April 16, when word of the resolutions reached Carbondale, the people of that town asked that they be repealed. A meeting was called that night in Marion, in response to the Carbondale request, which announced repeal. Since the persons involved on the 15th did not attend the repeal meeting, they maintained that repeal was ineffective. The resolutions were never put into effect and are only important as indications of Egypt's pro-Southern sentiment.

When Logan returned to Marion, he told Cunningham the resolutions were treasonous, but added:

> that he would suffer his tongue to cleave the roof of his mouth, and right arm to wither . . . before he would take up arms against his Southern brethren, unless it was to sustain the Government; and that if war was prosecuted solely for the purpose of freeing Negroes, he would not ground his arms but would turn and shoot them North.[52]

Logan was still the compromiser condemning both sides.

Through April and May, stories of Egyptian disloyalty increased. Missouri reported that 50,000 Illinoisans "opposed this inhuman, revengeful Lincoln war."[53] Governor Yates was flooded with letters outlining secessionist conspiracies in Egypt. One writer mentioned John Cunningham as leader of a group organizing a company to fight for the South. Another advised Yates that two-thirds of the people of Franklin County sympathized with the South and only lacked a leader.[54]

But there were also reports of Union sentiment in Egypt. John Olney wrote Yates from Shawneetown that, in general, Egyptians wanted the Union preserved. After the second Marion meeting, even the *Tribune* admitted that Union sentiment was strong in Egypt.[55]

While Egyptian public opinion vacillated, Logan kept silent. Then he determined to go to Springfield where a special session of the legislature was meeting. The session convened April 23,

[52]Erwin, *Williamson County*, 258.
[53]*Missouri Republican* (St. Louis), April 20, 1861.
[54]Griffin Garland to Richard Yates, April 23, 1861; W. G. Brown, *et. al*, to Yates, May 9, 1861, Richard Yates Mss., Illinois State Historical Library.
[55]John Olney to Yates, April 15, 1861, Yates Mss.; Chicago *Tribune*, April 17, 1861.

and two days later Douglas delivered a Union speech before a joint session. Logan did not hear the Douglas speech. He arrived in Springfield on Sunday, April 28, ready to see for himself the degree of Union sentiment in the capital.[56]

Logan's relations with Douglas, in Springfield, and his activities in general, have been the subject of much debate. Two Illinois politicians remember Logan as being hostile to the "Little Giant's" changing opinions. Gustave Koerner reported that for some time after the Douglas speech Logan denounced the senator. Usher F. Linder, a Democratic friend of both Logan and Douglas, wrote that after Douglas' address: "John A. Logan . . . took such mortal offense at the speech . . . that when he met him [Douglas] on the streets he actually refused to shake hands with him."[57]

After the war, reports of the Logan-Douglas feud persisted. The Chicago *Times,* then opposing Logan's candidacy, reported he vowed he would follow Douglas and denounce him from the stump.[58]

The most complete account of the split and of Logan's behavior came from Lanphier and the *State Register.* In a letter written in 1876, Lanphier accused Logan of being so "violent and incendiary" as to alarm Union Democrats who supported Douglas. The editor continued:

So intense was the alarm, in anticipation of the meeting of the legislature, and the fear of the influence of Logan and his associates upon its action, that a few days before the meeting, I was induced by friends here to telegraph Judge Douglas, at Washington, suggesting that there were 'grave reasons that he should be here at the meeting of the legislature.' Upon this he came. Logan was here, and everywhere about town abusive and vituperative of Douglas for the position he had taken; and to his face, in the most indecorous and offensive language, deprecated the course of Judge Douglas, saying that he (Douglas) had 'sold out the Democratic Party, but by ----you can not deliver it.' Not only of Judge Douglas, but of all Democrats who sustained him, Mr. Logan was equally abusive. Judge Douglas ad-

[56]*Illinois State Register,* April 29, 1861.
[57]Koerner, *Memoirs,* II, 124; Linder, *Reminiscences,* 345.
[58]Chicago *Times* in Chicago *Tribune,* Sept. 19, 1866.

dressed the legislature in one of the ablest speeches of his life and democracy came to his support, while Logan returned to Egypt, did his utmost to prevent the organization of the regiment called for that district, failed and finding the current running against him, through the persuasion of Gen. John A. McClernand, concluded to raise a regiment himself. . . . He continues to fight the war in his chosen line, but I have great hopes that the people of Illinois will elect a legislature next winter that will send him to the rear, where, in the quiet walks of private life, he may learn that the war is over between the North and the South.[59]

The veracity of Lanphier's accusation is open to question. The letter was written when Lanphier and Logan were in opposing parties, the editor trying to unseat Logan. As in many of these post-war accusations, truth is entangled in party politics. Furthermore, a close examination of the *Illinois State Register* in 1861 reveals no hint of disagreement between the paper and Logan. When Logan arrived in Springfield, the paper called him the "distinguished representative in Congress from the Ninth District." In June, when Logan finally defended himself, the paper denounced his detractors and supported him. In addition, Lanphier infers that Logan was in Springfield when Douglas spoke, and his own paper in 1861 announced Logan's arrival three days later.[60]

At the other extreme, Logan's defenders have mentioned no hostility between the two men. One author dated Logan's conversion to the Union cause from Douglas' April 25 speech.[61] Mary Logan went so far as to state that after Sumter it was Logan who became an intense Unionist leaving "Douglas and his party" behind.[62]

---

[59]Charles Lanphier to "a gentleman in Washington," n.d., Lanphier Mss., published in the Chicago *Times*, Oct. 31, 1876. The letter was written in opposition to Logan's candidacy for the U. S. Senate in 1877. This lengthy passage is reproduced here to give the partisan flavor of Lanphier's attack. Many authors have used parts of the letter without reproducing it in its revealing entirety. Milton, *Eve of Conflict*, uses it as evidence of Logan's anti-Douglas feeling without any comment on its role in post-war politics.

[60]*Illinois State Register*, April 29, June 21, 1861.

[61]Charles A. Church, *A History of the Republican Party in Illinois, 1854-1912* (Rockford, Illinois, 1912), 86.

[62]Mary Logan, *Reminiscences*, 68.

Logan himself denied a serious break with Douglas. He endorsed the story of their relations as told by D. W. Lusk. Lusk stated that the two men were in basic agreement, but that Douglas had recently campaigned in the South and knew better the seriousness of the threat to the Union. Logan called this estimate basically "fair and correct."[63] In this statement Logan does admit a slight difference of opinion with Douglas in the spring of 1861. There is reason to believe that the split, though not as deep as indicated by Lanphier, was more than Logan would have his readers think. A prominent Illinois politician, on the scene that summer in Springfield, added a reason for a difference of opinion between the two. Shelby Cullom indicated that Douglas' speech broke an understanding among Illinois' congressional Democrats to act together. Douglas' failure to consult with his fellow Democrats, before endorsing Lincoln's actions, angered them.[64] As late as April 18 Congressman James Robinson had written Logan: "I agree with you that the peace policy is the true policy for us."[65] Douglas' endorsement of the war naturally brought forth opposition.

In reading Logan's speeches of January and February, and his June letter to the *State Register*, the reasons for a split with Douglas can be seen. The breach had been growing since the 1860 election. As Douglas moved away from the South, Logan clung to his pro-Southern ideas. With secession, Douglas became increasingly aware of the futility of compromise while his Egyptian lieutenant continued to hope that compromise could be effected.

Logan, a practical politician, was still not sure of the views of his constituents. Pro-Confederate and, more important, peace sentiment was rife in southern Illinois. Robinson's letter is one example. Logan's law partner, Green, was also a peace man. He wrote Logan from Springfield condemning the war and Democrats like McClernand who endorsed war.[66]

---

[63]Lusk, *Politics and Politicians*, 175; Logan, *Conspiracy*, 265-270.

[64]Cullom, *Fifty Years*, 81. There is a typed, unsigned, three page note in the Logan collection in the Library of Congress which endorses Cullom's statement. It maintains that the Illinois Democrats went home with the idea of quieting "public apprehension," but that Douglas' speech to the assembly did the opposite. This angered Logan and brought on the feud. It is impossible to identify the author of the note.

[65]James Robinson to JAL, April 18, 1861, Logan Mss.

[66]W. H. Green to JAL, April 25, 1861, Logan Mss.

When Logan left Springfield in May, his relationship with Douglas is difficult to estimate. Logan said they parted in complete agreement.[67] The post-war Chicago *Tribune* repeated this story, but in May, 1861, an Egyptian paper told of an anti-Douglas faction in the Democratic Party, and called Logan "the most obnoxious and offensive of the gang."[68]

In early May Logan returned to Marion and soon was back on the circuit. He obtained a clearer idea of Egyptian public opinion, but did nothing to clarify his own position. There is one hostile report of Logan, at this time, published long after the war. A resident of Mt. Vernon, Edward V. Satterfield, claimed to have seen Logan, at McLeansboro, draw a knife and threaten to cut down the U. S. flag. This, like many other statements, came from a political opponent.[69]

May was an important month for Egypt and Logan. With peace impossible, Logan would soon be forced into a definite stand. His constituents were anxious to hear from their congressman. Refugees began pouring into Egypt from the South, and as the number increased, secession sentiment declined.[70] In May the first troops arrived in Egypt, causing considerable stir. About 4,000 men were stationed at Cairo by May 6, and on May 28 the first regiment of Egyptian troops was mobilized.[71] All this activity prompted one Egyptian journal to boast, "Illinois is changing poles. Cairo is taking precedence of Chicago."[72] With more and more troops moving into the section the possibility of secession or even a peace policy grew remote.

May was also the month in which pro-Southern sentiment in Egypt exploded again, and again enveloped Logan. For some time, rebel sympathizers had been considering the organization of an army to fight for the South. In early May

[67]Logan, *Great Conspiracy*, 269.

[68]Chicago *Tribune*, Sept. 19, 1866; Alton *Telegraph*, May 3, 1861. Linder says nothing to indicate that the two men parted amicably. Linder, *Reminiscences*, 345.

[69]Edward V. Satterfield to Ben Hill, Aug. 8, 1881 in the Bloomington *Daily Bulletin*, Aug. 10, 1881.

[70]*Illinois State Journal*, May 4, 1861.

[71]*Illinois State Journal*, May 6, 1861; *Report of the Adjutant-General of Illinois* (Springfield, 1863), 17, 18.

[72]Centralia *Egyptian Republic*, May 23, 1861.

two ardent secessionists, Thorndike Brooks and Harvey Hayes, began to organize troops. Their efforts were not very successful, and on May 25, despairing of raising more in Egypt, thirty-five men, brought together by Brooks and Hayes, started on foot for Paducah, Kentucky. They finally reached Mayfield, Kentucky, where they joined the 15th Tennessee Infantry.[73]

Logan was charged with complicity. These claims are redolent of politics. A letter often cited as evidence of Logan's activities in the Brooks plot, one of the few notes actually naming Logan as one of the conspirators, was written to Governor Yates by Patrick H. Lang. Lang, Republican postmaster at Marion, wrote:

> Your excellency has no doubt, ere this, been informed of the disunion feeling existing at Marion, Ill., brought about by disappointed politicians. Logan, Cunningham, Hundley, Pulley and others, have assisted in getting up a company for the so called 'Southern Confederacy.' The company so organized departed rejoicing in their treacherous mission of blood: and the men above named are making efforts for another company.

The letter ends with "Destroy this."[74] One day later another Egyptian Republican sent Yates a similar letter, but did not mention Logan.[75] A Republican in Democratic Egypt, Lang had to move his post office out of Marion.[76] He offers no definite proof of Logan's involvement. Blanket indictments of all Egyptian Democratic leaders were common in 1861. While Lang might have possessed information which he did not include in the letter, his note probably was merely a blow at opposition political leaders. Some political opponents did not credit the charge. The Republican *State Journal* later said Logan had nothing directly to do with organizing the men.[77]

On the other hand there is a great deal of evidence denying that Logan helped raise the company. Logan vigorously denied

---

[73]Erwin, *Williamson County*, 262.

[74]J. G. Randall, *Lincoln the President* (New York, 1946), I, 356; Patrick H. Lang to Yates, May 28, 1861, Yates Mss.

[75]Griffin Garland to Yates, May 28, 1861, Yates Mss.

[76]Erwin, *Williamson County*, 270.

[77]*Illinois State Journal*, June 15, 1861.

any part in forming the unit.[78] After the war he marshaled other testimony in his defense. Evidence consistently used against Logan was that his brother-in-law, Hibert Cunningham, was a member of Brooks' company. Young Hibe, despite pleadings from his family, joined Brooks and left with him on May 25. Mary, in despair, wrote her husband pleading with him to return to Marion. In this letter, which indicated Logan's absence when the company left, she warned, "I fear there will be some excitement and trouble growing out of those men leaving here." She concluded with a revealing comment indicating hostility toward the war and the Lincoln administration:

> The administration and his advisors have already begun their work of invasion, their arrogance and power have hurried them on in their progress . . . and the day will soon be here when every man must take sides in this conflict and never before were there two extremes more objectionable, for one can not honestly and honorably or justly endorse the course of the president.[79]

Further evidence of Logan's lack of knowledge of Hibe's decision came from Hibe himself. When Logan was accused of complicity by Democrats in the election of 1866, Hibe wrote Logan denying the charge. He was joined in this denial by A. H. Morgan, another member of the company, who added that Logan was not in Marion at the time.[80] However, to confuse the issue, Logan's sister Dorothy charged that he had furnished aid to pro-Southern forces in Egypt. Logan denied her charge.[81] The Logan family was a casualty of the war, and Logan's course of action earned the hostility of several of his brothers and sisters.

In addition to Cunningham and Morgan, of the Illinois rebels, Thorndike Brooks, their commander, later testified to Logan's innocence. In 1875 the charge appeared in the New York *World*. That paper produced an affadavit by one John

---

[78]JAL to D. L. Phillips, Oct. 20, 1864 in the Chicago *Tribune*, Oct. 25, 1864; *Illinois State Register*, June 21, 1861.

[79]Mary Logan to JAL, May 25, 1861, Logan Mss. See also Mary Logan's Diary for Jan. 20-Sept. 28, 1861, Mrs. Logan Mss., Library of Congress.

[80]Hibert Cunningham to JAL, Oct. 15, 1866; A. H. Morgan to JAL, Oct. 16, 1866, Logan Mss.

[81]Cole, *Era of the Civil War*, 402.

Wheatley which claimed Logan had not only organized the men, but led them to Kentucky. Logan wrote the paper charging that Wheatley was paid for the statement and had later withdrawn it. He asked the paper to print the Brooks letter, which it did. Brooks called the Wheatley story a "lie throughout," and denied that Logan had anything to do with organizing or aiding his company.[82]

Another charge made against Logan was that his actions were so treasonable that General B. M. Prentiss, Union commander at Cairo, ordered his arrest and made him report daily. In August, 1866, the general denied the charge, stating that his only talk with Logan came in August, 1861, when Logan returned to organize a regiment.[83] In June, 1861, however, an Egyptian paper reported a captain stationed at the railroad bridge over the Big Muddy River "told us that he did not think the people would keep quiet until LOGAN, the chief traitor among them was arrested. Said he was so smart that he covered his tracks and there could be nothing to get hold of him by."[84]

Perhaps the clearest view of Logan's role comes from two widely separated sources. Milo Erwin, author of *The History of Williamson County,* denied Logan aided in raising the company, and interviewed W. M. Davis, a member of the group. Davis, like Wheatley, had signed an affadavit saying he had joined the company at Logan's "advice." Erwin states that Davis told him "advice" was misleading, the wording of those who asked him for the affadavit.

> He [Davis] says that he did not think of going into the Confederate army until a few days before he started. Logan was not here [Marion] at that time, and of course could not have advised him to go. . . . He says that he did not swear nor mean that John A. Logan ever advised him . . . to go into the Southern army. . . .He says that what he means was that Logan, being a man of great influence in this county, and he believed that his sympathy was with the South, and in this way Logan influenced him to go South.[85]

[82]New York *World*, Mar. 16, 1875; Thorndike Brooks to JAL, Mar. 27, 1875, Logan Mss.
[83]*Illinois State Journal*, Aug. 24, 1866.
[84]Centralia *Egyptian Republic*, June 13, 1861.
[85]Erwin, *Williamson County*, 264-265.

Years later, Davis' statement was echoed by F. M. Woollard. In 1909, a student writing a thesis on Illinois in 1861, wrote Woollard for information. Woollard told his correspondent that, though Logan was an "extreme party man," he did not feel he had been guilty of treason. Woollard added that he met one of the men in the Brooks group who said nothing of Logan's direct involvement. He instead told Woollard "they told us that Logan would follow and command the regiment as soon as it could be raised."[86] It is reasonable to assume that Logan's popularity and pro-Southern ideas did assist in convincing some of the young hotheads that their course was wise. It is also likely that Logan's name was used in the recruiting campaign.

After his speech of April 25, Senator Douglas went home to Chicago and became seriously ill. In late May his condition worsened and on June 4 the Chicago *Times* mourned: "the foremost man in the nation is no more."[87] Douglas' death brought no public comment from Logan though he did serve on the committee to collect money to aid Douglas' family.[88]

Logan's silence continued amid charges that he was a secessionist. Tiring of the charges the Carbondale *Times* informed its readers that Logan merely advocated compromise instead of war.[89] Others asked for clear statements of his intentions. One paper advised Logan that the time for neutrality had passed and asked him to "come out and defend his position."[90] The "Egyptian Home Guards" demanded that Logan resign from Congress since he no longer represented the views of his constituents. The Carbondale *Times* again came to his defense, branding the resolutions "ill-timed" and passed without complete knowledge of Logan's position.[91]

From February to June, Logan's opinions had not appeared in the press. The time for compromise was long past. Soon he

[86]F. M. Woollard to E. L. Bost, April 22, 1909, F. M. Woollard Mss., Illinois State Historical Library. Smith in *Borderland in the Civil War*, 178, says: "As late as June [1861] Logan's name was used to secure volunteers for the Confederacy."

[87]Chicago *Times*, June 4, 1861.

[88]John B. Haskin to JAL, Aug. 6, 1861, Logan Mss.

[89]Carbondale *Times* in Quincy *Herald*, June 12, 1861.

[90]Shawneetown *Mercury* in *Illinois State Journal*, June 18, 1861.

[91]Carbondale *Times* in Chicago *Times*, June 21, 1861. The "Home Guards" resolutions were issued on June 8.

would have to return to Washington for the special session called by Lincoln. Since Sumter, Logan had been calculating the sentiments of his fellow Egyptians. By June it was evident southern Illinois would stand by the Union. On June 18, perhaps under McClernand's influence, Logan broke his silence.

The occasion was dramatic. At Camp Yates, near Springfield, a regiment commanded by Colonel Ulysses S. Grant faced the alternative of going home or reenlisting. Many had already gone home, and Grant, fearful of losing his command, asked McClernand to address it. McClernand arrived at the camp accompanied by Logan. Grant was aware of McClernand's unionism but hesitated to let Logan speak because of rumors of his secession sympathy. Finally, feeling McClernand could offset anything Logan might say, Grant agreed that both men speak.[92]

McClernand spoke first, and the hawk-faced congressman delivered as expected. Then he turned to the stockier Logan and introduced him: "Allow me, Illinoisans to present to you my friend and colleague in Congress, Hon. John A. Logan. He is gifted with eloquence, and will rouse you to feel as the Athenians felt when under the eloquent appeals of Demosthenes they asked to be immediately led against Phillip."[93]

Logan began by ridiculing the idea of going home without fighting a battle. He remarked, " 'You can't fall out now. If you go home to Mary, she will say, 'Why Tom, are you home from the war so soon?'

" 'Yes.'

" 'How far did you get?'

" 'Mattoon.' "[94]

This brought a roar of laughter, and Logan concluded with a forceful appeal which, Grant remembered: "breathed a loyalty and devotion to the Union which inspired my men to such a point that they would have volunteered to remain in the Army as long as any enemy of the country continued to bear arms against it. They entered the . . . service almost to a

---

[92]Ulysses S. Grant, *Memoirs* (New York, 1895), (2nd ed.), I, 195-197.
[93]*Illinois State Journal*, June 25, 1861.
[94]Lloyd Lewis, *Captain Sam Grant* (Boston, 1950), 429.

man."⁹⁵ Logan had taken his stand. There was no longer any doubt of his devotion to the Union.

Three days later he spoke again. For the first time, he defended himself against the charges of the spring. On June 3 "Josh" Allen who, like Logan, had been accused of fomenting secession in Egypt, denied the charges against Logan and himself. The *State Journal,* not satisfied with Allen's statement, asked Logan a series of questions.⁹⁶ Reading the queries, Logan wrote a heated reply. The long letter, printed in the *State Register,* June 21, branded as lies all reports of his aid to secession. Egypt secede? "Impossible and absurd." Noting that no substantial proof had been offered against him, he related his actions since returning from Washington:

> I have made three or four speeches while attending the courts in the ninth congressional district. In those speeches I very candidly deprecated the causes of our present troubles, and pointed to what appeared to me to be the concerted action between the abolitionists of the North and the secessionists of the South, to effect a dissolution of the Union. I said without disguise, as I say now, that the impertinent spirit of the anti-slavery party of the North was mainly chargeable for the state of feeling in the South.⁹⁷

He added he still thought, had Republicans exhibited a "proper spirit of compromise" in January and February, there would have been no need for coercion. "But while undisguised in the expression of opinion upon the policy of the administration, there was in no utterance of mine, an expression of disloyalty to the government." He defended Egyptians as loyal citizens. Men who followed Brooks into Kentucky he called "misguided boys."

Logan's defense drew applause from Union Democrats all over Illinois. It satisfied the *State Journal.* Its Cairo correspondent declared he knew Logan had never been a secessionist.⁹⁸ The June 18 letter stands as Logan's most effective defense in the confusing days of 1861. Frankly criticizing the

---

⁹⁵Grant, *Memoirs,* I, 197.

⁹⁶*Illinois State Register,* June 12, 1861; *Illinois State Journal,* June 10, 18, 1861.

⁹⁷*Illinois State Register,* June 21, 1861.

⁹⁸*Illinois State Journal,* June 25, 1861.

Lincoln administration, and continuing to speak for modera-
tion, his letter is far more credible than his post-war writings.

In late June only a few days remained before Logan's return
to Washington. He was still uncertain of his role in the war.
That he still entertained vague compromise hopes is evident
from his record in the special session. Nevertheless, Logan had
made clear his devotion to the Union and his opposition to
secession. He had set his course toward support of the war he
had desperately hoped could be avoided. Though there were
still doubts as to the wisdom of that course, there would be no
turning back.

CHAPTER VI

RALLY 'ROUND THE FLAG

A special session of the 37th Congress was called by Lincoln for July 4. Filled with uncertainty, Logan set out for the capital in late June. Illinois Republicans were still questioning his position, while the Democratic press rallied to his defense. The latter claimed the attacks came from "lying Republican newspapers" and denied that Logan was a secessionist.[1] Logan, denying aiding rebellion, had not come out for war. He spoke of patriotism and the fate of traitors, but dwelt on the horrors of civil war. His last speeches before entraining for Washington were intended to prepare his constituents for the "severing of party allegiance and enlistment in the army."[2] If this was his intent, he did it poorly. When Logan announced he would join the army, after his return to Illinois in August, his supporters were dismayed.

When Logan left Marion, Mary moved to Carbondale to be on the Illinois Central Railroad. There she could communicate with her husband rapidly by telegraph. Logan counted on his wife to keep the people informed of national conditions, as Logan saw them, so that his future course would cause a minimum of surprise and tension.[3]

On July 3, the day before the session began, Logan met Henry W. Blodgett, Illinois Republican. He excitedly told Blodgett of his intention to go to Lincoln and request a commission, all compromise efforts having failed. Accompanied by the Republican, Logan proposed raising a regiment, but the president advised him he could render greater service in Congress. Here, said Lincoln, Logan could use his influence among Democrats to secure votes for legislation to support the war. When Logan

[1]*Illinois State Register*, July 3, 1861; Carbondale *Times*, July 4, 1861.
[2]Mary Logan, *Reminiscences*, 90.
[3]*Ibid.*, 91, 206.

left, Lincoln promised that "authority would be given him later to raise a regiment."[4]

This interview with Lincoln would seem to indicate an end to Logan's wavering. His record in Congress and his letters to his wife belie this. He did not lend complete support to administration measures and continued to vote against bills he considered unwarranted. But he had almost abandoned hope of compromise. In despair, on the session's opening day, he wrote Mary:

> I can see no prospect of any adjustment of our difficulties. There is no one who will attempt to do anything. The Ky. and Mo. men all came here as solid as the Republicans for war, except Burnett, so you see that when from the South we get war, there is no use for northern men to sacrifice themselves by standing out against the storm. I shall act as consistently with my record as I can under all circumstances.[5]

On the session's first day, despite rumors of a protracted speakership fight, Republican Galusha Grow of Pennsylvania won the post. With no hope of victory, Logan voted for John S. Phelps of Missouri.

After the election of a speaker, the day's major business was the presidential message. Since April, Lincoln had been exercising unprecedented emergency powers. Many members of Congress felt that in his actions the president had been excessive. "These measures whether strictly legal or not," Lincoln replied on July 4, "were ventured upon what appeared to be a popular demand and a public necessity; trusting that Congress would readily ratify them."[6] The chief executive went on to trace the Sumter crisis and outline a program for the nation's preservation.

The president's message, with its call to arms, did little to mitigate Logan's feeling of dread. "I have been borne down

---

[4]George F. James (ed.), *Logan Monument Memorial Addresses* (Chicago, 1896), 58-61.

[5]JAL to Mary Logan, July 4, 1861, Logan Mss. Henry C. Burnett of Kentucky was later expelled from Congress and became a colonel in the Confederate army.

[6]James G. Randall and David Donald, *The Civil War and Reconstruction* (New York, 1961), 275.

with all the troubles that we feel," he wrote. Far from being a staunch administration supporter, he stated: "It seems the devil . . . has seized upon these infernal abolitionists and they would rather see us in a revolution than to modify their fanatical notions."[7]

Independence Day celebrations could not relieve his despondency. Fusillades resounded in the streets all day long, and a rumble of artillery rose from camps across the Potomac. After viewing a parade of 20,000 uniformed warriors on the 4th, and watching troops move, often drunkenly, about the city, he wrote Mary of his disgust at war hysteria. It was not safe, he complained, for women to appear on the streets. A few days later he thought "there can be no compromises, the South don't want any and the North would not make any."[8]

House committees were named July 8. Logan was renamed to the moribund Committee on Revisal and Unfinished Business, this time as chairman. He was also given a seat on the Committee on Invalid Pensions.[9]

Logan took little active part in the deliberations of the special session. His voice was rarely heard, and he hoped for a short session so he might "get home from the excitement."[10] When a motion was made July 8 to restrict business to defense measures, he agreed. Lovejoy introduced a resolution to repeal the Fugitive Slave Law. It was tabled 88 to 62, Logan voting with the majority. Another abolitionist move which failed proposed to instruct the Judiciary Committee to prepare a bill confiscating property of officeholders fighting against the government. Logan, who fought confiscation throughout the session, voted to table.[11]

Next day Lovejoy introduced a bill stating that it was no business of the army to return fugitive slaves. The bill passed, all Illinois Democrats voting "no."[12] Later that day the first military appropriations bills passed with Logan in support. He had resolved to vote for men and money to fight the war.

---

[7]JAL to John Cunningham, July 5, 1861, Logan Mss.
[8]JAL to Mary Logan, July 6, 10, 1861, Logan Mss.
[9]*Cong. Globe*, 37th Cong., 1st Sess., 22.
[10]JAL to Mary Logan, July 10, 1861, Logan Mss.
[11]*Cong. Globe*, 37th Cong., 1st Sess., 24.
[12]*Ibid.*, 32.

"I intend to give them a chance to preserve the government if it can be done. I do not think it can though I am willing they may try and then I cannot reproach myself that I was not willing for a trial," he told his wife.[13]

This change in Logan's policy was not generally known in Egypt. His law partner, W. H. Green, wrote: "the people of southern Illinois are looking to you and your action to guide them more than to any other man." Someone, he said, had started rumors that Logan supported the war and "the people, the bone and sinew of the land, the honest-hearted Democracy, are only fearful lest the rumors about you are true." He added that in Egypt Democrats were attacking Lincoln's emergency policies. All Egypt looked to Logan as their "Standard Bearer." "What Douglas was to the Democracy of the northwest, you are to the Democracy of Egypt." The rabid anti-war Democrat concluded with a caution. "For you to come out for the war is ruin to you politically."[14] His partner's letter left Logan more disturbed than ever. Support of the war might ruin him, but the war was under way and opposition to it might bring something worse. Logan was determined to go ahead with his intention of voting support for the war.

Logan was most active in the session's second week. He offered a resolution to print for distribution 20,000 copies of the Douglas eulogies delivered in the House July 9. He also introduced two private bills for the relief of citizens of southern Illinois. When Vallandigham introduced a resolution inquiring into the records of several House members who also held military commissions, the motion was tabled after heated debate. Logan, who later found himself in similar circumstances, voted against tabling.[15]

On July 13 one of the most intense debates of the session took place. Frank Blair offered a resolution to expel fellow Missourian John B. Clark from the House for having borne arms against the government. Logan joined Clark's defenders in an attempt to sidetrack the bill into the Committee on Elections. The maneuver failed and by a vote of 94 to 45 Clark was

---

[13]JAL to Mary Logan, July 16, 1861, Logan Mss.

[14]W. H. Green to JAL, July 9, 1861, Logan Mss.

[15]*Cong. Globe,* 37th Cong., 1st Sess., 93, 116.

expelled. Logan joined all Illinois Democrats, except McClernand, who did not vote, in opposition to expulsion.[16]

Two days later Logan and the Illinois Democrats demonstrated their mixed feelings in votes on resolutions by peace Democrat Ben Wood of New York, and war Democrat McClernand. Wood proposed a general convention of the states at Louisville on September 1 to "devise measures for the restoration of peace in our country." The proposal was tabled 92 to 51 with all Illinois Democrats voting against tabling. Later the same day, McClernand produced a resolution pledging the House to vote all means necessary to put down rebellion. Again Illinois Democrats presented a solid front. The McClernand proposal passed 121 to 5.[17] Thus Logan, like many northern Democrats, hoped for last minute compromise before major military action. Yet they were determined to vote war supports if mediatory efforts failed.

Throughout the session Logan complained of suppression of free speech. He wrote that no man was safe who spoke in any way opposed to war. He thought a "reign of terror" existed in Washington against peace advocates. "A man cannot express sentiments against the war without being scoffed and hissed," he complained.[18]

From the time Congress convened it was only a matter of days before the first great battle of the war was fought across the Potomac in Virginia. Logan, though disgusted at the presence of troops in the capital, determined to see the battle. As early as July 6 he told Mary it was his aim to join several congressmen in a martial excursion. He promised to sit "at a respectful distance to be out of danger."[19]

He and Illinois Democratic Congressman William Richardson went to General Winfield Scott to secure permission to follow the army to Manassas Junction. Logan cautioned Mary against mentioning the trip to Virginia to his constituents.[20] Having secured permits, the two men, accompanied by several other civilians, set out by carriage across Long Bridge and

---

[16]*Ibid.*, 117.
[17]*Ibid.*, 129, 131.
[18]JAL to Mary Logan, July 16, 1861, Logan Mss.
[19]JAL to Mary Logan, July 6, 1861, Logan Mss.
[20]JAL to Mary Logan, July 16, 1861, Logan Mss.

into Union camps in Confederate Virginia. When the House adjourned early on the 19th so that members could rush, in festive mood, to the battlefield, Logan had already attached himself to the 2nd Michigan and was marching through the sunny morning toward Bull Run.[21]

Logan's precise actions during the Bull Run campaign are difficult to trace. But there is enough evidence to indicate that he did not remain in Virginia until the great battle of the 21st. The 2nd Michigan, in the 4th Brigade, 1st Division of General Irvin McDowell's army, with whom Logan marched, broke camp near Centreville on the 18th and moved, on the Union left, toward Manassas Junction. The rebels had abandoned their lines at Centreville and the Union advance continued. After a short march, Colonel Israel Richardson ordered a halt to procure water. He and General Daniel Tyler, the division commander, decided on a reconnaissance down into the valley along Bull Run at Blackburn's Ford. Skirmishers and artillery support were pushed forward, and the 1st Massachusetts and 12th New York sent to reconnoitre.

Richardson ordered a charge on a Confederate position at the ford, and the New York regiment pushed forward into dense woods bordering the run. As the colonel ordered the 2nd and 3rd Michigan to advance, he discovered the New Yorkers streaming out of the woods in disorder. His left had caved in, but the center and right stood firm. Richardson proposed charging the ford with his three remaining regiments, when Tyler arrived and argued that further action was unnecessary. The shattered 12th New York finally regrouped up the hill, where an artillery battle was waged across the run for some time.[22] This skirmish left Confederates jubilant and brought gloom to the invaders. McDowell was afraid that the demoralizing setback would spread panic through his green units not yet in action.[23]

---

[21]Margaret Leech, *Reville in Washington* (New York, 1941), 99; Robert U. Johnson and Clarence C. Buel (eds.), *Battles and Leaders of the Civil War* (New York, 1887-1888), I, 194. The Second Michigan was led by Colonel Israel Richardson.

[22]*Official Records of the War of the Rebellion* (Washington, 1880-1901), Ser. 1, II, 313. Hereafter cited as *OR*.

[23]*Battles and Leaders*, I, 179.

During the engagement, Logan, forgetting his promise, moved forward with the troops. When the 12th New York charged, Logan accompanied it. He was a strange sight on the battlefield. Dressed in civilian clothes, with a plug hat pulled down tightly on his head, he picked up a musket and took a few shots at the Confederates. One observer remembered: "He was a man of alert and vigorous frame, swarthy complexion, long and heavy black moustache, and black eyes . . . and by language more forcible than polite, he strove to rally the men."[24] Logan did little fighting and spent most of his time under fire assisting wounded to the rear.

After the battle of the 18th Logan decided he had seen enough and returned to Washington, where he wrote to an anxious wife:

> I have just returned from three miles this side of Manassas, which is Bulls Run [sic] and was in the fight with a musket . . . and came out without a scratch. I came back black with powder and bloody from carrying off wounded soldiers . . . I am now glad that I went as I am not hurt and safely say that no man who saw me on the field will say that I wanted courage.[25]

Logan had accomplished his purpose. He had proved to his detractors that he was not afraid of war, though he deplored it. When the Union defeat of the 21st occurred Logan was in Washington. He avoided the ignominy of the panic-filled rush from Virginia.

When Logan returned from his baptism of fire he was determined to obtain an army commission. He had written Mary, before the battle, that if war continued he would rather be at the front than in Congress. "I feel very much inclined to go into the Army, not for the heart in the contest, but that if the Government is to be preserved to help do it," he told her.[26] On July 25 Logan completed his plans and wrote, "I want to join the army." He advised Mary he would not do so until he returned and talked to her. His family's opposition to the war

---

[24]Walter R. Houghton, *Early Life and Public Career of James G. Blaine with a Biography of Gen. John A. Logan* (Cleveland, 1884), 250. The description is by General Anson McCook of Ohio.
[25]JAL to Mary Logan, July 20, 1861, Logan Mss.
[26]JAL to Mary Logan, July 16, 1861, Logan Mss.

bore heavily on his decision. "I am desirous that our noble little daughter shall be known as the daughter of an honest and brave man. The stain upon our family must be wiped out."[27]

Mary, who knew the decision was coming, wrote him of the excitement created in Egypt by rumors he would return and raise a regiment. She had said nothing of his intentions. Commenting on Josh Allen's reception of the rumors, she remarked caustically that he seemed pleased at the possibility. Of Allen's motives she concluded, "Your going into the service of course . . . would vacate your seat in Congress. Oh man how treacherous thou art!"[28]

Once he had made up his mind, Logan wished for a rapid end to the special session. Unlike many members, however, he remained until adjournment. On July 22 he voted for Crittenden's resolution that the war was not to be waged for "conquest and subjugation," and would end as soon as "law is vindicated."[29] Logan continued to support measures to provide men and money to suppress the rebellion. He balked, however, at the proposed direct tax to raise revenue. When the bill passed, Logan voted against it.[30]

Even after Bull Run and his decision to join the army, Logan could not shake his wish for compromise. When S. S. Cox introduced a resolution to name a commission to meet with Confederate commissioners to discuss national difficulties, the House refused to suspend the rules to allow discussion. Logan, still clutching at vain hopes, voted to suspend.[31]

In the final week Logan remained, most of the time, a silent observer. On August 2 the confiscation bill was reported out of committee and subjected to lengthy discussion. Logan and Robert Mallory of Kentucky exchanged words with Thad Stevens of Pennsylvania, the measure's staunchest supporter. The two Western Democrats called the law unconstitutional, and Stevens defended it as a necessary wartime step. Logan

[27]JAL to Mary Logan, July 25, 1861, Logan Mss.
[28]Mary Logan to JAL, July 22, 1861, Logan Mss.
[29]New York *Times*, July 23, 1861.
[30]*Cong. Globe*, 37th Cong., 1st Sess., 331.
[31]*Ibid*.

later voted to table the bill but the attempt failed.[32] His final action of the session was to vote on another compromise proposal. Two days before adjournment Vallandigham and two Marylanders introduced a resolution to organize a committee to "make recommendations for constitutional amendments to restore mutual confidence." It was tabled with Logan voting "no."[33] Though determined to join the army, Logan felt no compromise possibility should be overlooked. He voted to the last for any proposal to stop the carnage.

Just prior to his return to Egypt, Logan indicated his future course to several previously ignorant of his intentions. A friend from southern Illinois, in Washington on business, visited the congressman and was told of Logan's plans to return and raise a regiment.[34] Back in Illinois, the circle of friends aware of his plans grew. Logan telegraphed a close friend, John H. White, informed him of his intentions, and asked him to announce that Logan would speak in Marion on his return. White, future lieutenant colonel of Logan's regiment, spread the word among close friends and had posters printed announcing the speech.[35] One Egyptian paper, still circulating the rumor of Logan's war support, informed its readers that Logan's first act upon returning would be to raise a regiment. It forecast Logan's elevation to brigadier general, in command of an Egyptian brigade, when enough regiments had been formed. This, it maintained, was an office for which Logan was "well fitted."[36]

Logan was also considered "well fitted" for a command by those in high places. "Well fitted" to bring increased support to the war effort rather than as a military leader. In the latter role his qualifications were unknown. When Logan visited the president on April 3, he had been promised a commission. On August 7, one day after the end of the special session, Lincoln

[32]*Ibid.*, 412, 415.
[33]*Ibid.*, 445.
[34]Halbert J. Strawn, "The Attitude of General John A. Logan on the Question of Secession in 1861," *Journal of the Illinois State Historical Society*, VI, No. 2 (July, 1913), 256-257.
[35]John H. White to JAL, Aug. 11, 1861, Logan Mss. Logan and White had talked of Logan's raising a regiment before Logan left for Congress. Erwin, *Williamson County*, 260.
[36]Jonesboro *Gazette*, Aug. 17, 1861.

wrote McClernand, who was to be a brigadier, that Logan was to command a regiment.[37] Four days later Governor Yates tendered Logan a colonelcy of one of the regiments to rendezvous at Camp Butler.[38] Lincoln's policy of proferring commands to political opponents, who would bring their followers into the war behind the government, was a wise one. In Logan's case it was an outstanding success.

The army talk had created hostile rumblings from Logan's anti-war friends. It was deemed wise for Logan to return and complete plans for the speech before going to the public. On August 18 Mary, who had moved back to Marion to aid in the preparations, drove to Carbondale to meet her husband. There she found he had missed a connection and would not arrive until the following morning. She drove back to Marion and was received by an angry crowd shouting for Logan. Williamson County Sheriff Swindell quieted the disturbance and told them to come back next day. That night Mary returned to Carbondale, and at 2 A. M. Logan arrived.[39]

When Logan first informed his friends of his intention to speak, it was felt wise to collect a few sure backers in Marion to support him. White and Swindell had collected a small group led by Dr. Samuel Mitchell.[40] The afternoon was hot when Logan walked to the town square, mounted a wagon, and began his address. His booming voice reached the limits of his audience as he began by tracing the national situation. He deplored action by extremists North and South. Then he slowly pictured the consequences of successful rebellion. Building to a climax, while some applauded and others listened in disappointment, he echoed Douglas' words of April 25:

> The time has come when a man must be for or against his country. . . . The Union once dissolved, we should have innumerable confederacies and rebellions. I, for one, shall stand or fall with the Union, and shall this day enroll for the war. I want as many of you as will to come with me. If

[37]Lincoln to McClernand, Aug. 7, 1861, in Abraham Lincoln, *Collected Works*, Roy P. Basler (ed.) (New Brunswick, New Jersey, 1953), IV, 477.

[38]Richard Yates to JAL, Aug. 11, 1861, Yates Mss.

[39]Mary Logan, *Reminiscences*, 93.

[40]*Ibid.*, 93, 97; George Smith, *Southern Illinois*, I, 563.

you say 'no,' and see your best interests and the welfare of your homes and your children in another direction, may God protect you.[41]

As the speech ended a man who had served with Logan in Mexico stepped forward and struck up a patriotic air on his fife. This was a prearranged signal and several of Logan's friends moved forward to volunteer. Enough men enlisted that day to form a company.[42] Many in the audience, on the other hand, disgusted with Logan refused to volunteer or support him in any way. A breach had opened that would never close. Many of those who had supported him became bitter personal and political enemies.

The estrangement from former political friends was not too difficult to bear; it was a natural hazard of politics. The treatment he received from his family was a different matter. Of this large group, only his young brother James shared Logan's Union sentiments at the outset of the war.[43] One brother, Tom, made clear his pro-Southern feelings, and Logan's brother-in-law, Dr. Israel Blanchard attacked the congressman for his advocacy of war.[44] His mother's hostility was most difficult to bear. When he went to Murphysboro, shortly after returning, Mrs. Logan received him coldly. She "upbraided" him for his abandonment of pro-Southern principles and he left sick at heart.[45]

Logan's decision to fight for the Union had an instantaneous effect on Egypt. When Logan, now called by some the "Little Egyptian Giant," offered his services, the Egyptian anti-war tide ebbed and quickly turned in favor of the government.[46] Within months, the section was supplying troops more rapidly than any other part of the state. Logan is credited by many with creating this change in Egypt's sympathies. Grant gave full credit to Logan: "Logan's popularity in this district was unbounded. He knew almost enough of the people in it by their

---

[41]Mary Logan, *Reminiscences*, 98.

[42]*Ibid*. This company became Co. C., 31st Illinois Infantry.

[43]Buel, *Standard Bearers*, 335.

[44]R. J. Wheatley to Yates, July 26, 1861, Yates Mss.

[45]Mary Logan, "Sketch of General John A. Logan," unpublished typewritten manuscript, Mrs. Logan Mss., Library of Congress.

[46]Cole, *Era of the Civil War*, 279.

Christian names to form an ordinary congressional district. As he went in politics, so his district was sure to go."[47]

Other contemporaries spoke of Logan's influence. James G. Blaine traced Egypt's enthusiastic support of the war to Logan's actions. Nicolay and Hay also spoke of Logan's influence in bringing his section to the government's support.[48] More recently Logan has been called one of the "most powerful of the Democrats in Illinois," and the congressman who could hold "the loyalty of his constituents as probably no other Illinois Congressman of his time."[49]

These estimates seem true. As a candidate for Congress in 1858 and 1860 Logan was elected by large majorities. While he said nothing in favor of the war, Egypt rumbled with discontent and lagged in rushing to the colors. After August, 1861, when Logan made his tardy decision to enter the contest, Egypt made a similar decision. Pro-secession activity continued in the section after August, 1861, but the overflow of enlistments from southern Illinois was unmatched throughout the state. Even Republican counties along the northern border lagged behind "darkest Egypt" in filling troop quotas.

It is possible that Logan, sensing a turn in public opinion, acted when he did to take command of the new trend before it passed by him. There was pro-Union strength before Logan's speech and it had grown from April to August. But it is also possible that Logan's decision helped create the turn in public opinion, and, as Grant maintained, win Egypt for the Union. It is certain that men flocked to the stars and stripes in ever increasing numbers after the Marion speech. This could have been a natural development. But the decision of a leader as popular as Logan, who had won great support in the past and continued to do so in the future, certainly had great effect on a section as uncertain as Egypt. They might have flocked to the colors anyway, but Logan's announcement hurried them on.

Logan's decision was a long time coming. A natural hatred

---

[47]Grant, *Memoirs*, I, 195-196.

[48]James G. Blaine, *Twenty Years of Congress, 1861-1881* (Norwich, Connecticut, 1886), II, 640; John G. Nicolay and John Hay, *Abraham Lincoln; A History* (New York, 1886), VII, 136.

[49]Lord Charnwood, *Abraham Lincoln* (London, 1921), 348; Lewis, *Sam Grant*, 429.

of abolitionists and sympathy for the South was tempered by a deep love of the Union. To a Jacksonian Democrat, which Logan considered himself, the Union's destruction was intolerable, but the coercion of one of the sections was also intolerable. Many factors contributed to his slow but irrevocable decision. His love of the Union and his conclusion that war alone could save it was important in determining his course. Like most Northern war-Democrats, he believed that the war was to save the Union and had nothing to do with freeing slaves. Logan agreed with the Chicago *Times*: "When the Democrats are in the field, disunionists will find it difficult to make this a war for the extermination of slavery, or the subjugation of the South. . . . It must be prosecuted for the sole purpose of sustaining the laws and the constitution."[50]

Practical politics played a significant role in Logan's resolution. He was accused of joining the army to play politics, a charge not without foundation. With Egypt seeming to swing toward the Union, Logan could lead it and retain political prominence there at the end of hostilities. In addition, a military career could be of great help politically. He was well aware of the uniform's hypnotic effect on voters. With McClernand, and many other Democrats in uniform, Logan joined to take advantage of military prestige. After all, he had used his Mexican War record, insignificant as it was, in past campaigns.

Finally, personal considerations had their importance. Logan's distress at the near-treasonous sympathy shown the rebels by his and his wife's family, left him determined to wipe out that disgrace. He wanted his daughter to be known as the child of an "honest and brave man." Joining the fight would help erase the stigma his family had acquired. He turned his face to the South as an enemy, but he entered the fray hesitantly and with grim forebodings.

---

[50]Chicago *Times*, Sept. 7, 1861.

CHAPTER VII

THE THIRTY-FIRST ILLINOIS

On July 22, after the Bull Run debacle, 13 new Illinois infantry regiments began organization. Two of these, the 29th and 31st, were to be formed in Egypt; colonelcy of the 31st went to Logan. When the command was officially proferred him August 11, Logan accepted, and as his first step in organizing the unit delivered the Marion address.

After Marion, Logan stumped southern Illinois, recruiting much as he had stumped for votes in 1858 and 1860. In his two congressional elections immense popularity and spell-binding oratory won Logan huge majorities. In August and September, 1861, similar methods brought Egyptians flocking to the colors. His speeches were all alike. "The Union must be preserved, join the army and save the nation."[1]

Expecting some hostility, Logan was surprised by the enthusiasm he encountered. He gradually shook off the gloom that had accompanied his decision to fight. Absorbed with details of raising troops, he "seemed almost happy."[2] Logan found little opposition and almost no difficulty in finding men. In some areas change was miraculous. When the first call was made in April, men who marched away were hissed and stoned by Democrats. When Logan and fellow Democrats took the recruiting trail, Southern sympathizers joined up and "no more was said about the horrible, unjust war."[3]

The call was always "save the Union." Some balked at fighting an abolitionist war, and Logan hastily assured recruits the struggle had nothing to do with freeing slaves. He promised to lead them home if the war became an abolition crusade.[4]

After a week's personal recruiting, Logan went to Spring-

---

[1]*Illinois State Register*, Aug. 14, 1861.
[2]Mary Logan, *Reminiscences*, 100.
[3]C. H. Kettler to Lyman Trumbull, Dec. 22, 1861, Trumbull Mss.
[4]Jonesboro *Gazette*, Feb. 28, 1863.

field to arrange the reception of his regiment at Camp Butler. Due to crowded conditions there, the rendezvous point was shifted to Camp Dunlap near Jacksonville. While Logan returned to Egypt to attend to final details and fill out the regiment, Judge I. N. Haynie, who had assisted in raising the unit, was sent to Camp Dunlap to take charge of the advance contingent of the 31st. Word of Haynie's activities reached Logan in Carbondale. Ever jealous of rank and power, Logan complained to McClernand: "I sent Judge Haynie some days ago, who desired to be Lt. Col. Though I find that since then, instead of doing anything like taking charge, he has been arranging with the folks in power there to be Col. himself, and has been trying to get some of the companies that I have raised from the stump."[5] Haynie never served in the 31st under Logan. He commanded his own regiment, the 48th, and cordial relations were restored.

By September 1 Logan's regiment, almost complete, was undergoing its first training at Camp Dunlap. Logan arrived to find men clothed in every variety of garment. They mounted guard without guns, drilled incessantly, and slept in straw without blankets.[6] When all had passed physical examinations, orders came to move to Cairo. Officers and men went by rail to Camp Defiance at Cairo where troop training began in earnest.

The men of the 31st had marched away from home to cheers, flowery words, and boundless enthusiasm. At Camp Dunlap they had experienced the first pangs of camp boredom. At Cairo routine camp life, though enlivened by wild rumors of impending action, brought restlessness and constant complaints. It had been an unusually hot summer, and early September offered little respite. Camp Defiance, at the point of land jutting south from Cairo, bounded by the two great rivers, was low, scorched, and uncomfortable. One author calls this narrow peninsula a "shining lance head, thrusting its way deep into the very vitals of slavery and rebellion." To men

---

[5]JAL to McClernand, Aug. 27, 1861, McClernand Mss.

[6]W. S. Morris, *History of the 31st Regiment Illinois Volunteers* (Evansville, Indiana, 1902), 17.

learning the art of war it was a steamy quagmire alive with mosquitoes.[7]

Most of the men arrived in summer clothing and did not receive uniforms until in need. Adequate weapons were also lacking, and ancient Belgian muskets were used to learn the manual, drill, and stand guard. Lack of proper equipment caused dissatisfaction and Logan and other regimental commanders were hard put to quell complaints.[3] Once a portion of the 31st refused to do duty, mutinied, and stacked arms. When informed, Logan roared, "Stacked arms! The devil they have! Well, I'll give them enough of stacking arms!" Stalking into camp, he put loyal companies under arms over the malcontents, who stacked and unstacked arms for 12 hours.[9]

Discipline continued to be a problem. Logan wrote often of the arduous duty of keeping troops reasonably content. He also continued to question the wisdom of his enlistment, fearing he had acted unwisely. However, he resignedly admitted, "It is done and I must make the best of it."[10] One difficulty was that many men in Logan's regiment had known him before enlisting, and persisted in calling him "John." These same old acquaintances plagued the colonel with pleas to go home when bad news arrived. The tyro regimental commander was busy refusing such requests.[11]

In good weather most of the time was spent drilling. Those who had served in the Mexican War were looked to for instruction. While Logan concerned himself with securing clothing and weapons, parade ground activities were conducted by Lieutenant Colonel John H. White. Soon regimental and company commanders obtained copies of Hardee's *Tactics* and citizens turned soldier diligently studied military theory written by a man they would face three years later in one of the war's

---

[7]Bluford Wilson, "Southern Illinois in the Civil War," *Transactions of the Illinois State Historical Society*, No. 16, 1911, 95; Augustus Chetlain, *Recollections of Seventy Years* (Galena, Illinois, 1899), 80; Chicago *Tribune*, May 28, June 8, 1861; Centralia *Egyptian Republic*, June 13, 1861.

[8]Mary Logan, *Reminiscences*, 105; Chicago *Times*, Sept. 7, 1861.

[9]William F. G. Shanks, *Personal Recollections of Distinguished Generals* (New York, 1866), 308.

[10]JAL to Mary Logan, Sept. 13, 1861, Logan Mss.

[11]Mary Logan, *Reminiscences*, 108.

great battles.[12] Journalists flocked to Cairo and wrote in glowing terms of the 31st: "The regiment . . . is composed of material that can be depended upon, the entire body being Democrats with the exception of twelve men. Logan . . . will command the entire confidence of his men."[13]

Until mid-September, Logan's regiment remained one company short of full complement. The deficiency was slowly filled. Most men of the regiment were Egyptians, but in Company K, last to be organized, men from northern Illinois, neighboring states, and even Canada, were enrolled. On September 18 the regiment was mustered into service. In the main, Logan's men came from the 9th Congressional District. Company A was from Perry County, Companies B and G from Saline, and C Company represented Logan's home county, Williamson. Company D from Johnson County, Company E from Union, F from Pulaski, and H from Alexander, rounded out the all-Egyptian units. Company I included some Egyptians but also numbered many from northern Illinois. The final group, Company K, so long in formation, was the most diverse. Regimental officers were all from southern Illinois. Logan's second in command was White, with Andrew J. Kuykendall, prominent Vienna Democrat, major, and Charles H. Capeheart, adjutant.[14]

Shortly after the mustering in, a ceremony was held presenting the 31st a regimental flag. Logan, replying to the presentation, spoke of preserving the Union and of the importance of free navigation of the Mississippi. "Should the free navigation of the Mississippi River be obstructed by force, the men of the West will hew their way to the Gulf with their swords."[15] The day after Logan's Civil War service officially began, a northern Illinois paper voiced an opinion now common among those previously critical of southern Illinois: "God bless Egypt. Her heart was right all the time."[16]

One week after final organization, Logan proudly wrote

[12]Morris, *31st Illinois*, 19.
[13]Jonesboro *Gazette*, Sept. 13, 1861.
[14]Morris, *31st Illinois*, 9.
[15]Carl Sandburg, *Abraham Lincoln, The War Years* (New York, 1939), IV, 18; Andrews, *Logan*, 397.
[16]Rockford *Republican*, Sept. 19, 1861.

Yates of his regiment's completion.[17] But time was needed to transform farmers and mechanics into soldiers. One disciplinary hazard was nearness to home and the descent of large numbers of civilians on Cairo. A British visitor discovered camps such a novelty and tents so unusual that "people come far and wide to see their friends under such extraordinary circumstances."[18] Requests for leave could be denied, but the "civilian army" departed only when forced by cold weather. Furthermore, sickness interfered with training. Several ailments swept the camp, but measles, which at one time infected about half the 31st, proved most bothersome. Drunkenness augmented command difficulties, and on October 11, McClernand, in command during Grant's absence, closed all "gambling saloons and bawdy houses." Despite these problems, discipline at Cairo in general was good, and preparations for action busily occupied the physically fit.[19]

Logan forgot some of his home troubles. But when Mary, still in Marion, sent word of family and friends, Logan's old doubts assailed him. For Mary, life at Marion was uncomfortable and dull. Pleading to be allowed to come to Cairo, she poured out her problems:

> Greater than all is the unnatural and piercing feelings our families feel about your being in the service. It makes it awful to be with them while you live; and when I think of many things you said and affirmations you made last spring in your speeches against war, I can trace the foundation of their feelings. They will never feel right the fact of your having to join with Republicans under Lincoln's administration to fight the South. . . . They will ever keep alive the bitterness which they will not hide.[20]

After several such plaints, Logan sent for her, and she spent October and much of November at Cairo.

The most prevalent feeling at Camp Defiance was expectancy. Rumors of attack circulated as early as April. It was

---

[17]JAL to Yates, Sept. 28, 1861, Yates Mss.
[18]William H. Russell, *My Diary North and South*, Fletcher Pratt (ed.) (New York, 1954), 174.
[19]William A. Pitkin, "When Cairo was Saved for the Union," *Journal of the Illinois State Historical Society*, LI, No. 3 (Autumn, 1958), 300, 302.
[20]Mary Logan to JAL, Sept. [?], 1861, Logan Mss.

predicted that Cairo, key to control of the upper Mississippi, would be site of the war's first great battle. By June, fear of attack receded to be replaced by expectation of Union advance. Many felt they were in the heart of enemy country and expected momentary action.[21] Rumor circulated wildly. It was well known that Confederates under General Leonidas Polk had occupied Columbus, Kentucky, and Belmont, Missouri, below Cairo, and commanded the river there. This placed Polk's force less than 20 miles away. In addition, rebel bands under Jeff Thompson prowled southeastern Missouri.

Grant was determined to drive Polk out of his Columbus bastion as the first step in opening the Mississippi. In late October he proposed a move against rebel fortifications there, but received no reply from General John C. Fremont commanding the military district including Cairo. After some delay and confusion, Grant was ordered on November 5 to demonstrate against Columbus. Concurrently Grant ordered a column under Colonel Richard Oglesby into Missouri to ferret out Jeff Thompson and stand ready to aid Grant's assault on Polk.[22]

On November 6 the anxiously awaited command came: "cook several days' rations and prepare for embarkation." Many in the 31st were hospitalized, and Logan was able to muster only 610 infantry and 70 cavalry, the horsemen attached to the regiment and led by Captain J. J. Dollins.[23] The regiment seemed in good spirits, attired in new uniforms and ready for a break in camp routine. Through a chilly, misty night, the 31st broke camp, marched to wharves and boarded the steamboat *Alex Scott*. The "civilian army" with cheers and tears, watched them go.

Grant's force numbered 3,114. The 31st Illinois was joined by Colonel N. B. Buford's 27th Illinois, and Colonel Phil

---

[21]John M. Adair, *Historical Sketch of the 45th Illinois Regiment* (Lanark, Illinois, 1869), 3.

[22]John A. Logan, *The Volunteer Soldier of America, with Memoir of the Author and Military Reminiscences from General Logan's Private Journal* (Chicago and New York, 1887), 620-621. The *Military Reminiscences* covering pages 617-696 are an excellent source for Logan's early military career, especially complete on Belmont and the Henry-Donelson campaigns.

[23]*OR*, Ser. 1, III, 287.

Fouke's 30th Illinois in the 1st Brigade under McClernand. The 2nd Brigade, led by Colonel Henry Dougherty, included the 22nd Illinois and 7th Iowa.[24] The *Alex Scott* was one of four transports, and the expedition was accompanied by two wooden gunboats, *Tyler* and *Lexington.*

Through darkness troops lined rails to watch Cairo's lights disappear as they rounded the bend near Wickliffe, Kentucky. Nine miles below Cairo, Grant's fleet tied up for the night along the Kentucky shore. The men shivered and slept fitfully on hard decks thinking of the morning's action. At 2 A.M. on the 7th, Grant, still unsure of his battle plan, received word Polk was concentrating men across from Columbus at Belmont, preparatory to reinforcing Confederate forces in Missouri. Grant at once decided to strike the reported assembly point at Belmont.

Belmont was an old steamboat landing around which clustered several wooden shacks. It lay beneath ominous cliffs on the Kentucky side, now surmounted by Polk's artillery. The Confederate camp at Belmont was located on river flats at an eastward bend of the Mississippi. The area, with the exception of several marshes, was heavily wooded, and slashed by numerous ravines, a product of the great New Madrid Earthquake of 1811. To protect themselves, the rebels had felled trees along the river bank. This served as cover and made protective observation from Columbus' heights easier. On the Kentucky side Polk commanded about 10,000 men and fortifications that made river passage suicidal. At Belmont, however, only a poorly supplied infantry regiment, mostly ill, six cannon, and a company of cavalry held the landing. Grant's information was faulty.[25]

When dawn broke on the 7th Grant's expedition moved down river. By 8:00 it arrived at Hunter's Farm, just around the bend from Columbus, and about two and one-half miles up river from Belmont, but concealed from both by a skirt of thick timber. Here the troops debarked in a cornfield and formed single line of march, 27th Illinois in the lead, followed

---

[24]*Battles and Leaders*, I, 355.
[25]*Ibid.*, I, 348.

by the 30th, 31st, 7th Iowa, and 22nd Illinois.[26] When troops landed, Logan was challenged by Buford for first place in the advance. He rode up to Logan exclaiming, "Colonel Logan, remember, if you please, that I have the position of honor." Logan instantly replied, "I don't care a damn where I am, so long as I get into this fight."[27] Surprise was lost when a detachment sent by Polk up the Kentucky bank discovered the Yankees and sounded the alarm. Quickly the Bishop-General sent General Gideon Pillow across with four regiments and later ferried a fifth to their aid.

While Polk acted promptly, the Union force, leaving five companies to guard the transports, wound up a narrow trail toward Belmont. *Lexington* and *Tyler* rounded the bend to keep Polk's gunners busy. Soon artillery thunder echoed off the Kentucky bluffs, giving Grant's infantry its first sound of battle. After a sharp exchange, the gunboats withdrew, unable to match rebel salvos.

After a short march Union forces reached a large cornfield and deployed in battle line. Skirmishers were thrown out and the entire force advanced. The 31st began in the center but was soon ordered to the extreme left.

At 10:30 Logan's Companies A and K met Pillow's men who had left the camp and were hurrying through heavy timber to halt Grant's advance. Shots were exchanged, the rebels gave way slowly, and Logan sent Captain E. S. McCook's Company I forward to join the line. With the rest of his command in support, Logan moved forward slowly, amid some confusion created by thick brush, into a marshy ravine. Enemy skirmishers poured fire on the advance and the regiment suffered its first casualties.[28]

When enemy fire increased, some confusion ensued as Logan and his officers struggled to form an even front and advance in orderly fashion. Uneven terrain and inexperience continued to make forward movement laborious. At last the men were

[26]*Battles and Leaders*, I, 350; *Official Atlas of the Civil War* (Washington, 1891-1895), Plate IV, Nos. 2, 3.

[27]Andrews, *Logan*, 397. This incident was reported by Kansas Congressman Lewis Hanback, a captain in the 27th Illinois.

[28]Morris, *31st Illinois*, 23.

ordered to "take to the trees and fight Indian fashion."[29] When momentarily stopped by withering fire, Grant ordered Logan to cease fire until the enemy position could be determined. While the 31st held fire, artillery crashed through trees overhead. Though these missiles caused few casualties, their roar unnerved Logan's raw troops who crouched in the thickets.

At Grant's order the advance continued. Soon Southerners counterattacked unsuccessfully several times. Once Logan feared he would be outflanked and was forced to extend his ranks toward the river on the left. Through the final 300 yards of forest the graycoats gradually retreated under hot fire from the Egyptians who "rallied under the gallant example of Colonel Logan."[30] On the edge of the woods McClernand ordered the left to charge, and opposition fled before it. Of this assault Logan wrote: "officers and men maintained as good a line and executed commands as well as could have been done by veteran troops."[31]

As center and right closed the vise, the 31st left cover for an open field in front of the enemy camp. Taking advantage of high ground overlooking rebel tents, Logan's men hurled fire on the retreating troops. Then Logan rode over to Fouke, and the two Democrats agreed to charge the rebels ensconced behind felled trees near the riverbank. Logan, eyes ablaze with excitement, sword in the air, rose in his stirrups roaring "charge." The troops hurtled the abatis and chased the enemy from his works. "The battle was hot, but for a moment. The enemy fled and the day was ours," wrote Logan.[32] In the charge one shot killed Logan's mount, sending the colonel sprawling; another shattered his pistol. He recovered, and still brandishing his sword, saw his men sweep the camp.

The 31st suffered many casualties. Logan ascertained his force's condition and discovered two company commanders badly wounded. These and other casualties were sent back to the transports. It was early afternoon, fighting had raged for two hours, the rebels had been routed and rushed headlong into the river where they crowded a narrow mud flat under a steep

---

[29]*Ibid.*
[30]*OR*, Ser. 1, III, 278. This is from McClernand's report.
[31]*Ibid.*, 288. This is from Logan's report.
[32]*Ibid.*, 288.

bank. Here they shouted "We are whipped!" to reinforcements arriving by ferry from Columbus.[33]

In a paroxysm of delight at having won the field, the Union troops lost their discipline. Both officers and men engaged in looting, many gorging themselves on Confederate rations. Others collected small arms, baggage, and horses.[34] While knots of men busied themselves looting, officers rode about and "at every halt delivered a short eulogy upon the Union cause and the achievements of the command."[35] No charges of contributing to discord are to be found against Logan, but it seems reasonable to assume that he, Fouke, and McClernand, politicians turned soldier, did not let the opportunity pass. However, Logan later boasted: "only one regiment of our troops, the 31st Illinois had retained its formation in ranks."[36]

Grant, furious, ordered the camp fired as a means of restoring order. As smoke and flames rolled down the river, officers struggled to reform their units. The conflagration had an immediate effect on Polk. Unwilling to give his Columbus batteries full play while Confederate troops were closely engaged in dense forest, he watched them retreat. With rebels cowering along the bank he had a clear shot at Union troops in the clearing. Furthermore, Grant's blaze gave Polk's gunners a target and they began to lob shells among their disorganized enemy.[37]

Nor was this barrage Polk's only countermeasure. After sending Pillow's reinforcement in the morning, Polk had been unwilling to weaken further his Columbus garrison. The Confederate general expected an attack on Columbus from the north, feeling the Belmont action was merely diversionary. When no assault threatened, and his troops were driven from the field, Polk sent three more regiments under General B. F. Cheatham to join the refugees and cut off Grant's retreat while Union troops frolicked.[38] They joined Pillow's defeated men and began to work up the bank to get between Belmont and Hunter's Farm.

---

[33]Shelby Foote, *The Civil War, a Narrative* (New York, 1958), I, 151.
[34]Morris, *31st Illinois*, 24.
[35]Grant, *Memoirs*, I, 223.
[36]Logan, *Volunteer Soldier*, 623.
[37]*Battles and Leaders*, I, 350; Morris, *31st Illinois*, 24.
[38]*Battles and Leaders*, I, 349.

Grant, alive to danger, saw Polk's ferry hauling Cheatham's men, "gray with soldiers from boiler-deck to roof," arrive on the Missouri side.[39] When told his retreat was being cut off, Grant angrily cried, "Well, we must cut our way out as we cut our way in."[40] The artillery cascade and word that they were surrounded quieted orators and halted looters, and a degree of order was restored. The command to return to Hunter's Farm was given and the race for safety began.

In forming the line of retreat, Logan was unsure of his position. Indecision passed quickly when he observed enemy troops in his rear. "I got my men in line poorly, but as best I could," he reported, when McClernand ordered him to cut his way through with the 31st. "I must confess I thought it a pretty hard task, though I felt complimented in getting the job, inasmuch as I was outranked by every colonel on the field."[41]

Obeying McClernand's command, Logan ordered McCook to lead with I Company. Moving rapidly though wooded ravines, Logan's regiment led the column for some distance without opposition. Then near the site of the morning's opening action, Confederates delivered scattered fire and momentarily halted the Egyptians. But before serious opposition could materialize, Logan's regiment reached the *Alex Scott* and clambered on board. The withdrawal had been so precipitous that Logan swore he would shoot anyone who shoved off before the entire regiment was on board.[42] While the rest of Grant's command climbed gangplanks in disorder, rebel infantry in trees nearby rained a steady fire on the retreating enemy. Once on board, the 31st lined the rail firing wildly into the woods, and kept shooting as the *Scott* rounded into midstream.

---

[39]Grant, *Memoirs*, I, 224.

[40]*Ibid.*

[41]*OR*, Ser. 1, III, 289. Robert Pearson of the 31st is reported in Andrews, *Logan*, 397, to have given this account of the order to retreat: "When Logan saw the position we were in and McClernand saw it, and the latter didn't know what to do, and made the remark, 'I don't know what we are going to do,' Logan said, 'You give me permission and I will show you what I will do.' McClernand said, 'All right you go ahead.'" Logan's own report written after Belmont negates this story completely.

[42]John A. Logan, *Speech of Major-General John A. Logan, on Return to Illinois after the Capture of Vicksburg* (Cincinnati, 1863), iii. Introduction to the pamphlet, from which this note comes, was written by "Mack" of the Cincinnati *Commercial*.

It was shortly after 4:00 when the boats shoved off, and for some time they were riddled with Confederate gunfire. Finally the two gunboats appeared and cleared the shoreline. The sun soon disappeared behind the Missouri flats, and without further opposition the fleet moved northward.

The return to Cairo was peaceful if uncomfortable. Cold night air was unpleasant to men who had thrown down blankets and overcoats during the advance and retreat. Hard deck planks and groaning wounded made sleep difficult.

All day long, battle sounds reached Cairo and streets and levees were crowded. About dawn "a light like a meteor" darted around the bend and the fleet materialized out of the darkness. Logan marched his regiment off the *Alex Scott* and back to camp where he was met by an anxious wife to whom he recounted details of the battle.[43]

Both sides claimed victory after Belmont. Casualty lists were revised several times before final accounts were made. The Union had lost 120 killed, 383 wounded, and 104 captured and missing. Ten of the dead, 70 wounded, and 18 missing came from Logan's ranks. Polk's loss totaled 105 dead, 419 wounded, and 117 missing or taken prisoner. Here neither side had the upper hand.[44]

There was much disagreement over Belmont's overall result. Some called the retreat an "ignominious withdrawal," and Egyptian anti-war Democrats used the battle for propaganda purposes.[45] Grant claimed complete victory, but the Chicago *Tribune* commented: "Our troops have suffered a bad defeat. . . . Our troops have been depressed if not discouraged."[46] The paper's appraisal was extreme and not generally supported by feelings at Camp Defiance. Those engaged at Belmont had immense respect for the grizzled general who took them out, fought them back when cut off, and remained behind until all were aboard ship. They had seen action, proved able soldiers, with the exception of one lapse, and had driven the enemy from the field. Southerners boasted of being able to whip five Yankees, but Belmont proved to Union troops' satisfaction

[43]Mary Logan, *Reminiscences*, 116.
[44]*Battles and Leaders*, I, 355; *OR*, Ser. 1, III, 275.
[45]Cole, *Era of the Civil War*, 266.
[46]Chicago *Tribune*, Nov. 8, 1861.

that "they were at least equal to the enemy man to man."[47] If they profited from Belmont's lessons, the battle would not be a total failure. Logan's regiment returned to Cairo rejoicing in its achievements, "self-reliant and confident." For months all that was needed to whip up enthusiasm was to command: "Belmont charge."[48]

On the other hand, Belmont accomplished little else. The Belmont landing remained in rebel hands and nothing had been done to dislodge Polk from Columbus.

For Logan the battle was an initiation to command. He proved a courageous, able, though inexperienced, regimental commander. McClernand's report spoke favorably of Logan, who inspired his men "largely contributing to the success of the day."[49] The 31st already devoted to Logan, whom it was beginning to call "Black Jack," had increased regard for its colonel. Logan now thought less about his decision to join the army, and more about preparing himself and his regiment for future action.

Routine camp duty returned, but enlivened by tales of battle, speculation of the next campaign, and arrival of new troops. The 31st was augmented by the 12th Illinois Cavalry.[50] But monotony took its toll. For three months after Belmont no order to advance came. Grant spent his time adding to his force and training it for a campaign slowly germinating in his brain.

Summer heat was succeeded by a lovely Egyptian autumn, which quickly passed bringing pinching cold. Winter decimated Cairo's "civilian army," thus aiding discipline, but other old amusements continued to lure restless troops. One soldier appeared at Logan's tent requesting a leave to meet his sister on her arrival in Cairo. The permit was granted but Logan, suspicious, sent two men to follow the soldier. Next morning he was found "quite drunk" and returned to Logan under arrest. Freely admitting his libations, the private drew a lecture from

[47]Logan, *Volunteer Soldier*, 625.
[48]Morris, *31st Illinois*, 26.
[49]*OR*, Ser. 1, III, 282.
[50]Harry Pratt (ed.), "Civil War Letters of Winthrop S. G. Allen," *Journal of the Illinois State Historical Society*, XXIV, No. 3 (October, 1931), 554.

Logan and was ordered to unearth a stump near the colonel's tent.[51] Despite such lapses, good order was general and Senator O. H. Browning, a camp visitor, was impressed by Logan's regiment on parade.[52]

Major problems facing Logan were outmoded weapons and inadequate clothing. Since September Logan and his fellow regimental commanders had struggled to obtain arms and supplies, and they were growing angry with frustration. Unable to secure satisfactory results in Egypt, Logan and Phil Fouke requested permission to go to Washington and New York to speed shipment before a major push began. Logan, telling Mary of his proposed trip, assured her, "I will return to remain with my Regiment until we are discharged from service."[53]

Boarding a train at Cairo, the two men arrived in Washington and were busily occupied renewing friendships and carrying out regimental business. Logan was still a member of Congress but he took no part in House debates. He felt the Republican Congress was "determined to ruin the country," and remarked to his wife, "I do hope that the time soon comes when another set of men will have the rains [sic] of government."[54] Unsure of his dual role, Logan investigated the possibility of retaining his seat while serving in the army.

> I cannot get pay for Member of Congress and Colonel at the same time and therefore I am not willing to do the duties of both without renumeration. I shall not resign my commission in the army after getting the boys into it, and to be candid with you I had rather fight anyhow now. . . . I feel desperate. Only for you and 'Dollie' do I want to live. I have no other friends outside my Regiment and with them I shall cast my fortune, either death or glory shall be mine.[55]

He did not officially resign from Congress until April.

Logan went to New York the first week in the new year, "annoyed to death with the business of getting guns." He

[51]Mary Logan, *Reminiscences*, 119.
[52]O. H. Browning, *The Diary of Orville H. Browning*, J. G. Randall and T. C. Pease (eds.) (Springfield, Illinois, 1925), I, 511.
[53]JAL to Mary Logan, Dec. 13, 1861, Logan Mss.
[54]*Ibid.*
[55]JAL to Mary Logan, Jan. 3, 1862, Logan Mss.

vowed he would not leave until the shipment was certain.[56] Accepting a promise of immediate shipment, he and Fouke returned to Washington where a letter from Mary awaited him. She reported rumors of Logan's impending promotion to brigadier. The promotion, she wrote, would be especially pleasing since it would place him on an equal footing with McClernand. Mary despised the latter as "aristocratic and overbearing. . . . It has always cut me deeply for *you* to be under him, he will never do you justice."[57]

Logan and Fouke stopped briefly in Washington before moving on to Illinois. A great movement was in the offing and the two soldier-congressmen wanted to participate. Logan had a long talk with Lincoln while in the capital. The president convinced him he would not "succumb to the abolitionists," but the colonel philosophically remarked, "the future must tell the tale."[58] Some believed Logan's hostility toward abolitionists had cooled since his enlistment. The *Illinois State Journal* reported his willingness to abolish slavery if necessary to restore the Union. In view of his talk with Lincoln this seems speculation.[59]

Logan and Fouke left Washington January 16 and a few days later were greeted by their regiments. The 31st had just returned from an expedition. Seven infantry regiments and eight cavalry companies, under McClernand, had left Cairo and ranged western Kentucky for two days. The 31st, commanded by White, marched 75 miles over icy, muddy roads, seeing no action, but suffering from exposure.[60]

When the regiment returned to winter quarters, its respite was abbreviated by Grant's plans for a large scale drive into Kentucky and Tennessee. Logan returned just in time to be advised of the project. A renewal of the river war was imminent.

---

[56]JAL to Mary Logan, Jan. 6, 1862, Logan Mss.

[57]Mary Logan to JAL, Jan. 5, 1862, Logan Mss.

[58]JAL to Mary Logan, Jan. 12, 1862, Logan Mss.

[59]*Illinois State Journal*, Dec. 14, 1861; JAL to Mary Logan, Jan. 12, 1862, Logan Mss.

[60]*OR*, Ser. 1, VII, 71; Morris, *31st Illinois*, 26.

CHAPTER VIII

HENRY AND DONELSON

Stretching from Columbus to Bowling Green, Kentucky, the Confederates had formed a line designed to hold Kentucky and defend Tennessee. In January, Union troops under General George Thomas had won a minor victory at the line's eastern end. Grant, having failed to dislodge the western flank, next proposed a drive at the line's center, which, if successful, would necessitate Confederate withdrawal from Kentucky and imperil Nashville. Grant's plan went to new district commander General Henry W. Halleck in January, and by month's end Halleck wired Grant to begin preparations. The order was unnecessary. Grant, already well prepared, moved immediately, and on February 2 Cairo bustled with marching men. Fifteen thousand troops boarded transports to launch a strike at the heart of Confederate strength in the West.[1]

The 31st Illinois was assigned to McClernand's 1st Division. The 1st Brigade, to which it was attached, was led by Colonel Richard Oglesby, a Republican politician-soldier. Joining Logan's regiment in the brigade were four other Illinois units: the 8th, 18th, 29th, and 30th regiments. The day before departure Logan hastily scribbled a note to Mary. He spoke fatalistically of his role in the war and, always thinking of his family, he concluded: "Tell mother and all the family good-bye for me. I have no unkind feeling toward anyone of them."[2]

When Logan's regiment boarded the *Minnehaha* to move down river, morale was high despite bleak weather. Many had stuffed their haversacks with sausage, cheese, and tobacco, bought on credit from a sutler, who was left on the levee watching his debtors sail up the Ohio.[3]

Grant's objectives, key to Confederate defense in the West, were two river forts, Henry on the Tennessee, and Donelson on

[1]*OR*, Ser. 1, VII, 578.
[2]JAL to Mary Logan, Feb. 1, 1862, Logan Mss.
[3]Morris, *31st Illinois*, 29.

the Cumberland. The two rivers flowed only twelve miles apart near the Kentucky-Tennessee border where the two forts were situated. Capture of the bastions would render hazardous further Confederate occupation of Kentucky. First objective was Ft. Henry on the Tennessee.

Grant's expedition steamed up the Ohio to Paducah at the juncture of the Ohio and Tennessee, and halted overnight. Next day the fleet turned into the muddy Tennessee, swollen by torrential rains, and sailed for Ft. Henry. Through a hazy morning Grant's fleet under Commodore Andrew Foote, steamed forward searching flooded banks for a landing.

Ft. Henry was an engineering monstrosity. It was built on low land near the riverbank, and heavy rains had so flooded the area that the fort was menaced by water as much as by Grant's army. But the inundation created a problem for Grant as well. Three miles north of the fort Panther Creek, now over its banks, made infantry movement perilous. To land south of the creek might put the army within range of Confederate batteries. Grant selected a debarkation spot north of the creek and landing began.

Logan's regiment, soggy with rain, watched the *Minnehaha* drift shoreward and moor alongside a sister ship. As the regiment marched across the bows of the adjoining ship, the men piled up their old muskets and each received a new Enfield rifle. Logan's Washington mission had borne fruit.[4]

Meanwhile, Grant had determined to launch a three pronged assault on General Lloyd Tilghman's garrison. One column would march up the west bank and seize high ground. This would give artillery a commanding view of Ft. Henry. The other half of Grant's land force, which included the 31st, would march around Panther Creek and strike the fort directly. The final prong was Foote's naval flotilla which would close and hammer the fort's batteries into silence.

Inside Henry the rebels uneasily watched the approach of their twin enemies. The water's rise had submerged six guns and only nine bearing on the river remained above the flood.[5] More distressing, however, was the blue clad deluge pouring

---

[4]*Ibid.*
[5]*Battles and Leaders*, I, 369.

down from up river. Tilghman at first decided on resistance
but as transports continued to land men he decided to abandon the fort, leaving a skeleton garrison to man the nine guns
and hold off enemy attack as long as possible. When Grant's
assault began February 6, only 56 men remained in the sodden
fortress.

At 11 A. M. that morning Logan, on horseback at the head
of the 31st, received Grant's order to advance. In concert, the
column west of the river moved out. As Logan sounded the
forward, sun broke through the haze. The men cheered this
sign and moved through bottomland skirting Panther Creek.
When they descended into the creek basin, the ground "became
reduced to the consistency of soft porridge," making movement difficult. For an hour Logan's men struggled through
the morass in silence, broken only by clatter of equipment, and
men's grumbling. Suddenly a roar shattered the silence, signaling the fleet's attack. Foote had held back, allowing the infantry a good start, then he closed on the fort. For a moment
Logan's column halted listening to the roar; then he urged the
men forward.[6]

For about an hour the advance was accompanied by thundering shells. Then all was still. Logan's column, unable to see any
of the artillery engagement, halted uncertainly, wondering if
Foote had been repulsed. When Logan ordered the advance
resumed they moved forward cautiously. McClernand sent out
scouts, who soon returned and announced that the rebels had
struck their flag. When Logan reported the news his men
cheered and pressed forward. Climbing a small hill they came
upon Ft. Henry's outlying breastworks, now abandoned. After
a brief stop, Logan urged his men on, and crossing a slough
near the fort, he rode in, first of the army to enter. Tilghman
had already surrendered to Foote's gunboats, but only 45 men
submitted with him. The remainder had escaped to Ft. Donelson. Grant quickly sent a dispatch to Halleck: "Ft. Henry is
ours. . . . I shall take and destroy Ft. Donelson on the 8th."[7]

Logan's regiment, inside Henry, rummaged about, discovered a number of gray uniforms, and donned rebel gray while

---

[6]Logan, *Volunteer Soldier*, 632.
[7]*OR*, Ser. 1, VII, 124.

they dried their own clothing. They also raided Confederate stores and feasted.[8] Logan, however, had little rest. At dusk he took a cavalry company and part of the 31st and moved down the road toward Donelson to ascertain the enemy's position. He returned to report the immediate terrain cleared of rebel troops.[9]

Grant's promise to take Donelson on the 8th was too optimistic. Grant found Donelson more formidable than Henry and decided overland attack without support from Foote's ships would be inadvisable. Therefore he sent the gunboats up the Tennessee and around to the Cumberland. Part of the army was put aboard, but the 1st and 2nd Divisions remained near Henry to march across the narrow neck of land between the two rivers. For five days Logan's regiment bivouacked in Ft. Henry waiting for the command to break camp. Logan was occupied much of the time leading cavalry detachments on scouting forays, several times pushing near the neighboring fort to report rebel activity.

The five-day delay gave Albert Sidney Johnston, Confederate commander in Tennessee, a chance to reinforce Donelson, which he did not use to advantage. It also gave Grant opportunity to increase his force, and by the 12th he was ready to move. McClernand met the commander on board his headquarters ship on the 11th and returned with orders to prepare to march next morning. The 12th dawned clear, sunny and cool, the first pleasant day since leaving Cairo. At mid-morning the 31st, in high spirits, began its march. The regiment marched light, carrying neither tents nor baggage wagons, but each man had two days' rations and 40 rounds of ammunition. Grant's column contained 15,000 men of the 1st and 2nd Divisions, led by McClernand and C. F. Smith respectively. Ten thousand had gone around with Foote, and 2,500 remained at Ft. Henry under Lew Wallace. Logan's men marched on the army's right, south of the main road between the two forts. By noon heat saturated dark blue uniforms with perspiration, and the men could no longer see use for heavy overcoats and blankets. The line of march left a wake of abandoned clothing.

---

[8]Morris, *31st Illinois*, 31.
[9]Logan, *Volunteer Soldier*, 636.

All thoughts of heat fled when, a little after midday, skir-mishers encountered fire from rebel pickets. This sporadic gunfire was accompanied by a deeper boom in the distance, indicating the flotilla's arrival. As the men scrambled up low hills, tents were visible on distant heights, and soon rebel works appeared, bristling with guns.[10] Nearing the rebel line, the Union army scattered like a giant fan, covering the rebel front from Hickman's Creek on the north to the outskirts of Dover, two miles south of Donelson. Logan's unit wheeled southward and by dusk was in place on the Union right be-tween two Illinois regiments, the 11th and 29th. As night fell, Logan's men were completing their investment.

Next morning Logan climbed a rise to observe the enemy lines. The 31st lay between Wynn's Ferry Road and Dover, a river hamlet two miles from the fort. Donelson and the rim of Confederate fortifications rested on a high bluff overlook-ing the Cumberland and rising menacingly above the Union line.[11] The rebel ridge was hacked with long yellow scars where the Confederates had dug emplacements.

His observations completed, Logan's regiment probed for-ward to find the most defensible positions. While this leisurely but sometimes dangerous game continued, suddenly to the left a volley roared out of the rebel works met by one from charg-ing Federals. McClernand had ordered a charge against a bothersome battery, and Colonel I. N. Haynie, Logan's old friend, led two Illinois regiments into a galling crossfire. Three times they advanced and three times they retreated. At last McClernand called them off. During the afternoon gunboats fired spasmodically and a clatter of picket fire continued. At sunset Logan's regiment settled down for the night in slightly better position after seeing little action.[12]

When night fell, Grant was disturbed by the failure of his shipboard division and the bulk of Foote's armada to arrive. He had fewer men than the besieged army, now commanded by General John B. Floyd. It was highly unorthodox to carry out siege operations while outnumbered, and Grant anxiously awaited his reinforcement.

---

[10]*Ibid.*, 647.
[11]*Official Atlas*, Plate XI.
[12]Logan, *Volunteer Soldier*, 649.

The army was disturbed by the prospect of a protracted siege. When Oglesby and Logan rode through camp after dark on the 13th, they found "one universal wish to meet the enemy and carry the fort."[13] Shortly after dark, tomorrow's problems were replaced by something more immediate. A drizzling rain began to fall, which quickly turned to sleet and blowing snow. The thermometer plunged to 20°, and tired and hungry men, their rations almost exhausted, lay down to sleep on the frozen ground. Camp fires were not allowed, and they huddled together, many without cover due to earlier folly.[14]

Friday, February 14, brought a gray dawn with Logan's men stamping in the snow to restore circulation. Dawn brought word that 2,500 men from Ft. Henry had arrived, and that Foote had reached Donelson and was unloading. Opposing forces now stood at 27,500 for Grant to 17,500 for Floyd. Grant was convinced his superiority made a breakout impossible, and he settled back to let Foote hammer the fort into submission.[15]

All morning skirmish fire was more subdued than on the previous day. Logan received orders to hold against a breakout while the flotilla went into action. At 3 o'clock Foote moved in while Logan stood on a snowy hill to watch. Guns boomed and shells screamed and thudded against the ironclads as Foote closed for action. Though initial salvos damaged the fort, the battle gradually turned against Foote. With four ironclads drifting, almost out of control, Foote called them back. Donelson was going to be tough to crack, and night fell again accompanied by bitter chill. The 31st had played a spectator's role, and the fleet's repulse had Logan gloomily discussing a long siege. Though the troops were again fireless and pelted by snow, the transports had brought some rations, and its hunger somewhat sated, the 31st lay on its arms through the freezing night.[16]

Inside the fort, Foote's repulse brought elation, but rebel chieftains, Pillow, Floyd, and Simon B. Buckner, were still pessimistic over their position. That night, while snow swirled

[13]OR, Ser. I, VII, 185.
[14]Logan, Volunteer Soldier, 650.
[15]Grant, Memoirs, I, 247.
[16]Logan, Volunteer Soldier, 653.

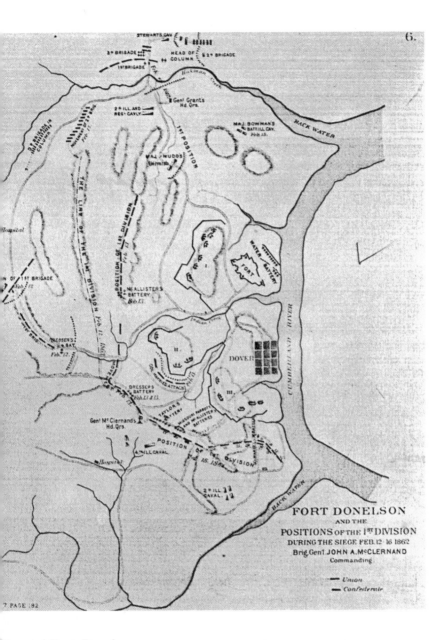

FORT DONELSON
AND THE
POSITIONS OF THE 1ST DIVISION
DURING THE SIEGE FEB. 12-16 1862
Brig. Gen! JOHN A. McCLERNAND
Commanding

———— *Union*
———— *Confederate*

Siege of Fort Donelson

From *Atlas to Accompany the Official Records*

about the town, the three rebels met in Dover and decided on
a breakout at daybreak. The assault was to be delivered south
of Dover where a road angled southward to Charlotte and on
to Nashville. Floyd ordered Pillow to mass his infantry against
the Union right, and Buckner to move his troops toward the
Union center to support Pillow and be ready to crash out
when the gate swung open. All night Confederate troops
moved, their jangle and rumble muffled by falling snow, unobserved by Federals wrapped together against the blast and
keeping poor watch.[17] At dawn Pillow was poised to kick open
the gate and fly for Nashville.

Logan spent another bitterly cold night on the ground and
arose stiffly to check his troops. Men struggled slowly to their
feet, prepared coffee, and rubbed their limbs to drive out the
night's stiffness. They had little time to collect themselves. As
if in answer to Union bugles, a rising crescendo of fire rapidly
swept back Federal pickets, as underbrush all along McClernand's front came alive with Pillow's gray coats.

Logan jumped on horesback and hurried to form the regiment to resist. Pillow's spearhead struck the extreme right
held by a portion of Oglesby's brigade and General John Mc-
Arthur's brigade. The assault quickly moved down the line,
enveloping Logan, whose pickets were driven in and who
found himself repelling a major frontal blow.

Logan's line was covered by smoky haze and blood reddened
the snow as rebel cannister tore gaps in its ranks. In the first
volley several fell dead and wounded. One of the dead, James
McIlrath, had gone into action by the side of his 17-year-old
son Robert.[18] Behind the line Logan and his staff, oblivious of
flying balls, remained on horseback urging the men against
the yelling rebels. Smoke hung like a cloud, and Logan was
unable to see his whole regiment flank to flank.

For three hours the battle surged back and forth. By
mid-morning Pillow had succeeded, by superior numbers, in
turning the right flank. McArthur's regiments ran out of ammunition and began to fall back on Oglesby's brigade. By 10
o'clock Oglesby's four Illinois regiments, having resisted nu-

---

[17]*Battles and Leaders*, I, 415.
[18]George Smith, *Southern Illinois*, II, 962.

merous attacks, were drifting backward, imperiling the entire Union right. Logan, hard-pressed all morning, now felt pressure mounting. Riding forward, he urged the regiment to hold fast. While shouting encouragement, a ball struck him in the left shoulder, and he slumped in the saddle. His staff quickly led him behind the line and urged him to retire to the hospital. Logan refused, his wound was bandaged, and he returned to direct the regiment.

Increased fire suddenly struck the 31st from the right, and Logan realized the entire Union line to his right had collapsed. His regiment, fighting for its life, was forced to repel assaults from right and front. He met the danger by ordering his right to fall back and form a right angle with the left to prevent the regiment being taken in the rear.[19] Lieutenant Colonel White galloped forward to lead the maneuver, and soon the regiment responding to shouted commands, stood ready to resist the new menace. Logan saw White riding among the men; then he saw him disappear beneath the smoke. News soon reached Logan that White had been killed by a rebel ball.[20]

With White's death, Logan moved forward again, his arm and shoulder streaming blood, to urge the regiment to hold its ground. To Logan's left Colonel W. H. L. Wallace, commander of McClernand's 2nd Brigade, looked off to the right from his position. He could see but one of Oglesby's regiments, the 31st Illinois, still in place, and resisting. "Through the smoke he could see Logan riding in a gallop behind his line; through the roar in his front and the rising yell in his rear, he could hear Logan's voice in fierce entreaty to his boys." The colonel screamed above the din, "Boys! give us death, but not dishonor!"[21]

For an hour the reformed 31st resisted Pillow's full onslaught, sustaining heavy casualties and running low on ammunition. Logan grew gradually weaker, and at times his men struggled on leaderless. Once in this final hour Logan, riding too near the lines, caught a ball in his thigh. By the time Logan took his second wound, the 31st had exhausted its ammunition

---

[19]OR, Ser. 1, VII, 177.
[20]Morris, 31st Illinois, 37.
[21]Battles and Leaders, I, 418; Dawson, Logan, 22.

and could no longer repel the enemy. Barely able to remain in the saddle, Logan decided to withdraw, believing further resistance suicidal. He sent a messenger to Lieutenant Colonel T. E. G. Ransom, of the 11th Illinois on his left, that ammunition was gone and he was retreating. Ransom moved toward the gap Logan's retirement would create and Logan brought off his regiment in good order.[22] He had held valiantly. General Pillow said, " 'had it not been for that regiment of regulars clothed in short blue jackets he would have made a Bull Run of it.' " Pillow was mistaken about the men being regulars, though they fought like veterans.[23]

Only after leaving the line would Logan agree to go to the rear. As he jolted to the hospital, he lay totally exhausted and severely weakened from loss of blood. Riding in an ambulance, Logan saw William Morrison, southern Illinois Democrat, also wounded. Logan inquired: " 'Bill, did you get a bad lick?' " Morrison replied: " 'Yes John. I think I got enough to go home and beat Phil Fouke for Congress.' "[24] Logan left behind a leaderless, shattered regiment, but one which had demonstrated discipline and courage.

When Logan left the field, the battle was by no means over. When the 31st retired, the Charlotte road stood open. Pillow hesitated, once the gate swung wide, afraid of a flanking counterattack while running the gap. At noon, though the line had been open for an hour, no one had gone through. Soon it was slammed shut.

For six hours, while the breakout attempt raged, Grant was absent, and Wallace and Smith, under orders not to change position, watched while McClernand's flank was rolled back. Grant had gone to visit wounded Commodore Foote with "no idea that there would be any engagement on land unless I brought it on myself."[25] After a conference with Foote, Grant began a slow ride back to the army, to be met by a staff officer who poured out the story of McClernand's repulse.

---

[22]OR, Ser. 1, VII, 187, 199; *Battles and Leaders*, I, 418.

[23]Morris, *31st Illinois*, 41.

[24]Sandburg, *Lincoln, War Years*, I, 461. Morrison did return and defeat Fouke, who had, unlike Logan, chosen to return to politics rather than retain his commission.

[25]Grant, *Memoirs*, I, 250.

Spurring his mount, Grant arrived behind the lines and quickly appraised the situation. He realized the rebels were trying to break out and ordered an immediate attack. Grant knew the Confederate right had been weakened to assist Pillow's drive, and he sent C. F. Smith's division forward to strike that flank. Then Wallace smashed the center and Grant rode to McClernand's division where he found men standing in small groups with no leader to direct them. Grant yelled, "Fill your cartridge boxes, quick, and get into line; the enemy is trying to escape and must not be permitted to do so."[26] Responding, McClernand's unit moved forward, and Pillow's men retired. Logan's regiment did not participate in the afternoon push. It was in reserve when Pillow was driven back into the entrenchments.

By dark Grant's army had regained its lost ground and even pushed forward in several places. The 31st was moved to the rear at nightfall and camped on a snowy hillside behind Smith's division. Logan's casualty list was long, 31 dead, 117 wounded, and 28 missing.[27] In addition to White, Captain James Williamson, the regiment's senior captain, had been killed. Logan lay in great pain in division hospital, weak from loss of blood, hunger, and exhaustion. He appeared so weak the attending physician was unsure of his recovery.[28]

Confederate elation turned to depression after failure to break Grant's siege line. Another council was held, and it was decided to surrender the fort, since Grant's afternoon attacks had placed Union guns in positions which would render further occupation hazardous. Floyd, Pillow, and cavalry commander Nathan Bedford Forrest took advantage of darkness and the river to escape, but Buckner and the bulk of the garrison remained to capitulate. That night, Buckner, who succeeded Floyd and Pillow, composed a note and sent a messenger to deliver it to Grant. A bugle rang out in the frosty air, and the messenger came through Smith's line and presented the proposed terms. Smith then went to Grant who had to be roused from a sound sleep. Grant read the note and jotted down his answer:

[26]*Ibid.*, 252.
[27]*OR*, Ser. 1, VII, 167.
[28]Andrews, *Logan*, 405.

Yours of this date proposing armistice and appointment of commissioners, to settle terms of capitulation is just received. No terms except an unconditional and immediate surrender can be accepted.

I propose to move immediately upon your works.[29]

Grant's reply angered Buckner. But, contenting himself with a protest, he surrendered. The Donelson victory was greeted throughout the North with great joy; Grant, dubbed "Unconditional Surrender," was a hero overnight. The long victory drought had finally ended, Bull Run was avenged, and Grant, holding two rebel forts and 15,000 rebel troops, stood poised to invade Tennessee.

While Sunday church bells pealed on the 16th announcing the sabbath and Grant's victory, Mary Logan, elated over the news but concerned for Logan's welfare, penned him a short note. "Be good my darling, I mean be religious and don't for your soul's sake be so profane. In the army a man must be careful or he will forget his dependence on a higher power."[30]

Logan was exercising his profanity and calling on a "higher power" at the same time. His shoulder wound was caused by a ball passing through the shoulder joint. Another ball smashed his holstered pistol and drove splinters into his side, nearly breaking his ribs. These two wounds caused intense pain. The third injury, a minor flesh wound in the thigh, was insignificant by comparison. Field surgeons felt it best to keep him as immobile as possible, and his left arm was strapped to his body to prevent movement.[31]

While Logan lay wounded, Ft. Donelson casualty lists raced over the telegraph. First lists to cross the Ohio were sketchy and inaccurate. The first list published in Egypt reached Mary at Murphysboro where she had recently moved. Glancing down to the 31st Illinois, she broke into sobs as she read the list of killed: "Colonel John A. Logan, Lieutenant Colonel John H. White."[32] She quickly recovered, and set out for Cairo determined to go to Donelson.

[29]*Battles and Leaders*, I, 427.
[30]Mary Logan to JAL, Feb. 16, 1862, Logan Mss.
[31]Mary Logan, *Reminiscences*, 125.
[32]*Ibid.*, 123.

News of Logan's death also reached Washington where it brought grief to old party comrades. A revised list numbering Logan among the wounded, prompted a friend to write from Washington: "If you could have heard the regrets over your reported death, yesterday, and the joy on ascertaining that you were only wounded, you would feel proud enough."[33]

At Cairo Mary also learned the truth, and she redoubled her determination to go to him. Orders, however, forbade civilians to board transports. Luckily, Mary encountered Colonel James Dunlap, McClernand's quartermaster, who pointed out a steamer about to embark and told her to board as a member of his family. Subterfuge was unnecessary, when she boarded and found the captain a man Logan had cleared of manslaughter several years earlier.

When Mary reached Donelson her steamer berthed alongside Grant's boat, the *New Uncle Sam*. Officers on the ship recognized her and assisted her over the rail, informing her Logan was below, having been brought on board at Grant's insistence. She descended and found Logan lying on a cot next to Colonel Ransom. After a tearful reunion she listened to Logan describe the 31st's heroism, and took steps to make him and Ransom more comfortable. For two weeks she kept vigil over the two colonels, until Ransom recovered and Logan was deemed fit to be moved. His doctors decided he could be taken North, and he sailed to Cairo, thence by rail and carriage to Murphysboro.

Logan left the 31st on garrison duty at Donelson where it remained through February and March. When danger had passed and Grant moved on toward Pittsburg Landing, relatives and friends poured down the Cumberland to view the scene of victory and visit the regiment.[34]

The river campaign was a giant step forward in Logan's military career. He had handled his men well under all conditions, and the 31st responded ably. Despite this splendid record, Egyptian political enemies, many of them former friends, continued to snipe from the rear. Nor were Logan's Republican enemies silent. Disgruntled at having many regimental commands go to their old adversaries, some Republican papers

[33]M. B. Brown to JAL, Feb. 18, 1862, Logan Mss.
[34]Morris, *31st Illinois*, 37.

lost no chance to attack the Democratic political soldiers. The *Missouri Democrat* claimed Logan's wound came from a boy in his own regiment. Another maintained Logan was not the hero at all, but gave credit to Colonel John Logan of Carlinville, "an approved Black Republican." Confusion was possible since John Logan commanded the 32nd Illinois, but his regiment was not engaged at Donelson.[35]

Grant might have been aware of these charges, but he ignored them in favor of his own observations. On March 14 he sent his report of the Henry-Donelson campaign to Secretary of War Edwin M. Stanton. At its conclusion he noted several officers for special commendation:

> I would particularly mention the names of Colonel J. D. Webster, 1st Illinois Artillery; Morgan L. Smith, 8th Missouri Volunteers; W. H. L. Wallace, 11th Illinois Volunteers, and John A. Logan, 31st Illinois Volunteers. The two former are old soldiers and men of decided merit. The two latter are from civil pursuits but I have no hesitation in fully endorsing them as in every way qualified for the position of brigadier-general, and think they have fully earned the position on the field of battle.[36]

The Egyptian press took up the cry and called for a general's rank for Logan, "the great representative man of Egypt." In late March the promotion arrived.

During March Logan rested and recovered from his wounds. He decided to resign from Congress, submitted his resignation, and on April 2 his seat was declared vacant.[37] As Logan started back to the front, Yates issued a proclamation calling for a special election for May 6 to fill Logan's seat. Many proposed Josh Allen, but Logan endorsed no one and departed, momentarily abandoning politics for his new career. Allen had written Logan February 18: "the government seems determined to go on its mad career," words with little meaning for a man lying badly wounded in defense of that "government."[38] Logan had created a breach with his old associate when he

---

[35] Jonesboro *Gazette*, Mar. 1, 8, 1862.
[36] *OR*, Ser. 1, X, pt. 2, 35.
[37] *Biographical Directory of the American Congress, 1774-1949* (Washington, 1950), 267.
[38] W. J. Allen to JAL, Feb. 18, 1862, Logan Mss.

joined the army; Allen's continued criticism of the war widened the breach.

By March's end Logan was ready to return to his command. Word filtered into Egypt of a major campaign in the offing and Logan rushed to rejoin the army. He was still unable to put his arm in his coat sleeve, but ignoring his wife's appeals, he left for Cairo where he hoped to find transportation to the front.[39]

On April 6 Logan was on his way down the Cumberland. Next day he reached Ft. Donelson where the 31st remained on duty. While preparing to embark the regiment, he heard of a great battle to the South, and loading the 31st on transports he steamed up the Cumberland to Paducah, then down the Tennessee to Pittsburg Landing. Logan arrived too late to fight at Shiloh, but in time to see the carnage.[40]

When Logan caught up with Grant, a new command had to be found for him, and on April 12 he was ordered to report to McClernand for assignment. The new brigadier was named commander of the 1st Brigade, 3rd Division, 17th Army Corps. His brigade included the 12th Michigan, and four Illinois regiments: 8th, 18th, 30th, and his own 31st, which he had specially requested.

The first phase of Logan's Civil War career concluded, he looked forward, for the moment, hopefully to the future. His mercurial temperament would soon return to gloomy pessimism, but in April, 1862, his hopes soared, both for his own advancement and quick end of the war. Logan had decided to put politics behind him and devote all, or nearly all, his time to his new life.

---

[39]Mary Logan, *Reminiscences*, 128.

[40]Morris, *31st Illinois*, 44; JAL to Mary Logan, April 2, 7, 15, 1862, Logan Mss. Logan is sometimes mentioned as being engaged at Shiloh, but he arrived three days too late. The mistake is probably due to the presence of Colonel John Logan and the 32nd Illinois at Shiloh. *Battles and Leaders*, I, 537-538.

CHAPTER IX

MONOTONY IN MISSISSIPPI, TEDIUM IN TENNESSEE

When Logan returned to the army, Grant was no longer in command. As a result of his actions at Shiloh, and Halleck's jealousy, Halleck had arrived from St. Louis to assume field command. Grant was to be his second in command, a position devoid of power. The change, and attacks on Grant because of alleged drunkenness, infuriated Logan who had become intimate with the victor of Henry and Donelson.[1] Grant was so disconsolate at the turn of events that General John M. Schofield found him packing to leave the army and go to St. Louis. Schofield dissuaded him, assuring Grant that he and Logan remained steadfast in his support.[2]

In addition to the Grant affair, Logan was concerned about other matters. He had promised on leaving Illinois to look for Hibert Cunningham, and persuade him to leave the Confederate army. On April 15 Logan wrote Mary of his failure to learn anything of her brother. Two weeks later, with the Union army moving toward Corinth, Mississippi, Logan heard that Hibe was at Corinth, and he renewed his promise to contact him.[3] The final source of dissatisfaction was Logan's continued service under McClernand, whom he had come to dislike intensely. This dislike, caused to some extent by political-military rivalry, was to increase in following months.

These matters, however, were forced into the background by arduous duties found in the new command. The brigade, formerly led by Oglesby, was in camp one mile north of Shiloh Church on the road to Corinth when Logan assumed command. From April 15 to the 24th, Logan was occupied in preparing his men for their role in the pursuit of the rebel army now commanded by General P. G. T. Beauregard and entrenched

---

[1]Mary Logan, *Reminiscences*, 128.

[2]Rutherford B. Hayes, *The Diary and Letters of Rutherford B. Hayes*, Charles R. Williams (ed.) (Columbus, Ohio, 1926), IV, 229-230.

[3]JAL to Mary Logan, April 15, 30, 1862, Logan Mss.

around Corinth 20 miles to the south. Logan knew most of the regimental commanders, having been closely associated with all units except the 12th Michigan in earlier campaigns. This familiarity eased his duties somewhat and relations were cordial, especially with the 31st Illinois. After Donelson, the 31st underwent a major command shakeup. Logan's promotion, White's death, and Major Kuykendall's resignation to return to Egyptian politics left a void filled by the promotion of three lieutenants. New regimental commander was Logan's old Mexican War comrade, "Doff" Ozburn.⁴ Logan felt it "is a great task to take charge of a Brigade, though I think I can get along."⁵ Concerning the impending campaign he informed two Illinois congressmen, "we are in front of a large rebel force, but when we will fight I cannot say, though when we do you will hear from Ills."⁶

April 24, preparations completed, Halleck ordered his forces to assemble for the movement against Corinth. Logan broke camp and moved two miles southward to a bluff overlooking Owl Creek where he constructed the first of many field fortifications ordered by the general commanding.⁷ For the next week Logan edged toward Monterey, a small town just north of the Mississippi line.

May arrived clear and pleasant, bringing Halleck's advance at last. On the 2nd, promising Lincoln he would stand before Corinth ready to strike the following day, he ordered the army to move. Halleck's force was immense; the left was commanded by John Pope, center by D. C. Buell, and right by George Thomas, with a reserve of three divisions under McClernand. The entire force totaled in excess of 100,000. Logan's brigade was in McClernand's reserve. When Halleck's order to advance reached McClernand, he had no commander for the 1st Division, so he gave Logan the post. Logan led the division for one day, when orders from army headquarters replaced him with General Henry M. Judah.⁸

---

⁴*OR*, Ser. 1, X, pt. 1, 758.
⁵JAL to Mary Logan, April 30, 1862, Logan Mss.
⁶JAL to Elihu Washburne and J. C. Robinson, April 18, 1862, Washburne Mss.
⁷*OR*, Ser. 1, X, pt. 1, 759.
⁸*Ibid.*

As the campaign began Logan, suffering from complications of his Donelson wounds, asked for a day's rest. On his day off he wrote Mary of the move on Corinth where he expected Halleck's force to encounter 120,000 rebel troops.[9] On May 4 he resumed his post.

Halleck shared Logan's estimate of enemy strength, sometimes figuring Beauregard's army to be even larger. Beauregard, entrenched behind strong breastworks, was able to muster only about 50,000 men, many of them ill. This overestimate, coupled with Halleck's naturally cautious nature, made the advance a snail-like affair which Logan labeled "the most ludicrous feature of the whole war."[10] A day's march covered only a few miles, and at nightfall the regiments dug fortifications to repel enemy attacks which did not come. Both officers and men, many of them used to Grant's slam-bang tactics, grew restive under "Old Brains." The movement was tedious and some feared it might turn into a summer-long siege. Perhaps the most unpopular feature was Halleck's insistence on daily construction of breastworks as his men inched their way south under a blistering sun.[11] The countryside from Shiloh to Corinth was hacked and scarred by endless lines of works, hastily constructed and abandoned by hot, angry troops.

On the 11th Logan finally crossed into Mississippi, using the road taken one day earlier by W. T. Sherman's division. That day, Logan's horsemen under Colonel William McCullough destroyed the Mobile and Ohio Railroad bridge over Cypress Creek and captured a locomotive which they ran into the creek. McCullough's men then moved on toward Purdy, where they encountered a rebel outpost which they scattered, clearing the town.

Following this action several days were spent without movement. It was not until May 21 that Logan received word to advance, and he moved his force, without opposition, to a position near Easel's House, vacated by Sherman the day before. Again forward movement halted, and Logan remained motion-

---

[9]JAL to Mary Logan, May 3, 1862, Logan Mss.

[10]Logan, *Volunteer Soldier*, 662.

[11]Adair, *45th Illinois*, 6.

less for another week. While he waited, in poor health and dissatisfied over the campaign, Logan wrote Mary, "I have been almost tempted after this fight is over, if I get through alive, to resign though I do not know what to do." He then complained of Halleck's lack of speed and of his division commander's incompetence. Judah he remarked, is a "perfect sapsucker, no sense at all."[12]

After six days in camp, Logan received his first chance for action. W. T. Sherman on the Union right, pushing close to rebel works, asked McClernand for a brigade and Logan was dispatched. On the 28th Logan moved his brigade to Sherman's extreme right. He was instructed to drive rebels from a fortified house and assist against Beauregard's left. Logan advanced to a new position in front of the rebel house. A strong demonstration was enough to convince the enemy his position was no longer tenable and he retreated.

The house taken, Sherman ordered Logan to throw out skirmishers and advance. Logan's skirmish line, moving forward slowly through scattered timber, exchanged shots with the enemy, but until late afternoon little damage was done by either side. At dusk the rebel picket line, obviously reinforced, suddenly rushed out of trees along Logan's front in an attempt to drive him back. His alert advance line, led by the 8th Illinois, poured a withering volley through the gathering dark and the rebel line fell back.[13]

At nightfall Logan's brigade stretched beyond Sherman's right, near the main line of the Mobile and Ohio Railroad. His men lay on their arms expecting further action, but the sultry summer night was peaceful. The night of the 28th was filled with speculation over Confederate plans. Reports of great commotion from Beauregard in Corinth raced through the army; many believed the sound of trains arriving followed by cheering indicated large reinforcements moving in from the South. Logan felt the rail activity had another significance. The Mobile and Ohio main line ran through Logan's sector, a few miles northeast of Corinth, and some of his men, old railroaders, walked up the tracks to listen to the far off noise.

[12]JAL to Mary Logan, May 22, 1862, Logan Mss.
[13]OR, Ser. 1, X, pt. 1, 741, 760, 761.

After listening for a moment some of the men put their ears to the rails to listen to the moving trains come and go. They became convinced that Beauregard was evacuating Corinth, claiming to be able to discern a difference between loaded and empty trains. The hum reaching them indicated empty trains rolling in and loaded cars moving out. They went to Logan, who came, listened, and agreed. He talked to McClernand and the two went to Grant. Grant, agreeing to the possible accuracy of the reported evacuation, took it to Halleck. "Old Brains" refused to credit the theory, still believing Beauregard was hauling in troops for an attack.[14]

In the morning Logan asked to be sent forward and was refused. Picket fire sputtered along Logan's front, but no attack having materialized, Logan was relieved and ordered back to the reserve at 1 o'clock. Three regiments had started for the rear when suddenly the clatter of rifle fire increased, and a solid line of gray clad soldiers burst out of the brush, driving in Logan's pickets. At first it semed as if Beauregard's full scale attack was beginning, but the 8th and 45th Illinois, volleyed against the Confederates and counterattacked. This show of force broke the foray and the enemy retreated through the sweltering afternoon. This was Logan's final action of the campaign. He was proud of the way his men had thrown back every rebel advance, exhibiting "true Western courage."[15]

When the rebels retired, Logan returned to his old camp with McClernand's reserve. That night explosions were heard from Corinth and at daybreak clouds of smoke spiralled up behind Confederate lines. Soon Logan heard that Pope's men had moved into town. Beauregard was gone, and Logan felt the victory merely "the barren honor of occupying an abandoned position."[16]

Logan's role in the Corinth campaign was minor, but carried out with ability. McClernand's report spoke well of his subordinate, and Sherman was impressed with Logan's behavior. Sherman reported: "I feel under special obligations to this officer who during the two days he served under me held the

[14]Logan, *Volunteer Soldier*, 666; Grant, *Memoirs*, I, 315; *OR*, Ser. 1, X, pt. 1, 757.
[15]*OR*, Ser. 1, X, pt. 1, 761.
[16]Logan, *Volunteer Soldier*, 667.

critical ground on my right."[17] Logan was gaining valuable
experience and was coming to be recognized as one of the better "political soldiers."

During the Corinth campaign Illinois politics seethed with
excitement, but Logan was unable to exert personal influence.
When an Illinois Democrat arrived at the front to ascertain
the degree of support among the troops for the Constitution
of 1862, he reported McClernand in opposition, but was unable
to find Logan, then attached to Sherman.[18]

May's political event with most interest for Logan, the race
to choose his successor, drew no statement from him. There
were six candidates in the field, the three leading contenders,
Josh Allen, S. S. Marshall, and I. N. Haynie, were Democrats
and one-time associates of Logan. Allen and Marshall were
peace Democrats, with Allen more of the extreme Copperhead
variety, and Haynie, who resigned his commission to enter
the race, supported war. Logan probably leaned toward Haynie, but he endorsed no one. Mary wrote favoring Marshall,
but Logan withheld comment entirely.[19] The degree of Logan's
influence in this election is difficult to estimate; it seems to
have been minor, but the result must have been disheartening.
When the votes were counted Allen had 4,795, Haynie 4,052,
and Marshall 4,000.[20] Certainly Haynie's defeat was a defeat
for Logan's brand of war Democracy and a victory for Egypt's
peace faction. But Logan seems to have been as unconcerned
with Illinois politics as he would ever be. In the war's final two
years he went home often to make his influence felt in the
state, but in 1862, after resigning from Congress, he appeared
to have renounced politics.

Beauregard's retreat left Confederate troops in western
Tennessee in a dangerous position and Halleck ordered Union
action to seize the region. Logan's brigade and a regiment
from Lew Wallace, the 78th Ohio, were named to move north
from Corinth and drive the rebel garrison out of Jackson,
Tennessee. This was more like Grant's kind of war, and in
early June Logan's men marched toward their objective. On

[17]OR, Ser. 1, X, pt. 1, 743.
[18]John Hill to Charles Lanphier, May 30, 1862, Lanphier Mss.
[19]Mary Logan to JAL, April 28, 1862, Logan Mss.
[20]Jonesboro Gazette, May 31, 1862.

June 7 they saw the town, nestled on the South Fork of the Forked Deer River loom up in the distance. His line formed, Logan threw out skirmishers, and ordered the advance. The outnumbered rebel garrison offered a hesitant defensive fire, then fled. Logan, riding at the head of his column, moved cautiously into Jackson, discovered the absence of armed opposition, and shot off a telegram to McClernand reporting capture of the town, with stores, two railroad depots, and the telegraph office.[21] Jackson, rail center of west central Tennessee, was center of a district whose command was given to McClernand. McClernand chose to remain with the bulk of the army near Corinth, and Logan remained in Jackson as post commander.[22]

The new duty brought Logan face to face with problems of occupying a district subject to raiding forays. Rumors of a rebel cavalry attack on Decaturville, 40 miles east of Jackson near the Tennessee River, forced Logan to send out several companies of cavalry and infantry. These raiders were supposed to be burning cotton, and Logan was instructed to capture incendiaries and turn them over to a military commission for trial. The rumor proved groundless and the expedition quickly returned.[23]

By the end of June, after several weeks at Jackson, Logan's men regarded the camp as a pleasant place. Their duties were varied enough by guarding bridges and railroads at various points to decrease camp boredom.[24] Logan was impressed with the district's beauty, though he found inhabitants "all hot 'secesh' and look daggers at us all." He also reported working harder than ever before, but he was "pleased with such a command·rather than a smaller one as it gives me position and I think I have given entire satisfaction."[25]

Politics continued to pursue Logan, who avoided the subject. In late June several Republican papers reported that Logan had told his troops, "he had been nosed around by Southern politicians long enough. He had seen enough of the cursed institution and he would not sheath his sword until it was

[21]*OR*, Ser. 1, X, pt. 1, 918.
[22]*Ibid.*, Ser. 1, XVII, pt. 2, 6.
[23]*Ibid.*
[24]Adair, *45th Illinois*, 6.
[25]JAL to Mary Logan, June 20, 1862, Logan Mss.

wiped from the land."[26] Logan denied this statement and declared that since he entered the army he had been too busy to deliver political speeches. He was still unwilling to endorse emancipation.[27]

By June the work of guarding lines of transportation was becoming tedious and nerve wracking. Some of Logan's troops at Humboldt, 17 miles northwest of Jackson, growing angry at verbal abuse from local citizens, looted part of the town. Logan was told to stop the pillaging and ordered to send an agent to punish offenders. But there was no time to investigate. On July 5 Logan received word that 300 of Confederate Colonel William H. Jackson's cavalrymen had moved into the district intending to destroy the railroad. To meet this threat he ordered out a detachment of cavalry under Major M. R. M. Wallace, supported by the 31st Illinois. They were to move to Brownsville, 30 miles west of Jackson, find Jackson and drive him out. Wallace's cavalry was to make frequent movements up the nearby Hatchie River, since Jackson was supposed to camp somewhere along the river. When Ozburn left at the head of the 31st, Logan, not wanting the Humboldt affair repeated, carefully instructed the colonel to stop straggling, enforce strict discipline, and protect private property.[28] Ozburn moved out, scoured the county, and found nothing. So it went through July, rumors, reports, expeditions dispatched, and no enemy found.

Logan heard rumors of a different nature by the middle of the month, and he wrote Mary that he momentarily expected to be sent to Virginia. Logan advised her that he did not want to go, preferring to remain in the West. Of Jackson, a "pretty place" a month earlier, he remarked, "there never was such a hole as this, it is insulting and impudent."[29]

For three weeks after he had sent Ozburn toward the Hatchie a deluge of reports of enemy forces operating around Jackson reached Logan. Rebel guerrillas were reported east of Jackson at Decaturville and Farmington, northwest at Poplar Grove, and east again along the Tennessee at Perryville. In

[26]Bloomington *Pantagraph* in *Illinois State Journal*, July 2, 1862.
[27]Jonesboro *Gazette*, July 26, 1862.
[28]*OR*, Ser. 1, XVII, pt. 2, 80.
[29]JAL to Mary Logan, July 10, 1862, Logan Mss.

each case Logan dispatched troops to disperse the raiders, but when his men arrived there were no rebels to be found. This prompt action, however, had prevented any serious damage in the district. Each time Logan repeated his cautions against seizing property. To Colonel Garrett Nevins of the 11th Illinois he added: "I desire you to use your endeavors to cultivate a conservative, friendly feeling with the people where you may be."[30]

Raiders finally struck the last week in July, divided Logan's force, and did considerable damage. On July 27 word of guerrilla activity around Bolivar, 30 miles south of Jackson, so alarmed McClernand that he ordered all Logan's force except two small regiments sent there. Logan protested that it weakened his garrison. On the 28th the heretofore phantom force of William "Cotton" Jackson took advantage of Logan's weakness and attacked the railroad between Humboldt and Jackson, burning the bridge over the Middle Fork of the Forked Deer River. In despair, Logan reported the attack to Grant and advised that he was sending a force to repair and hold the bridge. Of Jackson he telegraphed, "What will become of this place you can imagine. I shall hold it or be burned in its ashes."[31] Logan also reported the damage to McClernand. "I feared this when I was ordered to send from here nearly all the troops."[32]

All day the telegraph crackled as Logan and Grant exchanged messages. Grant advised Logan to keep a sharp watch for Jackson's further movements, assuring him reinforcements would be sent from Corinth if necessary. He then shot off a message to McClernand ordering him to return a portion of his forces at Bolivar, where they were not needed, to Jackson as soon as possible.[33]

Logan's complaints to Grant and McClernand and Grant's order to McClernand to send Logan's men back to Jackson, infuriated the touchy, ambitious McClernand. On the 29th McClernand and Logan kept operators busy tapping out charge and counter-charge, complaint and excuse, as the

---

[30]*OR*, Ser. 1, XVII, pt. 2, 115.
[31]*Ibid.*, 128.
[32]*Ibid.*, 129.
[33]*Ibid.*, 130.

smoldering rivalry between the two who aspired to Douglas' mantle as Illinois' leading Democrat, exploded. McClernand maintained Logan's force at Jackson was adequate to cope with the situation and called his telegram of the 28th a "gratuitous complaint."[34] Logan asked heatedly, "How could I guard against an attack north without anybody to leave here? Can I guard all the roads and property here with such a force as is left me and at the same time reinforce any of the points?" He again requested a reinforcement, telling McClernand he was doing all in his power to defeat Jackson. McClernand's next message reported another bridge destroyed, this time at Medon, south of Jackson, and he expressed surprise that Logan had not sent a reinforcement to the small garrison at Medon. Logan's reply reiterated his lack of troops, and assured McClernand there were troops at Medon, but not enough to drive off Confederate guerrillas. Taking offense at McClernand's intimation that he had been negligent and disobeyed orders, Logan wrote, "If I am to blame I can bear my part as well as any man. . . . I have no complaints to make of any kind, but will do my duty."[35]

While writing telegrams, Logan sent a cavalry force under Major Warren Stewart after Jackson. Stewart's force numbering only 75, caught up with Jackson's rearguard on the north bank of the Hatchie and routed them, taking ten prisoners. Pursuing, Stewart encountered Jackson's main body and was attacked and driven back toward Jackson. After Stewart's repulse, Logan was forced to weaken his Jackson garrison, even though his men at Bolivar had not returned, and send a combined cavalry and infantry force to push Jackson south of the Hatchie and into Mississippi. Logan cautioned Colonel Harvey Hogg, commander of the unit, to proceed carefully to prevent the Confederates from breaking through to Jackson. Hogg's column succeeded in driving the raiders out of Logan's district.[36]

Logan turned his attention to the civilians in his district. He was reasonably certain they had acted as infantry support for

---

[34]*Ibid.*, 133.
[35]*Ibid.*
[36]*Ibid.*, 136.

Jackson's strikes, and he moved to prevent repetitions. On receiving orders to extract an oath of allegiance to the government from all citizens in the area, Logan demanded the oath be taken. "Unless they do I will send them to Chicago," Logan threatened.[37] Many refused, and others swore and continued to aid rebel guerrillas. Most of the former, and those of the latter group who could be taken, were imprisoned until they took the oath and agreed to give no further aid to the Confederacy. Logan did his best to enforce the order, and civilian assistance to the enemy lessened around Jackson. On one occasion Logan, visiting a group of civilian prisoners in Jackson, asked them to take the oath, and all refused. He approached one of them, a middle aged farmer, and renewed his appeal. The man told Logan he had five boys in the Confederate army and rather than take the oath he would rot in prison. His loyalty impressed Logan and he went free.[38]

In mid-August rebel raiders reappeared along the Hatchie and Logan sent out column after column to pursue the elusive enemy. To these frustrations were added old problems of relations with McClernand and numerous complaints from both civilians and soldiers. "I am nearly worked to death and must get relief soon or I will break down," Logan complained. "I am almost tired of living in the army though I dislike to quit unless I could do it at some more proper time."[39] He asked for a 20-day leave and soon was on his way north by rail to Illinois.

Just before Logan left, politics reentered his life. On August 18 he received a letter from Republican O. M. Hatch, Yates' Secretary of State. The Republican, feeling Logan's war record and immense popularity would make him a winning candidate, asked him to return and run against Allen in Logan's old district. Hatch said nothing about party lables, but promised Republican support. Logan was better than peace-mongering Copperhead Allen.[40] Logan refused to endorse either party. "I

---

[37]JAL to Mary Logan, July 10, 1862, Logan Mss.

[38]R. S. Henry (ed.), *As They Saw Forrest* (Jackson, Tennessee, 1956), 80-81. This story was told by Mr. William Witherspoon.

[39]JAL to Mary Logan, Aug. 21, 1862, Logan Mss.

[40]O. M. Hatch to JAL, Aug. 18, 1862, Logan Mss.

express all my views and politics when I assert my attachment for the Union. I have no other politics now, and consequently no aspiration for civil place and power." Logan's letter indicated a desire to fight the war to a successful conclusion regardless of cost or "interest it may effect or destroy." He concluded, however, with what amounted to an endorsement of Yates' policies as he assured Hatch he "looked with pride and admiration on the continuance of the present able conduct of our State affairs."[41] While most Illinois Democratic leaders continued to attack Lincoln's conduct of the war, Logan was imperceptibly edging from anti-war Democracy to complete administration support.

When Logan arrived in Egypt he went at once to Carbondale where his family was living. Logan arrived shortly after his brother-in-law, Dr. Israel Blanchard, had been seized for opposition to the war and sent to Washington under arrest.[42] Despite political ferment caused by Blanchard's arrest and Allen's pre-election campaign, Logan vowed to spend his time with his family. His lone speech was delivered at Carbondale in response to a request from citizens of his new home. This address, similar to Logan's letter to Hatch, was basically a non-political statement in which he told Egyptians "party lines and partisan feelings should be swallowed up in patriotism."[43] When asked earlier what Logan would do in the fall political wars, Shelby Cullom had written, "Logan is quiet." This remained true, and Logan started back to Jackson without another public statement.[44]

Logan's return brought increased duties since McClernand had gone to Illinois to raise troops and Grant had given Logan command of the entire Jackson district. Logan's command included 23 regiments, stretched throughout the area.[45]

As if in honor of Logan's return, the rebels resumed their pyrotechnics the day he arrived in Jackson. The railroad bridge between Humboldt and Jackson, burned in July, was

[41]Dawson, *Logan*, 26-27.
[42]George Smith, *Southern Illinois*, I, 332.
[43]*Illinois State Journal*, Sept. 11, 1862
[44]S. M. Cullom to M. Hay, July 5, 1862, Cullom Mss., Illinois State Historical Library.
[45]Kenneth P. Williams *Lincoln Finds a General* (New York, 1956), IV, 67.

attacked again and set afire. This time, the fire was put out, and the rebels were driven off, losing their commander in the process. Logan's forces pursued the raiders in an attempt to take the whole force, but the party melted into the Tennessee hills. The remainder of September was spent, at Grant's orders, resting the men and guarding and repairing rail and wagon roads. Several times word reached Logan from along the Hatchie, south of Jackson, that large cavalry units were operating, but October arrived without further attacks.[46]

Difficulty arrived from a new quarter in late September with Lincoln's Emancipation Proclamation. Its effect on politics would be noted at the polls in November, and it took that long to affect the Westerners under Logan's command. The proclamation came as a surprise to Logan and his men, but was generally well received.[47] Some, however, agreed with the Egyptian paper which screamed, "The Niggers are free," and lashed out at Lincoln's change of war aims.[48] Of this group there were those who, recalling Logan's enlistment promise, expected to be led home, and when no such action was forthcoming, deserted. Logan privately confided to Mary, "The President's foolish message does us no good," but he said nothing publicly about emancipation, and continued to urge his men to fight to preserve the Union.[49]

October brought pleasant fall weather and an attack by Confederates under Earl Van Dorn and Sterling Price on Corinth. Logan was ordered to hold his position in west Tennessee against Confederate raiders, and keep Corinth's lines of communication open to the North. New units daily moved into Logan's district as Grant gathered his right wing for an advance on Vicksburg from the north. The 124th Illinois, recently organized, arrived at Jackson, October 9, and was reviewed by Logan, who was well pleased with the appearance of fresh troops.[50] Most welcome reinforcement was a company raised and captained by Logan's brother Tom, which joined

---

[46]*OR*, Ser. 1, XVII, pt. 2, 203, 231.

[47]Logan, *Great Conspiracy*, 498.

[48]Jonesboro *Gazette*, Oct. 4, 1862.

[49]JAL to Mary Logan, Dec. 12, 1862, Logan Mss.

[50]Richard L. Howard, *History of the 124th Regiment Illinois Infantry Volunteers* (Springfield, Illinois, 1880), 23.

the 31st. Logan had talked with Tom on his return in September, convincing him he should join the ranks.[51] As cool fall days passed, Logan's men enjoyed the break in combat and prepared for the rumored advance into Mississippi. Many had become friendly with the inhabitants and they visited homes and attended church. But there were always incidents that threatened the cordial relations Logan had tried so hard to create. A resident of Bolivar once came upon a soldier sitting in a garden on a sweet potato ridge digging potatoes with his bayonet. The Tennessean asked, "Is this the way you are going to convert us into good Union men?" Never looking up, the soldier replied, "No by God, this is the way we dig taters."[52]

"Tater digging" ended November 2 when Grant ordered Logan to move his command into Mississippi as the long awaited Vicksburg campaign began. On October 25 Grant was placed in command of the Department of the Tennessee, and he set in motion an advance on the great Confederate citadel on the Mississippi. He chose to move south through Mississippi, east of the river, driving scattered rebel forces back on Vicksburg as he went. Though October was relatively peaceful, the advance brought great relief after two and one-half months of fending off enemy raiders.

Grant's army numbered about 30,000 and he estimated his opposition under General J. C. Pemberton to be about the same. Grant's left wing was led by General James B. McPherson, the center by C. S. Hamilton, and the right by Sherman. Logan's division marched with McPherson's left. Pemberton was solidly entrenched south of the Tallahatchie River, but several rebel garrisons remained north of the river, and those at Holly Springs and Grand Junction merited Grant's attention.

As the campaign began Logan was named commander of the 3rd Division, 17th Army Corps, under McPherson. Logan's three brigades, led by Colonels Carroll Marsh and John D. Stevenson, both Illinoisans, and M. D. Leggett, able former chief of the 78th Ohio, included fourteen regiments, most of

---

[51]Green B. Raum, *A History of Illinois Republicanism* (Chicago, 1900), 526.

[52]Fritz Haskell (ed.), "Diary of Colonel William Camm, 1861-1865," *Journal of the Illinois State Historical Society*, XXVIII, No. 4 (January, 1926), 917.

which had served under Logan.[53] At 4 o'clock on a chilly November 2, Logan's division formed "with knapsacks and cartridge-boxes," and the advance began.

Two days later Logan moved into LaGrange, Tennessee, on the Mississippi Central Railroad. Here he remained for most of November, putting the railroad into running order and making certain Grant's line to the rear was secure. In addition to guard and repair duty, Logan drilled his men. Discipline was generally good and Logan took pains to make certain his men were well equipped. The recently arrived 124th Illinois began the movement without enough supply wagons, and Logan sent them more. "This affair gave General Logan a place in the hearts and confidence of our men which he never lost," observed the regimental historian.[54]

One of the few causes of distress was that men who, taking exception to the Emancipation Proclamation, resigned, were dismissed from the service, and sent home. While this did not constitute a great problem, it grieved Logan and led him to call emancipation "foolish."[55]

On November 28 Logan's division broke camp at LaGrange and moved with the Union left toward Holly Springs, Mississippi. All the following day Logan, moving along a narrow road, heard gunfire away to the southwest, but he encountered no opposition. Holly Springs, already taken, was reached on the 30th. Pemberton had pulled his entire force behind the Tallahatchie. After a brief halt at Holly Springs, which Grant designated his main supply depot, Logan advanced. On December 2 he was astir early and after a brisk morning march came in sight of formidable works north of the Tallahatchie. Instead of a powerful barrier occupied by Pemberton's force, Logan found works abandoned and Pemberton in rumored flight southward.[56] Grant, unwilling to attack Pemberton's strong river line, had sent a cavalry force up stream, crossed, and convinced the Confederate general he should fall back.

Grant quickly hurtled the Tallahatchie and moved his main

---

[53]*OR*, Ser. 1, XVII, pt. 2, 338.
[54]Howard, *124th Illinois*, 41.
[55]Haskell, "Diary," 923; JAL to Mary Logan, Dec. 12, 1862, Logan Mss.
[56]Richard Howard, *124th Illinois*, 42.

force south in pursuit toward Oxford. Logan's division, despite short rations and roads turned into a morass by fall rains, led the advance, and on December 3 it arrived in Oxford. Logan remained in the college town a few days, receiving supplies and preparing to spearhead the left flank southward. The army was forced to turn the state university's library into a hospital, and Logan found school officials bitterly hostile.[57] Ready to move again on the 12th, Logan's division advanced through rolling country toward the Yocona River. He marched without opposition and reached the Yocona, near Water Valley, to discover again an absence of Confederates. Logan was ordered to halt, make camp on the river, and await further instructions. Pemberton's continued withdrawal had caused a change in Grant's plans.

The Yocona was to be Logan's farthest line of penetration, the division camp there later being dubbed "Camp Turnabout." Logan's force lay along the river from the 11th to the 22nd, encountering few enemy troops. At Camp Turnabout he compiled his December report, finding almost 7,000 officers and men present for duty.[58] He scribbled a few lines to Mary, reporting, "I am well satisfied with my position and men," but added, "I would be glad if the war could be settled properly, and if the heads at Washington had any sense, and would have as much done on the Potomac as we have done, the rebellion would be ended."[59]

Still patrolling the Yocona region, Logan heard on the 19th of a Confederate raid on Jackson, Tennessee. Nathan Bedford Forrest had slammed into the area and ripped up the road between Jackson and Columbus, Kentucky, cutting off communications with the North. On the following day a second disaster struck the Union rear. Van Dorn's cavalry dashed into Holly Springs and set fire to Grant's supply depot.[60] His lines of communication severed and his supplies destroyed, Grant made the only possible decision, retreat. On the 21st McPherson told Logan to retire toward Oxford, seizing provisions to replace

---

[57]Ibid., 41.

[58]OR, Ser. 1, XVII, pt. 2, 512.

[59]JAL to Mary Logan, Dec. 12, 1862, Logan Mss.

[60]Grant, Memoirs, I, 360.

those destroyed by Van Dorn. These authorized seizures came
none too soon, for when Logan began his withdrawal some
units were already on short rations.[61] At 2 o'clock on the morning of the 22nd Logan asked his regimental officers to breakfast. After outlining the line of march, Logan launched into a
tirade against the rebellion in general, and Mississippi in particular, vowing that "he would burn every damned house in it
if he had command of it a couple of days."[62] At 7 o'clock Camp
Turnabout got its name and retreat began. Logan moved slowly through Oxford and spent a cheerless Christmas and New
Year's along the Tallahatchie. North of the river Logan was
sent by Grant to LaGrange to establish winter quarters. An
exhausted division dragged into the Tennessee rail junction as
1862, and the first act of the drama of Vicksburg ended.

------

[61]*OR*, Ser. 1, XVII, pt. 2, 453; Haskell, "Diary," 927; Morris, *31st
Illinois*, 52.
[62]Haskell, "Diary," 928.

CHAPTER X

HEWING THEIR WAY

"Should the free navigation of the Mississippi River be obstructed by force, the men of the West will hew their way to the Gulf with their swords," Logan had promised in 1861. Fifteen months had passed since Logan thundered his vow at the fledgling 31st Illinois, and the river remained closed. Grant had struck once at rebel forces north of Vicksburg, and his army had been cut off from the rear and repulsed. In January of the new year, Grant, forced to devote more attention to McClernand (who had his own ideas about who should lead the expedition) than to Pemberton, was busy moving troops down the Mississippi for another crack at the river fortress.[1]

Frustrated and denied victory east of the river, Grant had determined to approach Vicksburg from low country to the west. By the end of January he had a force on the river flats northwest of his objective, but high water made movement impossible. Deciding an advance was hazardous until March, Grant took steps to reinforce his assault force. He ordered McPherson to move Logan to Memphis where the 3rd Division would join the rest of the 17th Corps and steam down river to join Grant's van around Lake Providence, Louisiana. For some time Logan was unable to march to Memphis because of impassable roads. When his route cleared on the 17th Logan, "keen to go," broke camp and marched for Memphis.[2] On arriving, Logan was told that because of flooding down river landing would be perilous, and he was directed to await further orders. At month's end Logan's thirteen regiments had erected temporary winter quarters and were impatiently waiting for Grant's call.

January and February were the darkest months of the war for Logan. Since Donelson, his duties had been drudgery, with

---

[1] Grant, *Memoirs*, I, 367.
[2] *OR*, Ser. 1, XVII, pt. 2, 552, 569.

little chance for glory or advancement, and now it seemed as if there would be an interminable wait at Memphis. If the wait was too long Logan was afraid his command might disappear entirely. Desertions, a growing problem since September, were on the rise, and as long as the army remained motionless they increased. In desperation Logan wrote, "It takes all my time to keep the men in camp . . . the people, President and all, have gone crazy and I shall hold on to my command a while yet and see if all will not become sane again. If not I shall probably leave the army."[3] Logan, horrified to hear that the 109th Illinois, an Egyptian regiment, had mutinied at Holly Springs and was under arrest, feared a similar outbreak among his units.

While desertions increased and anti-war forces spread propaganda through his division, Logan was incapacitated. Damp, chill weather brought a recurrence of pain from his Donelson wounds and for a month he lay weak, feverish, and depressed.[4] On February 12, fearing wholesale mutiny, Logan issued an order to his troops. He assured them, "Your General still maintains unshaken confidence in your patriotism and devotion, and in the ultimate success of our cause." He expressed disgust at "treasonable" influences at work designed to create dissatisfaction. Logan especially deplored newspapers reaching the men containing false pictures of public sentiment at home. He concluded with a denunciation of deserters, calling on his men to stand by the flag.[5] Logan's message prompted the Jonesboro *Gazette*, a former friend, to take him to task for championing the war after it had become an abolition struggle, reminding him of his promise to lead his men home if abolition prevailed.[6] Even "Doff" Ozburn imbibed anti-war sentiment, and Logan confessed to Mary, "I want nothing to do with him."[7] The two men grew farther apart, and when Logan heard Ozburn say he had not come "to fight to free the Niggers," demanded his resignation.[8] Most of his men re-

---

[3]JAL to Mary Logan, Jan. 21, 1863, Logan Mss.
[4]Mary Logan, *Reminiscences*, 132.
[5]Order read to the 3rd Division at Memphis, Feb. 12, 1863, Logan Mss.
[6]Jonesboro *Gazette*, Feb. 28, 1863.
[7]JAL to Mary Logan, Jan. 21, 1863, Logan Mss.
[8]C. W. Balestier, *James G. Blaine; a Sketch of His Life, with a Brief*

mained in camp, however, and after Logan's plea of the 12th, Colonel John Stevenson pledged the troops' loyalty.[9]

After learning of Logan's illness, his wife received permission to go to Memphis, and brought a ray of light into the bleak winter. The couple first stayed at Logan's headquarters in the city at the Gayoso House, but in early February division headquarters was moved to the Lanier estate outside Memphis, and General and Mrs. Logan lived in the mansion. Mary was of great help during Logan's illness, acting as messenger and even reviewing troops. She remained until the division moved south and then returned to Carbondale.

By February 15, when Logan had recovered sufficiently to ride, the division stood ready to embark. The first transports arrived on the 8th, but until the 20th there were not enough to carry the whole division. On the 20th Logan marched his men aboard, and the transports turned down river toward Grant's army stretched snakelike across the river from Vicksburg. The grim interlude was over.

The division debarked at Lake Providence, about 35 miles north of Vicksburg, where it formed the northern extremity of Grant's line. The Louisiana lowlands around Lake Providence were dotted with flooded bayous. Towering over Grant's army, huddled in soggy bottomland, stood Vicksburg's armed cliffs. The Mississippi at Vicksburg meandered wildly through a series of hairpin turns, the most prominent of which thrust eastward into Mississippi like a giant finger. Grant realized a frontal attack on the bluffs would be madness and decided to undertake a series of experiments until he found a way to effect a landing on solid ground on the Mississippi side. He expected little from the time consuming activities of March and April, but they served to divert Pemberton, and keep Union troops busy.[10]

Grant's diversion included a number of attempts to get behind Vicksburg from the north through the Yazoo country, and several canal projects west of the river. The latter were aimed at by-passing Vicksburg's batteries and depositing the

---

Record of the Life of John A. Logan (New York, 1884), 257; Morris, 31st Illinois, 179. Ozburn was replaced by Edwin McCook.
    [9]Mary Logan, Reminiscences, 134.
    [10]Grant, Memoirs, I, 371.

army south of the city. When Logan arrived at Lake Providence troops already there had cut the levee and had been canal digging for almost a month. Lake Providence was part of the old bed of the Mississippi, but in 1863 it lay one mile west of the river. The lake, six miles long, joined a system of tortuous, tree clogged bayous which ran into the Tensas, Washita, and Red Rivers. If navigable for its entire length, this route could land Grant's army 400 miles south of Vicksburg at Port Hudson. On February 4 Grant returned to ascertain McPherson's progress and decided there was little chance of success. Nevertheless, he let the work continue "believing employment was better than idleness for the men."[11]

Logan's men, joining McPherson's miners, had little chance for idleness, and activity kept them in good spirits. Some dug while others explored the bayous in small boats. Several times they returned with reports of a practicable route through the winding waterways, but each time further investigation proved passage unsuitable.[12] One of Logan's brigades, under hard driving Colonel M. B. Leggett, also participated in a foray east of the river and north of Vicksburg, attempting to wriggle in behind Pemberton. This expedition, like several others there, failed and was called back. On March 27 Grant ordered the Lake Providence canal project abandoned and Logan's men, forced five miles up river by the lake's rising waters, set up a dry camp and waited for Grant's next move.[13]

Promotion occupied Logan's mind through the spring. During the advance into Mississippi the previous winter, Governor Yates asked Logan's promotion to major general.[14] Lincoln complied by sending Logan's name to the Senate, and that body, much to Logan's and Yates' distress, rejected the nomination. Undeterred, Logan pressed Yates for reconsideration, and the Illinois governor sent Lincoln a letter "in behalf of the State and of a large majority of her loyal people." Yates called the rejection "most unfortunate to the interest of the Government in my state and in the West generally." Yates was especially anxious to see Logan promoted because of the

[11]*Ibid.*, 374.
[12]*OR*, Ser. 1, XXIV, pt. 3, 96.
[13]*Ibid.*, Ser. 1, XXIV, pt. 1, 403.
[14]Dawson, *Logan*, 28.

influence such a step would have on Illinois' war Democrats.[15] A number of Logan's subordinates also penned letters to the president in his behalf. One, Colonel Jasper Maltby of the 45th Illinois, sent an appeal signed by the entire regiment to Elihu Washburne. Maltby asked a major general's stars for his "beloved and distinguished" commander as an evidence of political impartiality in making promotions. He cited Logan's excellent war record, his support of the government and his "shining example" to men under his command.[16] Lincoln again asked Logan's elevation, and he was promoted on March 13, the promotion to date from the previous November 29.

The Illinois Democratic press continued to show interest in Logan's "betrayal" of his party. Lanphier attacked Logan's February 12 letter, leading Logan to exclaim, "This does seem as if there was a determination to abuse me for everything."[17] Commenting on the same document, an Egyptian paper told Republicans who believed Logan had joined them, "Gen. John is as ardent a Democrat as he ever was, and he hates abolitionists as much as he ever did, but Gen. John wants to be promoted to Major General. . . . He hasn't fooled the Democrats for they never did think he amounted to much."[18]

While newspapers peppered Logan, stories attacking him swept through Egypt. Mary found herself rejected, subjected to stony silence from former friends, and forced to sit and listen to her husband called a thief and traitor. She finally refused to mention the war altogether, not even when told Logan was guilty of breaking seals on soldier's letters. Scarcely able to withstand the unremitting assault, she lamented: "Isolated from my kindred by this unfortunate trouble, torn from my husband by the same unholy cause . . . how can I say much with you on one side and a brother, whom I love dearly, on the other."[19]

In early April Logan completed the circle, moving from a bitter abolition foe to open advocacy of freedom for the slaves.

---

[15]Yates to Lincoln, Mar. 20, 1863, Logan Mss., copy.
[16]James M. Davis et al. to Lincoln, Mar. [?], 1863, Logan Mss.; J. M. Maltby to Elihu Washburne, April 2, 1863, Washburne Mss.
[17]JAL to Mary Logan, Mar. 10, 1863, Logan Mss.
[18]Jonesboro Gazette, Mar. 14, 1863.
[19]Mary Logan to JAL, April 6, Mar. 23, 1863, Logan Mss.

He had flirted with the idea of making such a statement for
several months, and the opportunity came when Adjutant-
General Lorenzo Thomas appeared at Lake Providence to
speak to the division on the government's policy of arming
Negroes. Thomas outlined the policy in a short, formal speech,
hissed and booed by many of the men. When Thomas finished
McPherson spoke briefly and introduced Logan. Roaring out
in his best stump style, Logan admitted he had been educated
to support slavery, but the war had opened his eyes. Slavocrats
had struck at the republic and slavery must be destroyed. Concentrating his appeal on the Egyptians of his old regiment
standing before him, he thundered:

> We must hurt the rebels in every way possible. Shoot
> them with shot and shells and minie balls, and damn them,
> shoot them with niggers. . . . And you my old 'Dirty-first,'
> you are willing even a colored man should shield you from
> rebel bullets. I know you are. So we'll unite on this policy,
> putting the one who is the innocent cause of this war, in the
> front rank and press on to victory.[20]

Instinctively, led by the 31st, the men cheered, and little was
said afterward against Negro troops. Thomas wrote, "I must
refer to the eloquent remarks of General Logan, who not only
fully endorsed my own remarks, but went beyond them."[21]

Logan's shift of position can be traced to two factors. He
was no dedicated abolitionist, but by 1863 he had concluded
that everything, even slavery, should be sacrificed if necessary
to save the Union. He also had politics in mind. His eye on
post-war politics, Logan was growing certain that a narrow
Egyptian view of national affairs would not win state-wide
office. Though his popularity might decline in Egypt, and even
there his enemies were more noisy than numerous, every
step away from rigid Egyptian Democracy brought him greater
praise from northern and central Illinois. His name, long
anathema in Springfield, Freeport, and Rockford, was now
greeted with cheers.

Shortly after Thomas left, roads became passable, and

[20]Richard Howard, *124th Illinois*, 65-66; Hayes, *Diary and Letters*,
IV, 302.
[21]*OR*, Ser. 3, III, 121.

Grant's mind bubbled with ideas. Unable to hit Pemberton from north or west, Grant determined to march down the Louisiana shore south of Vicksburg, cross, and strike from a new quarter. Having formulated his plan, Grant called a concentration of forces at Milliken's Bend. On April 15 McPherson ordered Logan to embark for the staging area as soon as transports arrived, A few days later the 3rd Division stood at Milliken's Bend ready to advance. His three brigades totaled thirteen crack regiments from Illinois, Indiana, Ohio, and Missouri.[22]

To ferry his men across the river south of Vicksburg, Grant was forced to send a fleet under Admiral David D. Porter down the Mississippi under Pemberton's guns. The success of this endeavor, despite some loss, led to a second try on the night of April 22. This sally was necessary to supply the army while waiting to cross. Grant called for volunteers to man the ships, asking for men with past experience on western waters. Five times more men offered their services than were needed, and of the force chosen almost all were from Logan's division. When Colonel Maltby asked for volunteers from the 45th Illinois, almost the entire regiment stepped forward. The zeal displayed was a tribute to spirit inspired by Logan and his regimental officers.[23]

While his volunteers dashed beneath Vicksburg's hulking cliffs, the bulk of Logan's division broke camp on the 25th and marched through bayou country toward Grant's projected crossing opposite Bruinsburg. Drenching rains hampered movement, but Logan kept a steady pace and on the 30th he reached the point where he was to cross.

Grant's plan of attack was now obvious to his subordinates, and they did not like it. Sherman, McPherson, and Logan strongly opposed this move on the grounds that an effective supply line to the rear could not be maintained and the whole force might be cut off and destroyed.[24] Grant, however, had

---

[22]*Ibid.*, Ser. 1, XXIV, pt. 3, 257. On the eve of the advance Brigadier General I. N. Haynie, longing for politics, resigned to be replaced as commander of the 1st Brigade by Brigadier General John E. Smith, but otherwise Logan's unit commanders were the same.

[23]Wilbur F. Crummer, *With Grant at Fort Donelson, Shiloh, and Vicksburg* (Oak Park, Illinois, 1915), 91.

[24]J. F. C. Fuller, *Grant and Lee* (Bloomington, Indiana, 1957), 87.

revolutionary ideas about supply lines. When Van Dorn put the torch to Grant's Holly Springs base, the army was forced to subsist off the country during its retreat. This policy was so successful that it gave Grant ideas. The concept was bold, reckless, and sure to be countermanded by Halleck, but Grant made sure Halleck knew nothing of his plans until it was too late to stop them. To confuse Pemberton, Grant ordered two diversions. He sent Sherman down through the Yazoo tangle feinting at Vicksburg from the north, and dispatched cavalry commander Benjamin Grierson on a hard riding sweep through Mississippi. This flurry of action sent Pemberton scurrying in all directions and rendered impossible effective stoppage of Grant's first move south of the city.

On the 30th McClernand's 13th Corps began crossing at Bruinsburg. That afternoon and night Logan's 1st and 3rd Brigades "bade farewell to Louisiana and its alligators."[25] Their crossing was accomplished without incident, but as Logan's artillery was being ferried after dark, two transports collided and one containing Battery G, 2nd Ilinois Light Artillery, sank, taking with it all the artillery, several horses, and three men. Though this accident slowed ferry work, the 2nd Brigade landed May 1. Before the 2nd Brigade landed, its fellow units were in action. Shortly after midnight on the 1st, McClernand's column encountered infantry and artillery fire on the road to Port Gibson and he halted to await daylight. When day came McClernand moved his troops down two roads toward Port Gibson about ten miles from Bruinsburg. Here he met Confederate General John S. Bowen, hurrying with 5,000 men to delay Grant's advance. While waiting for rations, Logan's two brigades heard distant booming, and as Grant arrived in Bruinsburg, a messenger from McClernand dashed in requesting aid. Grant sent Logan's 1st Brigade under Smith to the left, and Stevenson's brigade to reinforce McClernand's right. McPherson rode out with Smith while Logan joined Stevenson in jogging through the hot Mississippi sun toward the sound of battle. Smith, a veteran of Belmont, Donelson, and Shiloh, hurried as one old soldier recalled, "to help Mc-

---

[25]Osborn H. Oldroyd, *A Soldier's Story of the Siege of Vicksburg* (Springfield, Illinois, 1885), 3.

Clernand out of a scrape."[26] The terrain through which they moved was a broken series of wooded ridges separated by deep ravines choked with heavy timber and tangled undergrowth. Some of Smith's men fell by the wayside, overcome by heat, but most struggled on, bristling with fight after months of inactivity.[27] By noon wild Confederate artillery balls had begun to crash through trees around Smith's troops, and they soon reached McClernand's line. Bowen's rebels occupied a high ridge opposite McClernand and looked formidable behind natural fortifications. Smith quickly flung his advance units into the line, and Union troops slowly drove Bowen back. The Confederates retired to a hill where Bowen halted, hoping, with the aid of the terrain, to delay further Union advance. After a short exchange, Smith and McClernand decided to charge. Smith's entire force rose, fired, and raced through a hail of shots toward Bowen's line. The brigade struck like veterans, rolling Bowen back until he called a retreat. This charge was the first combat experience for the 124th Illinois, and it was disconcerted by balls that "struck uncomfortably close and made us cringe," but at day's end, Grant told regimental commander, Colonel T. J. Sloan, "I never want soldiers to do better."[28]

On McClernand's right, Stevenson's men, the 8th and 81st Illinois, 7th Missouri and 32nd Ohio, accompanied by Logan, stumbled through the broken country. This Union flank was stronger than the left, but Stevenson's men came in time to plug a hole in McClernand's line. Fighting was not as intense there. After an afternoon filled with the clatter of rifle fire, Bowen's left joined the retreat.

Guns stilled, Logan's men were exuberant at their success. First they cheered without knowing quite what they were cheering; then they cheered the 124th Illinois for behaving so well in its first fight. Logan and McPherson came up to be greeted with cheers, and when Grant rode along, the exclamations rose again. Behind Grant "on a couple of sorry looking secesh nags" came Yates and Washburne. The two politicians had recently come down river and they rode forward to ob-

[26]Adair, *45th Illinois*, 10.
[27]Morris, *31st Illinois*, 55.
[28]Richard Howard, *124th Illinois*, 79.

serve the battle. Washburne had even ridden toward the
enemy, but the sharp crack of muskets convinced him he should
remain in the rear. Emerging after Bowen's retreat he galloped up shouting, "Give it to 'em boys." His enthusiasm once
the enemy was silenced drew snickers from the men, but they
admitted, "You couldn't blame him much. He wasn't getting the
enormous sum of $13 per month to be shot at. A Congress-
man's salary didn't justify the sacrifice of being riddled with
bullets."[29] Despite this, and though "It wasn't our custom to
cheer for civilians," they gave Yates and Washburne "three
cheers such as they never got before or since."[30] How things
had changed. The army was in the field, confidently striking
through the heart of Dixie, and Grant told Halleck, "The army
is in the finest health and spirits."[31]

High spirits and carefree informality of Logan's men continued next morning as they swung into Port Gibson while
bridges over the South Fork of Bayou Pierre were burning.
The command stopped while Grant decided on his next move,
and a group of Logan's men, wandering through the streets,
found a quantity of blank currency. Signing large amounts,
privates left town feeling like bank presidents.[32]

Having reached Port Gibson and effected a firm landing east
of the river, Grant could have been expected to establish a
base of supplies and wait for N. P. Banks' force in Louisiana
to join him. A year earlier Grant might have stopped, but he
had the initiative and did not propose to drop it. Furthermore,
a halt might give Joe Johnston, in eastern Mississippi, time to
join Pemberton. Grant proposed to slash across the state,
separating the two enemy armies and drive Pemberton inside Vicksburg, thus sealing his fate. He moved even though
he had inadequate wagon trains, and orders went out to forage
liberally.

New bridges over the South Fork at Port Gibson were begun on May 2, but, not waiting for their completion, Grant
called on Logan and sent him to seek a quick crossing. Guided
by a helpful Negro, Logan went three miles upstream and

[29]Crummer, *With Grant*, 91.
[30]Adair, *45th Illinois*, 18.
[31]*OR*, Ser. 1, XXIV, pt. 1, 33.
[32]Oldroyd, *Soldier's Story*, 5.

forded. He found no enemy, moved across to the North Fork, and camped near Willow Springs. Logan, now leading the army, had attained high ground and was in the clear striking for Jackson. The men had no idea where they were going, but they reasoned Grant knew where he was taking them. With faith in their commanders as great as any army ever possessed, they were going to hack the Confederacy in half. "Logan," his men thought, "is brave, and does not seem to know what defeat means. We feel that he will bring us out of every fight victorious. . . . I have no fear of a needless sacrifice of life through mismanagement of this army."[33]

Rising early on the 3rd, Logan sent out foraging parties and prepared to cross the North Fork of Bayou Pierre. Some of Logan's men, on patrol along the peaceful stream, decided to take a swim before breakfast, and they were splashing happily when rifle fire kicked up jets of water. No one was hurt and Logan drove the marauding rebels off, crossed the bayou, and moved up a sandy road toward Hankinson's Ferry on the Big Black River. All afternoon retreating graycoats were herded along ahead of Logan's column, several times falling prisoner to advance units. Logan reached the ferry at dusk and camped along the Big Black for three days. Across the river Confederates had planted a battery and at daybreak on the 4th it opened on Logan's camp, sending men scurrying for cover. Logan brought his own artillery forward, and Union guns joined the booming chorus and silenced the rebel fire.

Rock Springs was the objective when Logan broke camp on the 7th. He reached the hamlet that evening and camped there for two days, thrusting ahead again on the 9th toward Utica. Forward movement slowed on the 9th and 10th due to the wait for supply wagons hauling necessities unprovided by the countryside, such as coffee, bread, and ammunition. Logan rumbled through Utica on the 11th bearing northeastward toward Raymond, certain the enemy would appear before he had gone much farther. At nightfall on the 11th, however, all remained peaceful, campfires were lit, and orders were passed to move out early on the 12th and seize the crossroads at Raymond.[34]

---

[33]Ibid., 15.
[34]OR, Ser. 1, XXIV, pt. 1, 35.

At 3:30 that morning, Logan, "gallant and irrepressible," led McPherson's line up the road with skirmishers thrown forward and cavalry riding the flanks.[35] By 10 o'clock skirmishers had encountered opposition, and reconnaissance discovered a considerable force, estimated by McPherson at 4-5,000, well posted, commanding the road and a bridge spanning a small creek. McPherson quickly ordered up Marcellus Crocker, who with Logan was considered by Grant the army's ablest division commander.[36] Before Crocker reached the battle, the contest had been decided. Raymond was Logan's private battle.

E. S. Dennis' brigade was leading Logan's division, and it arrived opposite the enemy first, followed by Smith and Stevenson. When the three units joined they stood on a hill overlooking a deep ravine cut by a small stream. From the hill they could see Raymond's clustered houses two miles away. Confederate General John Gregg had placed his skirmish line west of the creek and Logan's first wave of skirmishers dislodged it, forcing it to cross. Gregg's line now presented a menacing obstacle to attackers. Covered by the bank and thick brush, it lay along the creek and commanded an open hill down which Logan's forces must charge. Determined to strike immediately, Logan swung Smith's men to Dennis' right and leaving Stevenson in reserve he roared "charge!" Simultaneously he ordered Samuel DeGolyer's battery on the hill to bombard the enemy. When his guns began to thunder, several cooks, surprised near the front, broke for the rear carrying their utensils. One of them, kettle in hand, ran headlong into Logan who asked him where he was going. "Oh General," he quaked, "I've got no gun, and such a snapping and crackling as there is up there I never heard before." Chuckling, Logan let him pass.[37]

As the infantry charged, Gregg, swept the open space with a murderous fire, but "every man stepped promptly and majestically forward." Dennis and Smith soon reached cover behind a line of fence and timber overlooking the creek and Gregg's line, and for two hours the ravine was a bedlam of noise and death. During the lengthy exchange Logan moved Stevenson's

---

[35]Charles A. Dana and James H. Wilson, *The Life of Ulysses S. Grant* (Springfield, Massachusetts, 1868), 120.
[36]Grant, *Memoirs*, I, 416.
[37]Oldroyd, *Soldier's Story*, 17.

reserve brigade to Smith's right, placing his entire division in action, Dennis on the left, Smith in the center, and Stevenson on the right.[38]

Time after time Logan's men broke from behind the protection of the fence, only to be driven back by withering fire. Logan dashed up and down the line roaring at his men to hold their places, "firing the men with his own enthusiasm."[39] He constantly presented a clear target to rebel sharpshooters, and one shot his horse from under him. To Logan, behind the lines, it seemed as if Gregg was concentrating on Dennis. As he rode toward Dennis' flank, Logan encountered a tall, lanky soldier wandering alone in the rear. "General," drawled the soldier, "I hev been over on the rise yonder, and it's my idee that if you'll put a rigiment or two over thar, you'll get on their flank and lick them easy."[40] Thanking the man for his advice, Logan investigated the situation, saw the wisdom of the tall private's words, and spurred his new mount back to Stevenson. He detached the 8th Illinois and sent it to the left. It was just in time to support Evan Richards' 20th Illinois which had finally broken across the ravine and, bayonets out, was charging the rebels. Following the 8th and 20th, Logan's old "Dirty-first," some of its men plunging neck deep in water, clambered dripping up the bank, fixed bayonets, and pressed forward. Gregg's line, though punctured, was by no means broken, and he gave way grudgingly, subjecting Logan to a galling fire. To aid the 1st Brigade's drive up the hill, Logan moved DeGolyer's battery to the left and it smashed the enemy flank with terrible effect. Once Gregg tried to capture the battery, but the attackers were met by a wall of grape and cannister and they broke in disorder. At 3:30, with Smith and Stevenson fording the creek, Gregg, outnumbered and outgunned, fell back on Raymond in good order.[41] By 5 o'clock Logan and McPherson stood at Raymond's crossroads, but Gregg, retreating toward Jackson, was gone. The men pitched camp in the town and had

---

[38]*OR*, Ser. 1, XXIV, pt. 1, 645.

[39]Oldroyd, *Soldier's Story*, 17.

[40]Isaac H. Elliott and Virgil G. Way, *History of the Thirty-third Regiment Illinois Veteran Volunteer Infantry in the Civil War* (Gibson City, Illinois, 1902), 39.

[41]*OR*, Ser. 1, XXIV, pt. 1, 637; pt. 3, 873.

a chance to cheer. But there were fewer to do so; 66 lay dead in the smoking ravine, 339 were wounded, and 37 missing.[42]

Logan, disgusted at having failed to catch Gregg, nevertheless rejoiced at his victory. Fought entirely by his division, the small but intense engagement reflected his dynamic leadership and his growing ability as a tactician. Yet as he lay awake thinking of the day's events, he must have delighted in knowing that his men's knapsacks held their rightful share of marshal's batons.

Raymond was left behind on the 13th, but because of his long engagement the previous day, Logan gave up the lead to Crocker. Both divisions cut northward to Clinton on the Jackson-Vicksburg Railroad where they bivouacked. All night Logan busily destroyed railroad tracks near Clinton, and on the 14th followed Crocker toward Jackson. At 11 o'clock Crocker's advance units contacted Confederate skirmishers, drove them in on the main force, and Logan was sent in support. These rebels were commanded by Joe Johnston, just arrived from the east. Logan hurried forward his own skirmishers and moved his main force to Crocker's support, but Crocker's men pushed the rebels back. When Logan got up, there was nothing to do but cheer. Crocker had found enemy lines empty, and as Logan galloped up to join him the flag of the 49th Indiana waved from the capitol.

After dark Logan settled his men and sat with McPherson discussing the campaign. Soon several soldiers approached escorting a man recently come through the lines. This mysterious visitor, a Union secret agent, carried a message from Johnston to Pemberton, and McPherson hurried him off to Grant. Johnston, now Pemberton's superior, was ordering Pemberton to strike Sherman, encamped at Clinton. Grant immediately ordered McClernand, who had just reached Raymond, to slice in a northwesterly direction toward Bolton, and he sent McPherson and Sherman down the Jackson-Vicksburg Road to join him. On the 15th Logan hastened his men down the road toward Edwards' Depot, and camped that night seven miles west of Clinton.[43]

---

[42]Grant, *Memoirs*, I, 415.

[43]*OR*, Ser. 1, XXIV, pt. 1, 646.

As Grant moved his army toward Bolton to prevent a Confederate juncture and to drive Pemberton into Vicksburg, Pemberton was moving eastward hampered by conflicting orders. Jefferson Davis wanted Pemberton to hold Vicksburg at all costs while Johnston ordered him to leave Vicksburg and bring about a Confederate concentration. He had decided to try both, and he was moving toward Grant with 22,000 troops to smash Sherman's corps, thus delaying Grant, and then join Johnston. While neither Grant nor Pemberton was sure of his enemy's position, a clash was imminent.

When Logan reached Turkey Creek, he came up with General Alvin P. Hovey's division of McClernand's corps, and the two units moved forward past Bolton on the morning of the 16th. Hovey led, Logan next, followed by Crocker. At 10 o'clock Hovey's pickets met enemy advance units and discovered Pemberton in force along a ridge commanding the Union line of march. The ridge Pemberton had chosen, called Champion's Hill, was a low eminence running southwest to northeast, with one spur jutting southward from the northeast point. Near the hill, three roads leading from the east into Vicksburg came close together, two of them actually joining. Grant's army was moving down these three roads: Hovey's division and McPherson's corps on the right, two of McClernand's divisions in the center, and the other division, A. J. Smith, of McClernand, on the left. Sherman remained around Jackson destroying railroads and factories. Hovey, who had first made contact, formed his two brigades, threw out a skirmish line and prepared to fight. Meanwhile McPherson, riding with Logan, had encountered Hovey's wagons and sent for Grant to clear the road. Grant rode forward, ordered Hovey's train out of the way, and moved Logan and Crocker around to Hovey's right facing Confederates on the ridge. The men trotted forward until the heat made rest indispensable. Getting into position was hot work in more ways than one. Logan's 2nd Brigade, again commanded by Leggett, recently returned from a long illness, was raked by artillery fire as it moved through a small ravine to get into position. Once in line, Leggett told his men to lie down until the rest of the division came up. One of Colonel Manning Force's men in the 20th Ohio remembered: "The command was obeyed with alacrity, for bullets were already whizzing over our heads. I never hugged Dixie's soil as I have today."[44] Smith's brigade, on Leggett's right, had less trouble forming, and with Stevenson in reserve, Logan, on the union right, stood ready to strike.

Before Logan had all his men in position, Hovey launched the attack, and Logan quickly joined him, Leggett and Smith pushing forward in two lines. Rebel rifles crackled, sifting leaves down on the men's heads as they walked steadily forward. Logan, closely following his line, discovered Pemberton's troops strongly posted in the edge of thick timber up the ridge, their position further protected by a wooden fence. Riding to the rear, Logan called up DeGolyer's reliable artillerymen and they opened on the fence with grape and cannister. Round after round pounded into the structure splintering it and sending "rails and rebs in the air together."[45] DeGolyer's gory work completed, Logan sent in his infantry. Leggett found relatively easy going, but Smith, on the extreme right was forced to plow through a ravine clogged with thick growth and swept by enemy guns. Toiling upward was bloody business, but both brigades reached the fence, hurling the rebels back to a second and higher ridge. Ever mindful of a flanking attack, Logan placed Stevenson on Smith's right, and no sooner had the 3rd Brigade taken position than a five-gun battery began to throw shells down the hill. Stevenson, ordered to silence the guns, led his men through an "almost impassable" hollow and took the entire battery. At noon Logan rode to Stevenson's brigade where he was joined by Grant galloping up to examine the situation. Stevenson's movement had turned the rebel flank and actually cut Pemberton off from his only road of retreat, one leading along Baker's Creek between Champion's Hill and Vicksburg. This fact was unknown to Grant, and when Hovey, hard pressed in the center, asked for reinforcements, he told Logan to pull Stevenson back and close the entire division on Hovey.[46] Hovey's relief came none too soon, but it opened the road and the chance to capture a large part of Pemberton's army disappeared.

---

[44]Oldroyd, *Soldier's Story*, 22.
[45]*Ibid.*, 23.
[46]Grant, *Memoirs*, I, 433.

Moving back toward the Union center, Logan discovered Leggett, on Hovey's immediate right, hard pressed by rebel attackers who also soon moved down the hill toward Smith. Swedish Major Charles Stolbrand, Logan's artillery chief, noting the advancing enemy, rode to Smith crying, "Sheneral Schmitt dey are sharging you mitt double column. By damn it dey vant mine guns." Smith grimly replied, "Let 'em come, we're ready," and he ordered: "Fix bayonets!" As steel cleared scabbards, Logan and McPherson dashed up, the latter yelling, "Give them Jessee, boys, give them Jessee!" Logan added, "We are about to fight the battle for Vicksburg," and turning to his old regiment he roared: "Thirty-onesters, remember the blood of your mammas. We must whip them here or all go under the sod together. Give 'em hell."[47] One veteran thought this charge one of the finest he witnessed during the war. After a bloody battle in the ravine, rebel attackers reclimbed their hill, hastily scrambled down the open road to the rear and left the field to Grant.

When the fight was over, Logan, McPherson, and Grant were greeted with hysterical cheers. Two of Logan's brigades, completely exhausted, camped on the field, but a third, despite its fatigue, outstripped McClernand's troops in its pursuit of the retreating enemy. Logan's total loss at Champion's Hill was 407 killed, wounded, and missing. Logan in turn took 1,300 prisoners and 11 guns.[48]

Charles A. Dana was a special emissary to Grant's army from Washington, and his perceptive observations of leading participants of the Vicksburg campaign are among the best written. Dana, riding with John Rawlins of Grant's staff after Champion's Hill, came to Logan's headquarters and found him greatly excited. "Logan declared the day was lost, and that he would soon be swept from his position." Dana inquired later of Logan's unrealistic post-battle pessimism, and was told it was

simply a curious idiosyncracy of Logan's. In the beginning of a fight he was one of the bravest men that could be, saw no danger, went right on fighting until the battle was over.

---

[47]Morris, *31st Illinois*, 64.
[48]*OR*, Ser. 1, XXIV, pt. 2, 9.

Then after the battle was won, his mind gained an immovable conviction that it was lost. It was merely an intellectual peculiarity. It did not in the least impair his value as a soldier or commanding officer. He never made any mistake on account of it.[49]

Time after time this incurable pessimism overtook him, becoming one of his best known traits.

Later Dana further remarked of Logan:

Heroic and brilliant, he is sometimes unsteady. Inspiring his men with his own enthusiasm on the field of battle, he is splendid in all its crash and commotion. A man of instinct and not of reflection, his judgements are very apt to be right. . . . On the whole, few can serve the cause of the country more effectively than he, and none serve it more faithfully.[50]

Dana's opinion of Logan was shared by Grant. As his opinion of McClernand declined, Grant's admiration of Logan as leader and fighter increased. At Champion's Hill Logan struck hard and fought his men well, but McClernand held back, refusing to attack the left flank when his men might have sealed Pemberton's fate.[51] Grant surely agreed with the two men who wrote: "Logan exhibited every day, a constantly increasing aptitude for military command and the highest soldierly qualities, not only of courage and subordination, which latter McClernand did not possess and seemed incapable of acquiring."[52] McClernand's career was about to end, while Logan's military star was rising. Champion's Hill was a splendid victory, called by one "the decisive battle of the war."[53] Pemberton, separated from Johnston, had little choice but to take his crippled army back to Vicksburg, where his stubby pursuer and the all-winning Union army would lock the door.

Abroad early on the 17th, Logan led the corps toward the Big Black, but trailed two of McClernand's divisions who had the day's fight. Pemberton, instead of trying one final time to

[49]Charles A. Dana, *Recollections of the Civil War* (New York, 1898), 54.
[50]*Ibid.*, 67.
[51]Grant, *Memoirs*, I, 435.
[52]Nicolay and Hay, *Lincoln*, VII, 136.
[53]Williams, *Lincoln Finds a General*, IV, 379.

elude Grant and march to join Johnston, lay astride the river at the bridge. His men east of the river commanded a cleared field, but Grant's relentless army pounded across the open space, captured most of the defenders, tilted some into the river, and caused Pemberton's main body on the western heights to burn the bridge and retreat. Burned bridges never stopped Grant long, and on the 18th Logan crossed the Big Black on pontoons. Once across, Logan turned north, struck the Bridgeport-Vicksburg Road and marched all day, his men stepping out confidently. On the morning of the 19th, Logan struck Pemberton's outlying works, about two miles from the city, and he went into position in the siege line's center. His division lay between the wagon road and railroad to Jackson. That afternoon Grant ordered an assault and Logan's men charged, securing a few better positions. The attack was short and showed the effectiveness of rebel entrenchments.

Grant's investment completed by nightfall, his army coiled around Pemberton like a giant constrictor. The Union line ran from the river's U turn north of Vicksburg, to swampy lowland along river flats south of the city. Sherman's 15th Corps held the right or north; McPherson stretched out forming the center east of the city, with McClernand holding McPherson's left, south of Vicksburg. Pemberton's defensive line expertly took advantage of the rugged terrain around the city. The bluff overlooking the river on which Vicksburg is situated, lost its flatness as it stretched eastward to where Pemberton's men lay entrenched. There it was slashed by ravines, and Confederate rifle pits were arranged so as to make assault through this labyrinth of gullies extremely difficult. The Union army learned this on the 19th.

For two days after his first attack, Grant secured a supply line to bring bread and ammunition to his army. During this time Grant meditated on the possible success of a quick attack. His decision to try a frontal attack on the morning of the 22nd was based on several factors. Grant knew Johnston was somewhere in his rear, and he wanted to take Pemberton before Johnston arrived to complicate things. In addition Grant believed Pemberton's army, fresh from a series of defeats, was demoralized, while his own men, flushed with victory, were

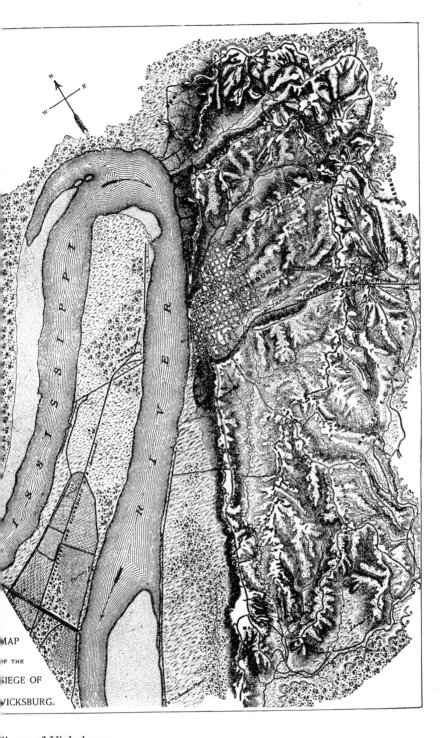

Siege of Vicksburg

From *Battles and Leaders of the Civil War*

confident.[54] Consequently he called his corps commanders, ordered them to synchronize watches, and strike at 10 A. M.

At 10 Logan shouted "forward," and the division, 1st and 3rd Brigades in advance, 2nd in reserve, leaped down the ravines, and rushed rebel riflemen. The attack was a total failure. Though pushed vigorously all along the front, Confederate sharpshooters cut holes in the blue line and Logan fell back leaving dead and wounded behind. On the left, McClernand saw some of his men reach rebel works, decided he was breaking through, and sent word to Grant that he could take Vicksburg if supported. Grant doubted McClernand's claim, but he sent the army forward again, remarking later, "This last attack only served to increase our casualties, without giving any benefit whatever."[55] Logan had ample reason to mourn Grant's decision to back McClernand. He suffered 359 casualties, 272 alone from the heavily engaged 3rd Brigade, and 81 from Smith's 1st. Most distressing was the death of Captain Samuel DeGolyer. As Logan charged, DeGolyer's 8th Michigan Artillery unlimbered and belched forth support for the infantry. The fiery Frenchmen, directing his men in clear view of rebel sharpshooters, was killed at his guns.[56]

The assault answered Grant's question as to the possibility of quick victory. Pemberton might be demoralized, but behind prepared fortifications even demoralized men could stop Grant's best. Sergeant O. H. Oldroyd wrote on the 23rd, "The weather is getting hotter, and I fear sickness. . . . If we can keep well, the future has no fear for us."[57] The repulse did not shatter Union morale but the men settled down for a long, hot summer.

For several weeks there were alarms that Pemberton would try to cut his way out, and McPherson warned Logan nightly to keep his pickets "particularly vigilant."[58] Finally with Grant's army approaching 75,000, fears of an assault vanished and men settled down to siege operations.

Life in the trenches was monotonous and hazardous, and

[54]Grant, *Memoirs*, I, 444.
[55]*Ibid.*, 445.
[56]*OR*, Ser. 1, XXIV, pt. 2, 155-156; 163-164.
[57]Oldroyd, *Soldier's Story*, 34.
[58]*OR*, Ser. 1, XXIV, pt. 3, 352.

men kept busy digging to make their lines strong. Daily existence was fraught with perils. Cooking rations in the front lines produced a curl of smoke twisting upward, usually followed by a torrent of enemy fire, often with fatal effect.[59] Water was scarce, wells yielded a muddy ooze, and men were forced to haul it from the Mississippi. As June's sultry weeks passed, Federal trenches inched toward enemy works. Every morning Logan's sappers crawled into an ingenious invention, the sap-roller, and excavating began. The sap-roller, two barrels lashed together, covered with willow saplings and daubed with earth, protected men while digging.[60]

Along Logan's main front elaborate fortifications were built of logs and dirt, with space between where sharpshooters pointed their deadly weapons. All day riflemen were busy, and Logan's artillery, on high ground in the rear, slammed countless rounds into rebel lines. At night naval batteries opened up, lighting the sky with lurid flashes. Mortar shells crisscrossed as they arched upward from the river, reminding men of shooting stars, before they fell on the beleagured city with a crash.[61]

Games and rumors occupied the men while deadly exchanges continued. By June 15 opposing lines were so close that one of Logan's men lobbed a hard-tack biscuit into trenches of the 3rd Louisiana. The biscuit, bearing the word "starvation," came back marked, "Forty days rations and no thanks to you."[62] Men of the 20th Ohio devised a method of luring enemy gunners from behind their parapets. Raising dummies a little above their rifle-pits, they waited until rebel riflemen raised their heads to fire; then a Union volley tore the rebel works, sometimes finding its mark.[63] Fraternization between the opposing armies occurred often, and men of Logan's 8th Illinois, planting a piece of light artillery on a rise behind the lines, were challenged by a single Confederate standing on top of his

[59]Adair, *45th Illinois*, 12.
[60]Crummer, *With Grant*, 103.
[61]Morris, *31st Illinois*, 71.
[62]Oldroyd, *Soldier's Story*, 54. This reminiscence comes from an appendix to Oldroyd's book written by W. H. Tunnard entitled, "Reminiscences of the 3rd Louisiana Infantry in the Trenches in Front of Logan's Division."
[63]*Ibid.*, 34.

fort's wall. Soldiers on both sides spent a short time talking through the quiet night, livened by an occasional shell from the river. Bidding each other good night they returned to their duties.[64]

Rumors were prevalent throughout the seige. Word of Confederate starvation inside Vicksburg was common; mule meat it was reported brought $1.00 a pound. A constant rumor was of Pemberton's breakout. At the same time reports that Johnston was coming with 50,000 to raise the siege were credited by some, scoffed at by others. Nevertheless, this fear was so real that McPherson ordered Logan on June 23 to have a regiment ready to march to Sherman's relief if the rumored attack occurred.[65]

While rumor flowed, and men lured the enemy to their deaths one day and exchanged gossip with them the next, the grim business of siege operations continued. Heat, dust, lack of water, and danger from whizzing missiles, made life tiresome and maddening. To men fresh from the war's most sensational series of flash victories, this was anti-climactic. Back to Logan came some of the wounded from Raymond, and veterans of subsequent action were amused at their timidity. "It is fun to see these newcomers dodge the balls as they zip along," chuckled one grizzled veteran.[66] A particularly dangerous spot was the main road from Logan's headquarters to Grant's command post. The road swung over a high bridge spanning a ravine, and rebels discovering that it was within range, assigned a sharpshooter corps to fire on all crossers. They were so effective that riders, Logan included, were forced to creep quietly to the edge of the cleared space and then spur their mounts across to make cover before the tattoo of minie balls began.[67] The historian of Logan's old 31st remembered "The hardships were not confined to Pemberton's lines. Continuous watching and exposure, scarcity of water, and a broiling sun, annoyed and sickened the assailants. The horrors of the siege

[64]Ms. Diary of Hiram C. Crandall, 5th Iowa Regiment, June 8, 1863, Civil War Diaries, Illinois State Historical Library.

[65]*OR*, Ser. 1, XXIV, pt. 3, 430.

[66]Oldroyd, *Soldier's Story*, 54.

[67]Sylvanus Cadwallader, *Three Years With Grant*, Benjamin P. Thomas (ed.) (New York, 1955), 101.

were everywhere visible."[68] Perhaps the best summary of the long days from May to July came in Second Lieutenant James S. McHenry's simple diary entry for June 19: "Fiting [sic] as usual. Hot and dry. Company lay in camp all day."[69]

Day after weary day they awaited Pemberton's surrender gazing at Vicksburg's courthouse and distant steeples. Most agreed with Sherman who pitied the poor families of the city, especially women and children.[70] Enlistments expired during the siege and many wanted to go home, "but go home they can not until our 'Rabbit is caught.'"[71] Somehow the 4th of July became a target date for Vicksburg's surrender, and men told themselves Union banners would fly in the city by Independence Day.

During the investment Logan became one of the army's greatest characters and perhaps, outside of Grant, its most popular leader. He flatly refused to remain in the rear and his headquarters, called "Siege Battery Logan," was thrust forward belligerently and perhaps ostentatiously toward rebel lines.[72] His first headquarters structure was unsuitable, and Logan had another built of timber filled with dirt, and containing loopholes for defense. It was the highest point in Logan's line and the most advanced point in Grant's army.[73] Though under constant fire Logan spent most of his time in it, despite a glancing wound in the thigh. He seemed determined to share the burden of the siege with his men.

A rough and ready camaraderie was maintained, and Logan, who knew many of his men by name, chatted with them as he moved up and down the trenches. Often a face was remembered from Illinois political days, and once, standing in front of his tent, a passing soldier jogged his memory. Logan ordered the man into the tent and asked, "See here sir, ain't you the man that gave me the damned lie at Enfield in 1860?" "Yes sir." "Well," said Logan, "it was a damned lie."[74]

[68]Morris, *31st Illinois*, 74.
[69]Ms. Diary of James S. McHenry, 2nd Illinois Cavalry, June 19, 1863, Civil War Diaries, Illinois State Historical Library.
[70]W. T. Sherman, *Home Letters of General Sherman*, M. A. DeWolfe Howe (ed.) (New York, 1909), 264.
[71]Oldroyd, *Soldier's Story*, 56.
[72]*OR*, Ser. 1, XXIV, pt. 2, 173.
[73]Ms. Crandall Diary, June 20, 1863, Illinois State Historical Library.
[74]F. W. Woollard to E. L. Bost, April 28, 1909, Woollard Mss.

Though in the lines by day, Logan often rode to Grant's headquarters at night. His visits were officially to see Grant, but in reality he went to share a convivial hour with Colonel William L. Duff, Grant's medical officer. These visits were pleasant intervals, and Logan made the most of them. One night a correspondent attached to Grant's headquarters came upon Logan, "with nothing on him . . . but his hat, shirt, and boots, sitting at a table on which stood a bottle of whisky and a tin cup." Logan was exuberantly playing the violin while a number of Negro roustabouts danced. When the dancers tired, Logan passed around the cup, taking a liberal portion for himself, and dancing continued through the night. "Yet he was not intoxicated from the beginning to the end of the war, so far as came to my knowledge," the astonished writer confessed.[75]

When Logan arrived before Vicksburg, Mary's letters caught up with him. Her first note reported people at Marion "picking your bones severely," but in general politics was quiet.[76] After the drive through Mississippi, with Logan's name echoing through the North, Mary gloated, "Everything is Grant and Logan." She was disgusted with fawning Republicans who had assaulted Logan in the past and now praised him.[77]

Logan's replies were short and irregular, usually broken off when he was called to duty. He simply assured Mary of his health, and spoke with uncertainty of the length of the siege. Sometimes he boasted of his division's nearness to rebel works, and he always spoke with confidence. There is an entirely different tenor to Logan's letters during the Vicksburg campaign. Gone was despair, pessimism, and constant threats to leave the army. Pride in the army's accomplishments and his role in them was obvious.[78]

Nor had Logan's role gone unnoticed. The Chicago *Tribune* admitted it had never been on "friendly relations" with Logan, but it called him "courageous, skillful, and full of pluck. . . . We echo the opinion of his superior that he is a whole division in himself."[79] Grant's opinion of Logan's ability had grown

---

[75]Cadwallader, *Three Years*, 67.
[76]Mary Logan to JAL, May 3, 1863, Logan Mss.
[77]Mary Logan to JAL, June 28, 1863, Logan Mss.
[78]JAL to Mary Logan, May 31, June 24, 1863, Logan Mss.
[79]Chicago *Tribune*, May 27, 1863.

since they crossed the river in May. When he recommended Logan for promotion to major general he wrote, "There is not a more patriotic soldier, braver man, or one more deserving of promotion in this department than General Logan."[80] Even the president, speaking of the army of the West, mentioned Logan as one of the ablest leaders of a campaign he considered "one of the most brilliant in the world."[81]

Writing of distinguished Union generals after the war, journalist William Shanks felt Logan's person had become enshrouded in myth. Logan, one of the most popular men in the army, said Shanks, had taken on an aura of romance. He had become "Black Jack" Logan with his rumored Indian ancestry, flashing eyes, drooping mustache, thundering voice, and proved courage. The role was one he loved to play.[82]

The only major action on the Union line between the assault of May 22 and Pemberton's surrender came from Logan on June 25. Mining became a major activity all along the front, and Logan pushed forward several tunnels in attempts to explode them, tearing a hole in the rebel line. Most were small excavations doing little damage, and some were discovered by defenders who hurled shells on the unfortunate miners. In mid-June, however, Logan determined to push a large tunnel that might break the Confederate line and lead to a general victory. It was pushed deeper than its predecessors and was unobserved by the defenders. Digging proceeded well into June, and on the 24th Logan was satisfied with its proximity to rebel lines. He told McPherson he was ready. The explosion was to go off at 3 o'clock on the 25th and Logan had his 1st Brigade poised to race through the breach once the mine did its work. The 45th Illinois was to lead with the 20th, 31st, and 56th Illinois in reserve. At 3 Jasper Maltby had his 45th set, while across the lines the enemy stood oblivious to impending doom. Suddenly a huge mass of earth surged upward, burying some defenders under mounds of dirt, killing others outright. "It seemed as if all hell had suddenly yawned," but the shock was shrugged off quickly and when Maltby charged, a murder-

---

[80]C. E. Macartney, *Grant and His Generals* (New York, 1953), 311.
[81]Lincoln to I. N. Arnold, May 26, 1863, Lincoln, *Collected Works*, VI, 230.
[82]Shanks, *Recollections*, 197.

ous fire greeted him.[83] As the troops bravely stumbled up the crater's sides, rifles, artillery, and grenades made the gap an inferno and the 45th fell back. In succession the three reserve units poured into the breach and were hurled back with considerable loss. Logan stood near the crater watching the carnage, murmuring, "My God! they are killing my bravest men in that hole."[84] Despite Union artillery support, an advance was impossible and Logan ordered his men out. Mining was abandoned as a way of opening Pemberton's line for infantry.[85]

The most famous event of the great explosion was the arrival of an unexpected visitor in Logan's camp. When the charge went off, several rebel soldiers were hurled into the air, and one Negro, working on Confederate works, was thrown toward Logan. Landing scared but unhurt, he was brought to Logan who asked him how high he went. "Dunno Massa, but I speck 'bout tree mile," he replied. The Negro remained with Logan as a servant, and marched into Vicksburg with him when the siege ended.[86]

July brought desperation to Pemberton, whose food was running low and who had abandoned all hope of escape. He called a council of his commanders and presented two alternatives: crash out, an almost impossible task, or surrender. Surrender won, and on July 3 a white flag went through Logan's lines to Grant. When the messenger went back to Pemberton, McPherson told Logan there would be no cessation of hostilities until the final terms were arranged. No one was taking any chances. But McPherson did ask Logan to clean up his men and put them in shape "so as to present a good soldierly appearance."[87]

That afternoon Grant called a meeting of corps and division commanders to query them on surrender terms. Most, including Logan, favored parole.[88] Later, accompanied by E. O. C.

---

[83]Oldroyd, *Soldier's Story*, 139.

[84]Crummer, *With Grant*, 141.

[85]*OR*, Ser. 1, XXIV, pt. 3, 456; *OR*, Ser. 1, XXIV, pt. 2, 293. Logan exploded another charge, with little effect on July 1.

[86]Dawson, *Logan*, 43.

[87]*OR*, Ser. 1, XXIV, pt. 3, 466.

[88]*Ibid.*, Ser. 1, XXIV, pt. 1, 115.

Ord, McPherson, Logan, and A. J. Smith, Grant walked to a hillside a few hundred yards from rebel parapets. There under a tree, Pemberton met his besieger. Men from both armies lined their works as the two commanders advanced, saluted, and talked. Standing with his three fellow officers, Logan looked out over lines where men exposed themselves in a way that would have invited sure death hours earlier. The meeting was brief and Union leaders returned to await Pemberton's decision.

Grant, unwilling to go through the cost and bother of sending Pemberton's garrison of 31,000 north as prisoners of war, offered parole. Next morning, a grim 4th for the Confederacy, prearranged signals, white flags draped along rebel lines, meant Grant's "Rabbit had been caught."

Logan's command, spruced up and ready to march, was designated lead unit for the advance into the city. McPherson suggested Maltby's 45th Illinois head the column and Logan heartily agreed.[89] The 45th stepped out with pride and Grant, Logan, and McPherson rode together as the army entered the battered city.[90] As they reached the courthouse, Confederate flags came down and the regimental flag of the 45th Illinois waved aloft. At sight of the Union banner "in a single moment the excitement became so great that you scarcely heard yourself talk. The whole division belched out in one glad shout."[91] Cheers rang through the shattered buildings and many broke enthusiastically into the "Battle Cry of Freedom."[92]

Logan was named by Grant temporary commander of the city with orders to provide guards to prevent prisoners from escaping and to protect against looting.

That night silence was so oppressive that many found it difficult to sleep, and others hardly able to realize the weary days had ended, sat around talking of home and an end to the war.[93] Next day, his duties as occupation chief just beginning, Logan wrote Mary: "The victory is the greatest triumph of

---

[89]*Ibid.*, Ser. 1, XXIV, pt. 3, 476.

[90]Adair, *45th Illinois*, 12.

[91]Ms. Unknown Soldier's Diary, 26th Illinois Infantry, July 4, 1863, Civil War Diaries, Illinois State Historical Library.

[92]Horace Greeley, *The American Conflict* (Chicago, 1867), II, 316.

[93]Ms. Crandall Diary, July 4, 1863, Illinois State Historical Library.

modern times. . . . My division has immortalized itself in the eyes of the whole army."[94]

These Westerners had done a great deal of "hewing" since October, 1861, and at last the "father of waters rolled unvexed to the sea." For Logan there had been great changes since the depression at Memphis five months earlier, and he wrote, "Daylight seemed to be breaking at last."[95]

---

[94]JAL to Mary Logan, July 5, 1863, Logan Mss.
[95]Logan, *Great Conspiracy*, 515.

CHAPTER XI

FORTY ROUNDS

Vicksburg lay in ruins and a multitude of problems confronted Logan as post commander. Though he held the position only sixteen days, his record was almost universally praised. Within a week of Vicksburg's fall Logan named a three-man committee composed of one Union officer, one Union chaplain, and one reliable citizen, to tour the town, discover needy cases, and issue provisions.[1] Logan received some visitors himself to ascertain their wants, and he was deluged with pleas for assistance.

Not all went smoothly, however, and Logan protested to Grant over "the manner in which Confederate officers are permitted to intimidate their servants in the presence of officers appointed to examine said servants." The policy of issuing passes to Negroes to go along with masters on trips outside of Vicksburg also brought a strong protest. Grant agreed with Logan's position and the practice was stopped.[2] Generally Logan's administration ran harmoniously and his troops behaved themselves so well that even Confederate observers remarked that Logan's division "conducted itself in an exemplary manner."[3]

A lull in the war having arrived, Logan ached to go home. Many have written that Logan went North in July, 1863, at the request of influential politicians. Some even include Lincoln on the list.[4] There is no evidence to support this. Yates had visited the army in front of Vicksburg and perhaps asked Logan to speak in Illinois, and Lincoln did show some interest in Logan's speeches later in the summer, but when Logan left the army he went home for reasons of health. Throughout the

---

[1]*OR*, Ser. 1, XXIV, pt. 3, 501-502.
[2]*Ibid.*, 483.
[3]Earl Schenck Miers, *Web of Victory: Grant at Vicksburg* (New York, 1955), 296.
[4]Andrews, *Logan*, 440; Dawson, *Logan*, 46; Mary Logan, *Reminiscences*, 141.

Vicksburg campaign old wounds bothered him, and on July 20, Special Orders 196, from Grant, gave leave so that Logan could "recover his health."[5] General John E. Smith relieved Logan as post commander and Logan started home.

In summer, 1863, anti-war feeling, despite the twin victories of early July, seemed on the increase. The new conscription order had been resisted violently in New York, and in the West Copperheadism appeared to be growing. Yet, Egypt's record of war support remained excellent. By early autumn, Egypt's ten southernmost counties, all from Logan's old district, had run up an excess of 50% over their troop quotas.[6] Nevertheless, anti-war sentiment remained strong there. Many deserters were rumored hiding in the region, and Brigadier General N. B. Buford wrote a fellow officer he had reason to believe there were 400 armed deserters in Williamson County.[7] Mary Logan also reported much activity from peace men, all of whom she labeled Knights of the Golden Circle. According to her, a "reign of terror" existed, and there were numerous threats of violence against Logan when he returned.[8] It was to this divided section that Logan, by 1863 a staunch war supporter, returned. He reached Cairo as the campaign for local offices was getting under way.

For a week Logan remained in Carbondale resting and visiting family and friends. After that brief respite, his leave turned into a whirlwind speaking tour. In his two previous trips to Illinois since war began, Logan had remained almost completely silent, but, by 1863, his earlier pessimism had turned to optimism and he took the stump to whip up war support. Many soldiers had been furloughed home after Vicksburg. Logan met them everywhere, and his audiences contained many men who had followed him against rebel guns. Groups of these servicemen called on him to address local gatherings to "set the citizens of this county *right* on the great issues of the day." Advising Logan that *"no other man can do it,"* writers spoke of fearful anti-war activities and begged him

---

[5]*OR*, Ser. 1, XXIV, pt. 3, 537.
[6]Cole, *Era of the Civil War*, 279.
[7]N. B. Buford to Jacob Ammen, June 4, 1863, Jacob Ammen Mss., Illinois State Historical Library.
[8]Mary Logan, *Reminiscences*, 141-145.

to speak. "From the respect they *once* entertained for you, they will listen to your admonition."⁹

Logan accepted several of these invitations, and on July 31 delivered one of his most famous speeches. Coming at the war's half-way point, this address at DuQuoin, Illinois, stands as a barometer of Logan's thoughts. "I do not propose to make a political speech. I am not canvassing this part of the country for the purpose of promoting any political organization," Logan began, his voice reaching the edge of a crowd of 5,000.¹⁰ "Since I have been in the Army I have at all times eschewed politics." Setting the stage in this manner, Logan turned away from partisan affairs to the war and the civilian's role. He demanded support from the home front and condemned all those who opposed the war and called it "unholy, unrighteous, or unconstitutional." Lashing out at the Knights of the Golden Circle, he called it "one of the foulest, most damnable, hellborn conspiracies that ever was organized."

Turning to the South, he maintained the only reason rebels gave for secession was Lincoln's election. Admitting he opposed Lincoln in 1860, Logan denied this as an adequate reason. He also denied the constitutionality of secession and attacked the Confederacy as the force that "stopped you men of the Northwest from taking your produce down to New Orleans." Returning to the Copperheads he sarcastically cried,

> they forget that Jeff Davis and his crowd are doing anything wrong. Oh no! They are honest people, they all go to church. But we [war Democrats] are a set of wicked devils. . . . I am for peace as much as any man can be, but I will tell you what sort of peace I am for. I am not for a piece of a country.

Logan discussed charges that Union troops had been ravaging the South. No one ever heard of an army in the field marching through an area without doing some damage. Things of that nature happened despite precautions. "The boys had nothing to eat but two crackers a day and half a ration of

---

⁹T. O. Spencer to JAL, July 30, 1863, Logan Mss.

¹⁰John A. Logan, *Speech of General Logan on Return to Illinois*, iv, 5. Logan's speech is 32 pp. long and all the quotations used come from it. The speech was translated into German and distributed to Germans throughout the Northwest.

meat. I told them to take hogs, chickens, and cows, and I'll do it again," he roared to the applause of listening troops.

He asked the rebels to acknowledge their allegiance to the Federal Government, stop the war, and "walk back as a whipped child" to be received again by a fond parent. But he cautioned his listeners: "I don't want any man to understand that I am striking at any party. I only strike at individuals who are trying to ruin the country." Then in a loud voice he challenged his former Democratic friends:

> I want them to tell me how they know I am an Abolitionist. . . . Why, I will tell you the reason. It is because we are in the Army and Abraham Lincoln is president. That is the reason. These men don't know enough or don't want to know that Abraham Lincoln because he is president, don't own the Government. This war ain't fighting for Mr. Lincoln. It is fighting for the Union, for the Government.

He said the fact that Negroes ran away did not make him an abolitionist. Of slavery: "That machine is gone up, played out. There is no doubt of that and the people of the North are not responsible. The Southern gentlemen have done it themselves." While on the subject of "Southern gentlemen," Logan demanded that at war's end the leaders of the rebellion be deprived of the constitutional rights they enjoyed before the war. He flatly opposed restoration of full rights, fearing a return to governmental control by the South.

Coming to the end of his long speech, Logan appealed to Northern citizens to discourage desertions. He asked families to say to the troops, "Go on boys, God bless you. . . . Be for your Government, in spite of what anybody may say." If Northerners were united, Logan believed, "and stood upon one platform, as we do in the army, this rebellion would be crushed in 90 days."

Finally, returning to politics, Logan again assured his auditors:

> I told you today that I did not intend to make a political speech, and would belong to no political party until the war is over. I meant just what I said, I am only for the Union, right or wrong. . . . I have learned in the army the best lesson I ever learned in the world. . . . I have stood for hours

under the hottest fire, where bullets were flying like hail, and cannon balls were whizzing past my head every moment. I have seen Republicans stand by my side and the Democrat and the Abolitionist. I have seen the Democrat shot down and buried in the same grave with the Republican and the Abolitionist. They are all fighting for the same country, the same ground, the same Constitution.

An immense roar greeted his final, "I thank you very kindly for your attention."

In this speech Logan seems to stand midway between parties. He still considered himself a Democrat, but he had no patience with Democrats who called for peace. Though a Democrat, he was willing to speak for Republicans who supported the war. His remarks made it evident that he was no fiery abolitionist, deeply concerned with the Negro's welfare, but his open advocacy of freedom for the slaves took him far beyond most western Democrats. Finally, Logan's sentiments on post-war terms for the South offer some hint of his growing hostility toward an easy peace which would allow Southerners again to control the Democratic Party and the nation. He had climbed the hill of public life a Democrat, but in 1863 Logan reached the divide. Thereafter he moved slowly toward the Republican horizon.

Logan's DuQuoin speech, circulated widely in pamphlet form, brought a flood of requests for speeches. A hundred citizens of Richview, Illinois asked him to speak to them "without distinction of party," and neighboring states joined the rush.[11] Logan covered Egypt with his words, speaking in Cairo and Carbondale to enthusiastic groups. All his speeches were circulated and used as campaign literature by local Union candidates. Abandoning Egypt in early August, Logan rode northward to Chicago, where he spoke on the 10th. A huge crowd assembled at Courthouse Square and Logan's appearance was greeted with wild cheers and doubtless a few unreported boos. This address was almost a replica of the DuQuoin talk as Logan told his audience he did not "propose to discuss party politics." He again dwelt on three main topics: Copperheads, Southern

---

[11] 100 Citizens of Richview, Illinois to JAL, Aug. 1, 1863, Logan Mss.; John Caldwell to JAL, Aug. 3, 1863, Logan Mss.

treason, and Northern civilians. Logan asked that Northern peace men be put in front of the Union army, "where they will get justice," and called for punishment of Southern "traitors."[12] This speech too was printed. Turned out by the Chicago *Tribune* in pamphlet form, it was circulated through the army and the Northwest at $2.00 a hundred.[13]

Logan's sweep through Illinois and his support of the administration reached Lincoln's attention when letters arrived asking for an extension of his leave. Several Republicans, convinced Logan was "doing much good to our cause here in Illinois," asked the president to let Logan tour portions of the state not yet visited. One writer who had spoken to Logan said he was writing because Logan "did not like to ask for the leave himself." This correspondent added, "Logan calls things by their right names and his speeches will do a world of good in this state as showing the spirit and temper of the army." In response to these requests, Lincoln asked Stanton to extend Logan's leave "unless you know a reason to the contrary." Stanton did not, and Logan stayed in Illinois until August.[14]

After another round of speeches, Logan returned to the army at Vicksburg where he resumed command of his division. He was not restored to command of the city's occupation forces since his veteran division was needed for other purposes. The division had seen a shift in brigade commanders while Logan visited Illinois. Leggett commanded the 1st Brigade, replacing Smith, Manning Force of the 20th Ohio led the 2nd Brigade, while Jasper Maltby led the 3rd. Logan's artillery remained under capable Major Charles Stolbrand.

Logan's first movement after his return was a reconnaissance into Louisiana in search of rebel raiders. The division crossed the river and marched about 90 miles to Monroe. It found hostile civilians, but no troops, and returned to Vicksburg in early September.[15] Most of the month Logan lay in camp doing picket and provost duty and working on fortifications.

---

[12]Ms. "Great Union Speech" at Chicago, Aug. 10, 1863, Logan Mss.; *Illinois State Journal*, Aug. 13, 1863.
[13]Philip Kinsley, *The Chicago Tribune: Its First Hundred Years* (New York, 1943), II, 282.
[14]Lincoln, *Collected Works*, VI, 382-383.
[15]*OR*, Ser. 1, XXX, pt. 2, 803-805.

In late September the efforts of John and Mary Logan bore fruit when Hibe Cunningham arrived at Vicksburg. He was welcomed coolly by Logan, who let him remain at division headquarters.[16] Mary was overjoyed and asked that Hibe come to Illinois, but Logan was determined to keep him at the front, perhaps to make amends for earlier actions. In October, with his command slated for an expedition into central Mississippi, Logan agreed to send Hibe to Illinois, exacting the promise that he return to the army.[17]

With the young man on his way north, Logan broke camp on October 14 and moved toward Canton, a small town north of Jackson, rumored base of Confederate guerillas. Logan's division joined James M. Tuttle's infantry division and a cavalry brigade, all under McPherson, in scouting the area. They were in the field for six days and skirmished several times with small bands of rebels, always driving them back. Unable to find large Confederate concentrations, McPherson moved his men back to Vicksburg where tiresome garrison duty began again.

Meanwhile, far east of Vicksburg at Chattanooga, great changes were taking place in the Western war. The Union army, beaten at Chickamauga, had fallen back to Chattanooga, where Bragg had it bottled up. Grant, inactive along the Mississippi, was sent to uncork the bottle. Sherman was named commander of the Army of the Tennessee and sent to reinforce Grant. Sherman's elevation left vacant permanent command of the 15th Corps (Frank Blair served as temporary commander) and on October 26 Grant wired Halleck recommending Logan's assignment to command Sherman's old corps.[18] One day later General Order 349 was signed by Stanton, and Logan received orders to report to Sherman in Chattanooga as major general commanding the 15th Corps.[19]

It took some time to complete the command change, and it

---

[16]There is no mention in Logan's letters or in Mary's *Reminiscences* as to the method of Hibe's escape from Confederate service. He simply appears at Logan's headquarters in October without further explanation.

[17]JAL to Mary Logan, Oct. 12, 1863, Logan Mss.

[18]*OR*, Ser. 1, XXXI, pt. 1, 739.

[19]*Ibid.*, 759, 768.

was not until November 15 that Logan boarded a steamer for the trip north. M. B. Leggett succeeded Logan as division chief, and the 3rd Division paraded for its ex-commander. At the review's conclusion, Logan, with deep feeling, addressed his old comrades of the Vicksburg campaign. He bade them an affectionate farewell and received a rousing ovation from men who were devoted to him because of "his uniform sympathy and kindness, his readiness to aid us in any emergency, his well recognized ability and soldierly qualities, and by his stern uncompromising patriotism." "General Logan," the division felt, "had greatly endeared himself to us all. We reposed almost implicit confidence in him . . . and parted with him with deep regret."[20]

To reach Chattanooga Logan had to sail to Cairo, up the Cumberland to Nashville, and then overland. The trip up-river was leisurely. Logan, reflecting on the send-off at Vicksburg, wrote Mary proudly, "You ought to have witnessed the scene at Vicksburg when I left my old division. The crowd gathered till the streets were filled and the air rang with farewells. . . . God blesses were enough to melt a stone. . . . If I can only win the confidence of my new command I am content."[21]

At Cairo, Logan waited a few days for transports, taking advantage of the stopover to deliver another Union speech. He was cheered by the success of the Egyptian Union candidates in recent elections and wrote Mary: "What does Josh and Co. think of the elections? Can they see it? If not they will some day soon I hope. The whole army is rejoiced at the happy result."[22]

Logan arrived too late to fight at Chattanooga. Grant had broken Bragg's vise when Logan reached southwestern Tennessee. When he caught up with his new command it was encamped near Chattanooga preparing to march to Knoxville to relieve General Ambrose Burnside's besieged garrison.

Temporary command of the 15th Corps was still in the hands of Frank Blair, like Logan a politician. When Logan arrived, he asked Sherman to let Blair lead the corps on the

[20]Richard Howard, *124th Illinois*, 158-159.
[21]JAL to Mary Logan, Nov. 16, 1863, Logan Mss.
[22]JAL to Mary Logan, Nov. 21, 1863, Logan Mss.; *Tribune Almanac, 1864*, 62. Seven Egyptian counties went Union in local elections in 1863.

march to Knoxville since he was familiar with it. In addition he felt Blair should have the honor of finishing the campaign. While he awaited the corps' return, Logan remained in the Chattanooga area. He wrote Mary forecasting a quick end after "one or two more decisive battles." If the rebellion continued after that "it will become a war of desolation and almost extermination." "All seem to feel," he wrote, "that much longer obstinacy on their part will justify any means to be used to destroy them."[23] Strange words from a man who had once favored compromise at any cost.

When Blair returned from Knoxville, the command change was made, and Blair, who was going to Washington to claim the House seat he had never resigned, turned over the corps to its new commander. Logan, Blair felt, "behaved very handsomely and I was not sorry . . . to relinquish the Corps . . . to one who had shown me such good feeling."[24]

Only two of the corps' four divisions returned with Blair on December 11; the others were still north of Chattanooga on the march. Logan did not wait for them to arrive, and taking one-half of his new command he marched them to Scottsboro, Alabama, corps headquarters. By the 17th the last two divisions had arrived and Logan had his first opportunity to view the entire corps. The 15th Corps, formerly led by Sherman, had an illustrious war career in the West. One soldier on being assigned to it wrote home, "we have just learned that now we are in the famous 15th Army Corps and we are very proud of it."[25] Logan intended to maintain that pride. When he took command, the corps' divisions were led by former Prussian officer, Peter J. Osterhaus; pre-war drill sergeant Morgan L. Smith; Logan's old friend, John E. Smith; and Sherman's boyhood friend, Hugh Ewing. The corps numbered 16,973 present for duty.[26]

Logan's first assignment on settling down at Scottsboro on the Tennessee River was the building and maintenance of a

---

[23]JAL to Mary Logan, Nov. 29, Dec. 4, 1863, Logan Mss.

[24]W. E. Smith, *The Francis Preston Blair Family in Politics* (New York, 1933), II, 171.

[25]Theodore F. Upson, *With Sherman to the Sea: The Civil War Letters, Diaries, and Reminiscences of Theodore F. Upson*, Oscar O. Winther (ed.) (Baton Rouge, Louisiana, 1943), 69.

[26]*OR*, Ser. 1, XXXI, pt. 3, 564.

pontoon bridge. He was also charged with selecting winter quarters at places where easy collection of supplies was possible. By a bitterly cold December 20 Logan's headquarters was established at Scottsboro, where he was joined by Ewing's 4th Division. Morgan Smith's 2nd was encamped slightly north at Bellefonte, while John Smith's 3rd lay west of Logan at Larkinsville. Osterhaus' 1st Division held Woodville a few miles west of Larkinsville.[27]

In late December, Sherman received permission to go home for Christmas. He sent Logan advice for disposition of the corps. If good weather lasted, Sherman wrote, Logan should place his army at Athens, Huntsville, Paint Rock, and Larkinsville, with outposts along the Tennessee covering fords and ferries. In addition to these instructions, Sherman told Logan, "I think I see one or two quick blows that will astonish the South."[28]

Sherman's instructions on troop distribution could not be carried out due to a drastic change in the weather. Logan pushed a brigade to Huntsville and sent Osterhaus with part of his command to explore Paint Rock and Flint River Valleys, but roads were too muddy to permit a major movement. Osterhaus' mission brought welcome news of a good supply of provisions in Paint Rock Valley.[29]

Christmas and New Year's Day passed accompanied by sleet and snow, but the first week of the new year brought some warmth to Logan's area. The heat was supplied by bridges fired around Huntsville by Confederate raiders. Four bridges were destroyed, but the raiders, believed to be operating along the Tennessee River across from Decatur, retired without doing further damage. Logan's greatest bother during January was the difficulty of securing rations. The area he occupied, thought at first to be bountiful, did not offer adequate provisions, and the railroad to Chattanooga and Nashville was undependable. He was finally forced to complain to Grant and advise him, "The men are suffering."[30]

By mid-January, despite the weather and a dearth of sup-

[27]*Ibid.*
[28]*Ibid.*, 459.
[29]*Ibid.*, 543.
[30]*Ibid.*, Ser. 1, XXXII, pt. 2, 24.

plies, Logan was forced into activity. Sherman had been sent by Grant into Mississippi to strike eastward from Vicksburg to Meridian. To prevent Confederate reinforcements from reaching General Polk at Meridian, Logan and General George H. Thomas, commander of the Army of the Cumberland, were ordered to feint toward Rome, Georgia. On the 24th, Morgan Smith moved his division from Bellefonte across the Tennessee toward Georgia. For eleven days he ranged the Alabama-Georgia border, destroying anything that would aid Confederate troops. After Smith returned, Logan reported to Grant that a great many people in eastern Alabama had expressed a desire to join the Alabama Union regiment.[31] Logan's feint was not successful in its purpose since Joe Johnston, Confederate commander in Georgia, had already sent two divisions to Meridian, but it kept him from dispatching others. Nor was the feint necessary to confuse Confederate leaders. Their intelligence reports in early February constantly mentioned Logan's 15th Corps as a part of Sherman's force in Mississippi. It was not until February 7 that they discovered their mistake.[32]

When Smith's men returned, Logan had shifted his headquarters to Huntsville and the corps was greatly reduced in number due to the absence of furloughed veterans. Cotton speculators had poured into the district and Logan was forced to proclaim: "All cotton speculators are ordered out of the limits of the 15th Corps."[33]

During the winter Logan received little news from home, but he did hear of a "Logan for Governor" proposal. The Republican Cairo *News* called for Logan as its party's candidate in 1864. Another party organ, printing the Cairo paper's endorsement, reported it had been told by an army friend of Logan's that the general did not care to run. The paper added that Logan did support the Union ticket.[34] "Logan for Governor" talk also filtered through the army. In late 1863 General John M. Palmer, another Illinois politician-soldier, at the front near Chattanooga, heard that "Logan stands a good chance for

---

[31]*Ibid.*, Ser. 1, XXXII, pt. 1, 128.
[32]Grant, *Memoirs*, II, 42; *OR*, Ser. 1, XXXII, pt. 2, 672, 688.
[33]*OR*, Ser. 1, XXXII, pt. 2, 192.
[34]Cairo *News* in Jacksonville *Journal*, Mar. 17, 1864.

governor. . . . He out of the way, Oglesby would start with the
advantage. . . . McClernand is rather under a cloud at present."[35] As events would prove, this prophecy was amazingly
accurate.

This speculation no doubt pleased Logan, but it did not lure
him from the army. Furthermore, the first week in February
he had little time to think of Illinois politics. No sooner had
Smith returned than Logan was ordered by Grant to march
his command northeastward into Tennessee. Grant decided to
strike General James Longstreet's Confederates near Knoxville, and Logan was ordered to send all troops, not needed to
guard the railroad, to Chattanooga to relieve Thomas there.
On the 11th, Logan started fourteen regiments toward Chattanooga, but the same day Grant cancelled Thomas' proposed
movement. He decided Longstreet would be best left alone.[36]
After changing his mind, Grant decided to start Thomas in
another direction, south against Dalton, Georgia. On the 12th
Grant ordered Thomas, reinforced by Logan's regiments, to
strike at Dalton, but "Slow Trot" Thomas held up his advance.
By the 21st Thomas still had not moved and Grant demanded
that he start immediately. Logan too was growing restive.
With Thomas stationary in Chattanooga, he wrote Grant "re-
spectfuly" requesting his troops' return as they were needed to
build and patrol the railroad.[37] Thomas finally moved on the
23rd and the enemy fell back without a battle, but with provisions hard to acquire, "Slow Trot" soon returned to Chattanooga. As soon as Thomas' expedition returned, Grant had
Logan's men detached and, badly fatigued, they rejoined Logan
on March 1.

While Logan was trying to get his men back from Thomas,
a new nuisance crept into his district. On the 26th he telegraphed Grant that a major of colored troops was at Huntsville "capturing Negroes with or without their consent." Logan
further commented that if these people were forced into the
army "it will entirely stop the cultivation of farms that were
being prepared for crops by loyal men." Grant immediately

[35]George T. Palmer, *A Conscientious Turncoat; The Story of John M.
Palmer, 1817-1900* (New Haven, Connecticut, 1941), 130.
[36]*OR*, Ser. 1, XXXII, pt. 2, 343; Grant, *Memoirs*, II, 43.
[37]*OR*, Ser. 1, XXXII, pt. 2, 461.

instructed Logan to stop the impressment and encourage farm-ing in the region.[38] In spite of these bothersome affairs Logan was able to write: "I am well and getting along first rate with my command."[39]

His relations with Huntsville's citizens, however, were a different matter and brought nothing but complaints. Logan was annoyed by locals in quest of permission to travel, and newsman Sylvanus Cadwallader reported riding to Nashville with several Huntsville ladies.[40] This incessant civilian bother prompted Logan to report: "This place, although a pleasant looking place, is the meanest place for complaints of citizens that I have ever seen."[41]

On March 3 an important shift took place in Union com-mand west of the Appalachians. Grant, promoted to lieutenant general, was ordered East to find a winning combination on the Potomac, and he recommended Sherman as his successor in the West. McPherson was brought from Vicksburg to re-place Sherman as head of the Army of the Tennessee, and command of McPherson's 17th Corps, at Grant's recommen-dation, was given to Logan.[42] The latter change brought a lengthy discussion before it was nullified. On March 15 the president wrote Grant asking that Frank Blair be returned to the 15th Corps and the army chief replied, "General Logan commands the corps referred to in your dispatch. I will see General Sherman within a few days and consult him about the transfer." On the 17th Grant advised Lincoln that Sherman consented to Logan's transfer to the 17th Corps and Blair's appointment to the 15th. Grant no doubt thought Logan would be happy to be reunited with his old division, still in the 17th Corps, but the transfer brought an appeal from Logan to the president nine days later. "I understand by the papers," Logan telegraphed, "that it is contemplated to make a change of com-manders of the 15th and 17th Army Corps, so as to transfer me to the 17th. I hope this will not be done. I fully understand the organization of the 15th Corps now . . . and earnestly hope

---

[38]*Ibid.*, 477.
[39]JAL to Mary Logan, Feb. 11, 1864, Logan Mss.
[40]Cadwallader, *Three Years*, 165.
[41]JAL to Mary Logan, Mar. 4, 1864, Logan Mss.
[42]Grant, *Memoirs*, II, 46.

that the change may not be made."[43] A week later when nothing had been done in the matter Logan wrote Mary calling the proposed switch "an act of injustice to me."[44] The following day Grant, unwilling to upset the western army in a command fight, notified Sherman that Blair would go to the 17th and Logan would keep the 15th.

While he struggled to retain the corps to which he had become attached, Logan kept sharp watch for rebels along the south bank of the Tennessee. There was a great deal of activity on the river around Whitesburg and a crossing seemed imminent. In mid-March, Nathan Bedford Forrest, the terror of isolated Union garrisons, was reported to command a large force operating out of Somerville, and Logan cautioned his commanders to "patrol the river well." On March 22, General Grenville M. Dodge, commanding the 16th Corps, telegraphed Logan that Forrest was reported preparing to attack Decatur the following day and tear up the railroad. The rebel assault did not develop, however, and the month ended peacefully.

At the end of March Logan, in excellent spirits, anxiously awaited initiation of Sherman's spring campaign. Winter's icy blasts had disappeared, and the dawn of a lovely Southern spring prompted Logan to tell Mary:

> I am now enjoying good health and feel buoyant as we prepare for an exciting campaign. . . . My command is in excellent condition and eager to be moving, which is much better for soldiers than lying in camps. When in camps they become indolent and study mischief, and not only study it but perpetrate it a good deal.[45]

The mischievous men of the 15th Corps were a colorful collection of western veterans. Logan's regiments were a potpourri of the great Northwest. Two regiments from Iowa's plains joined ten from Ohio. Missouri contributed eleven, many of them husky Germans who followed officers like Hugo Wangelin and Clemens Landgraeber. Indiana gave six Hoosier regiments, while one each came from Minnesota and Wisconsin. Closest to Logan's heart were the eleven Illinois units. Men

[43]OR, Ser. 1, XXXII, pt. 3, 156; Lincoln, Collected Works, VII, 248.
[44]JAL to Mary Logan, Mar. 30, 1864, Logan Mss.
[45]Ibid.

from Egypt marched side by side with central Illinois farmers and rowdy Irishmen from the streets of Chicago.

From one of the Irishmen, a veteran of the 26th Illinois, came a regimental song, taken from the popular war tune "Abraham's Daughter." Tired of the old words, the Gaelic troubadour sang:

"Oh, I belong to the Fifteenth Corps,
and don't you think I oughta?
For I'm going down to Washington
To court old Abraham's daughter."[46]

Pride in the corps and in the ruggedness of the western army was evident in the acquisition of a badge for the 15th Corps. When Hooker's 12th Corps reached Chattanooga from Virginia, another 15th Corps soldier, inevitably an Irishman, stopped to stare at the Easterners' corps badge, a five pointed star. "Are you all major generals?" he asked. They explained the star was their corps badge and inquired "What's your badge?"

The Irishman patted his ammunition pouch and replied proudly, "Badge is it? There be Jasus—forty rounds in the cartridge box and twenty in the pocket." When Logan took command of the 15th he heard the story and ordered an engraving of the box with "40 rounds" on it adopted as corps badge.[47]

While Logan's men sang their songs and perpetrated mischief, they took pride in their unit. Men of the 100th Indiana boasted of their "strict military life." "It greatly increased the efficiency of the Regiment and was for the good of the service," wrote the Hoosier regiment's historian.[48] To keep the men occupied instead of studying mischief when in camp, Logan supported Chaplain Joseph C. Thomas' plan to establish a loan library system. Logan wrote the chaplain that the reading plan met with his "hearty approval."[49]

[46]Upson, *With Sherman*, 100.
[47]Lloyd Lewis, *Sherman, Fighting Prophet* (New York, 1932), 317.
[48]E. J. Sherlock, *Memorabilia of the Marches and Battles in Which the One Hundredth Regiment of Indiana Infantry Volunteers took an Active Part, 1861-1865* (Kansas City, Missouri, 1896), 74.
[49]Carroll H. Quenzel, "Books for the Boys in Blue," *Journal of the Illinois State Historical Society*, XLIV, No. 3 (Autumn, 1951), 226.

By April time for reading books was running short. Sherman expected Grant to order his advance into Georgia on the 25th and he struggled to prepare his vast army of 100,000 for the campaign. Logan aided in cutting wood for the railroad, and in mid-April was told to collect his transportation and supply facilities, throw out surplus baggage, and place the corps in condition to march.[50]

In April, while Sherman worked to organize his men for the advance, a feud between Logan and George H. Thomas, commander of the Army of the Cumberland, erupted and was temporarily settled. When Grant went north in March to assume his new command, he asked Sherman to ride to Cincinnati with him to discuss future movements in the West. While Sherman was gone, Logan and Thomas scrapped. Thomas, in the Chattanooga area, ran the Nashville-Chattanooga Railroad and maintained close control over its use. When Logan discovered that Army of the Tennessee officers travelling over Thomas' tracks had to obtain passes from Thomas' headquarters, he exploded. "This brought on a conflict between Thomas and Logan, at first no bigger than your hand, but finally growing into a matter of considerable moment," wrote the onlooking Dodge.[51] Logan, ever jealous of his position, requested equal authority for all armies on military railroads. Sherman satisfied Logan by ordering his demands put into effect, and soothed Thomas by telling him "the slights were unintentional on your part."[52] Though Sherman's actions seemed to have ended the difficulty, Thomas and Logan maintained a hearty mutual dislike. The feud slumbered and would explode later with major consequences.

The Thomas affair settled, Logan devoted himself to preparations for the spring campaign. He had about 12,000 men in winter camps along the Huntsville-Larkinsville line, and by the last week in April they stood ready to march. Looking over his command, Logan proudly told Mary, "I think I have the best corps in the army and all seem to think well of me, and

[50]OR, Ser. 1, XXXII, pt. 3, 401.
[51]Grenville M. Dodge, *Personal Recollections of General W. T. Sherman* (Des Moines, Iowa, 1902), 9.
[52]Lewis, *Sherman*, 346; OR, Sec. 1, XXXII, pt. 3, 490.

desire no change to be made." Three weeks later, on the eve of the advance he wrote, "Everyone in good shape and think campaign may be a great victory."[53]

Logan's division commanders remained the same with one exception. Sherman's friend Hugh Ewing had asked for relief during the winter and had been sent to Louisville. When the Georgia campaign began, Sherman refused to restore Ewing, believing General William Harrow who had led the division through hard winter months should lead it into Georgia. Otherwise, Osterhaus and the two Smiths remained. On April 28 Logan received orders from McPherson to begin moving his command toward Chattanooga with full equipment.[54] John E. Smith's 3rd Division was assigned garrison duty along the railroad in Alabama and Tennessee, and disgustedly watched as Osterhaus, Morgan Smith, and Harrow moved their commands out toward a juncture with Sherman's entire force at Chattanooga.

The long winter's wait was over. Logan's veterans left arduous guard duty and marched to begin the campaign most of them were certain would end the war. They reached Chattanooga on May 5 and established camps where they deposited surplus baggage. On the 6th, Logan marched his men southward and halted at Lee's and Gordon's Mills on the south bank of West Chickamauga Creek. Sherman's sabre was raised; when it descended it would strike the heart of the Confederacy, bringing that proud foe to its knees.

53JAL to Mary Logan, April 6, 25, 1864, Logan Mss.
54OR, Ser. 1, XXXII, pt. 3, 524.

CHAPTER XII

FLANKING THE DEVIL

Spring had come to north Georgia when Sherman's army slashed southward May 7. The Army of the Tennessee swung through fields of wild flowers as it moved down the Union right. Sherman started 98,000 men in motion in three armies: Schofield's Army of the Ohio on the left, Thomas' Cumberlanders in the center, and McPherson's Army of the Tennessee on the right. To meet Sherman in this deadly springtime game Joe Johnston had mustered 60,000 veteran troops.

Johnston was a defensive master and his fortifications at Buzzard Roost Gap, near Dalton, were deemed by Sherman too formidable for a head-on assault. Therefore, while Thomas and Schofield occupied Johnston at the gap, Sherman began the first move in a series that came to be as formalized as a dance. He swung McPherson wide around Johnston's left and sent him racing for Resaca, a rail hub eighteen miles in the Confederate rear. The men of the Army of the Tennessee were to become Sherman's prize pedestrians and he hoped the rapid Tennesseans would cut off Johnston's rail line, forcing him out of the hills into flat country to the east where numerical superiority could smash the rebels.

Logan, moving on McPherson's left flank, marched to the western entrance of Gordon's Springs Gap, and the following day he shot the gap and passed through Villanow. That night he camped near the spot where Snake Creek cuts its way through Chattoogata Mountain. On the 9th Logan left most of his transportation at Snake Creek and marched through the gap "in fighting trim," moving along behind Dodge's 16th Corps.[1]

Logan moved forward until he reached the crossroads two miles southwest of Resaca where he halted and deployed to support Dodge. The 16th Corps advanced slowly hoping to

[1] OR Ser. 1, XXXVIII, pt. 3, 90. Dodge's Corps and Blair's 17th Corps joined Logan's 15th in forming the Army of the Tennessee.

sever the Confederate route of retreat. Word reached Sherman from McPherson that he was closing on Resaca and Sherman whooped, "I've got Joe Johnston dead!"[2] Events at Resaca proved otherwise. On approaching rebel lines, McPherson decided enemy fortifications were too strong for immediate attack and he fell back to await reinforcements. Disappointed, Sherman regretted the failure to cut off Johnston and rushed Thomas and Schofield toward Resaca. Johnston, ever cagey, slipped away ahead of Sherman and when the Union army united, Johnston was ready at Resaca. The delay on the 9th produced a controversial story of Logan's action. Shanks, New York *Tribune* correspondent, reported that Logan was "thoroughly disgusted" by McPherson's refusal to strike. Logan, insisted Shanks, demanded to be allowed to go forward immediately, promising he could take Resaca with his corps alone.[3] On the other hand, Logan himself later wrote: "The attempt to break the railroad at Resaca, and thus cut off the retreat of the enemy, failed, not because of the timidity of anyone, as has been unjustly suggested, but because the place was found so completely fortified."[4] When he wrote his report during the war Logan merely stated: "The movement not being successful, I fell back in the evening."[5] The difference in stories cannot be accounted for. It is perhaps due to Shanks' desire for a good story or Logan's post-war desire to protect his friend McPherson.

Logan fell back to Sugar Valley at dusk and drew up a line crossing the road from Villanow and guarding Snake Creek Gap. All day long on the 10th Logan held position in front of the gap. Skirmishing kept up a steady sputter of rifle fire and, fearing an attack that afternoon, Logan moved to a stronger position nearer the gap where he remained the next two days. While he was encamped in the gap, the rest of Sherman's army came down from the north and joined the Tennesseans.

On the 11th the corps dug defensive works and the follow-

2Lewis, *Sherman*, 357.
3Shanks, *Personal Recollections*, 308-309.
4Logan, *Volunteer Soldier*, 679. Resaca was completely fortified, but the works were held by a small force that probably could have been overwhelmed by the Army of the Tennessee.
5*OR*, Ser. 1, XXXVIII, pt. 3, 90.

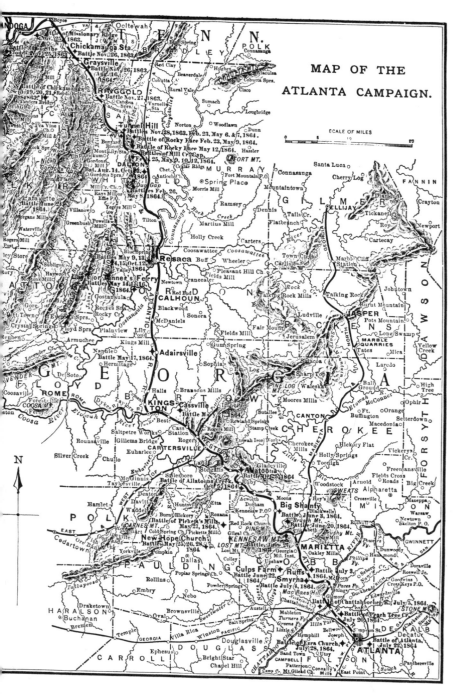

MAP OF THE

ATLANTA CAMPAIGN.

SCALE OF MILES

ta Campaign

Battles and Leaders of the Civil War

ing day, while Osterhaus and Harrow remained inside their works, Smith moved toward Resaca, joining Sherman's cavalry chief, Judson Kilpatrick, on reconnaissance. On the 13th Osterhaus and Harrow moved up to join Smith and by one o'clock Logan had the corps deployed in battle line. Osterhaus was on the left, straddling the Resaca Road, Smith on the right lay in a wooded field, and Harrow marched in reserve. Having formed his line, Logan threw out skirmishers and pushed forward. Rebel pickets gave way grudgingly and Logan followed over hilly ground, absorbing casualties from "rapid and effective" Confederate fire. When Logan left the timber and reached a row of cleared fields, he found rebel forces posted along a range of low hills commanding the open space. The enemy was protected by rifle pits and when Logan reached the clearing, rebel artillery opened up, doing some damage. Hurrying his own pieces up, Logan promptly silenced the enemy guns and ordered his whole line forward, Osterhaus on the left, Smith on the right, and Harrow in reserve. Confederate rifle fire failed to stop Logan's steady advance and he crossed the fields, climbed the hills, and drove the gray coats into Resaca. Spurring his horse forward, Logan discovered that his position overlooked Johnston's entire line, the town, and the railroad bridge over the Oostenaula River. Delighting in this vantage, Logan called for Stolbrand's guns. Placed in position on the crest, they opened a booming fire at the town "causing considerable confusion and interrupting the passage of railroad trains."[6] While his batteries sprayed the distant enemy they drew rebel fire in return. Balls began to find Logan's knoll and his staff scattered leaving Logan, Stolbrand, and Stolbrand's artillery lieutenant, Captain Francis DeGress, alone with the gunners. Showing little concern, they continued to expose themselves and Shanks marveled: "How they escape being struck I can not conceive."[7]

When night fell Logan halted the barrage and looked to corps deployment. He brought Harrow's reserve up on the left, left Osterhaus in the center, and placed Smith on the right. His line took advantage of the crests he had taken on the 13th

---

[6]*Ibid.*, 91.
[7]Shanks, *Personal Recollections*, 313.

and he had shallow rifle pits dug for protection. With most of Sherman's army before Resaca, Logan held the extreme right directly in front of the town.

Daylight on the 14th brought a renewal of sharp skirmishing and heavy artillery fire. Logan spent the 14th moving forward against stout opposition from Polk's Corps, occupying enemy lines along his front. While the remainder of Sherman's army moved into position, Logan kept up his fire to prevent reinforcements from leaving the Confederate left. During the skirmishing Osterhaus found a weak point and carried the heavily wooded valley in Logan's front near the Resaca Road. Then quickly the 12th Missouri took the bridge over Camp Creek, at the foot of Logan's position, giving him solid footing in timber between the Union line and Polk. Directly in front of Logan lay Polk's main line stretched along another range of hills, running from the Oostenaula River northward. Logan decided that, if taken, Polk's hills would put him only three-eighths of a mile from the railroad bridge, giving Sherman a point from which to sever Johnston's rail line.

Logan was supposed to move in force across Camp Creek and attack Polk on the following day, but he had plenty of light (it was 5:30) and he pushed his assaulting columns ahead. With rebel artillery pouring a withering fire on his lines, Logan hauled up Stolbrand's guns and they fired until enemy cannon fell silent. Then Logan ordered the advance, and two brigades, Charles Woods' and Giles Smith's, moved down the slope into the woods.[8] Camp Creek bridge could not accommodate all Logan's attackers, and some floated across on logs or waded up to their waists, sometimes their necks, holding their weapons overhead. It was about one third of a mile to the objective, but the terrain made going painfully slow. After crossing the creek, attackers still had to plow through marshy bottomland full of fallen trees. At 5:50, the slough behind them, Logan's line poised on the marsh's edge ready to strike. A bugle sent the two brigades racing at the double

[8]*Battles and Leaders*, IV, 301; *OR*, Ser. 1, XXXI, pt. 3, 564-565. Logan's brigade commanders were: in Osterhaus' 1st Division, Charles R. Woods, David Carskaddon, and Hugo Wangelin; in Smith's 2nd Division, Giles A. Smith, and Joseph A. J. Lightburn; and in Harrow's 4th Division, Reuben Williams, Charles C. Walcutt, and W. S. Jones.

quick up the rebel slope, cheered on by their watching comrades across the creek. Rebel infantry, well posted in shallow trenches, poured a deadly fire against the blue line, and fresh Confederate artillery, brought up to repel an attack, joined in smashing bloody holes in Union ranks. "But neither thicket, nor slough, nor shot, nor shell, distracted for a moment the attention of the stormers," Logan observed. By 6:30 Logan saw Union colors fly on the rebel summit and he watched as Smith and Woods deployed to resist counterattack. Entrenching tools were sent over, and Logan, fearful that the Confederates would attempt to retake the ridge, sent General Lightburn's brigade as support. Indications of a rebel attack proved correct when at 7:30, through a deepening dusk, Union skirmishers were driven in and Polk's men charged to retake the heights. Rebel attackers were met by a withering fire and withdrew to form for another try. This time greater Confederate numbers threatened to turn Union flanks, and Lightburn's men reached Smith and Woods just as the enemy swept forward. Lightburn had been able to locate the Union position from the red flame of muskets showing plainly through the night. Until 10 o'clock musket fire echoed across the hills and red musket flashes continued to puncture the dark. At 10:00, unable to dislodge Logan's advance, rebel flashes flickered out and "It was evident to the meanest comprehension among the rebels that the men who had double-quicked across to their hills that afternoon, had come to stay."[9]

Woods, Smith and Lightburn led their men gallantly and their loss of 102 killed, 502 wounded, and 14 missing was far less than the 92 prisoners and an estimated 1,500 killed and wounded suffered by the rebels. The chief importance of Logan's late evening victory was that Johnston, no longer able to use the bridge Logan's advance had placed under fire, was forced to build a new bridge over the Oostenaula.

Logan brought his entire command up after the battle ended, his new line running from the river's north bank along the ridge to the Resaca Road. At dawn the importance of the previous evening's struggle was obvious and Logan's artillery began to spray the town, bridge, and rebel lines. On the 15th

---

[9]*OR*, Ser. 1, XXXVIII, pt. 3, 93-94.

there was no advance as Sherman's lines kept up a steady fire and Johnston built his bridge and retreated. After dark on the 15th artillery continued to bang along the Union left, while the right remained silent. Anticipating withdrawal, Sherman ordered Logan's skirmishers to press the enemy all night and about daylight they found Polk's force gone. Smith's and Osterhaus' pickets moved into Resaca at dawn on the heels of the retreating enemy, driving Johnston's rear guard across the river.

Logan expected to be ordered to pursue the enemy and he moved his command across the river, but a messenger from McPherson found him and ordered a halt to await further orders. They came quickly and Logan struck westward to Lay's Ferry where he camped on the 16th. The next day he crossed the Oostenaula moving down the main road to Rome. Following Dodge's corps the afternoon of the 17th, Logan heard firing, and answering a call for assistance, rushed Osterhaus forward. The Prussian deployed, but crossing a low ridge, he discovered the enemy retreating, and Logan brought up Smith and Harrow. Logan camped at McGuire that evening and on the 18th swung away from Rome, moving southeastward toward Kingston.

Logan marched to Adairsville and then turned west again, crossing Gravelly Ridge in the afternoon. That night he camped at Woodland and moved out the following morning toward Kingston. Reaching that place, Logan found no opposition and camped on the Etowah River west of town. That afternoon Logan lost an invaluable member of his staff. Major Charles Stolbrand, Logan's artillery commander and close friend since Vicksburg, was sent at Logan's direction to examine surrounding territory. While his expert eye surveyed the terrain, picking out good artillery positions, a squad of rebel cavalry broke through the trees and before Stolbrand could mount, he was taken. The loss was a grievous one for Logan who had come to depend on the able Swede.[10]

At Kingston, Sherman ordered a brief halt. Logan took advantage of the stop to scribble two letters to Mary. Of Resaca he wrote: "My corps all behaved gallantly and received great

---

[10]*Ibid.*, 95. The major later escaped and returned to the corps.

credit by all who saw the charge and fight." Of the over-all campaign: "When Johnston will make a stand I do not know but think at the Allatoona Mountain." When the army paused at Kingston, Hibe came up from Chattanooga. He had rejoined Logan in Alabama in November, and had been working for a sutler in 15th Corps camps. Logan assured Mary of her brother's health and delighted in telling her, "He seems to take great interest in our success."[11]

When the army prepared to resume action on May 23, Logan, apprehensive of the future, wrote Mary. "I may fall," he told her, "and if so, I shall fall in a just cause and will be only one man added to the list of those who have laid down their lives in pure devotion to their country. . . . I want you to know that if I do not survive I have deposited with Col. John C. Smith, chief of the 15th Corps, $10,000 that he will pay you on demand."[12]

During his stay at Kingston, Sherman gathered supplies and tried to guess Johnston's next move. The little Scot who commanded the rebel army crossed the Etowah on the 21st and while Sherman rested, he set strong defensive positions along the railroad at Allatoona Gap. Just before Sherman resumed his advance, Johnston pushed Hardee's Corps westward to Dallas in expectation of another of Sherman's lightning-like flank movements.

The deadly dance began again on the 23rd. The bulk of Sherman's force was thrust south toward Johnston's line between Allatoona and Dallas, but the hard marching Army of the Tennessee looped wide again and walked for Johnston's flank. Logan, twenty days' rations packed into wagons, crossed the Etowah and marched for Van Wert. He made eighteen miles the first day out of Kingston and camped on Euharlee Creek. At dawn the corps rose, stepped out for Van Wert, cleared the town and bent eastward for Dallas. Marching was difficult due to heat and ragged terrain. The country between the Etowah and the Chattahoochee, slightly north of Atlanta, was desolate, with little sign of habitation. Unlike the piney

[11]JAL to Mary Logan, May 20, 1864, Logan Mss.
[12]JAL to Mary Logan, May 23, 1864, Logan Mss. He was quick to assure her the money was "no false or improper gain," he told her it came from a land deal.

hills north of the Etowah, growth here was scrubby and dense, and loose sand on hill slopes and quicksand-bordered streams slowed marchers.[13]

Pumpkin Vine Creek appeared on May 25 and Logan, drawing near Dallas, camped along the creek in line of battle expecting to find a large rebel force near the town. Next morning Logan heard heavy firing from the direction of Dallas and learned from deserters that Joe Johnston himself was at Dallas in force. Logan threw out flankers, pushed forward a strong skirmish line, and advanced cautiously. His cavalry and artillery fought a slight skirmish with enemy infantry west of Dallas, but they fell back and Logan marched through the town. Without a halt, he continued along the Powder Springs Road eastward. Two miles beyond the town Logan's skirmish line faltered and fell back, reporting a heavy Confederate concentration dug in behind strong field works along a low ridge. The corps halted and Logan sent forward skirmishers who felt out the rebel line and discovered that it lay north-northwest by south-southwest crossing Powder Springs and Marietta Roads.[14]

Logan's men were able to estimate rebel works at a glance and they accurately reported their strength to headquarters. One of them even presented his regimental commander a sketch of Hardee's entrenchments and the colonel forwarded the amazingly accurate information to the corps commander. Several days later the young man who made the drawing went to Logan with another sketch, this time of an enemy battery. Logan asked him in, examined his work, and opened his file book showing the soldier an order for a promotion for the young man who had sent in the sketch on the 26th. "Well that beat me," the soldier wrote, "General Logan treated me very nicely."[15]

Certain of his enemy's position, Logan ordered Harrow to the right, Morgan Smith in the center, and Osterhaus to the left where he joined Dodge's 16th Corps. After dark Logan ordered shovels broken out and his men, thankful that he had

---

[13]*Battles and Leaders*, IV, 306.
[14]*OR*, Ser. 1, XXXVIII, pt. 3, 95.
[15]Upson, *With Sherman*, 114.

waited until the sun went down, spent the night scraping works in the sandy Georgia hills.

That night Logan heard that Thomas had been engaged near New Hope Church, a few miles east of Dallas, and that Jeff C. Davis had come up to form on Dodge's left. Logan, Dodge, and Davis formed a solid blue wall facing Hardee's Corps. Logan, "like a horse ready for battle," was sure of a smashing victory on the 27th if Johnston chose to fight. At daybreak skirmish fighting began and all day long rifle fire, punctuated by artillery, continued. Logan, "intensely active on the approach of battle, his habitual conservatism in council changed into brightness, accompanied with energetic and persistent activity," momentarily expected to be ordered to charge, but no order came.[16] The only action of the 27th was an assault on Harrow's division which was promptly checked.

Clattering rifle fire ushered in the 28th and the scorching Georgia sun climbed high to hover over two sweating, bleeding armies. Early in the day, Sherman decided to move his army eastward, and McPherson was told to withdraw and march toward the Union center near New Hope Church. Hot skirmish action made it impossible for McPherson to pull out, and he spent the morning and early afternoon fending off rebel forays. At 3:30 the army commander tried to extricate his men, but Hardee, moving quickly, poured out of the woods and stormed forward. McPherson stopped the withdrawal and turned to face Hardee's entire corps.

Logan, "growling at the situation," hurried forward to rally his corps. He galloped down the line alone, coatless, forming units to resist, roaring his commands above the din of Confederate musketry.[17] First blow came on Harrow at the weakest point in Logan's line. Harrow's division lay across the Villa Rica Road where the road wound down the backbone of a ridge in terrain difficult to fortify. Hardee's assault struck this point, sweeping in skirmishers from Colonel Charles Walcutt's 2nd Brigade and overrunning three guns of the 1st Iowa Battery.

---

[16]Oliver Otis Howard, *The Autobiography of O. O. Howard* (New York, 1907), I, 557.

[17]Andrews, *Logan*, 452. This account comes from Brigadier General George A. Stone's description of the battle in a Mt. Pleasant, Iowa paper, Jan. 17, 1884.

With the enemy only eighty yards from their works, Walcutt's men fired volley after volley across the plateau, the deadly fire preventing rebels from turning the Iowa guns on Union works. The fighting in front of Walcutt was murderous. His four regiments "stood unflinchingly at their guns," led by Walcutt, "who stood on the parapet amid the storm of bullets, ruling the fight."[18]

Seeing the battle storm on the right, Logan galloped to Walcutt waving his sword in the air, his red undershirt showing beneath his torn uniform tunic. Disorganized groups converged on Logan asking for their regiments and officers. Logan thundered at them, "Damn your regiments! Damn your officers! Forward and yell like hell!"[19] With the 1st Iowa's guns still in rebel hands, Logan mounted a counterattack by rallying Harrow's division to retake the battery. He jumped his horse over the works, followed by shouting troops racing into a hail of rebel fire. Logan, struck in the left forearm by a rebel ball, saw the men claim their guns and hurl the enemy back.[20]

His arm supported in a hastily torn sling, Logan rode back to the line followed by the cry, "Black Jack's wounded." He continued to ride along the front urging his men to repel new assaults. Several times Hardee rallied against Harrow, but each time he was turned back. Shortly after Confederate attackers first struck Harrow, they swept in on Smith and Osterhaus, but the ground in front of the latter two was more favorable for defense and after several advances Hardee retired. The engagement lasted only one hour, but its intensity can be measured in the casualties. Logan lost 30 killed, 295 wounded, and 54 missing. He took 97 prisoners and estimated Hardee's total loss at 2,000.[21]

Following the battle McPherson reported Hardee "handsomely repulsed" by the 15th and 16th Corps. Logan, his wound troubling him only slightly, exultantly reported to

---

[18]OR, Ser. 1, XXXVIII, pt. 3, 96. This is in Logan's report.

[19]Stone in Andrews, Logan, 452.

[20]Upson, With Sherman, 109.

[21]OR, Ser. 1, XXXVIII, pt. 3, 96. Logan's estimate of enemy casualties is a trifle high, but Logan did bury many rebel dead in front of his works after the battle.

Mary, "Since the fight of Saturday, the men are all enthusiasm and think I am all they want to command them."[22]

On the 29th, in compliance with Sherman's orders, Logan attempted to withdraw and move to the left, but once again Hardee's demonstrations caused Logan to march the corps back into the works. All day and most of the night Confederate fire continued. Several times after dark, skirmish action seemed about to turn into full scale attacks. From 11 o'clock until 3 A.M. musket fire lit up opposing lines and Union commanders gave up attempting to change position. On May 30, Sherman rode over to McPherson to ascertain Hardee's intentions. Sherman, McPherson, Logan, and Sherman's artillery chief, Colonel W. H. H. Taylor, mounted a high point on Logan's line, despite rebel fire, to survey opposing lines. Rebel balls began to move uncomfortably close to the knot of Federal officers, and before they could retire, one tore through Logan's sleeve and struck Taylor in the chest. Logan's wound was insignificant and Taylor was saved by a thick memorandum book in his pocket. The ball merely broke several of the colonel's ribs.[23]

When June arrived, Logan was on the move eastward toward New Hope Church and Acworth. From the 1st to the 5th skirmishing was continuous as rebel lines at New Hope remained stationary. On the 5th Logan's probing pickets found enemy lines abandoned and he pushed on toward Acworth. Johnston's withdrawal from Allatoona and Acworth gave Sherman control of the railroad as far south as Big Shanty and Kenesaw Mountain, and he called another halt around Acworth to bring forward supplies and complete rail communications with Chattanooga.

While he lay at Acworth, Blair's 17th Corps came up and Logan went over to see his old comrades of the 3rd Division. "I rode along their line," he told Mary, "and it caused the wildest enthusiasm you ever saw." He concluded caustically, "They do not think much of General Blair."[24]

From the 6th to the 9th Logan lay south of Acworth in

[22]JAL to Mary Logan, May 30, 1864, Logan Mss.
[23]W. T. Sherman, *The Memoirs of W. T. Sherman* (New York, 1875), II, 45.
[24]JAL to Mary Logan, June 8, 1864, Logan Mss.

battle line. May's hot, dry weather disappeared in June and Logan's encamped corps was pelted almost daily by heavy rain, often followed by sun which turned woods into a steam bath. On the 10th Acworth was left behind and Logan, with Smith leading the way, joined the army's march southeastward toward what Sherman believed to be Johnston's new position. After a short walk, they found gray clad skirmishers posted behind rail piles just south of Big Shanty Station. Johnston's pickets were dislodged by Logan's artillery and he moved forward only to be stopped shortly by the defensive master's newest line of works.

Johnston, now only about twenty miles from Atlanta, had erected his new line along three rugged hills, Kenesaw, Pine, and Lost Mountains, guarding the rail line south. A quick look convinced veteran Union campaigners that Johnston had dug formidable parapets and "heavy masses of infantry could be distinctly seen with the naked eye."[25] Johnston seemed prepared for battle, and Logan, on the Union left facing Kenesaw, edged his men toward the rebel heights. He reached the hills' outcrop by the 13th. Here shovels came out and Logan dug his works, the men scooping out the muddy clay, accompanied by incessant rain and booming guns. For a week, digging, light skirmishing, and constant artillery exchanges occupied weary, sodden troops. Logan inched up the hill wherever possible, but was forced to detach Smith and Harrow and send them to the left to aid in repelling what looked like Johnston's attempt to flank Sherman. Harrow's division was engaged there on the 15th, losing 45 men killed and wounded. On June 19 Johnston gave up his first line on Kenesaw and moved farther up the hill, allowing Logan to advance to the mountain's base. From the 20th to the 25th, positions remained unchanged and fire was almost continuous during daylight hours. Logan's line during this period had Osterhaus on the right, connecting with Dodge's 16th Corps, Smith on the left, joining Blair, and Harrow in reserve. Logan's corps occupied the center of the Army of the Tennessee, which held Sherman's left.

While opposing armies ceased the flank-withdrawal-flank pattern so well developed since early May, and prepared for

[25]Sherman, *Memoirs*, II, 51.

what seemed to be a head-on collision, reporters with the army ground out copy on the campaign's leaders. Logan was described by a New York journalist as

of middle stature, compact, well-knit frame. He has a glorious pair of dark eyes, that scintillate beneath his heavy brows, and dark hair. A heavy, curved mustache covers his well formed mouth. Such is his appearance, and his fighting qualities are in accordance.

The Northern public read that Logan's "military career is full of dashing heroism."[26]

"Dashing heroism" was useful in Logan's next engagement, the assault on Kenesaw. If Sherman had followed his established policy he would have thrown out the Army of the Tennessee, flanked Johnston and raced for Atlanta, but he decided differently. Johnston's mountain line was strong on the flanks but weak in the center. Sherman felt that if he made a breach in the center, his spearhead could wheel toward the flanks and overwhelm Johnston's position.[27]

After the war Logan was the source of another story of Sherman's reasons for assaulting Kenesaw. Logan told Donn Piatt, who disliked Sherman, that the western commander struck the mountain because of jealousy of Grant. Logan described a meeting in Sherman's tent on the 26th in which Sherman, reading a newspaper's war reports, grew angry at the attention given Grant's eastern army and determined to win headline space for his command.[28] Whatever the reason, Sherman told his army commanders to prepare their men for an attack at 8 o'clock on the morning of the 27th.

Logan spent the night of the 26th moving his men into position for their bloody climb up the rebel hills. He put Lightburn, Giles Smith, and Walcutt in his assault force under former Indiana schoolmaster, Morgan Smith. Smith had orders to charge the south and west faces of Little Kenesaw. Then Logan went to his tent and dashed off a letter to Mary. "John-

---

[26]David P. Conyngham, *Sherman's March Through the South* (New York, 1865), 54.

[27]Sherman, *Memoirs*, II, 60.

[28]Lewis, *Sherman*, 375. Sherman's biographer thinks that there is an element of truth in Logan's story.

ston," he wrote, "has a strong position entrenched strongly on high mountains. We have to climb there and then assault earth works of a very formidable character. Our men are in good heart, though they have a bloody road before them."[29]

The road was bloody indeed. Early on the 27th Sherman's artillery began working along the hills, its shells producing white puffs where they struck Johnston's heights. At 8 o'clock artillery stilled and Logan, sitting tensely on his horse, "Old John," cried "Charge!" Many of the soldiers had grave doubts about the ascent in the face of 25,000 rifles and 50 cannon, but the order brought immediate action and men started up. Thomas' Cumberlanders climbed in formal battle columns, but McPherson's Tennesseans moving in loose Indian formation suffered fewer casualties and advanced more rapidly.

As soon as Logan broke cover, his three brigades, in two lines, drew enemy fire. Toiling upward was deadly business, but Logan's attackers took and held two lines of rebel rifle pits on the hill's side. Feeling further attempts at enemy lines futile, John Palmer of Thomas' 14th Corps told his men to lie down and rode over to Logan to tell him the mountain could not be carried. Logan replied the 15th Corps could go farther than any unit, and he urged his men up again.[30]

Logan rode up the mountain, bullets falling about him, driving his men forward. However, Johnston's works on the crest defied the Federals. The torrent of rebel fire was bad enough, but the terrain made further attack certain death. "After vainly attempting to carry the works for some time, and finding that so many gallant men were being uselessly slain, I ordered them to retire to the last line of works captured, and placed them in a defensible condition for occupancy," Logan reported.[31] Pioneers went up the hill and by nightfall Logan's line lay dug in along the hillside slightly below Johnston's crest and higher than any other corps. About dusk Confederates attempted to dislodge Lightburn, but were driven back with heavy loss. Dark arrived, guns growled into silence; Logan improved his works and counted his loss. In the rela-

---

[29]JAL to Mary Logan, June 26, 1864, Logan Mss.
[30]Palmer, *Personal Recollections*, 205.
[31]*OR*, Ser. 1, XXXVIII, pt. 3, 99.

tively brief action Logan lost 80 killed, 506 wounded, and 17 missing.[32]

The next day Sherman reminded Palmer that Logan had gone 100 yards farther than the 14th Corps. Palmer bristled and told Sherman he could have gone as far as Logan, but it would have cost 100 more useless casualties.[33]

Once up the hill there was no further advance. For four days rifle and cannon fire continued, but Sherman ordered no new assault. On July 1 the old dance began again with the Army of the Tennessee in its familiar role. Swinging to the right, McPherson marched toward Schofield to aid the Army of the Ohio in flanking Johnston's formidable position. From Logan, Morgan Smith pulled out on the 1st with Harrow and, Osterhaus prepared to follow on the 2nd. Just as Harrow and Osterhaus began their swing to the west McPherson rode up to Logan with word that Johnston had abandoned his lines on Kenesaw. Instead of following Smith, the 1st and 4th Divisions swept past Kenesaw on the left and entered Marietta taking 200 prisoners. Sherman's flank movement had caused another retreat. It seemed to men in both armies as if the endless game of cat and mouse might go on forever. One frustrated Confederate soldier, taken prisoner by Logan's 103rd Illinois, gave vent to his exasperation at Union strategy. "Sherman'll never go to hell," he drawled, "He will flank the devil and make heaven in spite of the guards."[34]

Reaching Marietta, the last significant town between Union troops and Atlanta, Logan deployed to cover the town, remaining there until July 4. Then he pulled out, marching to the army's right. That night Morgan Smith's division rejoined Logan, and on the 5th and 6th, the corps advanced slowly toward the Chattahoochee River, Johnston's last natural barrier north of Atlanta. On the 7th, Logan moved into Union lines along Nicajack Creek erected by Jeff C. Davis when he drove

---

[32]Among the dead was Colonel Rigdon S. Barnhill of the 40th Illinois, shot while leading his men against the crest. Jacob D. Cox, *Atlanta* (New York, 1882), 127.

[33]Palmer, *Personal Recollections*, 205

[34]H. H. Orendorff *et al.* (eds.), *Reminiscences of the Civil War from Diaries of Members of the One Hundred and Third Illinois Volunteer Infantry* (Chicago, 1905), 74.

the rebels across the 5th.[35] For five days Logan lay north of the creek as both sides remained generally inactive.

While Logan lay opposite Johnston, rain abated and his men were bathed by a scorching sun. However, most of them were in good spirits. They had driven Johnston to the gates of Atlanta and by early July they "began to find blackberries and green apples . . . so we live quite good again."[36] Their respite ended on the 12th.

When Sherman began to edge flankers across the Chattahoochee, Johnston gave up the river line and fell behind Peachtree Creek. Now came the time for Sherman to set his racehorse army in motion again. Crossing the Chattahoochee, Sherman started Thomas and Schofield directly at Johnston, but he took McPherson and swung him from the right to the extreme left, a fifty mile march. This movement led Sherman to call McPherson's army his "whip-lash."[37]

Logan pulled out on the 12th, raced back through Marietta, and wheeled northeastward for Roswell where he was to cross the Chattahoochee. On the 14th he made Roswell with one division and waited for the other two to come up the next day. Crossing the river on the 15th was made hazardous by a thunderstorm which broke while the 15th Corps was on the bridge. A bolt struck near the bridge knocking down several of Logan's men, but movement proceeded and that night the damp corps dug fortifications on the Atlanta side.[38]

Logan remained in camp across from Roswell on the 16th and got off two letters. He had written Mary earlier: "My command was 1st on Kenesaw and in Marietta, but that will make no difference unless I was a West Point officer." This is Logan's first complaint against Sherman's favoritism for professional soldiers. On the 16th he wrote:

Sherman is a strange man and seems to fight a portion of the army at a time, which is certainly of disadvantage to

[35]Jeff C. Davis to John M. Palmer, Jan. 4, 1866, Jefferson C. Davis Mss., Indiana State Historical Library, Indianapolis.

[36]James D. Padgett (ed.), "With Sherman Through Georgia and the Carolinas: Letters of a Federal Soldier," *Georgia Historical Quarterly*, XXXII, No. 4 (Dec., 1948), 298.

[37]Lewis, *Sherman*, 381.

[38]Dodge, *Sherman*, 17.

us. I should not complain however, for I am sure that he has
given me enough to do since with him, and he has certainly
said as little about it as he possibly could in his dispatches.[39]

Logan had never been as close to Sherman as he had to Grant,
and this first evidence of dissatisfaction was to become a bitter
conflict in the next two weeks.

Logan wrote another letter on the 16th to Governor Yates.
Hibe Cunningham was still with the corps, and Logan asked
Yates for a captain's commission on his staff for the young
man, assuring the governor, "I am well satisfied that he has
finally relented and feels a deep interest in our success."[40]
Logan's plan for Hibe met with Mary's hearty approval, and
within the month he had his commission and was leading
Union troops against his former comrades.

On the 17th Logan moved forward again, reached Nancy's
Creek where he drove in skirmishers, and marched for Decatur. That night he learned that Sherman's old dance partner
was no longer in command. Jefferson Davis, no longer able to
stand Johnston's policy of withdrawal, removed him and replaced him with John B. Hood. McPherson had known Hood
at West Point and he told Sherman, and later Logan, that the
new Confederate commander was impetuous where Johnston
had been cautious. Terpsichore was overthrown; Mars now
ruled.

[39]JAL to Mary Logan, July 14, 16, 1864, Logan Mss.
[40]JAL to Richard Yates, July 16, 1864, Logan Mss.

CHAPTER XIII

SHERMAN IS A BRUTE

Mcpherson sent Logan racing for the Georgia Railroad on July 18. By dusk, operating in the shadow of Stone Mountain, Logan reported the railroad, Hood's link with the East, destroyed for a considerable distance. The following day Logan's agile command headed for Decatur. It struck the railroad east of town and worked westward tearing up track. That night Logan bivouacked on Decatur's north side, only five miles from Atlanta. July 20 brought Logan closer to Atlanta. He left everything except his ammunition wagons at Decatur and pushed for Hood's lines. That day, while Hood struck Sherman's main line along Peachtree Creek, Logan's artillery lobbed shells toward the city's spires. Logan entrenched in that position on the night of the 20th, and on the 21st set his lines: Smith in the center, flanked by Harrow on the right, and Osterhaus on the left.[1] Slight skirmishing occupied Logan on the 21st, but he spent most of his time strengthening his position with earthworks.

While Logan dug works on the night of the 21st, Hood was stealthily moving four divisions toward the Army of the Tennessee. The battered Texan, now charged with Atlanta's defense, had been smashed by Thomas on the 20th, but, undaunted, he decided Sherman's left flank might be turned by a quick strike near Decatur. Logan's men were astir early in the morning. It was drizzling rain when they rose, and before rations were handed out skirmish fire began, driving them into their trenches.[2] After a short time skirmish fire flickered out and Logan advanced scouts who reported rebel skirmishers had abandoned lines opposite the 15th Corps. Logan reported this withdrawal to McPherson and was ordered to send Mor-

---

[1]OR, Ser. 1, XXXVIII, pt. 3, 101-102. Osterhaus' 1st Division was temporarily under the command of Charles Woods while the Prussian recovered from illness.
[2]Morris, *31st Illinois*, 103.

gan Smith forward to occupy the vacated trenches. Smith's advance completed, Logan received word from McPherson that Sherman believed Hood was evacuating Atlanta, and Logan was to lead the pursuit. Before the order to march could be given, it was evident to Logan that the rebels were still along his front in force. Enemy fire rose in a sudden torrent and a rebel shell burst within twenty feet of where Logan and Mc-Pherson stood observing the action. "General, they seem to be popping that corn for us," Logan remarked to the army commander.[3] By 10 o'clock there was no longer any doubt. Confederate entrenchments in front of Thomas and Schofield were found partially vacant and word reached Logan and McPherson that Hood's men were moving to the left in force.[4]

McPherson immediately halted the ordered advance, put Logan back in his lines, and rode off to Sherman. He found the general in the rear, told him of his fear of a strong assault against the left, and received Sherman's endorsement for the change of plans he had made. The two generals met briefly, and McPherson returned to his men.[5] For some time McPherson and his staff rode along behind the Army of the Tennessee observing the placement of the Union lines. Then at noon a sudden cannonade erupted on McPherson's extreme left. The general rounded up his staff and galloped off toward the portentous rumbling.

The first assault struck General Thomas Sweeny's division of the 16th Corps and then crashed into the 17th Corps division of General Giles A. Smith. Some of Smith's skirmishers had been picking blackberries in the damp woods and they came hurtling back over Union works. Smith, recently elevated to division command and transferred out of Logan's corps, was the target for Hood's artillery and infantry, and Logan rode toward the flank to assess the danger. McPherson was riding in the same direction, but Logan turned back before he met the

---

[3] Dawson, *Logan*, 61.
[4] *OR*, Ser. 1, XXXVIII, pt. 3, 102.
[5] *Military Essays and Recollections. Military Order of the Loyal Legion of the United States, Illinois Commandery* (Chicago, 1891), I, 311. This account of the final meeting between McPherson and Sherman was written by Col. William E. Strong of McPherson's staff. It runs counter to the story, long accepted, of the dramatic final meeting between the two men.

army commander. However, McPherson soon sent word to Logan to send a brigade to fill the gap between the 16th and 17th Corps. Logan quickly sent Colonel Hugo Wangelin's brigade of the 1st Division.

When McPherson reached the point of attack, the danger was evident. Hardee's Confederate corps had slashed out of a stand of timber into the left flank. All that saved the Union wing from being outflanked was that as Hardee charged, Dodge's men, started in motion earlier by McPherson, were swinging into position on the extreme end of the line. When Hardee assaulted, he met part of the 16th Corps head-on rather than (as the Confederates expected) the rear of Blair's unit. Better to discover his enemy's position, McPherson rode to the left of the 17th Corps line. He had ridden a short distance when a squad of rebel horsemen burst through the trees and ordered McPherson and his signal officer, the only person with him, to halt. The general refused and, urging his horse toward the Union line, was brought down by a rebel volley. The aide was chased off, leaving the general's body in enemy hands. Some of Blair's men heard the volley and ran forward to help McPherson. As one soldier ran toward the scene he was told McPherson was dead. "I wouldn't believe it, but it was too true."[6] Blair himself heard the volley and rushed McPherson's adjutant, then at 17th Corps headquarters, to Logan and Sherman with the news that McPherson was either killed or wounded. Sherman was stunned: "The suddenness of this terrible calamity would have overwhelmed me with grief, but the living demanded my whole thoughts."[7]

Sherman acted quickly to provide McPherson's successor. He directed Logan, the senior corps commander, to assume command of the Army, ordering him to hold at all costs, and promising reinforcements if necessary.[8] Logan turned corps command over to Morgan Smith and rode rapidly to the sound of firing on the left. He was determined to recover McPherson's body. A nearby soldier heard "Logan say he would have McPherson's body if he sacrificed every man in the 15th

---

[6]Byron R. Abernethy (ed.), *Private Elisha Stockwell, Jr., Sees the Civil War* (Norman, Oklahoma, 1958), 91.
[7]*OR*, Ser. 1, XXXVIII, pt. 1, 73.
[8]Sherman, *Memoirs*, II, 77.

Corps."[9] Soon a group found McPherson and brought the remains back to Union lines.

This accomplished, Logan rode on. When he reached the part of the field hit by Hardee's first attack, firing had slackened and he looked over the position. The 16th Corps held the extreme left, Blair the center, and Logan's old corps the right. The Union line formed a right angle with Dodge and Blair forming one side and the 15th Corps the other. Strongest point on the line was held by General M. B. Leggett, commanding the 3rd Division, 17th Corps. It was a slight rise called Bald Hill (named Leggett's Hill after the battle) and it gave Leggett a vantage from which he could observe Hardee's movements. Logan told Blair to make certain Leggett was not driven off the hill and turned to the Army's weakest spot. Between the 16th and 17th Corps was a gap in the line in a wooded area providing excellent cover for enemy attackers. It had been created because Dodge had not had time enough to set his men completely before the enemy charged. Logan acted quickly to plug the hole. He ordered Dodge to swing out his right to connect with Wangelin's brigade; Blair was ordered to move the brigade on his left over to link up also with Wangelin. Logan called for Colonel James S. Martin's brigade of the 2nd Division, 15th Corps, to reinforce the threatened sector.

Before Dodge and Blair could make the necessary changes, Hardee's men debouched from the trees and charged the 17th Corps again. After a severe struggle the attack was repulsed only to be followed by another and still another. Blair's men gave ground slowly, fighting on both sides of their works. By 3 o'clock Giles Smith's division had been forced to give ground, creating a dangerous pocket on the Union left.

All this time the 15th Corps, holding the right, had not been attacked. At 3:30 the right felt its first shock, the 2nd Division meeting and hurling back the first line of General B. F. Cheatham's gray attackers. But the 15th Corps had been weakened by the loss of troops sent to the left, and a gap along the railroad cut offered an avenue of attack. Under cover of the smoke of battle, a rebel column marched up the cut and appeared in

[9]Abernethy, *Stockwell*, 91.

the Union rear before anyone saw it. The right of the 15th Corps, forced to fall back to avoid annihilation, had to leave two batteries in rebel hands. Logan, having ridden to Dodge's Corps, when told of the danger on the right, raced back to his old command. Before leaving Dodge he asked the 16th Corps leader for a brigade to assist the right. "He came to me as we were in the habit of doing, Logan, Blair, and myself," wrote Dodge, "when one was hard pushed and the other was not. We sent troops without orders where they were most needed."[10] Logan took Colonel August Mersey's brigade of the 16th Corps and Colonel Martin's brigade when he returned to the right.

Arriving there, Logan found the 15th Corps struggling to change position to avoid a debacle. The rebel spearhead had driven a wedge between General Charles R. Woods' division and the rest of the corps. Woods had closed on Schofield's Army of the Ohio on his right, but the opening the rebels had made grew wider, seriously imperiling the entire Union flank. Logan brought up Major Clemens Landgraeber's battery; the gunners, soon enforced by artillery from Schofield, compelled the enemy to take shelter.

The cannonading having given them a chance to reform, the divisions of the right were ready to counterattack. Woods and General William Harrow rushed men forward, and Morgan Smith's old division, now led by General J. A. J. Lightburn and supported by the 16th Corps reinforcements, joined the charge. As the men advanced, Logan rode along the lines, his black hair streaming, waving his hat in the air. As they charged he cried, "McPherson and revenge boys!" The blue lines moving forward began to chant "Black Jack! Black Jack!" as they fought against a hail of rebel fire. The fierce assault successfully hurled back the Confederates, and the lost batteries were retaken. By 4:30, after a costly struggle, the right had recaptured its old position.

Only two more attacks remained, and the first one poured out of the woods at about 5 o'clock in front of Blair. Rebel troops reached Blair's lines and "The flags of two opposing regiments would meet on the opposite sides of the same works, and would be flaunted by their respective bearers in each

[10]Dodge, *Sherman*, 19-20.

other's faces. Men were bayoneted across the works and officers, with their swords, fought hand-to-hand with men with
bayonets."[11] For forty-five minutes the bloody engagement
raged around Blair's works before Hardee retired.

At 6 o'clock the final assault began, again directed against
Giles Smith and Leggett on the left of the 16th Corps. Smith's
line was driven back by superior numbers, but Wangelin, still
supporting Blair's corps, advanced to Smith's support. These
two units and Leggett's men hurled back the onslaught. Wangelin's four Missouri regiments were the deciding factor as
the fight raged through the dusky woods. His brigade managed
to strike the enemy flank, drove it in, and threatened the entire assault line. This check, and confusion brought on by falling night, led to a final retreat. Night fell, firing ceased, and
the Army of the Tennessee stood battered but in position. This
battle proved the Army of the Tennessee was "panic-proof."[12]

Writing his report of the Battle of Atlanta, Logan felt Hood
"did not succeed due . . . to the lateness of the hour at which
the attack was made, a lack of concert in his movements, . . .
but more than all these to the splendid bravery and tenacity
of the men and the ability and skill of the officers of the Army
of the Tennessee." Logan added that McPherson "was an earnest patriot, a brave and accomplished officer, and . . . a true
gentleman."[13]

While Logan was being pounded, the remainder of Sherman's army stood immobile. Sherman ordered Thomas to attack when he discovered Hood's main force opposite the
Tennesseans, but "Slow Trot" moved forward, found what he
felt were strong entrenchments, and fell back. Years later
Sherman said Atlanta should have been taken on the 22nd, but
he was unwilling to blame anyone for failure to do so.[14]

Skirmish fire lasted long into the night. Logan set his army
in its old position and called Blair and Dodge to his headquarters. The three men stood under an oak near the railroad
and discussed the battle. They agreed Thomas and Schofield

[11]*OR*, Ser. 1, XXXVIII, pt. 3, 582-583.
[12]Nicolay and Hay, *Lincoln*, IX, 272.
[13]*OR*, Ser. 1, XXXVIII, pt. 3, 28.
[14]G. M. Dodge, *The Battle of Atlanta and Other Campaigns* (Council
Bluffs, Iowa, 1910), 49-50; Dodge, *Sherman*, 21.

should send troops to relieve some of the most battered units, and Dodge went to Sherman with the request. The Iowa general arrived and delivered the appeal. Sherman replied, "Dodge, you whipped them today didn't you?"

"Yes sir."

"Can't you do it again tomorrow?"

"Yes sir," said Dodge, saluted, and rode back to his command.[15]

This interview, illustrating Sherman's faith in the men of his old army, might have been the source of a rumor that filtered through the army:

> Gen. Logan sent to Sherman for reinforcements. Sherman's answer is said to have been 'No sir, not a man. If I had 50,000 men here and did not know what to do with them, you should not have a man. You have lost those works and *you must retake them.*' And he did retake them.[16]

Dodge returned with Sherman's actual reply and Logan set his men to strengthening their works. When Hood did not renew his assault on the 23rd, Logan took the opportunity to entrench himself against future attack.

Sherman, Logan, and most Union leaders were happy at the result of the 22nd's action. They, of course, mourned McPherson, but many felt Hood's failure would force him to abandon Atlanta. Yet General John Palmer of Illinois, perhaps seeing in Logan's new acclaim the rise of a potential political opponent, thought differently. "The newspapers will be filled with the details," he wrote his wife; "Logan will be announced as the saviour of the army. While really the battle need not have been fought if our troops had been ready for battle."[17]

The period of calm following the battle gave Sherman time to think about a commander for the Army of the Tennessee. Thomas came to see him on the 23rd to talk about McPherson's successor. He expressed opposition to Logan, admitting Logan "is brave enough and a good officer, but if he had an army I

---

[15]Dodge, *Sherman*, 19-20.

[16]Ira B. Read, "The Campaign from Chattanooga to Atlanta as Seen by a Federal Soldier," Richard B. Harwell (ed.), *Georgia Historical Quarterly*, XXV, No. 3 (September, 1941), 273.

[17]John M. Palmer to Maggie A. Palmer, July 24, 1864, Palmer Mss., Illinois State Historical Library.

am afraid he would edge over both sides and annoy Schofield and me." The old railroad difficulty at Chattanooga still rankled and Thomas supported General O. O. Howard for the post.[18] Sherman argued that Howard, having come from the East, might be opposed by the Westerners, but Thomas insisted.

" 'If you give it to Logan,' said the solemn Thomas, 'I should feel like asking to be relieved.' "

" 'Why Thomas,' exclaimed Sherman, 'you would not do that?' "

" 'No,' said Thomas slowly, 'I would not, but I feel that army commanders should be on friendly terms and Logan and I cannot. Let the President decide it.' "

"Sherman snapped, 'No, it is my duty and I'll perform it.' "[19]

The discussion continued. General Joseph Hooker, senior corps commander in the entire army, was considered and rejected immediately. Few could get along with the former commander of Union forces in Virginia, and talk inevitably returned to Howard. Finally Sherman made up his mind. On July 26 he wrote home, "Poor Mac, he was killed dead instantly. I think I shall prefer Howard to succeed him."[20]

He wanted to maintain harmony between his army commanders at all costs and he regarded Thomas' advice highly. Sherman later wrote:

> General Logan had taken command of the Army of the Tennessee by virtue of his seniority, and had done well; but I did not consider him equal to the command of three corps. Between him and General Blair there existed a natural rivalry. Both were men of great experience, courage and talent. Both were politicians by nature and experience, and it may be that for this reason they were mistrusted by regular officers like Generals Schofield, Thomas and myself.[21]

Sherman considered Logan more than adequate in a fight, but was not certain of the amateur's ability to run all the technical

---

[18]Jacob D. Cox, *Military Reminiscences of the Civil War* (New York, 1900), II, 308; Sherman, *Memoirs*, II, 85; Lewis, *Sherman*, 388.

[19]Lewis, *Sherman*, 388. In contrast, Sherman on July 24 wrote to General H. W. Slocum: "The President must name [McPherson's] successor." *OR*, Ser. 1, XXXVIII, pt. 5, 245-246.

[20]Sherman, *Home Letters*, 303.

[21]Sherman, *Memoirs*, II, 85.

aspects of a protracted campaign. He was about to wheel the Army of the Tennessee over to the right flank and was unsure of Logan's ability to carry off this intricate movement.

Howard's name was sent to the War Department and on the 27th the one-armed Howard, known as the "Christian Soldier" relieved Logan. "Black Jack" resumed command of the 15th Corps.

Howard's appointment stirred up a hornet's nest in Sherman's army. Hooker was infuriated and resigned. On hearing the news, "Fighting Joe" wrote Logan: "I asked to be relieved from duty with the army, it being an insult to my rank and service. Had you retained the command I could have remained on duty without the sacrifice of honor or principle."[22] Logan, thoroughly disappointed, refused to follow Hooker and he gave way to Howard. Logan's disappointment was shared by many in the Army of the Tennessee. Dodge felt that the army "had in it material to command itself." Shortly after Logan's removal, Dodge went to Sherman's headquarters and found Logan sitting on the porch:

> He hardly recognized me as I walked in, and I saw a great change in him. I asked General Sherman what the change in commanders meant, why Logan was not left in command. As everyone knows, Logan's independence and criticisms in the army were very severe, but they all knew what he was in a fight, and whenever we sent to Logan for aid he would not only send his forces, but come himself; so, as Blair said, we only knew Logan as we saw him in battle. Logan could hear every word that was said between Sherman and myself. Sherman did not feel at liberty to say anything in explanation of this change. He simply put me off very firmly, but as nicely as he could, and spoke highly of General Howard. . . . I went away from the place without any satisfaction, and when I met Logan on the outside, I expressed to him my regrets, and I said to him: 'There is something here that none of us understand,' and he said: 'It makes no difference; it will all come right in the end.'[23]

[22]Joseph Hooker to JAL, July 27, 1864, Logan Mss. For an account of the entire struggle for command of the Army of the Tennessee see: James P. Jones, "The Battle of Atlanta and McPherson's Successor," *Civil War History*, VII, No. 4 (December, 1961), 393-405.
[23]Dodge, *Sherman*, 21-22.

FROM A PHOTOGRAPH.

GENERAL O. O. HOWARD.   GENERAL WM. B. HAZEN.   GENERAL W. T. SHERMAN.   GENERAL HENRY W. SLOCUM.
GENERAL JOHN A. LOGAN,   GENERAL JEFF. C. DAVIS.   GENERAL J. A. MOWER.

William T. Sherman and his staff, 1864

m *Battles and Leaders of the Civil War*

The "something" Dodge could not understand Logan felt he
understood completely. Logan believed, a belief he held until
he died, that he was replaced because he was not a West Point
graduate. Sherman's *Memoirs* did little to convince him otherwise. It seemed to substantiate Logan's opinion. "I regarded
both Generals Logan and Blair as 'volunteers' that looked to
personal fame and glory as auxiliary and secondary to their
political ambition, and not as professional soldiers." Though
he insisted elsewhere he had not been partial to any class, his
words indicate differently.[24] Sherman was particularly dis-
tressed by his political generals' periodic visits North for political purposes and preferred to have commanders he could
depend on to stay with the army.[25]

Logan seemed to bear little ill will toward Howard personally. After the war he called Howard, then head of the Freedmen's Bureau, a "noble officer."[26] Howard in turn was impressed by Logan's return to duty despite his disappointment.
He took every opportunity to praise Logan's ability and courage.[27]

Sherman's decision was a difficult one since his "heart
prompted him to name Logan, whose battle conduct entitled
him to command the army that was already his in spirit."[28]
But his uncertainty as to Logan's command capabilities and
his unwillingness to offend Thomas led him to his eventual
resolution. That he felt badly about Logan and was obvious
from the tributes he paid him during the rest of the campaign.
On the day Howard was named, Sherman wrote Logan:

> I fear you will be disappointed at not succeeding perma-
> nently to the command of the army. I assure you in giving
> prejudice to General Howard I will not fail to give you every
> credit for having done so well. . . . Take a good rest. I know
> you are worn out with mental and physical work. No one
> could have a higher appreciation of the responsibility that

---

[24]Sherman, *Memoirs*, II, 86.
[25]*Ibid.*, 145.
[26]John A. Logan, *Relief of the Suffering Poor of the South* (Washington, 1867), 5.
[27]Howard, *Autobiography*, II, 16.
[28]Lewis, *Sherman*, 389.

devolved on you so unexpectedly and the noble manner in which you met it.[29]

Further impressed by Logan's refusal to rush northward with Hooker, Sherman concluded, "If I can do anything to mark my full sense at the honorable manner in which you acted in the battle and since, name it to me frankly and I will do it."[30] In mid-August when Sherman wrote his report of the campaign, he told Grant: "General Logan admirably conceived my orders and executed them. . . . General Logan managed the Army of the Tennessee well during his command." On the change of command, Sherman wrote: "I meant no disrespect to any officer, and hereby declare that General Logan submitted with the grace and dignity of a soldier, gentleman, and patriot, resumed command of his corps, and enjoys the love and respect of his army and his commanders."[31]

Though Logan carried his disappointment into post-war politics, his 1864 actions won admiration from all. Logan had vowed to leave the army only when the rebellion had been crushed, and on July 27 Hood's plainly audible picket fire told Logan that time had not come. He had come to fight, but he could not forget.

When Howard replaced Logan the Army of the Tennessee was in the midst of moving to Sherman's right. Logan had begun the movement as army commander and when he returned to the 15th Corps it was almost complete. Sherman had swung his foot cavalry to the west and it took its new position opposite Hood's lines at Ezra Church. On the morning of the 28th, as Logan's men climbed the ridge on which Ezra Church was situated, Hood struck again. At first only skirmish fire, accompanied by low rumblings from rebel artillery, broke the morning's silence. Then Hood stepped up his fire, rebel shells smashing trees where Logan lay. Several men, unnerved by the cannonade, ran for the rear, but Logan, "greatly animated, rushed for all stragglers with drawn saber, and assisted by his officers, drove them back to their commands."[32] At 11:30 rebel

[29]W. T. Sherman to JAL, July 27, 1864, Logan Mss.
[30]*Ibid.*
[31]*OR*, Ser. 1, XXXVIII, pt. 5, 522-523.
[32]Howard, *Autobiography*, II, 22.

fire exploded and Sherman, two miles away, exclaimed, "Logan is feeling them, and I guess he has found them."[33]

Out of thick brush along his front rushed gray clad attackers hitting hard at Logan's right and center. The corps had not had a chance to dig trenches along the ridge, but the height of its position aided the men in hurling back Hood's warriors. The first assault, in good order and great strength, failed to dislodge a single portion of Logan's line. The confident 15th, nervousness gone, stood firm in a manner that led Howard to comment, "I never saw better conduct in battle."[34] Their first advance repulsed, the Confederates retired, reformed, and about 1 o'clock started up again. The second assault was turned back, but three more times Hood's battered troops climbed the hill only to be driven back. Fighting was intense. Hood's ranks were decimated as Logan's men unloosed a torrent of fire.

Once in the afternoon Logan's line, hammered severely in several places and weakened due to heavy casualties, showed signs of giving way, but Logan raced down the front roaring, "Hold 'em! Hold 'em!" His men rallied, but Logan felt it necessary to call on Dodge and Blair for aid and six regiments from the 15th's sister corps went into line. Only darkness brought an end to Hood's assaults. The 15th Corps fought Ezra Church almost alone. Logan sustained 50 killed, 439 wounded, and 73 missing.[35] Enemy loss was much heavier, and Hood's second failure in less than a week to crack the Tennesseans discouraged him from another immediate fight. The following day as pickets exchanged shots, one of Logan's men shouted across the lines, " 'Well Johnny, how many of you are left?' " " ' Oh! about enough for another killing.' "[36]

Logan had again fought his men ably. Sherman lauded Logan's "conspicuous" behavior and Howard, who remained in the rear so that Logan might garner the laurels, wrote: "The general commanding the Fifteenth Corps . . . was indefatigable, and the success of the day is as much attributable to him as to any one man."[37]

[33]Lewis, Sherman, 399.
[34]OR, Ser. 1, XXXVIII, pt. 3, 86.
[35]Ibid., 105.
[36]Cox, Atlanta, 186.
[37]OR, Ser. 1, XXXVIII, pt. 1, 78; OR, Ser. 1, XXXVIII, pt. 3, 86.

Despite these plaudits and his undeniable success in battle, Logan was disconsolate and angry at what he felt was failure to give him due credit. Three days after Ezra Church he wrote Mary: "Whether I will get any credit for these fights I can not tell, but guess not." He complained, "Were I from West Point these two fights would make me more reputation than Sherman ever had before this campaign, but I do not expect it."[38] A week later he wrote:

On the 28th I had the hardest fight of the campaign with my corps alone and gained a great and complete victory, but will get no credit for it. West Point must have all under Sherman who is an infernal *brute*. As soon as this campaign is over I think I shall come home, at least I will not serve longer under Sherman.[39]

As Logan won successes in the Atlanta campaign, the colorful stories surrounding him continued to grow. He became an idol, and men "cheered and leaned forward to touch his stallion," as he galloped along the lines.[40] Combat correspondents found him good copy, and while they rather disliked Sherman, they delighted in stories about Logan. A New York writer felt that "Logan by his dashing, kind manner, might create enthusiasm among troops, but Sherman or Thomas never."[41] It is certain the general loved the adulation and encouraged the journalists.

Following Ezra Church, Logan dug strong defensive works. July passed and August arrived with the corps still in position west of Atlanta. Almost no action occurred until the 3rd when Harrow fought a brief skirmish. One week later Osterhaus moved forward slightly, capturing 60 prisoners after a short contest.

On August 4 Logan lost his veteran lieutenant Morgan Smith. Smith had been wounded at Chickasaw Bayou in December, 1862, and constant exposure so weakened him that he had to be sent north. Lightburn led the 2nd Division until a new commander, William B. Hazen, arrived. The new brigadier

---

[38]JAL to Mary Logan, July 31, 1864, Logan Mss.
[39]JAL to Mary Logan, Aug. 6, 1864, Logan, Mss.
[40]Lewis, *Sherman*, 400.
[41]Conyngham, *Sherman's March*, 48.

rode into camp just as Logan and his staff were sitting down to supper. Hazen reported of his new associates: "The staff was very numerous, and, as I found afterward, very efficient. Most of them were young men. It was the first time I had met Logan, and I was most agreeably impressed by him, both as a soldier and as a man, and have never had reason to change the first impression."[42]

While Logan awaited renewal of action, he complained to Mary of his treatment at Sherman's hands. "I do feel it as sensitively as any one can, and so does the whole army and they speak of it in very severe terms, but the good sense of it is for me to say not a word but go on and do my duty to my country." He expressed disgust at the rise of peace sentiment in the North:

> from the papers it seems that at home . . . there will be trouble yet though I hope not. The people are crazy. Just now when the rebels are almost exhausted, they can not increase their armies any more, and if we can only get the proper quota to fill our ranks it must be crushed, yet, at home they cry of peace.[43]

August was a quiet month as Hood and Sherman played a giant game of bluff. Hood sent Fighting Joe Wheeler's horsemen at Sherman's rail link with the rear, but they were unable to do serious damage. In the lines around Atlanta Hood seemed unwilling to hazard another attack. Sherman was content to put Atlanta under siege. Union guns daily screamed and whistled their deadly salvos into the city. "The Yankees . . . are 'pegging away' with their cannon and the picket's keep up a regular noise from one end of the line to the other, something like *cutting cord wood*," reported a rebel private.[44] As his guns "pegged away," Sherman edged his army around the city on the west to cut off Hood's rail lines, enveloping Atlanta like a giant octopus.

Logan's 15th Corps was the spearhead of one of the tenta-

---

[42]William B. Hazen, *Narrative of Military Service* (Boston, 1885), 280.

[43]JAL to Mary Logan, Aug. 21, 1864, Logan Mss.

[44]J. I. Cain, "The Battle of Atlanta as Described by a Confederate Soldier," Contributed by Andrew F. Muir, *Georgia Historical Quarterly*, XLII, No. 1 (March, 1958), 110.

cles slowly extending southward. Its objectives were two railroads running south from Atlanta. Logan started moving on the night of the 27th, and though it rained all night, Logan, "as wide awake by night as by day," kept his men rolling and they reached Camp Creek by the 28th.[45] Osterhaus led the way on the 29th as Logan probed forward on the Army of the Tennessee's left. Dodge and Blair had the roads, but Logan's pioneers, hacking their way through dense woods, kept up a steady pace. On the 29th Logan hit the Atlanta and West Point Railroad and spent the day tearing up rails. The men burned ties, twisted rails, and broke telegraph wire. The job was done so well that Logan pronounced the destruction complete.[46]

Jonesboro was the objective on the 30th, and Logan crossed a number of creeks as he sweated toward Hood's last rail line, the Macon and Western. Before noon a detachment of cavalry under Hibe Cunningham, now a captain wearing blue instead of gray, struck rebel cavalry vedettes and drove them back. The corps, Hazen leading, came up quickly and by 3:30 it had reached the Flint River about a mile from Jonesboro and the railroad. At the river Logan found a strong enemy force rushed by Hood to keep the railroad open. Logan sent Hazen to join Judson Kilpatrick's cavalry in securing the bridge across the Flint and rushed his whole command across when it was in Union hands. It was midnight before the entire corps had crossed and Logan found the best ground available and dug in. The new man, Hazen, held Logan's left, and Harrow the right. Osterhaus was in reserve with Kilpatrick's cavalry. All night trains chugged into the town as Hood, surprised by Sherman's movement, rushed to hurl back the Yankees and protect the railroad.

As he sat in his tent on the quiet night before battle, Logan's mind went back to an incident of the day. As his men had moved forward they encountered a clearing surrounding a log cabin. An old "cracker" woman came out but retreated when she saw Union troops. The cabin was badly scarred by shell fire and entering troops found the woman's daughter lying on the bed with a new born child. Someone proposed baptism and

---

[45]Howard, *Autobiography*, II, 32.
[46]*OR*, Ser. 1, XXXVIII, pt. 3, 107.

sent for a chaplain. The request was heard by Logan who wanted to know why a chaplain was needed. When he heard, he rode off with the clergyman. On arriving in the clearing a Union doctor told him, "General you are just the man we're after."

"For what?"

"For a godfather," replied the doctor.

Logan went inside, ordered his men to leave some of their rations, and held the child while the chaplain went through the ceremony. The baby, whose father had been killed fighting with the Confederate army in Virginia, was christened "Shell-Anna," and Logan left a gold coin as a gift. As he rode away from this interlude in the war, Logan posted a guard to make certain the women were not disturbed by stragglers.[47]

When dawn broke on the 31st, Logan roused his men to be ready for immediate attack. He sent two regiments from Osterhaus to bolster Hazen and got one brigade from the 16th Corps. With this one exception the day's fight was the private property of the 15th Corps. All morning Logan's pioneers under Captain Herman Klosterman erected stronger positions. At noon Logan stood ready to receive an attack, and he ordered his guns to shell the railroad depot and Confederate lines. It was not until 3 o'clock that an answering fire came from enemy artillery. After a 15-minute barrage rebel infantry charged Logan's entire line. Hazen bore the brunt of enemy assaults, but Klosterman's shovellers had done their job well and from strong works Logan poured "the most terrible and destructive fire" he had ever witnessed. Logan, as usual galloping along the line looked across the field, saw his opponent, General Patton Anderson, riding fearlessly into the mouth of withering Federal fire. He later observed that Anderson "did all that a commander could to make the assault a success. . . . I could not help but admire his gallantry, though an enemy."[48]

The first Confederate attack broke but was succeeded by two others. The final strike was made hesitantly by men who seemed to have had enough dying while trying to hammer the sturdy Tennesseans into submission. At dusk rebel fire sput-

[47]Dawson, Logan, 76-80.
[48]OR, Ser. 1, XXXVIII, pt. 3, 109.

tered to a stop and Logan took stock of his position. He had lost only 154 men while Confederate loss in prisoners alone exceeded that figure.

On September 1, Logan, busy with artillery fire to support Jeff C. Davis' 14th Corps, heard that Schofield had cut the Macon and Western between Atlanta and Jonesboro. That night unusual sounds drifted southward from Atlanta. At about midnight Logan heard rumblings from the city 26 miles away. Again about 4 o'clock more faint explosions roused Logan, but they soon died away. At dawn Logan rose to find enemy trenches vacant, and by 10 o'clock rumors that Hood had abandoned Atlanta reached men at Jonesboro. All day long Sherman cautiously approached the city, unwilling to expose his army needlessly. All was quiet from the Georgia rail center, and Sherman wrote Schofield, "Nothing positive from Atlanta, and that bothers me."[49] After midnight the happy truth finally arrived. The sounds of the previous night were sounds of Hood's evacuation. The rebel army was gone. General Henry W. Slocum had already telegraphed Stanton: "General Sherman has taken Atlanta," but it was Sherman's message of the 4th that is best remembered: "Atlanta is ours and fairly won."[50]

When word reached the troops pandemonium ensued. Cheers rang through the woods and Logan and his staff congratulated each other on the success of the great campaign. For a time cheers had to be suppressed since Sherman had ordered Logan to pursue the retreating enemy. Sherman called off the chase on the 5th and Logan marched to East Point where he set up camp and rested his men from four months of almost constant action.

At East Point Logan wrote his report to Sherman. Evidencing great pride in his corps, Logan wrote: "The officers and soldiers of my command have performed the duties of the campaign willingly and earnestly; in no instance has a disposition other than to face the enemy been exhibited." Logan reported his casualties at 650 killed, 3,538 wounded, and 633 missing.[51]

49*Ibid.*, Ser. 1, XXXVIII, pt. 5, 774-775.
50*Ibid.*, 763, 777.
51*Ibid.*, Ser. 1, XXXVIII, pt. 3, 111.

The capture of Atlanta had a great effect on a North starved for concrete victory. For months Grant and Sherman had advanced, but neither had won a triumph which could bring joy and hope to the nation. J. G. Randall has written:

It is hard to exaggerate the effect of this news. To the average Northerner, weary with hope deferred after years of frightful loss, it seemed the most important achievement of Union arms in the year 1864. To Lincoln and the Republicans, under blame for a blundering and 'hopeless' war, it was a godsend.[52]

Logan's role in the Atlanta campaign had been an active and significant one. He had been the most dashing corps commander in an army of able leaders, and his fame travelled throughout the nation. Due to his friendly relations with the press, probably no officer in the army except Sherman and possibly McPherson had garnered more fame in the four months in Georgia. Despite this acclaim, Logan sat in his tent on September 13, writing his campaign report, a disappointed man. His words do not reveal this feeling or his hostility to Sherman, but he deeply resented the refusal to preserve him as McPherson's successor.

The campaign over, Sherman's mind began to think of the next move against Hood. Logan's thoughts moved in other directions. As after Vicksburg, a lull gave Logan a chance to go home and parlay his military fame in the political arena. Logan had "flanked the devil" in Georgia; now he was ready to begin a head-on assault against political "devils" in Illinois.

---

[52]Randall and Donald, *Civil War and Reconstruction*, 426.

CHAPTER XIV

LOGAN IS CARRYING EGYPT

As Sherman's legions struck deep into the heart of the Confederacy, political events of 1864 gathered momentum. Union failure to end the war in the spring and summer increased the clamor for peace and made Democratic chances of unseating Lincoln in the fall appear excellent. Furthermore, Republican politicians were not helping their own cause. Factional strife between Lincoln and the Radicals brought on Salmon P. Chase and John C. Fremont booms. Both movements failed to be followed by a Lincoln victory in June at Baltimore. Tennessee Unionist Andrew Johnson was named Lincoln's running mate. The Baltimore platform called for a united effort to put down the rebellion and demanded abolition of slavery.

The Democrats met in Chicago August 29 to choose their nominees. Both war and peace men were included in the convention, and a war Democrat, General George McClellan, and a peace man, George Pendleton of Ohio, were the party's candidates. The platform was composed by the peace faction and called the war a failure. It demanded peace as soon as possible.

In Illinois, Democrats seemed to be ahead in the spring and summer. They nominated James Robinson for governor while Republicans chose Richard Oglesby. In Egypt Josh Allen was certain to receive the Democratic nomination for Congress from the 13th District, Logan's old seat. For a time the Republican candidate was in doubt, but in July Andrew J. Kuykendall, an old comrade of Logan's in the 31st Illinois and a former Democrat, won the nomination to oppose Allen. The *Illinois State Register* greeted Kuykendall with hostility: "The miscegens of the 13th district have nominated that patriotic 'war democrat' Kuykendall for Congress. Good Lord Kuyk, what can one man be? We don't think you'll find your 'war democracy' a very paying card in Egypt."[1]

1*Illinois State Register*, July 8, 1864.

Logan kept his eye on the political scene as he fought through Georgia. As early as March he had written his wife, "I understand that Josh Allen will soon . . . commence his canvass for Congress. I do hope that Haynie will run against him and beat him. He can do it and God knows it would do me good to hear of his defeat."[2] Logan said little else about politics until nominations had been made and then he struck at Allen again. "Josh Allen wrote me a letter, the infernal scoundrel, merely wanting me to write a letter to him saying that I was not for Kuykendall. I shall not answer his letter, but hope Kuykendall may beat him of which I have no hopes."[3]

In August and September, as national candidates were nominated and politics moved to stage center, Logan was deluged with political letters. Two old Democratic friends, Charles Lanphier, editor of the *State Register*, and Democratic journalist, James W. Sheahan of Chicago, wanted Logan to speak for the Democrats. Lanphier asked him to campaign for four days in Springfield: "They are pressing us here, have all the money, and with the pride about 'Lincoln's home,' they will turn heaven and hell to beat us."[4] Sheahan wrote after McClellan's nomination, requesting Logan's endorsement of McClellan. He asked:

Will you refuse both [party and country] when they jointly ask your voice in this election? In God's name Dear Logan, by all your hopes for your country and yourself, let not the Democracy ask your arm and be refused. . . . That party gives us a *rational* and a *national* platform, will you refuse to give your voice in behalf of our Hon. soldier, patriot, Democrat, and Statesman, McClellan?

P. S. Lincoln has gone to the devil. Illinois will give Mc[Clellan] 35,000 majority.[5]

A Democrat from New York, friend of Democratic Congressman J. B. Haskin, several times wrote Logan suggesting that the general be a candidate for vice-president on the Democratic ticket.[6] Logan seems to have ignored these pleas entire-

---

[2]JAL to Mary Logan, Mar. 4, 1864, Logan Mss.
[3]JAL to Mary Logan, Aug. 6, 1864, Logan Mss.
[4]Charles Lanphier to JAL, Aug. 7, 1964, Logan Mss.
[5]J. W. Sheahan to JAL, Aug. 31, 1864, Logan Mss.

ly. Until Atlanta fell he showed no indication that he would participate in the election in any capacity.

In September an old friend and a Republican congressman wrote Logan to ask his support. I. N. Haynie regretted Logan's absence from Egyptian politics, and accurately stated the general's feelings when he wrote, "I am sure that you cannot be a disinterested spectator of a field in which you were in days past so conspicuous a leader." Haynie told Logan Egyptian Democrats were nothing but peace men, but hoped at least six counties in Logan's old district might give Union majorities.[7] Three days after Haynie's report, Republican Congressman Elihu Washburne wrote Logan from Washington. He congratulated him on his role in Sherman's victory and turned to politics. The Chicago platform, he commented, "proclaims the experiment of war has been a failure, that you and the noble soldiers who have been fighting under you have accomplished nothing." Washburne expressed the wish that Logan might go to Illinois and campaign for Lincoln. "We want your clarion voice to echo over our state and arouse the Union and patriotic people to the salvation of the country."[8]

Washburne's appeal for Logan's support was seconded by the president shortly afterward. If Lincoln wrote Logan a personal letter the document has disappeared, but Logan wrote long after the war, "When I left on leave after the Atlanta campaign to canvass for Mr. Lincoln, I did it at the special and private request of the then president. This I kept to myself and have never made it public."[9]

The request for Logan's leave that Sherman received came from Stanton, no doubt with Lincoln's approval. On September 20 Sherman remarked caustically to Howard, "There seems a special reason why he should go home at once."[10] Though military success had made Sherman more cooperative in sending soldiers home to take part in political campaigns, he still complained: "our armies vanish before our eyes and it is useless to complain because the election is more important than the

6F. G. Young to JAL, July 27, Aug. 12, 1864, Logan Mss.
7I. N. Haynie to JAL, Sept. 9, 1864, Logan Mss.
8Elihu Washburne to JAL, Sept. 13, 1864, Logan Mss.
9JAL to W. T. Sherman, Feb. 18, 1883, Logan Mss.
10OR, Ser. 1, XXXIX, pt. 2, 426.

war."[11] In his *Memoirs* Sherman wrote curtly, "General . . . Logan went home to look after politics."[12] On September 21 Logan turned over corps command to Osterhaus and bade his men good-by. He told them they could "feel safe" under Osterhaus, and was loudly cheered when he boarded the train.[13]

Before Logan decided to return, both parties were claiming his support. The *State Register* advised Illinois Democrats that Palmer, McClernand, Logan "and other distinguished and influential gentlemen who have not, of late, acted with the Democratic party, will give their influence to secure the election of Gen. McClellan."[14] Several days later the Republican *State Journal* questioned the *Register's* claim in light of all that had been said against Logan by Illinois peace men. The paper intimated that Logan and other war Democrats would back Lincoln.[15] Later, when they were sure of Logan's support, Illinois Republicans did not claim Logan had abandoned the Democrats. Rather they continued to call him a "war Democrat" to win increased support from Democrats.[16]

Logan's journey northward took about a week, and when he reached Illinois, the Democrats announced his arrival with no mention of politics. The *State Journal,* on the other hand, blared in a banner headline: "Gen. John A. Logan Coming Home." It claimed, "He will be enthusiastically welcomed by every loyal man in Illinois."[17]

Logan had said so little about his probable course that even his wife was not sure whom he would support. He had written nothing concerning politics except opposition to Allen, but from this she felt he would stump for Lincoln. Logan's brothers thought he would come out for McClellan. In her *Reminiscences* Mary Logan tells of a bet she made with one of them. A span of mules was the prize won by Mary when her husband spoke for the president. The mules were used to pull the Logan's carriage around Egypt.[18]

---

[11]Sherman, *Home Letters*, 314.
[12]Sherman, *Memoirs*, II, 130.
[13]Upson, *With Sherman*, 133.
[14]*Illinois State Register*, Sept. 6, 1864.
[15]*Illinois State Journal*, Sept. 8, 1864.
[16]*Ibid.*, Sept. 21, 1864.
[17]*Illinois State Register*, Sept. 27, 1864; *Illinois State Journal*, Sept. 24, 1864.
[18]Mary Logan, *Reminiscences*, 178.

Logan's first speech was scheduled for Carbondale on October 1. Before that appearance, few were certain which candidates would be beneficiaries of Logan's "clarion voice." Two days before Logan took the stump Josh Allen wrote him from Marion. Allen spoke of Logan's "extensive influence" and asked, "if compatible with your sense of duty and conviction of right," that he back McClellan. Allen assured Logan his "true friends" were Democrats. Logan's former law partner did not ask support for his own candidacy, but concluded, "No one would hail with greater delight than myself the era when your relations and mine should be as of your [sic]."[19]

Logan reserved his answer for the rostrum. On October 1, dashing off a note to Republican leaders, "I will be in Springgeld on the 5th of October ready for duty," he walked to Carbondale square. He had been swamped with questions since he reached the city but had parried them all. Logan looked appropriately tired when he mounted the platform on a warm fall day and looked out on familiar faces.[20]

From the first words it was evident he would not support McClellan. He delivered a tirade against "men among us who sympathize with the infamous and damnable treason." He spoke of his Democratic background but refused to "act with or support any man or set of men, no matter by what name they may be called, that are not in favor of exhausting all the men and means under the control of the Government in order to put down this accursed rebellion." His familiar voice rising to a roar, he said:

> When I find the leaders of the party I acted with, betraying the trust of the people reposed in them; when I find them repudiating the doctrine of Jackson, who was for hanging traitors to the highest tree . . . and for preserving the Union at all hazards, either with blood or without it, I am compelled to follow you no farther. I cannot go with you into the precincts of treason and disloyalty.

The crowd roared as he finished: "I will act with no party who

---

[19]Josh Allen to JAL, Sept. 29, 1864, Logan Mss.

[20]Mary Logan, *Reminiscences*, 170. Mrs. Logan estimated the Carbondale crowd at 20,000, no doubt a slight exaggeration.

is not in favor of my country, and must refuse to support the nominees of the Chicago platform."[21]

After the Carbondale speech Logan boarded a train for Springfield. A ceremony complete with cannon and speeches was to have greeted the Egyptian, but a downpour interfered. Several hundred braved the rain to greet Logan and hear Governor Yates say, "Napoleon never had a better or prouder General than John A. Logan." Logan responded telling the gathering there were only two sides, patriots and traitors, and declared his determination to fight the Chicago platform.[22]

The *Illinois State Register* greeted Logan's arrival sarcastically, saying he had "reported for duty" to the abolitionists. It asked the former Democratic congressman how it felt to be supporting men who had called him "Dirty Work" in 1861. Lanphier's paper professed to be mystified by Logan's traitorous conduct to his old party.[23]

On October 5, Logan closeted himself with Republican leaders to work out a schedule of sixteen speeches. Most of these were to be in Egypt, with an occasional foray into northern Illinois.[24] The same night in Springfield, Logan delivered his second speech, almost a reiteration of the Carbondale address. He again called on Jacksonian Democrats to act as "Old Hickory" would have in preserving the Union. He added, "I believe Mr. Lincoln is a devoted patriot struggling honestly to preserve this country." "He has done some things that I have not thought best," Logan continued without specifying, "but that he has tried faithfully to sustain the Constitution . . . is a position . . . no man can gainsay." Of Lincoln's running mate, Logan said, "If Lincoln should die this man Johnson has brains enough to run the machine. He is a patriot, a soldier, and a statesman. . . . I am for these men whether I have a friend left in the Democratic party or not."[25]

The *State Register* stepped up its attack on the apostate, reiterating the 1861 Republican charge that Logan had raised troops for the South. Lanphier wrote, "John, we should be

[21]Alton *Telegraph*, Oct. 7, 1864; Carbondale *New Era*, Oct. 12, 1864.
[22]*Illinois State Journal*, Oct. 5, 1864.
[23]*Illinois State Register*, Oct. 5, 1864.
[24]*Illinois State Journal*, Oct. 6, 1864.
[25]*Ibid.*, Oct. 6, 7, 1864.

sorry to think you couldn't fight any better than you talk."[26] Then the paper implied that Logan's campaigning constituted desertion from the army. It reported the Confederate attempt to cut off Sherman's line of communications, "Yet Major Generals Logan and Palmer . . . are in Illinois making speeches for Lincoln." Democrats everywhere took up the cry and Logan was condemned for playing politics when he should have been at the front.[27]

Logan left Springfield and spoke in Belleville on October 10, then moved on to Centralia and DuQuoin. At DuQuoin, scene of his 1863 address, Logan was joined by Oglesby. Haynie tried to get Yates to join the group, but the governor was unable to attend.[28] At DuQuoin Logan reminded his listeners of his earlier address, and endorsed Oglesby for governor. Logan followed Springfield Republican Shelby Cullom on the 15th at Clinton, and launched his first attack on Josh Allen. Allen, Logan claimed, had proposed dividing Illinois into two parts in 1861, the Southern part to join the Confederacy. Logan stated that he refused to join Allen's plot and "told him that he would see any man who would attempt such a project hanged as high as Haman."[29]

Logan's Egyptian speeches continued to strike at Allen. While he endorsed Lincoln and Oglesby, he worked even harder for Kuykendall. In August he was pessimistic of Kuykendall's chances, but in October his hopes soared. He wrote his wife, "I spoke yesterday to a large crowd, mostly Republicans. . . . This district [the 13th] is now safe I think."[30]

Alton, center of Egyptian Republicanism, furnished Logan's audience on October 20, and he told it he was ready to go to any length to put down the rebellion. "I am willing to subjugate, burn, and I had almost said exterminate rather than not put down this rebellion. I am in favor of taking Negroes. I have no conscientious scruples concerning slavery; but the South has violated its contract."[31] Moving into deepest Egypt,

[26]*Illinois State Register*, Oct. 7, 8, 1864.
[27]*Ibid.*, Oct. 16, 1864.
[28]I. N. Haynie to Richard Yates, Oct. 7, 1864, **Yates Mss.**
[29]*Missouri Democrat* (St. Louis) in *Illinois State Journal*, Oct. 17, 1864.
[30]JAL to Mary Logan, Oct. 19, 1864, Logan Mss.
[31]*Illinois State Journal*, Oct. 21, 1864; Alton *Telegraph*, Oct. 21, 1864.

he spoke at Jonesboro, Cairo, and Benton. In Jonesboro he returned to the subject of Allen:

Now let me say a few words about this man Allen. I know him well and a greater traitor and humbug walks not unhung. When the war first broke out, and at about the time I returned from Congress to this district, in order to raise a regiment and to enter the field and service of my country, I met Josh Allen stalking about the Southern part of the State, trying to turn it over to the rebels; and he made a proposition to me to stump the district for the Confederacy to induce the Southern half of Illinois to secede with me, and I told him I'd see him in Hell first.[32]

This brought a heated denial from Allen. He proclaimed his innocence and professed astonishment at Logan's charge. "I pronounce the charge . . . unqualifiedly false—false in its conception by him, and dastardly in its repetition by the poor parasites of ill-gained power."[33]

Logan echoed Allen in denying charges of treason. He wrote a note dealing with these charges to Egyptian Republican D. L. Phillips, which was printed in the Chicago *Tribune*. Logan called these allegations "false in every particular," and denied he had ever assisted any man to go South. His opponents were slandering him because he had stood by his country while they aided rebels.[34] The Jonesboro *Gazette* defended Allen and berated Logan, its former hero, calling him a "mysterious combination of buffoonary and blackguardism," and pointing to Logan's pro-Confederate attitude in 1861.[35]

The campaign, bitter all over Illinois, was especially intense in Egypt where Logan and Allen traded accusations at every opportunity while Kuykendall was forgotten much of the time. Logan concluded most of his addresses with appeals in Kuykendall's name and bore the brunt of the campaigning. Though Kuykendall spoke regularly, it was obvious that if Allen were to lose Logan would be the chief reason.

Pennsylvania, Indiana, and Ohio chose state officers in October in elections indicative of the November result. Republicans

---

[32]*Illinois State Journal*, Oct. 29, 1864.
[33]Jonesboro *Gazette*, Nov. 4, 1864.
[34]JAL to D. L. Phillips in Chicago *Tribune*, Oct. 25, 1864.
[35]Jonesboro *Gazette*, Oct. 29, 1864.

ran well in October and forecast complete victory the following month. Many troops had been furloughed to aid Lincoln's cause, and Logan everywhere met comrades from the Army of the Tennessee. The week before election day, Logan swung through Harrisburg, Vienna, and Metropolis, then left the state for one big Union speech in Evansville, Indiana. Lincoln estimated Illinois in the McClellan column during the final week. Washburne had written of "imminent danger of losing this state," but just before election day he wrote a worried president, "Logan is carrying all before him in Egypt."[36]

The nation voted on November 8, and the next day even Lanphier's paper admitted "the returns so far look unfavorable for the Democracy."[37] Returns soon indicated a national landslide for Lincoln, for McClellan was able to carry only Kentucky, Delaware, and New Jersey as the president amassed a 400,000 vote majority. Illinois wound up safely Republican by 30,736 votes. In addition Oglesby beat Robinson, and eleven of the state's fourteen seats in Congress went to Republicans.[38]

Congressional and presidential races in Egypt were exciting to the end. The 13th District, always Democratic, went Republican. Kuykendall defeated Allen 11,742 to 10,759. Allen won nine counties to six for Logan's candidate, but Kuykendall won several by landslides. Johnson County, which had given Logan immense majorities as a Democrat, voted for Kuykendall, 1,225 to 367, but Logan's native county, Jackson, refused to follow his lead and went to Allen.[39] Even the neighboring 12th District became Republican. There W. R. Morrison, Logan's wounded comrade of Donelson, was beaten by Republican Jehu Baker, for whom Logan had campaigned. The Lincoln-McClellan race in the 13th was also evidence of Logan's electioneering ability and popularity. In a district that had soundly defeated him in 1858 and 1860, Lincoln won a close race.[40]

Most were willing to credit Logan for the section's amazing

[36]Sandburg, *Lincoln, War Years*, III, 275.
[37]*Illinois State Register*, Nov. 9, 1864.
[38]Cole, *Era of the Civil War*, 328.
[39]*Illinois State Journal*, Nov. 21, 1864. Jackson voted for Allen 1,201 to 789.
[40]*Ibid.*, Nov. 22, 1864. Lincoln won 11,714 to 10,926.

political reversal. Washburne's words were echoed by the *Illinois State Journal* and Alton *Telegraph*. The latter felt:

The Union party is indebted in a great measure to him for the glorious result. . . . He it was that went to the field of battle and came back covered with glory, and exposed the machinations of Josh Allen. To this fact then, more than any other, this glorious triumph over Copperheadism is attributable.[41]

After the war the Chicago *Tribune* recalled "how he revolutionized Egypt in the fall of 1864."[42] In 1864 newly elected Governor Oglesby joined these voices as he thanked Logan for

the generous and very effective cooperation and support of your heart and tongue in the late canvass. This however, General is but a small part of the rich results of your noble efforts in behalf of the whole cause. I feel sure your bold attacks in Egypt . . . will never be forgotten nor cease to be honored by all Illinois.[43]

Election over, Logan thought of his return to the army. During October, unknown to Logan, he was proposed by both Stanton and Grant as Rosecrans' successor as Union commander in Missouri. Logan's name was dropped, however, because of his political activities.[44] Although he was exhausted and complained of an "inflammation in the throat," he wrote Sherman asking if he should come back at once, but Sherman, about to march to the sea, replied, "It is not possible to overtake your command. Remain at home until you recover."[45] To obtain an extended leave Logan wrote Lincoln. He asked thirty additional days and for permission to visit Washington on his way back to the army.[46] Lincoln granted the leave, subject to Sherman's approval, and added, "If in view of maintaining your good relations with Gen. Sherman . . . you can safely come here, I shall be very glad to see you."[47] Logan spent a few days resting in Illinois.

[41]Alton *Telegraph*, Nov. 18, 1864; *Illinois State Journal*, Nov. 15, 1864.
[42]Chicago *Tribune*, Aug. 6, 1866.
[43]Richard Oglesby to JAL, Nov. 20, 1864, Logan Mss.
[44]*OR*, Ser. 1, XLI, pt. 4, 3, 126.
[45]*Ibid.*, Ser. 1, XLIV, 465.
[46]*Ibid.*, Ser. 1, XXXIX, pt. 3, 751.
[47]*Ibid.*

Never quiet for long, he was off again in mid-November. He traveled to Chicago and delivered a Union speech before returning to Springfield and Egypt at month's end. Logan's extended leave and his trip to northern Illinois may have been prompted by a sudden "Logan for Senator" movement. Letters written two months later indicate Logan's interest in the senatorship, but in November he stuck to his vow to "eschew politics" and returned to the army before the legislature met.[48] I. N. Haynie was interested in promoting Logan's candidacy. He arranged with the editor of the Mt. Vernon *Unconditional Unionist* to mention Logan as Egypt's senatorial favorite, promising to send a copy of the endorsement to every paper in the state. Haynie told Logan, "It is my design to stir things up hot."[49] Several other papers took up the *Unionist's* call for Logan, but the *State Journal* was not carried away.[50] It supported Yates for the Senate but announced its admiration for Logan whom it believed would not be a candidate. Democrats, smarting under the election defeat, accused Logan of thinking more about the senatorship than the war.[51] When Yates was finally elected, Logan was on his way back to resume command. Haynie, disappointed at Logan's refusal to stay in Springfield until the legislature met, wrote Mary: "There is no question but that the senatorship was within his grasp if he had been able to be present during the contest. All parties concede that Genl. Logan will be invincible two years hence."[52]

In early December the politician became a soldier again. With Lincoln's permission he began his trip to Washington. Logan's activity in Illinois in 1864 was significant. He supported Union candidates and opposed those he felt favored peace. His speeches rang with appeals for war support, but mentioned few other issues. Abolition and Reconstruction were almost completely ignored. It is difficult to call Logan a Republican in 1864. He was obviously a Unionist, one of many prewar Democrats who joined Republicans behind Lincoln under

---

[48]JAL to Mary Logan, Jan. 20, 22, 1865, Logan Mss.
[49]I. N. Haynie to JAL, Nov. 19, 25, 1864, Logan Mss.
[50]Two of Logan's supporters were the *Central Illinois Gazette* (Champaign), Dec. 2, 1864 and the Carbondale *New Era* in *Illinois State Journal*, Dec. 12, 1864. See also *Illinois State Journal*, Nov. 26, 1864.
[51]Jonesboro *Gazette*, Dec. 24, 1864.
[52]I. N. Haynie to Mary Logan, Jan. 4, 1865, Logan Mss.

the Union banner. But to date Logan's conversion to Republicanism from 1864 is misleading. In his speeches and letters he did not seem to think of himself as a Republican. Logan was regarded by others as a "war Democrat," or a "Unionist." "Black Jack" arrived in Washington in December, spent several days in the city, and went out to City Point, Virginia, to see Grant. The two friends greeted each other cordially and talked over old times in the West. There was little time for reminiscing, however, for Grant had something on his mind. Since Logan had returned to Illinois there had been important developments at the front. Sherman had left Atlanta and was somewhere in the interior of Georgia, striking for the sea. When Sherman left Atlanta he sent part of his army under Thomas back to Tennessee to stop Hood's invasion. The Confederate chief had decided to slash northward hoping to draw Sherman out of Georgia. When Logan met Grant, Hood was outside Nashville besieging Thomas, and the "Rock of Chickaamagua" showed no inclination to attack his besiegers.[53]

Thomas felt he had ample reason to wait. His cavalry did not have sufficient mounts, and when they got them, bad weather made cavalry movement impossible. One of Thomas' lieutenants reported, "Men and horses were seen falling whenever they attempted to move across country."[54]

In Washington, where the ice hazard was not fully appreciated, Thomas' superiors were first anxious and then angry. Grant wired Thomas several times in early December urging him to attack, and by the 11th he threatened Thomas with removal.[55] Stanton and Halleck joined in Grant's demands and the Secretary of War telegraphed Grant, "Thomas seems unwilling to attack because it is hazardous, as if all war was anything but hazardous. If he waits for Wilson to get ready, Gabriel will be blowing his last horn."[56]

Finally, on the 13th, Thomas still waiting, Grant decided to send Logan to relieve him.[57] Logan held a high place in Grant's mind; the army commander thought of him as a "vig-

[53]Stanley F. Horn, *The Decisive Battle of Nashville* (Baton Rouge, Louisiana, 1956), 59-62; *Battles and Leaders*, IV, 440-474.
[54]Cox, *Reminiscences*, II, 352-353.
[55]Grant, *Memoirs*, II, 259.
[56]*OR*, Ser. 1, XLV, pt. 2, 84.
[57]*Ibid.*, 171.

orous fighter." The two men talked over the Nashville situation and Logan was on his way by midday.[58] He was directed "not to deliver the order or publish it until he reached there, and if Thomas had moved then not to deliver it at all."[59]

"Black Jack" raced to Washington and entrained for the West.[60] He reached Cincinnati next day and Louisville on the 15th. Grant himself, still anxious, decided to follow Logan. He was in Washington ready to depart when he heard of Thomas' victory. With Logan in Kentucky and Grant on his way, Thomas attacked. In a two day contest the deliberate Thomas smashed Hood's invaders.

Logan had no reason to go on. He telegraphed Grant on the morning of the 17th, "People here jubilant over Thomas' success. Confidence seems to be restored. I will remain here to hear from you. . . . It would seem best that I return to join my command with Sherman."[61] Two days later Grant ordered Logan to report to Washington on his way back to the South.[62]

The Nashville affair was a subject of much discussion after the war. Logan's magnanimity in not rushing to relieve Thomas, who had supposedly been unfair to Logan in Georgia, drew praise. Mary Logan embellished this story with a claim that Logan stopped at Cincinnati and sent a staff officer to Thomas, telling him of Logan's mission and urging him to attack.[63] This story seems a fabrication, repeated by Logan's friends. Colonel Henry Stone, of Thomas' staff, stated that Thomas was totally ignorant of Logan's mission.[64] If Logan warned Thomas he was disobeying Grant's order not to "publish" the mission until he arrived. It was also said by Logan's friends that the general stopped in Kentucky when he could have reached Nashville in time to seize command.[65] This story

---

[58]Horace Porter, *Campaigning with Grant* (New York, 1897), 348.
[59]Grant, *Memoirs*, II, 259.
[60]Logan says in *The Great Conspiracy*, 602, that he went to see Lincoln on his way west. His letters do not indicate that he saw the president until his return. The urgency of the situation would surely have prevented a visit to Lincoln on his way to Nashville.
[61]*OR*, Ser. 1, XLV, pt. 2, 230.
[62]*Ibid.*, 265.
[63]Mary Logan, *Reminiscences*, 187.
[64]*Battles and Leaders*, IV, 456.
[65]Mary Logan, *Reminiscences*, 187; Logan, *Volunteer Soldier*, 67. The latter is from C. A. Logan's introductory memoir in *The Volunteer Soldier*.

was accepted by such post-war writers as Senator George Hoar, who called it an act of "magnanimous self-denial."[66] It would have been impossible for Logan to have reached Nashville ahead of Thomas' attack. This is an example of war tales, many either false or wrongly interpreted, used by Logan in post-war politics. None seem to have had greater currency than that of Logan's self-sacrifice at Nashville.[67]

Logan returned to Washington on December 23 and went to see Lincoln. In November when Logan asked to see the president, Washburne conveyed the request to Lincoln: "Genl. Jack Logan sends word to me that he wants to go to Washington . . . to see you about certain matters he does not wish to write about." What these "matters" were Logan never stated. While in Washington he wrote Mary, "I will see the President . . . and do the best I can in matters."[68] Nowhere does the general clarify his mysterious mission. His only report of the meeting came long after the war and it sheds no light on the mystery. He mentioned a conversation with Lincoln about the war:

> He had an absolute conviction as to the ultimate outcome of the war, the final triumph of the Union army; and I well remember with what an air of complete relief . . . he said to me, referring to Grant—'We have now at the head of the armies, a man in whom all the people can have confidence.'[69]

Following the Lincoln conference, Logan, the political arena once again thrust into the background, prepared to return to Sherman and the war.

---

[66]George F. Hoar, *Autobiography of Seventy Years* (New York, 1903), I, 236-237.

[67]Many of Logan's friendly biographers also reported that Logan commanded the 15th Corps in Sherman's March through Georgia.

[68]Lincoln, *Collected Works*, VIII, 105; JAL to Mary Logan, Dec. 23, 1864, Logan Mss.

[69]Logan, *Great Conspiracy*, 602.

CHAPTER XV

THE YEAR OF JUBILO

One topic of conversation in the Logan-Lincoln talks was a message from the president to Sherman. Logan was to be the messenger. When Sherman arrived at Savannah in December he telegraphed an anxious Lincoln, "I beg to present you as a Christmas gift the city of Savannah."[1] The answer Logan carried began, "Many, many thanks for your Christmas gift."[2] Logan boarded a warship and sailed to Savannah, arriving on January 6. He was welcomed by Sherman and, shaking off seasickness, reported to Mary, "This is the most beautiful city I have ever seen, it looks like a garden full of flowers."[3]

To the cheers of the 15th Corps Logan resumed his command. He relieved Osterhaus, congratulating the able Prussian on his leadership through Georgia. The corps staged a review to welcome "Black Jack," and an Illinois chaplain wrote: "The 15th Army Corps was reviewed today by Genl. Sherman. . . . Genl. Logan is here and presents the finest military appearance of all."[4]

Composition of the Army of the Tennessee had changed since Logan left Atlanta. The 16th Corps had been dissolved and merged into the 15th and 17th. Logan gained a fourth division commanded by General John M. Corse. His three old units remained virtually the same.[5]

The first week of the new year brought a resumption of Sherman's campaign. He decided to strike northward through the Carolinas toward Virginia where he and Grant would combine to crush Lee. Between Savannah and Virginia stood a battered rebel army, again commanded by Johnston, and miles

---

[1]Sherman, *Memoirs*, II, 231.
[2]Lincoln, *Collected Works*, VIII, 181.
[3]JAL to Mary Logan, Jan. 8, 1865, Logan Mss.
[4]George Compton Diary, Jan. 7, 1865, Civil War Diary Mss., Illinois State Historical Library.
[5]Sherman, *Memoirs*, II, 268-269. Charles Woods led the 1st, Hazen the 2nd, and John E. Smith the 3rd. The command totaled 15,765 officers and men.

of terrain made for defensive action. Sherman's men would have to march through long stretches of swamp filled to overflowing by torrential rains. Though the march would be no lark, as the stroll through Georgia had been, the men were ready to start. Every step seemed to bring victory nearer.

Logan spent a few days working on Savannah's defenses. After Blair's corps started into South Carolina, Woods' division of Logan's corps began embarkation. The division marched to Fort Thunderbolt south of the city and boarded transports on the 10th. Logan was anxious to have all his men in Beaufort, South Carolina, as soon as possible. Therefore he ordered Woods to move by all means available. Seizing anything that would float, Woods reached Beaufort by the 13th. He was followed by Hazen who had most of his unit there by the 17th. Woods and Hazen went into camp at Beaufort, a town with "a dilipadated appearance and . . . very full of Negroes."⁶ With these two divisions away safely, Logan received a change of orders. Blair had advanced from Beaufort to Pocotaligo and reported enemy troops in retreat. He scouted the area across river from Savannah and decided troops could be moved overland. Sherman ordered embarkation suspended and Logan's men moved back to Savannah.⁷

Smith's division was set to cross the pontoon bridge over the Savannah River January 19, but the evening of the 18th brought a fierce rainstorm, pronounced by natives the worst in twenty years. Despite the deluge Smith began crossing and managed to get one brigade across before flooding made further crossing impossible. At this juncture Logan ordered Smith to push on to Pocotaligo with the half of his command on the South Carolina side, while the remainder of his division was in camp at Beaufort. On the 26th Logan transferred corps headquarters to that town. His last division, Corse's, was sent with General Henry Slocum's left wing up river to Sister's Ferry where it was to cross and march toward Hickory Hill where the entire corps was to rendezvous.

Before he left Savannah Logan wrote home. He remarked on the Illinois senatorial election, pronouncing Yates' victory

⁶Sherlock, *100th Indiana*, 109.
⁷*OR*, Ser. 1, XLVII, pt. 1, 221.

the result he expected. He also indicated disappointment at the failure of his own candidacy, blaming his supporters for not working hard enough. "I do feel as though I was somewhat neglected by those who should be under some obligations to me," he told his wife. This indicated more than passing interest in the election and seems to mean he would have resigned his commission if elected.[8]

Through soggy lowlands Logan's partial command moved toward Pocotaligo on the 27th. Despite the weather, marching was rapid and the men moved through "a low wet country which was a picture of desolation."[9] Most of the troops were determined to make South Carolina, called by many the "Hell hole of secession," howl, and many cheered and sang patriotic songs when they crossed into the Palmetto State.

By month's end Logan joined Smith's brigade at Pocotaligo, and the three divisions moved along the south bank of the Big Salkehatchie River toward Hickory Hill. Now they were in inhabited country, and foraging by "bummers" began. Daily, soldiers moved out ahead, behind, and to the side of the column, collecting supplies. A jingle, popular in the army, expressed the attitude toward "bumming":

'My boys can live on chicken and ham,
For everything that we do find
Belongs to Uncle Sam.'[10]

The last day of January Logan's corps moved through McPhersonville, and before the column cleared the town it was in flames. This was the first example of a harsh and often needless pattern already established in Georgia and many times repeated in the Carolinas. Logan, like Sherman, publicly deplored the wanton destruction, but seems to have made little effort to stop it. As Logan moved toward Hickory Hill he found many trees felled by retreating rebels, but his own mounted infantry detachments quickly cleared them and moved on.[11] The first days of February, Confederate cavalry appeared to harass

---

[8]JAL to Mary Logan, Jan. 20, 22, 1865, Logan Mss.

[9]Sherlock, *100th Indiana*, 187.

[10]John G. Barrett, *Sherman's March Through the Carolinas* (Chapel Hill, North Carolina, 1956), 54.

[11]*Henry Hitchcock, Marching With Sherman*, M. A. DeWolfe Howe

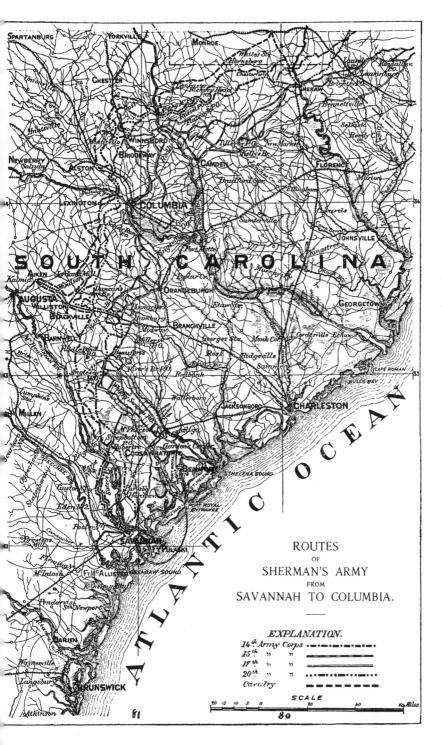

ROUTES
OF
SHERMAN'S ARMY
FROM
SAVANNAH TO COLUMBIA.

EXPLANATION.

14th Army Corps		
15th " "		
17th " "		
20th " "		
Cavalry		

SCALE

Sherman's March through the Carolinas

From *Battles and Leaders of the Civil War*

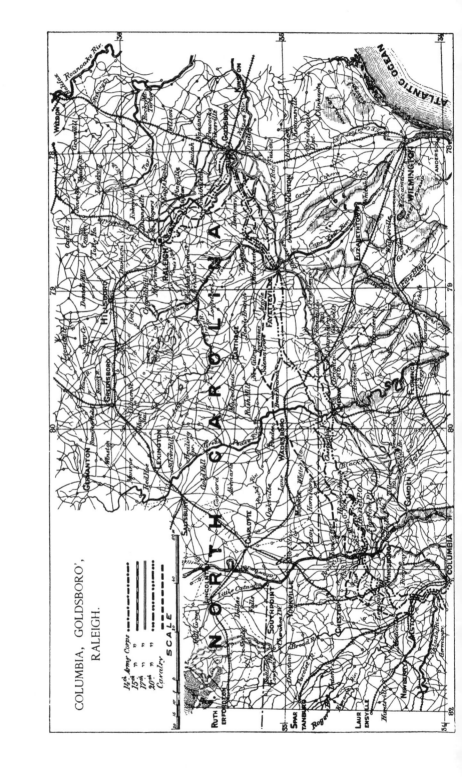

COLUMBIA, GOLDSBORO', RALEIGH.

the corps. Logan's men yelled, "You'd better get out, this is the Fifteenth Corps," and routed them.[12]

Corse failed to join Logan on February 2. He reported trouble crossing the Savannah River and was ordered to march with Jeff C. Davis' 14th Corps until it caught Logan.[13] Accompanied by Sherman, Logan left Hickory Hill and pushed toward Beaufort Bridge over the Big Salkehatchie. Corduroying was necessary, and grumbling artillerymen struggled to move guns over the morass. That night they camped in a field near Duck Creek and Logan sent Sherman an interesting captive of the day's advance, a "white slave." Sherman first feared the man was a spy, but his story was corroborated by a Negro slave. Logan, it was reported, was very interested in the case and declared, "This alone would have made an abolitionist of him."[14]

Logan began crossing the Big Salkehatchie on the 5th. Retreating enemy troops had destroyed the bridge and Logan's pioneers worked all day with pontoons. By nightfall the command had crossed, and Logan and Sherman shared a house used as Wheeler's headquarters the night before.[15]

Smith in the lead, Logan plodded on toward the Little Salkehatchie the following day. On reaching the stream Smith drove Wheeler's skirmishers across and discovered the bridge destroyed. He also found rebel works on the north bank occupied by a force ready to stop his crossing. The 3rd Division deployed in battle line facing rebel works, and Logan sent his two mounted infantry regiments in quest of a ford from which they could flank the enemy. While they searched, Woods' division was ordered up to support Smith, and the two units stood ready to attack. Logan, waiting word from his reconnaissance, rode toward the rear where he met Sherman and his staff. "Those fellows are trying to stop us at the creek down there, and damned sassy they are acting about it," he told Sherman.[16]

(ed.) (New Haven, Connecticut, 1927), 236.
 [12]Lewis, *Sherman*, 489.
 [13]Jeff C. Davis to John M. Palmer, Jan. 4, 1866, Davis Mss.
 [14]Hitchcock, *Marching With Sherman*, 248.
 [15]Conyngham, *Sherman's March*, 306.
 [16]Hitchcock, *Marching With Sherman*, 258.

Scouts could find no ford, so Logan decided on a frontal assault. Union troops occupied a high bluff overlooking rebel fortifications. The Confederate position, though much lower than Logan's, was defensible since its front was covered by the stream and a tangled swamp. The Little Salkehatchie could be forded opposite Wheeler's line, but it would mean a direct charge likely to be costly. Logan decided to fight anyway and called on Smith's 2nd Brigade, led by Colonel C. R. Wever, to attack. Wever's men charged across the stream and waded the muddy swamp in face of enemy fire. They cleared Confederate works and chased enemy troops back to an open field a mile to the rear. The rest of Smith's command waded across and dispersed the enemy.[17] Until dark the corps forded while pioneers erected a bridge for artillery and wagons.

At 6 o'clock the following morning, after a night of drenching rain, the corps marched toward Bamberg and the Charleston and Augusta Railroad. Sherman expected stiff resistance at the railroad, but none was found when the corps reached the tracks at noon. Logan put Hazen to work ripping up ties and rails, and before dark one mile of track had been totally destroyed.[18] Next day was spent destroying more track and scouting ahead to the next water barrier, the South Edisto. Colonel W. S. Jones returned at dusk to report bridges down and the river high.

On the 9th Logan swung slightly westward and camped, covering approaches to sites of two recently destroyed bridges. Pontoons were built on the 10th, and that day and the following morning were spent hurtling the river. High water extended far back into the woods and Logan's men "worked incessantly, often with cartridge boxes and haversacks suspended to their necks."[19] At dark Corse's division came up after an arduous struggle to catch the corps. Corse encountered high water at the Savannah River and was delayed for days. When he caught up, Logan wrote, "At last I found my whole corps together, unimpaired in usefulness."[20]

More water and rebel opposition loomed ahead. The North

---

[17]*OR*, Sec. 1, XLVII, pt. 1, 224.
[18]Hazen, *Narrative*, 357.
[19]Howard, *Autobiography*, II, 109.
[20]*OR*, Ser. 1, XLVII, pt. 1, 225.

Edisto was reached before noon, and a line of works appeared on the north bank. Logan spread his corps, sending Jones' brigade and Hazen's division to cross up and down stream from the rebel position. Many forded in water chest deep and others floated over on fallen trees. As soon as the gray coats found Logan's men on their side they broke, throwing down weapons in their flight. Logan took 80 prisoners, losing only one killed and five wounded. By night the entire corps had forded, but once over, a mile-wide swamp remained. Officers and men, including Logan, "waded with cheerfulness and enthusiasm."[21] Though a number of waterways remained between the 15th Corps and Columbia, it had spanned its last significant barrier in front of the South Carolina capital.

Sherman, who had ridden with the 17th Corps for several days, rejoined Logan on the 13th. Marching was easy for two days and by the morning of the 15th Logan, approaching Congaree Creek, stood less than ten miles from Columbia. Scouts reported enemy works north of the creek, and Woods' division was sent to take them. As they had done twice earlier, Logan's men flanked the enemy. Rebels abandoned their line with a rush, but a rear guard tried to burn the small bridge Logan had been unable to cross because of enemy fire. Wet timbers would not ignite, Confederates fled, and Logan crossed, racing for Columbia. He met a large force of Wade Hampton's rebel cavalry in the afternoon, but Woods advanced and it gave way without fighting. Logan reached the Congaree River that night and bivouacked opposite the capital of the "Hell hole of secession." During the night rebel artillery shelled 15th Corps camps, doing little damage except to sleep. At dawn Logan stood ready to fight the battle for Columbia.

Approaching the city, Logan found the bridge over the Congaree destroyed and his pioneers told him their pontoons would not reach across. This necessitated crossing the Saluda and Broad Rivers. Opposite Columbia these streams join to form the Congaree, and the 15th Corps prepared to cross the Saluda to a narrow point of land between it and the Broad. The Confederate army showed no sign of giving up Columbia, and while Logan's men bridged the Saluda, DeGress' guns pounded

---

[21] Hazen, *Narrative*, 357.

the capital. Across the Saluda, Logan's advance pushed on toward the Broad, attempting to seize the bridge before it was demolished. Near the river it was stopped by Wheeler's rear guard, fortified by gin. The rebels, emboldened by their potations, held position until the bridge was on fire; then they rushed through flames to safety. Logan's lead troops could only sit and watch as the structure flamed and fell hissing into the river.[22]

After dark Logan camped in the narrow triangle between the two streams. The following morning, Woods leading, he began to cross the Broad. By 7:00 pontoons were down and the corps marched. Colonel George A. Stone's brigade crossed rapidly and reached the city before the 15th Corps had crossed. It was he who received the surrender from the mayor.[23] After threatening to fight, rebel leaders decided to abandon the city.

Before noon, led by Sherman, Howard, and Logan, the 15th Corps filed into the city. As the men marched they sang:

'Hail Columbia, happy land
If I don't burn you, I'll be damned.'[24]

A journalist watching the procession remarked, "John A. Logan, too was there, with his dark, almost bronzed countenance, and fiery, commanding eye, the true type of the dashing general."[25]

In Columbia order degenerated and men ran out of control. Logan maintained that the citizens received his soldiers with "bucketfuls of liquor, and negroes, overjoyed at our entrance, piloted them to buildings where wine and whiskey were stored, and for a while all control was lost."[26] General Slocum wrote, "A drunken soldier with a musket in one hand and a match in the other is not a pleasant visitor to have about the house on a dark, windy night."[27]

By dark fires had sprung up all over the city, and Sherman, lying down to rest, was roused by cries and flickering shad-

---

[22]Barrett, *Sherman's March Through the Carolinas*, 62.
[23]*OR*, Ser. 1, XLVII, pt. 1, 227.
[24]George W. Pepper, *Personal Recollections of Sherman's Campaigns in Georgia and the Carolinas* (Zanesville, Ohio, 1866), 311.
[25]New York *Herald*, Mar. 18, 1865.
[26]*OR*, Ser. 1, XLVII, pt. 1, 227.
[27]*Battles and Leaders*, IV, 686.

ows.[28] The origin of the flames is still a mystery. Sherman, Howard, and Hazen reported cotton bales on fire as the army entered the city, but Wade Hampton denied it emphatically.[29] Logan and Woods, who led the march, mention no such flames in their reports.[30] No matter what the origin, a strong wind blew all day, and after dark drunken soldiers raced about the city applying the torch.[31] Wind fanned the flames and a lurid nocturnal glare hung over the doomed city. Emma LeConte, South Carolina college girl, observed the scene with horror: "Two corps entered town . . . one, the diabolical 15th which Sherman had hitherto never permitted to enter a city on account of their vile and desperate character. . . . The devils as they marched past, looked strong and well-clad in dark, dirty-looking blue."[32]

With fire busily consuming the business district, Logan joined Howard and Woods in an attempt to fight its spread.[33] Sherman joined them about 11 o'clock and they worked feverishly to stem the inferno. Many soldiers, camped outside the city, ran back to help "Generals Logan and Howard in their fruitless attempts to extinguish the flames and save the city."[34] Man was impotent against the blaze and it had to burn itself out. Toward morning Logan had enough sober men to quell rioting and stop incendiaries, but fire had destroyed much of Columbia.

Of Logan's personal incendiary activities there are conflicting accounts. His headquarters was the beautiful home of Hampton's father-in-law, John C. Preston. When the Ursuline Convent burned, Sherman sent the Mother Superior and her charges to the Preston House for refuge. As the procession of little girls marched in, some claimed Logan was preparing to fire the house. Furthermore, South Carolina tradition, perhaps

28Sherman, Memoirs, II, 284-286.
29OR, Ser. 1, XLVII, pt. 1, 21; Sherman, Memoirs, II, 280; Hazen, Narrative, 349; Earl Schenck Miers, The General Who Marched to Hell: William Tecumseh Sherman and His March to Fame and Infamy (New York, 1951), 314-316.
30OR, Ser. 1, XLVII, pt. 1, 227-243.
31OR, Ser. 1, XLVII, pt. 1, 227; Battles and Leaders, IV, 686.
32Emma LeConte, When the World Ended: The Diary of Emma LeConte Earl Schenck Miers (ed.) (New York, 1957), 43-44.
33Howard, Autobiography, II, 122.
34Morris, 31st Illinois, 150.

truth, held that "Black Jack" had "sworn mightily" when handed Sherman's order.[35] In Logan's defense, Hazen stated the mansion received excellent care.[36] At any rate the home was standing when Union troops left the city.

Incendiarism was not the only charge brought against Logan by South Carolinians. Another diarist, Mrs. Mary Boykin Chesnut, reported being told how a "Yankee General, Logan by name, snatched a watch from Mrs. McCord's bosom."[37] This is the only mention of this incident and it was possibly one of thousands of such stories that followed Sherman's wake, some fact, some fancy.

While Columbia smoldered, Hazen and Corse spent the 18th ruining 15 miles of the Columbia branch of the South Carolina Railroad. The city was quiet except for occasional bursts of lingering flames and an occasional explosion as Logan's men destroyed enemy stores. One of these explosions occurred when members of the 63rd Illinois, carting ammunition from the arsenal to the river, let one box fall, igniting a whole wagon of shells. Four men were killed and 20 wounded in the mishap.[38]

Marching orders were issued on the 20th, and next morning the corps moved out. As his men wound their way toward Winnsboro, Logan heard them singing:

'John Brown's body lies mouldering in the grave,
But his soul goes marching on.'[39]

Instead of swamps, Logan found himself in hilly, barren uplands with little forage for men or animals. He pressed on rapidly, crossing the Wateree River on the 22nd. The enemy did not appear, and on the 23rd Logan decided to divide his column. Woods and Smith were to move toward Cheraw by a direct route while Hazen and Corse were to swing eastward to Camden. The two columns were to link up at Pine Tree Church. Troops advancing on Camden found the town unde-

---

[35]M. B. Chesnut, *A Diary from Dixie*, Isabella D. Martin and Myrta Lockett Avary (eds.) (New York, 1929), 358.

[36]Hazen, *Narrative*, 352.

[37]M. B. Chesnut, *A Diary from Dixie*, Ben Ames Williams (ed.) (Boston, 1949), 499. The earlier edition of the Chesnut diary cited above and published twenty years before Mr. Williams' edition, does not name the "Yankee General."

[38]Conyngham, *Sherman's March*, 330.

[39]Upson, *With Sherman*, 150.

fended and, after destroying Confederate stores, they turned north. The corps reformed on the 25th and moved on toward Cheraw. First obstacle since leaving Columbia proved to be swollen Lynch's Creek about thirty miles south of Cheraw. Rains had made the stream "too wide to be bridged, too deep to be forded." Logan's infantry waded the creek up to their armpits, but trains could not cross. As Logan's pioneers struggled in vain, a "slight *contretemps*" developed between Logan's pioneers and Howard's army engineers, both impatient at their failure. Logan sent Howard a note threatening to "make no further effort to cross that ugly stream," unless Howard withdrew his engineers. Howard simply wrote back, "The commanding officer of the 15th Corps will obey every lawful order." When the two met 20 minutes later nothing further was said.[40] It took eight days for waters to subside enough for wagons to pass and then bread and ammunition had to be raised off wagon beds.

Movement was still painfully slow due to flooding, but despite this obstruction Logan moved into Cheraw on March 4. The army stopped there, on the banks of the Great Pee Dee, until the 5th, when it crossed the river. While the advance halted, a pleasant interlude took place at Blair's headquarters. Blair was joined by Sherman, Logan, and their staff officers escaping the rain. Glasses of wine were handed around, a violin was produced, and Logan sang and played for the appreciative group.[41]

The only music from the 6th to the 8th was creaking wagon wheels and pattering rain as the army trudged toward the North Carolina line. It rained almost constantly, and when Logan crossed into North Carolina on the 8th roads had become almost impassable. Corduroying was necessary most of the time and anyone wandering off the road was certain to mire. Fayetteville was reached on the 12th, and when they went into camp there to take a few days rest, "the men had been soaking wet for about sixty hours, with nothing to eat but cold rations. . . . The sufferings of the officers and men, as well as the animals was very great."[42]

[40]Howard, *Autobiography*, II, 131-132.
[41]S. H. M. Byers, *With Fire and Sword* (New York, 1911), 182.
[42]Sherlock, *100th Indiana*, 206.

While the army rested, engineers erected pontoons over the Cape Fear River. When Corse led Logan's corps out on the 14th, it moved toward Bentonville. Corse met rebel cavalry on the 15th but shoved it back, and mud was the only impediment until the 19th.

On the move early on the 19th, Logan struck directly for Everettsville, across the Neuse River from Goldsboro. The usual flooded terrain slowed the column somewhat, but pioneers cleared the way, and before noon Logan reached a crossroads three miles south of Cox's Bridge over the Neuse. He considered the spot valuable and set Wever's brigade in position across the road facing the bridge until the rest of the corps could come up. That afternoon heavy cannonading suddenly boomed up from the south. Logan ordered Smith to entrench and moved Woods and Corse up to his support. Hazen, some miles to the rear, was told to go in the direction of the cannonading. It proved to be Slocum's left wing under fire at Bentonville where he had encountered Johnston's whole force.

After dark Logan received a change of orders; Sherman decided to strike the Confederates at Bentonville. He told Logan to leave one brigade at the bridge and sent the remainder of his command to Slocum. Up at 5 o'clock, Woods led, followed by Corse and Smith, with Wever left to cover the bridge. Enemy pickets appeared before Logan had moved very far, and Woods threw out skirmishers and advanced. Periodically Logan fired a cannon, and Slocum, at Bentonville, knew the 15th was moving to his support. At Mill Creek, halfway to the field, rebel cavalry appeared in force and dismounted, fighting behind prepared fortifications. Woods drove them from a series of these barricades and soon the corps was close enough to hear the rattle of musketry from Slocum.[43]

Logan's advance had been on Johnston's rear, and had it been done silently the Confederates might have been taken by surprise. Silence was impossible and skirmishing announced Logan's coming. Johnston had ample time to shift to meet the new threat. He bent his left back, and Logan, forming the Union right, found Johnston's new position running along a

---

[43]OR, Ser. 1, XLVII, pt. 1, 235.

ridge through thickly wooded country.[44] At 4 o'clock Woods and Corse moved up to a point near Johnston, and by dark they were firmly in place. On the left they connected with Jeff C. Davis' 14th Corps, heavily engaged on the 19th.

On the 21st Logan probed forward at daylight, but found the enemy still in force. Heavy rain began in the morning and continued all day, making artillery movement almost impossible. Hazen splashed up in the morning and went into position on Woods' left. In the meantime Blair's 17th Corps had gone into the line on Logan's right, putting the 15th in the Union center. By noon Logan's gunners had wrestled several cannon into position, and they opened a little later with great effect. At 1 o'clock Sherman ordered Logan to send skirmishers forward to keep pressure on Johnston. Men from Woods, Hazen, and Corse clambered down the slope and charged through the gray haze made bright by rifle flashes. They overwhelmed rebel skirmishers and took their advance line of rifle pits. Through the afternoon Confederates tried to retake the pits, but their guns growled into silence at dusk, having failed completely.[45]

During the night Johnston, having done little to stop Sherman or inflict damage on the Union army, retreated. In the morning Woods' lead units found the retreat bridge still burning. Woods moved back to his old line, and Logan left him at Bentonville with orders to hold position all day and then follow the corps north. Marching was easier after Bentonville. Hazen led the corps back to Cox's Bridge, then on to Goldsboro where the army encamped on the 27th.

Goldsboro marked the terminus of Sherman's Carolina campaign. The army began refitting there for a new move northward into Virginia. It had struggled through miles of difficult country since leaving Savannah and a halt was badly needed.

The Goldsboro respite was a pleasant one with men lolling around camp "luxuriating in the spring weather."[46] Some went to church; others went into town to see what diversion it might

---

[44]Barrett, *Sherman's March Through the Carolinas*, 177-178.

[45]Jay Luvaas, "Johnston's Last Stand—Bentonville," *North Carolina Historical Review*, XXXII, No. 3 (July, 1956), 332-358.

[46]Barrett, *Sherman's March Through the Carolinas*, 193.

offer and found none. While the army waited, countless appeals for aid poured in from the surrounding country. Logan was confronted by a planter claiming to be a British subject. The man asked protection and Logan answered: "What the hell, then, are you doing here if you are? The boys will take every hog and chicken you have, though you are a British subject. British subject be hanged."[47]

In addition to trouble from outsiders, a minor dispute erupted in the Union camp. Logan and Blair felt that Sherman's chief commissary officer had been incompetent in outfitting the men, especially with shoes. They sent a protest charging him with "utter incompetency and inefficiency." Sherman replied, "Generals Blair and Logan don't know of the difficulties arising from mud banks, storms at sea, difficulties of navigation, etc."[48] There the matter rested.

By April 5 Sherman felt that the army was rested and supplied sufficiently to begin another campaign. On the 5th orders went out to be ready to move in five days. The army was to drive across the Roanoke River, use Norfolk as a supply base, link up with Grant, and launch one great assault on Lee.[49] Before he could move, word that Richmond had fallen reached the army. Sherman quickly changed his plans and ordered an advance on Raleigh and Johnston.

News of Richmond's fall was greeted with wild rejoicing. Generals toasted victory while enlisted men went wild. In the camp, "such cheering, shouting, gunfiring, band playing, etc. I never heard before." The same soldier wrote, "I can't think what to say this time only 'Three times three and a Tiger for Grant and his army.' "[50]

The army broke camp on the 10th and moved on Raleigh. Sherman wrote on leaving Goldsboro,

> Poor North Carolina will have a hard time, for we sweep the country like a swarm of locusts. Thousands of people may perish but they now realize that war means something

[47]Conyngham, *Sherman's March*, 344-345.
[48]*OR*, Ser. 1, XLVII, pt. 3, 28-29.
[49]Sherman, *Memoirs*, II, 341-342.
[50]Padgett, "Letters of a Federal Soldier," *Georgia Historical Quarterly*, XXXIII, No. 1 (March, 1949), 75, 77.

else than vain glory and boasting. . . . The entire army has new clothing, and with soap and water have made wonderful changes in our appearance.[51]

The change was indeed miraculous. Grimy marchers were scrubbed, and though more swamps lay ahead, they moved with a more sprightly step. Weather was better and stories raced through the army bringing smiles to confident men. One of these was the tale that became a standing joke during the march. Logan, it was said, had offered a reward for a dead cavalryman, blue or gray.[52] Infantrymen who had seen Kilpatrick's cavalry dash along, but who found themselves doing the fighting, roared at Logan's joke.

Logan's line of march toward Raleigh lay through Lowell Factory and Pineville. Sherman warned him not to destroy the factory, hoping less pillaging might aid in bringing a quick surrender. During the night of the 11th more news arrived from Virginia—Lee had surrendered. Sherman shot off a congratulatory telegram to Grant and bands blared, guns roared, and bottles came out. In the 15th Corps pandemonium broke loose. Sergeant Theodore Upson wrote, "We had a great blow out at Hd Quarters last night," and described singing and drinking far into the night.[53]

Lee's capitulation further altered Union plans; Sherman was determined to begin immediate negotiations with Johnston. Logan moved his happy troops into a quiet, evacuated Raleigh on the 14th and camped three miles north of the city. His "bummers," feeling an end of their activities near, took advantage of a last chance and "a large number were found dead drunk by the roadside."[54]

For the next few days Sherman and Johnston met, trying to arrange an end to hostilities. While the army awaited word of the negotiations, an unexpected and terrible piece of news arrived. On April 17 a telegrapher rushed to Sherman with a coded message. Lincoln had been assassinated. Sherman cautioned his officers to keep the message a secret until he could

---

[51]Sherman, *Home Letters*, 342.
[52]Bell I. Wiley, *The Life of Billy Yank: Common Soldier of the Union* (Indianapolis, 1951), 327.
[53]Upson, *With Sherman*, 164-166.
[54]Orendorff, *103rd Illinois*, 205.

write an announcement. That night he returned from a talk with Johnston and published word of the assassination.[55]

Before releasing the news, Sherman set heavy guards in Raleigh and ordered his commanders to maintain order. Most of the men were angry but not violent; some talked of inscribing "Lincoln's Avengers" on their flags. A small mob of about 2,000, however, decided to take action. Shouting threats to burn the city, they marched toward the North Carolina capital. Just outside town, Logan galloped up and ordered them back to camp. They stopped, listened, and went on. At this point General Jacob D. Cox, whose troops stood guard in the city, felt "We . . . feared we might not be able to save the city from vengeance."[56] Logan, roaring angrily, threatened to order the artillery to rake them with cannister. This stopped the enraged troops and they returned to camp.[57] Raleigh escaped Columbia's fate.

The day after word of Lincoln's death arrived, welcome news reached the army; surrender terms had been arranged, subject to approval from Washington. During the 17th and 18th Sherman had consulted his generals, and Logan was most vocal in favoring surrender on almost any terms. He told Sherman the whole army dreaded another long pursuit, and insisted Jeff Davis be allowed to escape if that was one of Johnston's conditions.[58]

Though Logan and Blair urged Sherman to end hostilities without approval from Washington, he forwarded his terms. Their liberal nature met a hostile reception and they were rejected. On the 26th a new set of terms, approximating Grant's terms to Lee, was agreed upon. This time they were accepted and Johnston's army laid down its arms.

Union troops went wild again. Major Hitchcock described the festive scene at Sherman's headquarters in the governor's mansion on the night of the 26th:

> a crowd of officers have been sitting and standing all evening on the portico in front . . . and a little while ago looking through the front windows . . . one could see Grant and

[55]Sherman, *Memoirs*, II, 351.
[56]Cox, *Reminiscences*, II, 465.
[57]Upson, *With Sherman*, 167.
[58]Sherman, *Memoirs*, II, 351-352.

Sherman sitting at the center table, . . . stopping now and then to talk earnestly with other general officers in the room —Howard, Schofield, 'Johnny' Logan, and Meigs.[59]

In the week that brought peace, Logan wrote his wife, starved for news of Sherman's army. "We have just heard of the terrible tragedy in Washington and it has very much exasperated the army," he wrote two days after turning back "Lincoln's Avengers." One day after Johnston gave up, he told Mary, "It is terrible that he [Lincoln] should be taken off at such a time." In his note of the 27th Logan exhibited his first interest in his post-war career. "They want to make me a Brigadier in the regular army," he wrote, "but I think I shall quit the business and try peaceful associations for a while, and see how I will be used by the country and that may determine me as to the army."[60]

"All foraging will cease" read general orders on the 27th. The same orders cautioned corps commanders to stop all "bumming" and set each unit's line of march northward. Logan was to move to Washington with the right wing by way of Louisburg, Lawrenceville, Petersburg, Richmond, Fredericksburg, and Alexandria. Howard asked that the march be made a "model one for propriety of conduct," and Sherman warned, "Punishment for entering or pillaging houses will be severe and immediate."[61]

It was a joyous group of veterans that stepped out for Washington on the 29th. The men crossed the Tar River in early May and moved into Virginia. A 15th Corps chaplain reported: "The citizens, ladies in particular, seemed very indignant—yet *crest fallen*. Gen. Logan said he loved to shake the old flag at them."[62]

An area much like battered Vicksburg came into view on the 6th. Logan reached Petersburg, scene of Grant's siege, and the corps camped for several days. Logan reported to Mary, "There is no more necessity for troops south more than small

[59]Hitchcock, *Marching With Sherman*, 316. Grant had come down to visit Sherman shortly after the surrender.

[60]JAL to Mary Logan, Apr. 19, 27, 1865, Logan Mss.

[61]*OR* Ser. 1, XLVII, pt. 3, 324, 326.

[62]George Compton Diary, May 3, 1865, Civil War Diaries, Illinois State Historical Library.

numbers in each state. These people are thoroughly whipped."[63]

On leaving Petersburg for Richmond, Howard received an order from Halleck: "Your command will be encamped at or near Manchester and not be permitted to enter Richmond until prepared to march through the city."[64] This was taken as an insult by the Westerners who wanted to look at the Confederate capital. Army of the Potomac guards were posted to keep Logan's men out, and his soldiers pelted the guards with stones. On the 11th when the army was ready, it marched through Richmond. When it swung by Halleck's headquarters, elaborate by Western standards, a ragged Westerner broke ranks to spit tobacco juice on the immaculate guard's boots.[65]

North of Richmond, Logan struck for Alexandria. Sherman told Logan not to rush things, but to arrive at Alexandria one or two days before the scheduled "Grand Review" of the 24th. Sherman poured out his bitterness against Halleck and the despised Easterners. The cause was the insult at Richmond.

> The manner of your welcome was a part of a grand game to insult us—us who have marched 1,000 miles through a hostile country in mid-winter to help them. We did help them and what has been our reward?
>
> Your men were denied admission to the city, when Halleck had invited all citizens (rebels of course) to come and go without passes. If the American people sanction this kind of courtesy to old and tried troops, where is the honor, satisfaction and glory of serving them in constancy and faith? If such be the welcome the East gives to the West, we can but let them make war and fight it out themselves.

Disgusted with the alien Easterners, Sherman turned his thoughts to a more appreciative land:

> I know where is a land and people who will not treat us thus—the West, the Valley of the Mississippi, the heart and soul of the future strength of America, and I for one will go there.... Chew the cud of 'bitter fancy' as you ride along, and when events draw to a conclusion we can step into the ring.[66]

---

[63]JAL to Mary Logan, May 6, 1865, Logan Mss.
[64]*OR*, Ser. 1, XLVII, pt. 3, 421.
[65]Lewis, *Sherman*, 566.
[66]*OR*, Ser. 1, XLVII, pt. 3, 477-478.

While Logan moved through Virginia, events took place that made possible his elevation to command of the Army of the Tennessee. On the 12th Howard was named head of the Freedmen's Bureau and Logan designated temporary chief of the Tennesseans. A week later Sherman asked for Logan as permanent army commander, and on the 23rd "Black Jack" assumed command.[67] Before final word came, Logan, pessimistic after Atlanta, wrote Mary, "Gen. Howard has been assigned to the 'darkie' bureau . . . and I am told that I am to command the army, but God knows I am sure I shall not ask it, as I have been treated so once before, I have nothing to expect at the hands of these men."[68]

For a time it seemed Logan's prediction might be true. Howard still intended to lead the army's march into Washington. Several days before the review, Sherman asked Howard to relinquish command. Howard told Sherman he had fought the army since Atlanta and had a right to lead it. Sherman answered, "I know it, but it will be everything to Logan to have this opportunity." "Howard, you are a Christian," he continued, "and won't mind such a sacrifice." Howard replied, "Surely if you put it on that ground, I submit." Sherman later thanked Howard, adding, "I do think it but just to Logan."[69] This time he would not be disappointed. Logan would lead the Army in the Grand Review.

The last few days of the march turned into a scenic tour. Men saw the Fredericksburg battlefield and Mt. Vernon before reaching Alexandria on the 20th.

Rivalry between Eastern and Western armies continued in camps across from Washington. Sherman was afraid his ambling Westerners, so unused to anything like great crowds, would look like a rabble. On the 23rd the Eastern army was reviewed by the president and an immense crowd. The following day was the West's turn.

Early on the 24th the troops crossed Long Bridge into the city, gaping at the Potomac and the Capitol Dome in the distance. By 9 o'clock Logan and the Army of the Tennessee were

---

[67]Ibid., 532, 562.

[68]JAL to Mary Logan, May 20, 1865, Logan Mss.

[69]Howard, Autobiography, II, 210-211.

in position behind the Capitol building. Sherman rode past to the head of the procession and the men "snickered to see Uncle Billy 'dressed up after the dingy carelessness of years.'"[70] Howard rode up to join Sherman, and Logan and his staff moved to the head of the army. The Tennesseans were to lead followed by the Army of Georgia. First in line in Logan's army was the 15th Corps, trailed by the 17th.

At 9 a cannon boomed, bands blared "The Star Spangled Banner," and Sherman urged his horse forward. "Stage fright stuck in plowboys' throats. The roofs and trees were black with people." Bunting and flags waved everywhere and long streamers proclaimed: "Hail to the Western Heroes . . . Hail, Champions of Belmont, Donelson, Shiloh, Vicksburg, Chattanooga, Atlanta, Savannah, Bentonville, Pride of the Nation."[71]

Sherman, still apprehensive, dared not look back until he reached the Treasury. Then he turned: "The sight was simply magnificent. The column was compact, and the glittering muskets looked like a solid mass of steel."[72] As Sherman turned in the saddle, cheers were deafening. The Army of the Potomac was on old story in Washington but the Westerners were novel and the crowd welcomed them warmly.

Leading the column came Logan who was recognized, along with Blair, as former congressmen and applauded wildly.[73] Grant's aide, Horace Porter, saw "Logan, 'Black Jack,' riding at the head of the Army of the Tennessee, his swarthy coal-black hair giving him the air of a native chief."[74] Most watchers greeted Logan with hurrahs, but one observer, Miss Marian Hooper, later Henry Adams' wife, thought "Howard looks finely with his one arm; and General Logan, with Indian blood in his veins—very little of anything else, I should think."[75]

When Logan reached Sherman and Howard near the stand, the three rode together, hearing "loud and prolonged acclamations of applause."[76] In front of the stand the three turned and

[70]Lewis, *Sherman*, 573.
[71]*Ibid.*, 574.
[72]Sherman, *Memoirs*, II, 377.
[73]Leech, *Reville*, 416.
[74]Porter, *Campaigning With Grant*, 510.
[75]Marian Hooper Adams, *The Letters of Mrs. Henry Adams, 1865-1883*, Ward Thoron (ed.) (Boston, 1937), 9.
[76]New York *Times*, May 25, 1865.

took the review. Emotion welling up inside, Logan saw able Charles Woods, handsome Bill Hazen, and longtime associate, John E. Smith, ride past. Then Frank Blair's Corps, and Logan watched Leggett, Giles Smith, and with them Logan's old division. Striding by went the 45th Illinois, the 30th, and Logan's old regiment, the 31st. Mary Logan wrote later, "It looked as if the great republic was on dress parade."[77] Sherman called it his happiest moment, and Logan describing the glorious scene, spoke with pride when he told Mary, "The Army of the Tenn. . . . excelled the Potomac army in appearance and marching."[78]

Almost everyone agreed. The Westerners looked taller, more rawboned, and walked with a springier stride. Logan's pride was overflowing as he led the great army through the capital. He had come a long way since his uncertain words to a divided crowd from a wagon in the square of a small Illinois town in August, 1861. But what would he do now? There would be time to think of that later; now was the time to bask in the applause of a grateful republic. The moment might not come again and Logan could hope the republic's gratitude would endure. But on a pleasant spring day in May, 1865, those hearty Westerners were marching down Pennsylvania Avenue. An old friend of Sherman's sat in the stand and said as he watched the army, "They march like the lords of the world."[79] That night a New York journalist wrote his headline story: "The great display is over. Sherman's two armies—the most superb material ever molded into soldiers—have passed in review."[80]

---

[77] Mary Logan, *Reminiscences*, 193.
[78] JAL to Mary Logan, May 26, 1865, Logan Mss.
[79] Lewis, *Sherman*, 576.
[80] New York *Times*, May 25, 1865.

CHAPTER XVI

I WILL NEVER AFFILIATE

Peace did not immediately end Logan's military duties. As commander of the Army of the Tennessee he had to manage its separation from service. Since the army was composed mostly of Westerners, headquarters was shifted to Louisville, and in June troops began to move there. In addition to the Tennesseans, Logan inherited Westerners in the Army of Georgia, and ten Western regiments from the Army of the Potomac were on their way to Louisville to be mustered out.[1]

Before Logan joined his men, he delivered his first post-war address. Several Union generals, Logan among them, travelled to New York for a mass meeting June 7. Grant was in the city to receive its adulation, but the taciturn lieutenant general said little. Orations were left to men like Blair and Logan. The meeting, held at Cooper Institute, was called to express confidence in the "character and patriotism of President Johnson, and to pledge support . . . to the measures of his administration."[2] It was evident that administration forces were endeavoring to tie to themselves those war Democrats, replete with military prestige, who had supported Republicans during the war. These men had to be secured before they wandered into the Radical camp.

The Cooper Institute meeting brought out an enthusiastic crowd to see the heroes. It thundered a welcome for Grant as he marched in, stood for a moment, and departed without saying a word. Noise at the rear announced the arrival of Logan and Blair, and Sherman's two "political generals" strode to the platform. Blair spoke first, and when he concluded, loud shouts for Logan brought "Black Jack" to his feet. Logan thanked the people for coming and launched into comments on the president:

---

[1]*OR*, Ser. 1, XLIX, pt. 2, 1029.
[2]New York *Times*, June 7, 1865.

So far as his administration has developed I certainly have no fault with it. What there may be to object to in the future I don't know; but if there is anything objectionable, then, as a matter of course, and as the questions arise the country will have a right to decide for themselves whether the president is in the right or in the wrong. The great questions that have been before the people for the last 4 years are now settled, the rebellion is suppressed; slavery is forever dead.[3]

This statement came after Johnson's presidential plan of restoring the states had been announced. Logan's remarks seem to indicate an endorsement of Johnson's plan.

Logan went on to deny the congressional theory that former Confederate states had been out of the Union and should be treated as territories. "If those States, by making war on the government, have become territories, then we must admit that Davis did really establish a government," and Logan was unwilling to do that. This again endorsed Johnson's theory of Reconstruction. Turning to punishment of rebel leaders, Logan roared that Davis and his associates should be convicted of treason and punished. He did not specify the degree of punishment. Returning briefly to Presidential Reconstruction, Logan said,

I maintain this as being correct doctrine, that President Johnson has the right to exercise power as is necessary to assist in putting the machinery of these states in motion. He has the right for the time being to appoint a man or govern. When he does that and they organize, the State is then in existence, not only as it has been, but can exercise the functions that it did before in the government of the nation.

The remainder of Logan's speech concerned foreign problems. He referred to aid given Confederates by the English and demanded payments of what later were called the "*Alabama* claims." On French interference in Mexico, Logan demanded Maximilian's resignation, but opposed an American military expedition. His address ended in a bedlam of applause.[4]

[3]*Ibid.*, June 8, 1865.
[4]*Ibid.*

Logan's speech seemed to line him up with the president. But did it? This June address is the only public statement in which Logan took a clear stand during the first 14 months after the war. Though he spoke many times, he made no public endorsements of either side until June, 1866. For the next year he watched, waited, and studied political trends before openly supporting either side in the great Reconstruction debate.

Logan left New York and joined the army at Louisville. When he arrived he began to enforce strict discipline.[5] Though there were some reports of vandalism in June, the press reported, "Notwithstanding the large number of soldiers around our city, good order generally prevails."[6] Most of the month was spent mustering out veteran regiments. Orders came from Grant on the 23rd to step up the pace, and soon much of the army was on its way home. Logan reiterated strict warnings to units leaving Louisville to behave themselves. Officers were told men were liable to punishment until finally separated at state rendezvous points.[7] The business of discharging thousands of men, all of whom wanted to go home at once, led Logan to comment, "My duties now are more arduous than since the war. There is so much discontent among the soldiers and so many things to do." There was no chance for glory in this and every chance for dissatisfaction. Mindful of the future and good relations with veterans, Logan wrote: "They will forget all that the man has ever done unless in the last instance he looks to their interest."[8] Logan worked to make sure his Western troops, especially Illinoisans, left his command with happy recollections. Every man was a potential vote.

July was an active month. In severe summer heat mustering out continued. Sherman arrived to inspect the command, and wrote Grant "All are to be mustered out forthwith. I am glad of it, for I think many . . . will soon tire of the tedium of civil life and be anxious to enlist in the regular army."[9] A banquet was held in Sherman's honor and he left Louisville satisfied with operations.

[5]OR, Ser. 1, XLVII, pt. 3, 589-590. There had been some difficulty with troops around Washington disturbing citizens.
[6]Louisville Democrat, June 13, 1865.
[7]OR, Ser. 1, XLIX, pt. 2, 1047.
[8]JAL to Mary Logan, June 28, 1865, Logan Mss.
[9]OR, Ser. 1, XLVIII, pt. 2, 1050.

Logan, flooded with civilian complaints, soon issued a stern warning concerning "wanton depredations . . . upon both white and colored citizens." In July there was a noticeable change for the worse in the troops' behavior. Street fights, robbery, assault, and vandalism marred civil-military relations. In addition discipline was breaking down in regimental camps. A member of Logan's old regiment struck an officer and was sent to jail for three months.[10] To prevent these outbreaks, Logan told his subordinates to keep troops out of Louisville.[11]

An opportunity to speak came to Logan July 22. He condemned slavery as a degrading, socially stagnating institution that "dwarfs the energies of the people, and is a stumbling-block in every respect." He asked Kentuckians to adopt the 13th Amendment and forever wipe out slavery. To the amendment's opponents, who called its advocates supporters of "Negro equality," Logan exclaimed: "The 'Negro equality' talk against the amendment is all a bugbear and humbug. I don't consider a 'nigger' my equal." He maintained the war had been fought to free slaves and all should be liberated. Concerning Negro suffrage, Logan thought Kentucky could "do as she pleases." The Constitution expressly gave every state "the right and power to regulate the privilege of suffrage for itself."[12]

In late July, Reconstruction, army affairs, and politics were overshadowed by a personal event. The Logans expected a baby in the summer. Mary's letters assured the general all was well and wished he could be in Carbondale when the baby was born. He thought he might not be able to come home before early August.[13]

Logan had written in May that he wanted to leave the army, and July 17 he wrote: "I have determined to resign as soon as I can." Of the political scene he observed: "From the way politics seem to be moving . . . I can not say that I will have anything to do with them again."[14]

[10]Louisville *Democrat*, July 14, 19, 1865.
[11]*OR*, Ser. 1, XLIX, pt. 3, 1080.
[12]New York *Times*, July 30, 1865.
[13]JAL to Mary Logan, July 9, 1865, Logan Mss.
[14]JAL to Mary Logan, July 9, 17, 1865, Logan Mss.

War Department orders accelerated separation, and Logan expected all troops to be on their way home by August 1. With his army disappearing, Logan delivered the customary farewell address.

> The profound gratification I feel in being authorized to release you from the onerous obligations of the camp, and return you laden with laurels to homes where warm hearts wait to welcome you, is somewhat embittered by the painful reflection that I am sundering the ties that trials have made true.

He recounted the army's victories and mentioned his connection with it. "Although I have been but a short period your commander we are not strangers; affections have sprung up between us during the long years we have passed through together." Logan paid tribute to McPherson and asked the army to bear itself as well in peace as in war.[15]

In Carbondale, on July 24, Mary bore a 13 pound boy. The child, healthy from the first, was baptized Manning Alexander Logan.[16] The general heard the good news and started for home immediately, his duties completed at Louisville. He reached Carbondale July 28 and saw his son for the first time. His wife was doing well and it was a happy homecoming.

Orders followed Logan telling him to report for duty and he decided to resign, "there being," he wrote Stanton, "no necessity for my services longer. . . . Matters of pecuniary interest . . . demand my attention."[17] The War Secretary replied: "Your telegram tendering the resignation of your commission was received this morning and submitted to the President, who directs me to say that it is accepted. Allow me to express my regret that the service will lose so gallant and patriotic a soldier."[18] Almost four years to the day from his enlistment, Logan returned to civilian life.

[15]New York *Times*, July 23, 1865.

[16]Ms. "Sketch of the Life of John A. Logan, Jr.," by Mary Logan in Mary Logan Mss., Library of Congress, n.d. The boy changed his name from Manning to John A. Logan, Jr. His mother wrote, "He inherited all the intensity and enthusiasm of his father's nature."

[17]*OR*, Ser. 1, XLIX, pt. 2, 1100.

[18]*Ibid.*, 1101.

He had his eyes on a higher post than the one he left for the field. He remembered Haynie's prediction that the Senate seat would be his in 1866, and aimed for it. For the time being, however, Logan was not sure which party could put him there. Through 1865 he stood uncommitted. At first he dabbled in Egyptian real estate and took a few local law cases, but politics remained his paramount concern.[19]

One month after his son's birth, restless as usual, Logan left for Springfield and the State Fair. From Springfield he went to Jacksonville, Decatur, and Chicago. From Chicago he wrote Mary,

> I have had such a pleasant time. Everywhere I have been the people seem glad to see me and unless I am very much fooled I will have but little trouble when the time comes in securing any position I may desire. The fairs all going on now, I think I had better avail myself of this opportunity to see the people.[20]

He saw them all over the state, and was hailed everywhere as Illinois' greatest soldier after Grant. There was every reason to believe a bright political career was dawning. While he watched political tides, Logan considered a second choice, law practice in a large city. He decided to move his family out of Egypt, preferably to Chicago, if his political expectations turned out badly.[21]

As Logan travelled the fair circuit, his interest developed in veterans' organizations. In North Carolina, in the war's last weeks, Logan and several other officers conceived the idea for a Society of the Army of the Tennessee. The organization, a fraternal society to keep alive wartime friendships, was one of the earliest such groups to appear. By 1866 it was holding annual conventions. The society remained primarily a non-political organization, but it gave Logan ideas of the political possibilities of such groups.[22]

After a swing through Illinois, Logan returned to Carbon-

[19]Newsome, *Jackson County*, 177.
[20]JAL to Mary Logan, Aug. 27, Sept. 2, 1865, Logan Mss.
[21]Ms. "Sketch of the Life of John A. Logan," by Mary Logan, Mary Logan Mss., n.d.
[22]Mary R. Dearing, *Veterans in Politics: The Story of the Grand Army of the Republic* (Baton Rouge, Louisiana, 1952), 70; Dawson, *Logan*, 96.

dale. Mary had hoped peace would bring him home for good, but, pleading necessity of travel to make a living and watch political currents, Logan left for the East in October. He went to New York and spent five months there and in Washington speculating in cotton and stocks.[23]

Never letting pass a chance to speak, Logan addressed large crowds in New York and New Jersey. Both states were holding local elections, and Logan endorsed Union men. In Jersey City he talked of the significance of the war: "It has been decided according to the doctrine of Andrew Jackson, that the sovereignty of the United States is paramount." He adroitly straddled on Reconstruction. Of the Union Party, in which he claimed membership, Logan stated, "The Union Party, what is it? Is it mere Republican or Democrat or Abolition? No, it is not this limited. It is that party, which organized in the hour of the nation's peril, preserved it till the safety was secure."[24] It was such speeches that led one historian to comment, "His speeches were mere rodomontade. He denounced slavery and bombastically lauded the soldier boys; . . . but his speeches reveal nothing of his politics."[25]

In November Logan found himself confronted by a new problem. On the 14th he received a commission from Johnson naming him minister to Republican Mexico, possibly hoping to win Logan's support by the move. Logan, his eye on the Senate, never seriously considered acceptance.[26] He was inclined to refuse at once, but Grant advised him to at least talk to Seward before declining.[27] Logan wrote the Secretary of State that he would withhold his decision until mid-December. Logan suggested another appointment if time was important, since he intended to decline.[28]

Press reports of Johnson's offer reported Logan's hesitancy from the first. An Egyptian paper wrote that Logan had advised the mayor of Carbondale that he did not intend to go to

[23]Chicago *Tribune*, Jan. 2, 1877; JAL to Mary Logan, Nov. 4, 1865, Logan Mss.
[24]New York *Times*, Oct. 31, 1865.
[25]Howard K. Beale, *The Critical Year* (New York, 1930), 110.
[26]Andrew Johnson to JAL, Nov. 14, 1865, Logan Mss.; Mary Logan, *Reminiscences*, 203.
[27]U. S. Grant to JAL, Nov. 23, 1865, Logan Mss.
[28]JAL to W. H. Seward, Nov. 29, 1865, Logan Mss.

Mexico.[29] The New York *Times* did not comment on the merit of Logan's selection, but it saw significance in the move: "The appointment of Major General Logan to be Minister to the Mexican Republic is a new notice to Maximilian that his imperial rule will not be recognized."[30] The capital press thought Logan's acceptance doubtful and that the general regarded the appointment as a demonstration in favor of Juarez rather than an intention of actually sending him to Mexico.[31]

Comment from France mentioned the absurdity of sending a minister to a defunct government. Laughing at the picture of Logan vainly searching for Juarez' seat of government, a French paper said, "It is said that Mr. Logan comprehends the ridiculous position in which he is placed, and will refuse it, preferring to be a . . . Senator."[32] Johnson's cabinet heard that one French diplomat was "scared out of his wits" by Logan's appointment.[33]

His mind already made up, Logan went to Washington in December. He had several interviews with Johnson and Seward and declined officially.[34] Johnson then offered the mission to Japan. Honshu was a long way from the Senate and Logan refused again.[35] While Logan was in Washington he talked to Republicans as well as Democrats. One Republican, Elihu Washburne, offered to back Logan for the Senate.[36]

In 1866 Logan continued to speculate in cotton and politics. The best sources of Logan's political speculation in these days of indecision are his letters to his wife, which reveal a policy of watchful waiting. In January he wrote, "I am saying nothing in politics nor will I until the proper time." The following month he reported from Washington, "Political matters are in a perfect stew here. . . . Congress abusing Johnson and he abusing Congress so that nothing can be done." A little later he vowed again to say nothing about Reconstruction through

[29]Centralia *Sentinel*, Nov. 23, 1865.

[30]New York *Times*, Nov. 17, 1865.

[31]*National Intelligencer* (Washington), Nov. 21, 1865.

[32]*Courier des Etats Unis* in *National Intelligencer*, Nov. 20, 1865.

[33]Gideon Welles, *The Diary of Gideon Welles* (New York, 1960), Howard K. Beale, ed., II, 401.

[34]JAL to Mary Logan, Dec. 12, 1865, Logan Mss.

[35]Mary Logan, *Reminiscences*, 203.

[36]JAL to Mary Logan, Dec. 12, 1865, Logan Mss.

the winter and spring. In April: "Johnson seems determined to force the Copperheads into power again, all things look blurry and I fear matters in Illinois, they look ugly."[37]

Illinois politicians were growing restive. In April, Yates received a letter from an Egyptian Republican asking the senator to influence Logan.

> Our future success here depends very much on the position Gen. Logan shall take. I should like to know very much what he will probably do. Josh Allen and his old opponents here are all out for Johnson. . . . If Logan shall go with them, the 13th district is lost to us beyond doubt.[38]

By early May a slight shift developed in Logan's tone. He may have decided Johnson's cause was doomed, and chose to oppose the president for that reason alone. However, other factors seem to have contributed to this switch. Logan was disgusted at seeing many former Confederates in Washington during the winter. Alexander Stephens, he reported, "comes here . . . and makes the platform on which Johnson and his friends will soon stand. . . . The propositions reported by the Committee on Monday as amendments to the Constitution are right and if Mr. Johnson opposes them, as I understand he will, he is entirely over with the Copperheads." Logan expressed surprise at his wife's statement that people in Illinois were in doubt as to which party he would support. Contradicting all his letters in which he had told of scrupulously avoiding political issues, he wrote, "Everybody here knows how I have stood all winter and it does appear strange that anyone should question it for a moment." He refused to consider running for Congress from the 13th District. "If I am not worthy of something more, I want nothing . . . I have had no favors from Johnson nor do I want any."[39] Though no word of this change reached the public for a while, Logan had all but decided to join the Republicans.

While Logan worked in the East, Mary grieved at a renewal of his pre-war life. She hoped he would return in the spring and looked forward to a family vacation in the summer. Lo-

[37]JAL to Mary Logan, Jan. 18, Feb. 19, Mar. 5, April 29, 1866, Logan Mss.

[38]Jesse Bishop to Richard Yates, April 17, 1866, Yates Mss.

[39]JAL to Mary Logan, May 2, 1866, Logan Mss.

gan, on the other hand, looked to the summer as a time to campaign. Certain she would never find happiness, Mary complained:

> I have struggled for ten years with an untiring devotion to help you and be all you wanted. I loved my home and tried by might and main to make it pleasant the short visits you have made to it, but failing to make it tolerable scarcely to you as you well know my Darling, you have never spent *an evening* with me and made me feel you were happy. . . . You have been in excitement for so long, a quiet domestic home has no charm for you. . . . Alas like all my past anticipations of pleasure, it is all over and so I will give up and do the best I can.[40]

Mary's letter brought protestations that his absences were in the family's best interest. In every letter he promised to return as soon as possible.

Family trouble, political indecision, and business ups and downs harassed Logan. But he was busy with another matter, the Grand Army of the Republic. Legend has it that the G. A. R. was started by an idealistic army chaplain and an army doctor for social reasons. A recent study indicates the real founder was Governor Oglesby, with Logan as collaborator.[41] Chaplain Benjamin F. Stephenson and Doctor William J. Rutledge participated, but as tools in the hands of Illinois politicians. Best evidence of the G. A. R.'s political overtones is a letter from Stephenson to Logan written in 1868 in which the clergyman promised: "I will keep you posted on the internal workings of the Capitol for I will be on the inside of everything without anyone suspecting that I take any interest in it. . . . I have been too long a politician to not know how to keep my secrets."[42]

Oglesby had most to do with the group's start since Logan was in the East. But Logan was apprised of the plan and worked with Oglesby. The two men were primarily interested in unseating Senator Lyman Trumbull, and saw the Grand Army a means to that end. Oglesby believed Logan had a good

---

[40]Mary Logan to JAL, Mar. 15, 1866, Logan Mss. In her *Reminiscences*, Mrs. Logan paints a picture of serenity and joy during this period.
[41]Dearing, *Veterans*, 81-84.
[42]B. F. Stephenson to JAL, Jan. 30, 1868, Logan Mss.

chance to defeat Trumbull and backed him. Trumbull's workers soon got wind of the plan and told the senator of the plot.[43] Though no letters between Logan and Oglesby, dealing with this affair, remain in the Logan collection, Oglesby's support, and the founding of a potent Republican veterans' organization seem to have been influential in swinging Logan away from the Democrats. He had been immensely popular with troops during the war, and veterans, well organized, could convert this popularity into peacetime office.

The Grand Army's Illinois founders organized their first post in April, and by August, 56 had been formed. Two months later, before the November election, the number was 157. Political intentions were veiled, but the Chicago *Tribune* reported in August that it held the balance of political power in several counties.[44]

With the G. A. R. burgeoning, and Oglesby working for him, Logan broke his long silence in June. On the 28th at Cairo he spoke for three hours, and while he said nothing clearly announcing his party stand, his address left little doubt. Hs castigated the traitorous rebels, calling for their perpetual banishment from public office. Logan spoke in favor of the Freedmen's Bureau, but said nothing about Johnson.[45]

Logan reserved a definite statement for his Independence Day oration at Salem. There, at a soldier's picnic, Logan joined Sherman and Oglesby on the speaker's platform. He spoke for the entire Radical program, denounced Presidential Reconstruction, and on his conclusion Oglesby welcomed him into Republican ranks.[46] This address was Logan's first real contribution to "Bloody Shirt" oratory, the style he and other Radicals made famous. His words ring with condemnation of the Democrats as a party of Southern rebels and Northern Copperheads. Both the Cairo and Salem speeches were printed and distributed by the Chicago *Tribune* as campaign documents.[47] Logan had made up his mind; he was no longer a Democrat.

[43]S. W. Munn to Lyman Trumbull, May 27, 1866, Trumbull Mss.
[44]Chicago *Tribune*, Aug. 27, 30, 1866.
[45]*Illinois State Journal*, July 3, 1866.
[46]Centralia *Sentinel*, July 5, 1866.
[47]Kinsley, *Chicago Tribune*, II, 44.

The state's Democratic press greeted Logan's July 4 speech and his alliance with the Republicans with derision. They called the Salem meeting the "smallest kind of a pot house political gathering," and branded Logan's address a "rehashed political tirade." Democrats further informed the public that Logan's mother, who was still a Democrat, attributed her son's political defection to "bad company."[48]

Logan went to Springfield for the first state Grand Army convention. He hoped to be elected state commander and use the organization to support his senatorial ambitions. Logan's plans failed when a new challenger entered the fray and won the post. John M. Palmer, leader of Sherman's 14th Corps, also had senatorial ambitions, and had become interested in the G. A. R. Palmer was a popular leader and close friend of Chaplain Stephenson. The July 12 meeting was not public, and no records exist to shed light on its deliberations. But one of Trumbull's friends provides the reasons for Logan's defeat. Norman B. Judd reported that a majority of delegates opposed Logan because of a feeling he was still on the fence and would support Johnson if enough patronage was forthcoming.[49] Logan's loss made it evident that Illinois Radicals had decided to back Palmer rather than Logan.

Logan went back to Washington. Cotton speculation was one reason and politics another. He endorsed Congressional Reconstruction and urged the lawmakers to remain in session to defeat the president. Logan also addressed a veterans meeting and attacked Johnson as a tool of Copperheads.[50] He was anxious to return to Illinois before the Republican state convention in August, and told Mary he intended to make several speeches beforehand.[51]

Through July Trumbull's supporters schemed to nominate Logan as congressman-at-large.[52] The incumbent was S. W. Moulton, and many delegates favored his renomination. In July, talk of Logan for congress spread, and announcements of county delegations instructed for the general appeared

48*Illinois State Register*, July 6, 13, 1866.
49Norman B. Judd to Lyman Trumbull, July 11, 1866, Trumbull Mss.
50*Illinois State Journal*, July 17, 21, 1866.
51JAL to Mary Logan, July 21, 1866, Logan Mss.
52Dearing, *Veterans*, 89-91.

daily. Several papers opposed the movement and deprecated the attempt to railroad Moulton out of his seat.[53]

The Democratic press greeted every mention of Logan with old stories of rumored sympathy for secession. An old friend spoke of Logan's attempt to raise troops for the Confederacy. His former associates revived his pre-war nickname and broadsides against "Dirty Work" were a regular feature of Democratic editorial pages.[54]

Republican delegates converged on Springfield, August 8. Logan had returned a week earlier and made several talks. Most Republican journals were adamant in their demands that a soldier be on the party ticket. The Chicago *Tribune* warned that if this were not done, the Copperheads might corral the veteran vote.[55]

The boom for the House nomination took Logan by surprise and disappointed him. He still cherished the Senate seat, and was silent for a time about the lesser post. On convention eve, however, following an editorial maintaining his "name would be a tower of strength to the ticket," Logan said he would accept if nominated.[56]

When the convention met, Green B. Raum, close friend of Logan's from Egypt, was elected president and nominations began. There was little doubt of Logan's victory from the first. A motion was made that he be nominated by acclamation. Moulton rose, removed himself as a candidate, and pledged his support. In a storm of cheers the convention stampeded to Logan. Responding to calls for a speech, the general rose and in the fashion of many victorious nominees, said he had "come to the city not anticipating the honor, but merely to see and listen." Logan then called the Democrats traitors and said the Republicans must carry on the movement to save the country. Waxing eloquent in the best "Bloody Shirt" manner, he attacked Johnson and lauded efforts of "patriotic" congressmen to upset the president's plans. Logan thanked the delegates, paid his respects to Moulton, and retired.[57]

[53]Belleville *Advocate* in *Illinois State Journal*, July 27, 1866.
[54]Jonesboro *Gazette*, July 21, 28, 1866; *Illinois State Register*, Sept. 1, 1866.
[55]Chicago *Tribune*, Aug. 3, 1866.
[56]*Ibid.*, July 6, 8, 1866.
[57]*Illinois State Journal*, Aug. 9, 1866.

"Black Jack's" selection was greeted with Republican applause. Most papers felt Logan's campaign would be so vigorous as to sweep other party candidates into office with him. All looked forward to a great majority for Logan, the "man for whom the loyal masses have a deep regard."[58] Trumbull forces were delighted at his victory.[59] Logan prepared to run a strong race for the House seat, but he had not given up the Senate. He looked forward to January when the legislature convened. A November victory might help his candidacy in January.

The Democrats took delight in Logan's discomfort. The *State Register* reported Logan "did not appear to feel at all complimented at this questionable nomination of Trumbull's." His former associates renewed their attacks on Logan's prewar record, advance evidence of the bitterness of the campaign.[60]

Springfield held a rally the day after the nominations, and Logan brandished the "Bloody Shirt." Of Johnson, the man he lauded in 1864, Logan said: "When all things were created, in the creation it was necessary to have animals for all kinds of work, and when the Almighty looked around for a demagogue he found Andrew Johnson and made him."[61]

Logan and Oglesby left Springfield to attend a soldiers' mass meeting at St. Louis. Here they joined Wisconsin Governor Lucius Fairchild, Indiana Governor Oliver P. Morton, and Missouri Governor Thomas C. Fletcher, all Radicals, in a political conference. President Johnson got wind of this conclave and sent an investigator, Charles O'Beirne, to report on the meeting. O'Beirne produced startling information that the western Radicals intended to use the Grand Army as a military organization to enforce their program. They even discussed appointing a dictator, the President was told. Logan's correspondence reveals nothing of this conspiracy, but several reliable witnesses substantiate O'Beirne's report.[62]

Leaving St. Louis, Logan went to Chicago to begin his cam-

---

[58]*Illinois State Journal*, Aug. 9, 1866; Chicago *Tribune*, Aug. 9, 1866; Chicago *Republican*, Aug. 9, 1866.
[59]George T. Brown to Lyman Trumbull, Aug. 16, 1866, Trumbull Mss.
[60]*Illinois State Register*, Aug. 8, 15, 1866.
[61]New York *Herald*, Aug. 10, 1866.
[62]Dearing, *Veterans*, 104-106; Beale, *Critical Year*, 377. O'Beirne's reports are in the Andrew Johnson Mss., Library of Congress.

paign. A large crowd greeted him at the station, and a reception was held where Logan delivered a speech out of the usual mold. To influence the veteran vote, Logan adopted the 15th Corps badge as his campaign badge. Veterans flocked to hear him remind them that it was their duty to defeat the "Copperhead" Democrats as they had vanquished Confederate troops.

From Chicago Logan returned to the state capital and drew up his itinerary. He was scheduled to tour northern Illinois in late August, swinging in to the central part of the state in September. While he denounced them from the stump, the Democrats struck back. The Chicago *Times* called him a "political courtesan" who "prostituted" himself for office. Lanphier dredged up Logan's speech against Governor Bissell and used it as campaign material.[63]

At month's end, the Democrats held their own convention and named Logan's opponent. They steered away from peace men, and Colonel T. Lyle Dickey, veteran of several Western battles, won. Dickey's military record convinced Democrats they had a strong ticket and they called the former colonel a "distinguished veteran," who "presents a striking contrast to the brawling, blatant demagogue, the foul-mouthed, profane, obscene mercenery selected by the Radicals as his opponent."[64] Democrats determined to keep up a barrage of this anti-Logan vituperation.

Quick to pounce on Dickey's claim as a military hero, Republicans greeted his nomination with a preview of the campaign's bitterness.

> We believe Col. Dickey did go to war as Colonel of a regiment, but we are not certain he was ever heard from after he got in. On the contrary, if we are not mistaken, he won but few laurels . . . his fighting being confined to guarding bridges in Tennessee; and after a brief and inglorious career, he threw up his commission and came home in disgust, either because he was not made commander-in-chief, or because of Mr. Lincoln's proclamation of emancipation.[65]

[63]Chicago *Times* in *Illinois State Journal*, Aug. 18, 1866; *Illinois State Register*, Aug. 14, 1866.

[64]*Illinois State Register*, Aug. 30, 1866.

[65]*Illinois State Journal*, Aug. 30, 1866.

These unfair attacks on an able cavalry colonel launched the struggle.

September found Logan speaking in northern Illinois counties where his name produced a torrent of abuse before the war. He spoke to large crowds, and at Galena, Grant's home, he denounced Democratic claims of Grant's support. Logan held that Grant's every act made it evident he stood behind the party that saved the Union.[66]

On his way into central Illinois for speeches at Joilet and Ottawa, Logan detoured to South Bend, Indiana, where he addressed an immense crowd of soldiers. His malignant tongue lashed out at Johnson and cheered such Hoosier Radicals as Oliver P. Morton and Schuyler Colfax. This was the sort of "Bloody Shirt" harangue that later prompted a 14-year old Indiana farm boy, Albert J. Beveridge, to envy. The future senator wrote, "Next day, following the plow, with my bare feet, I wondered if I could ever talk so wonderfully."[67] Logan's appearance is credited with greatly aiding Republican candidates in Indiana.[68]

Logan's first Egyptian oration came at Carbondale, September 13. He arrived home to find Mary, her woes momentarily forgotten, caught up in the excitement of the canvass. Raum had been nominated for Congress from the 13th District against Josh Allen; and Logan, Raum, and Oglesby joined in hammering the Democrats. The day before Logan's speech, his opponents reached their peak of abuse. A Chester weekly hoped to deliver Illinois, already disgraced by " 'such a dishonest, radical, lecherous, blasphemous, and drunken, dirty, beastly thing as Dick Oglesby,' " from " 'that low vulgar, dirty, and hypocritical Logan. Maggots would sicken on him.' "[69] Logan countered with his own castigation of Dickey, Allen and the "nest of traitors" that supported them. Veterans of Vicks-

---

[66]Chicago *Tribune*, Sept. 2, 1866. Democratic reasons for reporting Grant's Copperhead connection, Logan declared, was their desire to destroy his chances for the Presidency in 1868.

[67]Thomas J. Pressly, *Americans Interpret Their Civil War* (Princeton, New Jersey, 1954), 45.

[68]Beale, *Critical Year*, 391; O. J. Hollister, *The Life of Schuyler Colfax* (New York, 1887), 295.

[69]Chester *Picket Guard*, Sept. 12, 1866 in Cole, *Era of the Civil War*, 403.

burg heard Dickey called the man who rushed home in June, 1863, to speak "at a peace meeting, invoking the people to crush you into powder, should you dare to do an act of offensive war against the traitors."[70]

A new development enlivened the Logan-Dickey battle in late September. On September 1, W. H. Green, Logan's ex-law partner and a peace Democrat, wrote McClernand a suggestion for Dickey's campaign. McClernand promptly sent a copy to Dickey. Green advised the colonel to "invite Logan to a joint discussion extending all over the State." The Egyptian Democrat told Dickey, "I might give many reasons in favor of my suggestion, but will only mention one. That is, Logan cannot ever do himself justice in a joint discussion and will do much less damage in such discussion."[71] Dickey decided the plan had merit and made the proposal to Logan. An agreement was reached for three meetings: at Carbondale on September 28, Macomb, October 9, and at Decatur, October 16. Logan was to open with an hour speech at Carbondale, to be followed by Dickey for 90 minutes. Logan was then to conclude with a 30 minute rebuttal. The procedure was to be reversed at Macomb, and returned to at Decatur.[72]

The first debate brought a huge crowd to Carbondale.[73] The gathering was tumultuous, divided about equally between adherents of the rivals. Logan's opening was the usual "Bloody Shirt" message. He said he joined the Republicans only when he discovered the Democrats were the party of treason. Dickey's speech was calm and dignified compared to the intemperate assaults on Logan by some of his followers. "I stand before you today as the advocate of that good old Constitution that our fathers made and intrusted to our care." He struck at Logan's pre-war voting record, and spent some time on charges that Logan conspired with the rebels. Logan's rebuttal

---

[70]Chicago *Tribune*, Sept. 20, 1866.

[71]W. H. Green to John McClernand, Sept. 1, 1866; John McClernand to T. Lyle Dickey, Sept. 5, 1866, W. H. L. Wallace-T. Lyle Dickey Mss., Illinois State Historical Library.

[72]Ms. of an agreement signed by Logan and Dickey, Sept. 19, 1866, Logan Mss.

[73]*Illinois State Journal*, Oct. 1, 1866. The *Journal* estimated the number at 10,000, probably not too far off, owing to the nature of the occasion and the fact that the Grand Army was out in force.

was a denial of these charges, and an attack on Dickey's war record. This denial brought Logan's sister Dorothy, Mrs. Israel Blanchard, to her feet shouting that Logan aided her husband in support of rebellion. Logan denied the charge and vowed to gather proof in his defense.[74] On Reconstruction, the two men spoke for opposing sides, Dickey for Johnson, Logan for the Radicals.

After the candidates left Egypt, Logan's opponents there decided to let the "skeleton of Logan's past . . . stalk forth among his admirers."[75] The Cairo Democrat published nine charges of secessionist activity against Logan. The paper charged "Logan entered the war . . . for the same reason he entered politics,—to get office." Other Democratic journals took up the cry, and Logan's actions in 1861 became an issue in 1866. Josh Allen charged Logan with attempting to bring about the secession of southern Illinois, and the Democrats produced a member of Brooks' company willing to testify that Logan had participated in the group's formation.[76]

Dickey seemed to have little to do with these attacks. He made them occasionally, but his campaign concentrated on issues rather than personalities. Reconstruction was his primary interest, and he backed the presidential plan. Despite Republican charges of Dickey's incompetence and cowardice as a soldier, calm Republicans admitted, "He was a modest, brave, and efficient commander of cavalry."[77]

While his opponents scattered their charges, Logan struggled to obtain counter evidence. He found little time for the task and Mary had to undertake the search. The general moved into western Illinois in October, speaking in Quincy on the 6th. Before going to Macomb and the second joint debate, he crossed into Iowa and spoke at Keokuk. Back in Illinois, he called Johnson an "accidental president" and shouted, "Andrew Johnson has been swinging around the circle for weeks and making a blatant ass of himself."[78]

The Macomb and Decatur debates were like the Carbondale

[74]Cole, Era of the Civil War, 402.
[75]Ibid., 400.
[76]Cairo Democrat, Oct. 2, 21, 1866.
[77]Chetlain, Recollections, 198.
[78]Illinois State Journal, Oct. 4, 1866.

meeting. At Macomb, Dickey stuck to Reconstruction, and
Logan called for harsh treatment of the Confederate states.
"We have the power to give rights which they have forfeited,"
he roared, "and I propose that we give them—when we get
ready."[79] At Decatur the audience was pro-Logan. The G. A. R.
had bands present, and the general's every statement brought
cheers. Defending himself, Logan averred, "As long as I saw
a chance to avert war I voted and worked for peace, but the
instant the first gun was fired, I left the Democratic Party and
went with loyal men to suppress the rebellion."[80] In light of
events five years earlier, this was an exaggeration. Before the
Decatur meeting, Dickey asked for another debate in which
he might open and close, but Logan, pleading a full schedule,
declined.[81]

If his protestations from the stump did not reassure his followers of his innocence of secession activity, Logan was certain the evidence would. On October 14 he sent Mary a draft
of a statement he wanted several Egyptian Democrats to sign.
The allegation denied Cairo *Democrat* charges.[82] Mary had
difficulty getting the document signed. Finally her father and
seven others agreed to sign. Shortly after Mary had rushed the
statement into print, however, two of Josh Allen's lieutenants
persauded six of the men to remove their names. Mary wrote
her husband that the men reported they were still "willing to
swear you never furnished them any encouragement . . . but
they did not want anything done to injure *Josh Allen* and their
cause."[83] On the 27th the Cairo *Democrat* published a story by
the reluctant six claiming Mrs. Logan had printed their names
without their consent.[84]

This denial hurt Logan in Egypt, but he was quick to counter with what he had. Hibe Cunningham and A. H. Morgan,
two members of Brooks' company, wrote letters denying Logan's complicity and the notes were published.[85] The *Illinois*

[79]*Ibid.*, Oct. 12, 1866.
[80]*Ibid.*, Oct. 17, 1866.
[81]T. Lyle Dickey to JAL, Oct. 16, 1866, Logan Mss.
[82]JAL to Mary Logan, Oct. 14, 1866, Logan, Mss.
[83]Mary Logan to JAL, Oct. 22, 1866, Logan Mss.
[84]Cairo *Democrat*, Oct. 27, 1866.
[85]Hibert Cunningham to JAL, Oct. 15, 1866; A. H. Morgan to JAL,
Oct. 16, 1866, Logan Mss.; Centralia *Sentinel*, Nov. 1, 1866.

State Journal also produced a number of letters from Egyptian Democrats who announced their political opposition to Logan, yet denied he had supported secession.[86]

The charges of treason angered Logan. He wrote his wife, "unless my conduct in the army is sufficient to satisfy the people with me they can go to thunder." Furthermore, he vowed to save his last speaking dates for Egypt in an effort to save the district for himself and aid Raum against Allen.[87]

When November arrived Logan spoke in Anna on the 1st, Tamaroa on the 2nd, and Murphysboro on the 3rd. His last address, a joint appearance with Raum, came at Marion on the 5th. Logan spent little time on issues, but lashed out at Dickey and Allen as Copperheads. Election day was the 6th, and Logan seemed safely ahead. Dickey had stumped the state, calmly discussing the issues. His supporters had spent their time making a feeble appeal for the soldier vote, and, when that seemed to fail, attacking Logan. "Black Jack" campaigned tirelessly, speaking all over the state to large crowds. The Grand Army appeared everywhere and the veteran vote alone seemed enough to sweep Logan into office. The general touched Reconstruction only when he cried out at the folly of turning the nation over to traitorous Democrats. His appearances were intemperate while Dickey's were calm. Illinois, like most midwestern states, was in no mood to support Democrats. Logan rode the crest of a Radical wave.

Vote counting showed a Logan trend that never stopped. The day after the election the Chicago *Tribune* reported that city safely in the Republican camp, and Logan ahead by 9,000 votes in Cook County.[88] Everywhere the story was similar. Logan swept through Boone County 1,646 to 165, and Winnebago, where his name had long brought jeers, went to Logan 3,375 to 407. He won 65 counties to Dickey's 37, and few of Dickey's majorities were as large as Logan's. Statewide, the vote was 203,045 for Logan to 147,455 for Dickey, a comfortable 55,590 majority.

The 13th District brought the closest race, but even there

[86]*Illinois State Journal*, Oct. 29, 1866.
[87]JAL to Mary Logan, Oct. 27, 1866, Logan Mss.
[88]Chicago *Tribune*, Nov. 7, 1866.

Logan edged the colonel. Dickey won eight of fifteen counties, but Logan took the total vote 13,515 to 12,938. While Logan won Egypt, his fellow Republican also triumphed. Raum whipped Allen 13,459 to 12,890. Even the 12th District, also Egyptian, voted Republican.

Republicans exulted in their victory, claiming it the nation's greatest for the Radicals. The *Tribune* pronounced Logan's majority unexpectedly large. Egyptian Republicans boasted that their victories indicated Logan's "revolution" of 1864 "would not go backwards, and that the district had actually become Radical." They were willing to credit Logan with the result. "No man," they felt, "has ever before made such a thorough and effective canvass in the State." This opinion is conceded by Howard K. Beale who wrote: "A large factor in the success of Illinois Radicals was the personal popularity and tireless campaigning of General Logan, by sheer dint of personality he swung the two 'Egypt' districts . . . to the Radical side."[89]

Democrats had little to say. They cheered Jackson, Logan's native county, and proclaimed, "Johnny can 'sell out,' but he can't deliver the Democracy of Old Jackson."[90]

After the election, Logan returned to the East and business. He intended to remain there until mid-December and return for the Senate fight. One report stated that Logan's trip was undertaken to "induce the impeachment of the President."[91] Logan's letters, however, merely concern business and his political aspirations. Before his wife could lament his absence, Logan assured her, "I am doing all I can . . . to get some money for us, and you must not complain at me." He reported several large fees in the offing, but wanted to return for the legislative vote before taking the cases.[92]

The last week in December Logan arrived in Illinois. He had reported from the East that letters from political friends indicated his senatorial chances were poor. Nevertheless, he resolved to "make the best fight I can."[93] In early December his

[89]Carbondale *New Era*, Nov. 22, 29, 1866; Beale, *Critical Year*, 392.
[90]Jonesboro *Gazette*, Nov. 13, 1866.
[91]*Illinois State Journal*, Nov. 17, 1866.
[92]JAL to Mary Logan, Nov. 29, Dec. 7, 1866, Logan Mss.
[93]JAL to Mary Logan, Nov. 22, 1866, Logan Mss.

hopes turned for the better, and he wrote, "I do not intend to be beat [sic] for Senator, have written everybody, and will do all I can."[94] His letters went to Illinois Republican legislators and their answers brought disappointment. Most said they would vote for Trumbull, and Logan considered withdrawing. He and Oglesby had both coveted the Senate seat, and both had urged John Palmer to join the fight against Trumbull.[95] The three generals, however, were ineffectual allies, and their efforts against Trumbull were inadequate. A Palmer supporter wrote that better preparation before the delegates had been instructed could have unseated Trumbull.[96]

The three generals were prominently mentioned as candidates all through November and December. An Egyptian journal endorsed Logan daily. This paper claimed Logan's sweeping November victory gave him the right to the seat.[97] Other reports placed Trumbull in front, followed by Logan, Palmer, and Oglesby. The Democrats, despairing of victory for one of their own, predicted a Logan triumph.[98]

In Springfield Logan found he had little chance to win. He joined Oglesby in an effort to throw the election to Palmer, a military man and more Radical than Trumbull. "I got out of the race," he wrote, "as I was determined not to be beaten and ruin my future prospects. . . . I am working hard to help elect Palmer . . . but am fearful we will not succeed."[99] His fears were realized when Trumbull won.

Logan went East shortly after the election determined to practice law until Congress convened. Mary decided to remain in Carbondale until Logan took his seat. For six weeks he worked hard in Washington, although his letters reveal business was not going well. Just before Congress met, Logan travelled to Connecticut to give the New Englanders an example of his "Bloody Shirt" style.

Returning from the North, Logan arrived on March 3. The

94JAL to Mary Logan, Dec. 1, 1866, Logan Mss.
95John M. Palmer to John Mayo Palmer, Nov. 10, 1866, Palmer Mss.
96J. D. Ward to John M. Palmer, Dec. 25, 1866, Palmer Mss.
97Carbondale *New Era*, Jan. 3, 1867.
98*Illinois State Journal*, Nov. 28, 1866; Jonesboro *Gazette*, Nov. 24, 1866; *Illinois State Register*, Nov. 10, 1866.
99JAL to Mary Logan, Jan. 9, 1867, Logan Mss.

following day he went to the Capitol for the swearing ceremony. The last time he had sat in the chamber he was a
Democrat, but now he took his seat among the Republican
desks that overflowed across the center aisle after the 1866
landslide. He was welcomed by old enemies George Boutwell,
John Covode, and John Bingham. James G. Blaine remembered his arrival as a "noteworthy addition" to the House.[100]
Military figures were widely evident in the chamber. Logan
found former generals Rutherford B. Hayes, James A. Gar-
field, and Ben Butler. From Illinois, Logan joined Republicans
Ebon Ingersoll, Shelby Cullom, and Elihu Washburne, the latter being the only member of the state's House delegation who
sat with Logan in 1861.[101]

At noon the chair gaveled for order and new members took
the oath. When Logan rose and was sworn in, veteran members watched the man they remembered as an intensely partisan young Democrat return as an equally partisan Republican.
What were Logan's thoughts as he completed his journey
across the aisle, a journey few in American politics have
made? Did he remember a speech delivered in this same chamber in 1859 by a freshman Democrat:

> I came here as a Democrat, and I expect to support a
> Democrat. I may have differed with gentlemen on this side
> of the House in reference to issues that are passed; but God
> knows that I have differed with the other side from my
> childhood, and with that side I will never affiliate so long as
> I have breath in my body.[102]

In 1867 he found himself on the "other side." Logan completed
the oath, took his seat, and a few moments later voted for
speaker. In the contest between his pre-war friend Scott Marshall, a Democrat, and Schuyler Colfax, Logan voted for Colfax—a Republican.

---

[100]Blaine, *Twenty Years*, II, 287.
[101]*Cong. Globe*, 40th Cong., 1st Sess., 2, 4.
[102]*Ibid.*, 36th Cong., 1st Sess., pt. 1, 86.

BIBLIOGRAPHY

I. PRIMARY MATERIALS

MANUSCRIPTS:
Ammen MSS. Papers of Jacob Ammen, Illinois State Historical Library, Springfield.
Civil War Diaries MSS. Diary of an Unknown Soldier, 26th Illinois Infantry, Illinois State Historical Library, Springfield.
Compton MSS. Diary of George Compton, Illinois State Historical Library, Springfield.
Crandall MSS. Diary of Hiram Crandall, Illinois State Historical Library, Springfield.
Cullom MSS. Papers of Shelby M. Cullom, Illinois State Historical Library, Springfield.
Davis MSS. Papers of Jefferson C. Davis, Indiana State Library, Indianapolis.
Gillespie MSS. Papers of Joseph Gillespie, Illinois State Historical Library, Springfield.
Ingersoll MSS. Papers of Robert and Ebon C. Ingersoll, Illinois State Historical Library, Springfield.
Lanphier MSS. Papers of Charles Lanphier, Illinois State Historical Library, Springfield.
Dr. John Logan MSS. Papers of Dr. John Logan, Illinois State Historical Library, Springfield.
John A. Logan MSS. Papers of John A. Logan, Library of Congress.
Mary Logan MSS. Papers of Mary Logan, Library of Congress.
McClernand MSS. Papers of John A. McClernand, Illinois State Historical Library, Springfield.
McHenry MSS. Diary of James S. McHenry, Illinois State Historical Library, Springfield.
Ozburn MSS. Papers of Lindorf Ozburn, Illinois State Historical Library, Springfield.
Palmer MSS. Papers of John M. Palmer, Illinois State Historical Library, Springfield.
Trumbull MSS. Papers of Lyman Trumbull, Library of Congress.
Wallace-Dickey MSS. Papers of W. H. L. Wallace and T. Lyle Dickey, Illinois State Historical Library, Springfield.
Washburne MSS. Papers of Elihu B. Washburne, Library of Congress.
Woollard MSS. Papers of F. M. Woollard, Illinois State Historical Library, Springfield.
Yates MSS. Papers of Richard Yates, Illinois State Historical Library, Springfield.

GOVERNMENT DOCUMENTS:
Federal:
U.S. Bureau of the Census. *Seventh Census of the United States: 1850.*
U.S. Bureau of the Census. *Eighth Census of the United States: 1860.*
U.S. *Congressional Globe.* 1859-1867.

U.S. Department of War. *Atlas to Accompany the Official Records of the Union and Confederate Armies.* 2 vols. Washington: Government Printing Office, 1891-1895.

U.S. Department of War. *The War of the Rebellion: A Compilation of the Official Records of the Union and Confederate Armies.* 129 vols. Washington: Government Printing Office, 1880-1901.

State:

Illinois. Adjutant-General. Elliott, Isaac H., ed. *Record of the Services of Illinois Soldiers in the Black Hawk War, 1831-1832, and in the Mexican War, 1846-1848.* Springfield, Illinois: Journal Co., 1902.

Illinois. Adjutant-General. *Report of the Adjutant-General of the State of Illinois, 1861-1862.* Springfield, Illinois, 1863.

Illinois. *House Journal.* 1853, 1857.

Illinois. *Private Laws.* 1853.

NEWSPAPERS:

Alton *Courier*, Alton, Illinois.

Alton *Telegraph*, Alton, Illinois. Also appears as Alton *Telegraph and Democratic Review.*

Baltimore *Sun*, Baltimore, Maryland.

Bloomington *Daily Bulletin*, Bloomington, Illinois.

Cairo *City Gazette*, Cairo, Illinois.

Cairo *Democrat*, Cairo, Illinois.

Cairo *Sun*, Cairo, Illinois.

Cairo *Times and Delta*, Cairo, Illinois. Also appears as Cairo *City Times.*

Carbondale *New Era*, Carbondale, Illinois.

Carbondale *Times*, Carbondale, Illinois.

Central Illinois Gazette, Champaign, Illinois.

Centralia *Egyptian Republic*, Centralia, Illinois.

Centralia *Sentinel*, Centralia, Illinois.

Chicago *Republican.*

Chicago *Times.*

Chicago *Tribune.* Also appears as Chicago *Press and Tribune.*

Illinois State Journal, Springfield, Illinois.

Illinois State Register, Springfield, Illinois.

Jacksonville *Journal*, Jacksonville, Illinois.

Jonesboro *Gazette*, Jonesboro, Illinois.

Louisville *Democrat*, Louisville, Kentucky.

Marion *Intelligencer*, Marion, Illinois.

Missouri Republican, St. Louis, Missouri.

Mound City *Emporium*, Mound City, Illinois.

National Intelligencer, Washington, D. C.

New York *Herald*

New York *Times.*

New York *World.*

Oregon *Argus*, Oregon, Illinois.

Quincy *Daily Whig and Republican*, Quincy, Illinois. Also appears as Quincy *Weekly Whig.*

Quincy *Herald*, Quincy, Illinois.

Rockford *Republican*, Rockford, Illinois.

Salem *Advocate*, Salem, Illinois.

Shawneetown *Illinoisan*, Shawneetown, Illinois.

BOOKS:

Adair, John M. *Historical Sketch of the 45th Illinois Regiment.* Lanark, Illinois: Carroll County *Gazette* Printers, 1869.

Adams, Marian Hooper. *The Letters of Mrs. Henry Adams, 1865-1883.* Ward Thoron, ed. Boston: Little Brown, 1937.

Angle, Paul, ed. *Created Equal? The Complete Lincoln-Douglas Debates of 1858.* Chicago: The University of Chicago Press, 1958.

Battles and Leaders of the Civil War. Robert U. Johnson and Clarence C. Buel, eds. 4 vols. New York: The Century Co., 1887-1888.

Blaine, James G. *Twenty Years of Congress, 1861-1881.* 2 vols. Norwich, Connecticut: Henry Bill Publishing Co., 1886.

Browning, Orville Hickman. *The Diary of Orville Hickman Browning.* T. C. Pease and J. G. Randall, eds. 2 vols. Springfield, Illinois: Illinois State Historical Library, 1925, 1933.

Brush, Daniel H. *Growing Up With Southern Illinois, 1820-1861.* Milo M. Quaife, ed. Chicago: R. R. Donnelley & Sons, 1944.

Byers, Samuel Hawken Marshall. *With Fire and Sword.* New York: Neale Publishing Co., 1911.

Cadwallader, Sylvanus. *Three Years With Grant.* Benjamin P. Thomas, ed. New York: Alfred Knopf, 1955.

Carr, Clark E. *My Day and Generation.* Chicago: A. C. McClurg & Co., 1908.

Chesnut, Mary Boykin. *A Diary from Dixie.* Isabella D. Martin and Myrta Lockett Avary, eds. New York: Peter Smith Co., 1929.

_____. *A Diary from Dixie.* Ben Ames Williams, ed. Boston: Houghton, Mifflin Co., 1949.

Chetlain, Augustus L. *Recollections of Seventy Years.* Galena, Illinois. Gazette Publishing Co., 1899.

Conyngham, David P. *Sherman's March Through the South.* New York: Sheldon & Co., 1865.

Cox, Jacob D. *Military Reminiscences of the Civil War.* 2 vols. New York: Charles Scribner's Sons, 1900.

Cox, Samuel S. *Three Decades of Federal Legislation, 1855-1885.* Providence: J. A. and R. A. Reid, 1885.

Crummer, Wilbur F. *With Grant at Fort Donelson, Shiloh, and Vicksburg.* Oak Park, Illinois: E. C. Crummer Co., 1915.

Cullom, Shelby M. *Fifty Years of Public Service: Personal Recollections.* A. C. McClurg, 1911.

Dana, Charles A. and James H. Wilson. *The Life of Ulysses S. Grant, General of the Armies of the United States.* Springfield, Massachusetts: Bill Co., 1868.

Dana, Charles A. *Recollections of the Civil War.* New York: D. Appleton Co., 1898.

Dodge, Grenville M. *The Battle of Atlanta and Other Campaigns, Addresses, etc.* Council Bluffs, Iowa: The Monarch Publishing Co., 1910.

_____. *Personal Recollections of General William T. Sherman.* Des Moines: n. p., 1902.

Erwin, Milo. *The History of Williamson County, Illinois.* Marion, Illinois: n. p., 1876.

Grant, Ulysses S. *Personal Memoirs of U. S. Grant.* 2 vols. 2nd ed. New York: The Century Co., 1895.

Halstead, Murat. *Caucuses of 1860.* Columbus, Ohio: Follett, Foster Co., 1860.

Hayes, Rutherford B. *The Diary and Letters of Rutherford B. Hayes.* Charles R. Williams, ed. 5 vols. Columbus, Ohio: The Ohio State Archaelogical and Historical Society, 1922-1926.

Hazen, William B. *Narrative of Military Service.* Boston: Ticknor Co., 1885.

Henry, Robert S., ed. *As They Saw Forrest.* Jackson, Tennessee: McCowat-Mercer Press, 1956.

Hitchcock, Henry. *Marching With Sherman.* M. A. DeWolfe Howe, ed. New Haven, Connecticut: Yale University Press, 1927.

Hoar, George F. *Autobiography of Seventy Years.* 2 vols. New York: Charles Scribner's Sons, 1903.

Houghton, Walter R. *Early Life and Public Career of James G. Blaine, Including a Biography of General John A. Logan.* Cleveland: N. G. Hamilton & Co., 1884.

Howard, Oliver Otis. *The Autobiography of Oliver Otis Howard.* 2 vols. New York: The Baker and Taylor Co., 1907.

Howard, Richard L. *History of the 124th Regiment Illinois Infantry Volunteers.* Springfield, Illinois: H. W. Rokker Co., 1880.

James, George F., ed. *Logan Monument Memorial Addresses.* Chicago: n. p., 1896.

Johnson, Charles B. *Illinois in the Fifties.* Champaign, Illinois: Flanigan-Pearson Co., 1918.

Koerner, Gustave P. *Memoirs of Gustave P. Koerner.* 2 vols. Cedar Rapids, Iowa: Torch Press, 1909.

Le Conte, Emma. *When the World Ended: The Diary of Emma Le Conte.* Earl Schenck Miers, ed. New York: Oxford University Press, 1957.

Lincoln, Abraham. *The Collected Works of Abraham Lincoln.* Roy P. Basler, ed. 9 vols. New Brunswick, New Jersey: Rutgers University Press, 1953.

Linder, Usher F. *Reminiscences of the Early Bench and Bar of Illinois.* Chicago: Legal News Co., 1879.

Logan, John A. *The Great Conspiracy, Its Origin and History.* New York: A. R. Hart, 1886.

————. *Relief of the Suffering Poor of the South.* Washington: Chronicle Printers, 1867.

————. *Speech of Major General John A. Logan on His Return to Illinois after the Capture of Vicksburg, with an Introduction by "Mack" of the Cincinnati Commercial.* Cincinnati: Loyal Publications of the National Union Association of Ohio, Caleb Clark Printer, 1863.

————. *The Volunteer Soldier of America.* Chicago and New York: R. S. Peale Co., 1887.

Logan, Mary S. C. *Reminiscences of a Soldier's Wife.* New York: Charles Scribner's Sons, 1913.

————. *Thirty Years in Washington.* Hartford, Connecticut: A. D. Worthington & Co., 1901.

Military Essays and Recollections. Military Order of the Loyal Legion of the United States, Illinois Commandery. Chicago; n. p., 1891.

Morris, W. S. *History of the Thirty-first Regiment Illinois Volunteers, Organized by John A. Logan.* Evansville, Indiana: Keller Publishing Co., 1902.

Newsome, Edmund. *Historical Sketches of Jackson County, Illinois.* Carbondale, Illinois: Edmund Newsome, 1882.

Oldroyd, Osborn H. *A Soldier's Story of the Siege of Vicksburg.* Springfield, Illinois: H. W. Rokker, 1885.

Orendorff, H. H., *et al.*, eds. *Reminiscences of the Civil War from Diaries of Members of the One Hundred and Third Illinois Volunteer Infantry.* Chicago; n. p., 1904.

Palmer, John M. *Personal Recollections of John M. Palmer.* Cincinnati: R. Clarke Co., 1901.

Pepper, George W. *Personal Recollections of Sherman's Campaigns in Georgia and the Carolinas.* Zanesville, Ohio: Hugh Dunne, 1866.

Porter, Horace. *Campaigning With Grant.* New York: The Century Co., 1897.

Proceedings of the Conventions at Charleston and Baltimore of the National Democratic Convention. Washington: National Democratic Executive Committee, 1860.

Russell, William Howard. *My Diary North and South.* Fletcher Pratt, ed. New York: Harpers, 1954.

Shanks, William F. G. *Personal Recollections of Distinguished Generals.* New York: Harpers, 1866.

Sherlock, E. J. *Memorabilia of the Marches and Battles in Which the One Hundredth Regiment of Indiana Infantry Volunteers Took an Active Part, 1861-1865.* Kansas City, Missouri: Gerard-Woody Co., 1896.

Sherman, William T. *Home Letters of General Sherman.* M. A. DeWolfe Howe, ed. New York: Charles Scribner's Sons, 1909.

_____. *Memoirs of General W. T. Sherman.* 2 vols. 1st ed. New York: D. Appleton & Co., 1875.

Stockwell, Elisha. *Private Elisha Stockwell, Jr., Sees the Civil War.* Byron R. Abernethy, ed. Norman, Oklahoma: University of Oklahoma Press, 1958.

Tribune Almanac. Chicago: *Tribune* Publishers, 1864, 1866.

Upson, Theodore F. *With Sherman to the Sea: The Civil War Letters, Diaries and Reminiscences of Theodore F. Upson.* Oscar O. Winther, ed. Baton Rouge, Louisiana: Louisiana State University Press, 1943.

Way, Virgil and Isaac H. Elliott. *History of the Thirty-third Regiment Illinois Veteran Volunteer Infantry in the Civil War.* Gibson City, Illinois: The Regimental Association, 1902.

Welles, Gideon. *The Diary of Gideon Welles.* 2 vols. Howard K. Beale, ed. New York: W. W. Norton & Co., 1960.

ARTICLES:

Haskell, Fritz, ed. "Diary of Colonel William Camm, 1861-1865," *Journal of the Illinois State Historical Society,* XXVIII, No. 4, January, 1926.

Kimmel, H. E. "Sixty-sixth Wedding Anniversary of Daniel Gill and Lucinda Pyle Gill, DuQuoin, Illinois," *Journal of the Illinois State Historical Society,* XVII, No. 3, September, 1924.

Muir, Andrew F., contrib. "The Battle of Atlanta as Described by a Confederate Soldier," *Georgia Historical Quarterly,* XLII, No. 1, March, 1958.

Padgett, James, ed. "With Sherman Through Georgia and the Carolinas: Letters of a Federal Soldier," *Georgia Historical Quarterly,* XXXII, No. 4, December, 1948, March, 1949.

Pratt, Harry, ed. "Civil War Letters of Winthrop S. G. Allen," *Journal of the Illinois State Historical Society*, XXIV, No. 3, October, 1931.
Read, Ira B. "The Campaign from Chattanooga to Atlanta as Seen by a Federal Soldier," Richard B. Harwell, ed. *Georgia Historical Quarterly*, XXV, No. 3, September, 1941.
Strawn, Halbert J. "The Attitude of General John A. Logan on the Question of Secession in 1861," *Journal of the Illinois State Historical Society*, VI, No. 2, July, 1913.

II. SECONDARY MATERIALS

BOOKS:

Andrews, Byron. *A Biography of General John A. Logan: With an Account of His Public Service in Peace and War.* New York: H. S. Goodspeed, 1884.
Appleton's Annual Cyclopaedia and Register of Important Events.
Balestier, Charles W. *James G. Blaine: A Sketch of His Life, with a Brief Record of the Life of John A. Logan.* New York: R. Worthington, 1884.
Barrett, John G. *Sherman's March Through the Carolinas.* Chapel Hill, North Carolina: University of North Carolina Press, 1956.
Bateman, Newton and Paul Selby. *Historical Encyclopedia of Illinois and a History of Sangamon County.* Chicago: Munsell Publishing Co., 1912.
Beale, Howard K. *The Critical Year.* New York: Harcourt, Brace, 1930.
Biographical Directory of the American Congress, 1774-1949. Washington: Government Printing Office, 1950.
Brownell, Baker. *The Other Illinois.* New York; Duell, Sloan and Pearce, 1958.
Buel, J. W. *The Standard Bearers: the Authorized Pictorial Lives of Blaine and Logan.* Philadelphia: W. H. Thompson, 1884.
Charnwood, Lord. *Abraham Lincoln.* London: Constable & Co., Ltd., 1921.
Church, Charles A. *A History of the Republican Party in Illinois, 1854-1912.* Rockford, Illinois: Wilson Bros. Co., 1912.
Cole, Arthur C. *The Era of the Civil War.* Vol. III, The Centennial History of Illinois. Springfield, Illinois: Illinois Centennial Commission, 1919.
Cox, Jacob D. *Atlanta.* New York: Charles Scribner's Sons, 1882.
Davidson, Alexander and Benjamin Stuve. *A Complete History of Illinois from 1673 to 1884.* Springfield, Illinois: H. W. Rokker, 1884.
Dawson, George Francis. *Life and Services of General John A. Logan as Soldier and Statesman.* Chicago and New York: Belford, Clarke Co., 1887.
Dearing, Mary R. *Veterans in Politics: The Story of the Grand Army of the Republic.* Baton Rouge, Louisiana: Louisiana State University Press, 1952.
Eddy, T. M. *The Patriotism of Illinois.* 2 vols. Chicago: Clarke & Co., 1865-1866.
Fite, Emerson D. *The Presidential Campaign of 1860.* New York: Macmillan, 1911.
Foote, Shelby. *The Civil War: a Narrative, From Sumter to Perryville.* New York: Random House, 1958.

BIBLIOGRAPHY 293

Fuller, J. F. C. *Grant and Lee*. Bloomington, Indiana: Indiana University Press, 1957.
Gray, Wood. *The Hidden Civil War: The Story of the Copperheads*. New York: Viking Press, 1942.
Greeley, Horace. *The American Conflict*. 2 vols. Chicago: G. & C. W. Sherwood, 1865-1867.
Harris, N. Dwight. *The History of Negro Servitude in Illinois: and of Slavery Agitation in that State, 1719-1864*. Chicago: A. C. McClurg, 1904.
Hollister, O. J. *Life of Schuyler Colfax*. New York: Funk and Wagnalls, 1887.
Horn, Stanley F. *The Decisive Battle of Nashville*. Baton Rouge, Louisiana: Louisiana State University Press, 1956.
Kinsley, Philip. *The Chicago Tribune: Its First Hundred Years*. 2 vols. New York: Alfred Knopf, 1943.
Kittredge, Herman E. *Robert G. Ingersoll: A Biographical Appreciation*. New York: Dresden Publishing Co., 1911.
Knox, Thomas W. *The Lives of James G. Blaine and John A. Logan*. Hartford, Connecticut: Hartford Publishing Co., 1884.
Leech, Margaret. *Reville in Washington*. New York: Harpers, 1941.
Lewis, Lloyd. *Captain Sam Grant*. Boston: Little, Brown & Co., 1950.
_____. *Sherman, Fighting Prophet*. New York: Harcourt, Brace Co., 1932.
Lusk, David W. *Politics and Politicians of Illinois, 1856-1884*. Springfield, Illinois: H. W. Rokker, 1884.
Macartney, Clarence Edward. *Grant and His Generals*. New York: The McBride Co., 1953.
Miers, Earl Schenck. *The General Who Marched to Hell: William Tecumseh Sherman and His March to Fame and Infamy*. New York: Alfred Knopf, 1951.
_____. *Web of Victory: Grant at Vicksburg*. New York: Alfred Knopf, 1955.
Milton, George Fort. *The Eve of Conflict: Stephen A. Douglas and the Needless War*. New York: Houghton, Mifflin, 1934.
Nevins, Allan. *The Emergence of Lincoln*. 2 vols. New York: Charles Scribner's Sons, 1950.
Nicolay, John G. and John Hay. *Abraham Lincoln, a History*. 10 vols. New York: The Century Co., 1886.
Palmer, George T. *A Conscientious Turncoat: The Story of John M. Palmer, 1817-1900*. New Haven, Connecticut: Yale University Press, 1941.
Pressly, Thomas J. *Americans Interpret Their Civil War*. Princeton, New Jersey: Princeton University Press, 1954.
Randall, James G. and David Donald. *The Civil War and Reconstruction*. Boston: D. C. Heath Co., 1961.
Randall, James G. *Lincoln the President*. 4 vols. New York: Dodd, Mead Co., 1946-1955.
Raum, Green B. *A History of Illinois Republicanism*. Chicago: Rollins Publishing Co., 1900.
Rogers, Cameron. *Colonel Bob Ingersoll*. Garden City, New York: Doubleday, Page Co., 1927.
Sandburg, Carl. *Abraham Lincoln, the Prairie Years*. 2 vols. New York: Harcourt, Brace Co., 1926.

————. *Abraham Lincoln, the War Years.* 4 vols. New York: Harcourt, Brace Co., 1939.

Sheahan, James W. *The Life of Stephen A. Douglas.* New York: Harper & Bros., 1860.

Smith, Edward C. *The Borderland in the Civil War.* New York: Macmillan, 1927.

Smith, George W. *A History of Southern Illinois.* 3 vols. Chicago: Lewis Publishing Co., 1912.

Smith, William E. *The Francis Preston Blair Family in Politics.* 2 vols. New York: Macmillan, 1933.

Stevens, Frank E. *The Life of Stephen A. Douglas.* Springfield, Illinois: Illinois State Historical Society, 1924.

Stringer, Lawrence B. *History of Logan County, Illinois.* Chicago: Inter-State Publishing Co., 1886.

Vallandigham, James L. *A Life of Clement L. Vallandigham.* Baltimore: Turnbull Bros., 1872.

Wiley, Bell I. *The Life of Billy Yank: Common Soldier of the Union.* Indianapolis: Bobbs-Merrill, 1951.

Williams, Kenneth P. *Lincoln Finds a General.* 5 vols. New York: Macmillan, 1949-1959.

ARTICLES:

Auchampaugh, Philip G. "The Buchanan-Douglas Feud," *Journal of the Illinois State Historical Society,* XXV, Nos. 1, 2, April, July, 1932.

Baringer, William E. "Campaign Technique in Illinois, 1860," *Transactions of the Illinois State Historical Society,* No. 39, 1932.

Cross, Jasper W. "The Civil War Comes to 'Egypt,'" *Journal of the Illinois State Historical Society,* XLIV, No. 2, Summer, 1951.

Holt, Robert D. "The Political Career of William A. Richardson," *Journal of the Illinois State Historical Society,* XXVI, No. 3, October, 1933.

Hubbart, Henry C. "'Pro-Southern' Influences in the Free West, 1840-1865," *Mississippi Valley Historical Review,* XX, No. 1, June, 1933.

Luvaas, Jay. "Johnston's Last Stand—Bentonville," *North Carolina Historical Review,* XXXII, No. 3, July, 1956.

Pitkin, William A. "When Cairo was Saved for the Union," *Journal of the Illinois State Historical Society,* LI, No. 3, Autumn, 1958.

Quenzel, Carroll H. "Books for the Boys in Blue," *Journal of the Illinois State Historical Society,* XLIV, No. 3, Autumn, 1951.

Stenberg, Richard R. "An Unnoted Factor in the Buchanan-Douglas Feud," *Journal of the Illinois State Historical Society,* XXV, No. 4, January, 1933.

Wilson, Bluford. "Southern Illinois in the Civil War," *Transactions of the Illinois State Historical Society,* No. 16, 1911.

UNPUBLISHED MATERIALS:

Cross, Jasper W. "Divided Loyalties in Southern Illinois During the Civil War," unpublished doctoral dissertation, University of Illinois, 1942.

Hawkins, May Strong. "The Early Political Career of John A. Logan," unpublished masters thesis, University of Chicago, 1934.

Wallace, Joseph. "A Biography of John A. Logan," unpublished manuscript in the Illinois State Historical Library, Springfield.

INDEX

Marshall, Samuel Scott, 22, 72, in the House, 25-26, 30, 32, 34, as an Egyptian Democratic leader, 35, supports Logan for the House, 36, at Charleston Convention, 52, runs to succeed Logan in the House, 138, nominated for Speaker of the House in 1867, 286
Martin, James S., 215-216
Maryland, 1n, 98
Massac County, Illinois, 15
Massachusetts, Civil War units:
1st Infantry, 96
Matteson, Joel, 27
Mattoon, Illinois, 88
Mayfield, Kentucky, 84
Maximilian, Emperor of Mexico, 265, 271
McArthur, John, 125
McClellan, George B., 230-231, 233-234, 238
McClernand, John, 26, 56, 67, 75, 87, 105, 130, 132, 139, 144, in the 36th Congress, 42-43, friendship with Logan, 46, voted on for speaker, 47, stands with Logan as a moderate, 50, and Charleston Convention, 52-53, endorses Douglas, 59, Logan and McClernand split over compromise, 73, supports Lincoln administration, 82, and discipline at Cairo, 108, addresses Grant's regiment, 88, commissioned brigadier general, 100, 103, Battle of Belmont, 110-116, Logan's hostility toward, 118, 133, at Henry-Donelson campaign, 121-128, and Corinth campaign, 134, 136-137, opposes Illinois Constitution of 1862, 138, disputes with Logan around Jackson, Tenn., 141-143, conflicts with Grant, 150, and Vicksburg campaign, 157-158, 163-164, 166, Grant's opinion of, 167, and siege of Vicksburg, 168-169, mentioned for governor of Illinois, 189, and election of 1864, 233, and election of 1866, 280
McCook, Anson, 97n
McCook, E. S., 111, 114
McCullough, William, 135
McDowell, Irvin, 96
McHenry, James S., 172
McIlrath, James, 125
McIlrath, Robert, 125
McKean, James, 56
McLeansboro, Illinois, 83
McPherson, James B., 155, 194, 229, 268, and first Vicksburg campaign, 146, 148, and 1863 Vicksburg campaign, 153, 156-158, 161-164, 166, and Vicksburg siege, 168-169, 171, 174-176, and march to Canton, 184, commander of the Army of the Tennessee, 190, invasion of Georgia, 195-211, at Resaca, 196-199, at Kenesaw Mountain, 208-209, estimate of Hood, 211, Battle of Atlanta, 213-214, death of, 214
McPhersonville, South Carolina, 246
Medon, Tennessee, 142
Meigs, Montgomery, 259
Memphis, Tennessee, 150-152, 177
Meridian, Mississippi, 188
Mersey, August, 216
Metropolis, Illinois, 22, 238
Mexican War, 5-7, 106, 134
Mexico, 265, 270-271

Union County, Illinois, 20, 59, 62
Upson, Theodore, 257
Ursuline Convent (Columbia, South Carolina), 251
Utica, Mississippi, 160

Vallandigham, Clement L., 48, 50, 55, 59n 94, 99
Vandalia, Illinois, 1, 3
VanDorn, Earl, 145, 148-149, 157
Van Wert, Georgia, 201
Vicksburg, Battles for, 145-146, 149-150, 152-153, 156-157, 159, 164, 166-169, 171-173, 175, 178-179, 183-185, 188, 190, 200, 229, 259, 262, 279
Vienna, Illinois, 107, 238
Villanow, Georgia, 195-196
Virginia, 1, 96-97, 140, 192, 227, 244, 255, 257, 259-260

Walcutt, Charles C., 198n, 203-204, 207
Wallace, Lew, 122, 138
Wallace, M. R. M., 140
Wallace, W. H. L., 126, 128, 131
Wangelin, Hugo, 191, 198n, 214-215, 217
Washburne, Elihu, 55, 66, 69, 75, 154, 158-159, 232, 238-239, 271
Washington, D. C., 40-41, 46-47, 55-56, 58, 63, 65-66, 70, 80, 88-91, 95, 97, 117, 120, 130, 144, 148, 166, 186, 192, 232, 240-243, 258-259, 261-263, 270-272, 275, 285
Washita River, 153
Wateree River, 252
Water Valley, Mississippi, 148
Wayne County, Illinois, 76
Webster, J. D., 131
West Point (U.S.M.A.), xxii, 31, 210-211, 221, 224
Wever, C. R., 248, 254
Wheatley, John, 86
Wheeler, Joseph, 225, 247-248, 250
White, John H., 128-129, 134, helps with organization of 31st Illinois, 99, named lieutenant colonel of 31st Illinois, 106-107, leads 31st in Logan's absence, 118, killed at Donelson, 126
Whitesburg, Alabama, 191
Wickliffe, Kentucky, 110
"Wide-Awakes," 60
Wiley, Ben L., 36, 38
Willard's Hotel, 74
Williams, Reuben, 198n
Williamson, James, 128
Williamson County, Illinois, 6, 76, 100, 107, 179
Wilson, James H., 241
Winnebago, County, Illinois, 283
Winnsboro, South Carolina, 252
Witherspoon, William, 143n
Wood, Ben, 95
Wood, Fernando, 53
Woodland, Georgia, 200
Woods, Charles, 198-199, 212n, 216, 244-245, 247, 249-252, 254-255, 263

James Pickett Jones, a native Floridian, is Distinguished Teaching Professor of History at Florida State University. He received his BA, MA, and PhD degrees from the University of Florida. Jones has published numerous articles on Civil War history. His contributions have appeared in such journals as *Civil War History, Mid-America,* the *Journal of the Illinois State Historical Society,* the *Florida Historical Quarterly,* the *Missouri Historical Review,* and the *Lincoln Herald.* In addition to *"Black Jack,"* Jones's books include: *John A. Logan, Stalwart Republican from Illinois* (1982) and *Yankee Blitzkrieg: Wilson's Raid through Alabama and Georgia* (1976).

Shawnee Classics

A Series of Classic Regional Reprints for the Midwest

"Black Jack"
John A. Logan and Southern Illinois
     in the Civil War Era
James Pickett Jones

A Woman's Story of Pioneer Illinois
Christiana Holmes Tillson
Edited by Milo Milton Quaife